Feminist Waves, Feminist Generations

Life Stories from the Academy

Hokulani K. Aikau
Karla A. Erickson
Jennifer L. Pierce, Editors

D1521128

University of Minnesota Press | Minneapolis | London

Chapter 2 was previously published as "Who and Where We Are," in Toni McNaron, *Poisoned Ivy: Lesbian and Gay Academics Confronting Homophobia* (Philadelphia: Temple University Press, 1997); copyright 1997 Temple University Press; all rights reserved; reprinted with permission of Temple University Press. Chapter 3 previously appeared as Anne Firor Scott, Sara Evans, Susan Cahn, and Elizabeth Faue, "Women's History in the New Millennium: A Conversation across Three Generations, Part I," *Journal of Women's History* 11, issue 1 (1999): 9–30; reprinted with permission from Indiana University Press. Chapter 4 was previously published in *Qualitative Sociology* 26, no. 3 (2003): 397–425; reprinted with permission from Springer Science and Business Media. Chapter 7 previously appeared in *Think Again*, published in 2003 by the New York State Gay Black Network, Inc., and AIDS Project Los Angeles; reprinted with permission.

Published by the University of Minnesota Press
111 Third Avenue South, Suite 290
Minneapolis, MN 55401-2520
http://www.upress.umn.edu

LIBRARY OF CONGRESS CATALOGING-IN-PUBLICATION DATA
Feminist waves, feminist generations : life stories from the academy /
Hokulani K. Aikau, Karla A. Erickson, and Jennifer L. Pierce, editors.
p. cm.
Includes bibliographical references and index.
ISBN 978-0-8166-4933-4 (hc : alk. paper)
ISBN 978-0-8166-4934-1 (pb : alk. paper)
1. Feminism and higher education—United States. 2. Feminism—United
States. 3. Feminist theory—United States. I. Aikau, Hokulani K., 1970–
II. Erickson, Karla A., 1973– III. Pierce, Jennifer L., 1958–
LC197.F48 2007
378.0082–dc22   2007004969

Printed in the United States of America on acid-free paper

The University of Minnesota is an equal-opportunity educator and employer.

12 11 10 09 08 07   10 9 8 7 6 5 4 3 2 1

Feminist Waves, Feminist Generations

Contents

Acknowledgments

WE are fortunate in having worked on this project at the University of Minnesota. The community between and among feminist scholars in the College of Liberal Arts as well as the Graduate School and the Humanities Institute provided both intellectual and material support throughout the work on this volume. Numerous friends and colleagues across the college generously gave us productive comments along the way, including Anne Carter, Anna Clark, Lisa Disch, Kirsten Fischer, Jean O'Brien, Gabriella Tsurutani, Pam Butler, Susan Craddock, M. J. Maynes, David Noble, Riv-Ellen Prell, Janet Spector, and Anne Truax.

We presented an early draft of the introduction to the Comparative Women's History Workshop in the Department of History. The faculty and graduate students who attended provided wonderful feedback, and we are especially grateful to Ann Waltner, who served as discussant for our paper. The Center for Advanced Feminist Studies supported this project by hosting a special symposium on "Feminist Generations at Minnesota" to celebrate its twentieth anniversary; Hokulani Aikau, Karla Erickson, Sara Evans, Peter Hennen, and Wendy Leo Moore all had the opportunity to present versions of their personal narrative essays to an enthusiastic audience. For material support, Jennifer Pierce received a Grant in Aid for Scholarly and Creative Activity from the Graduate School (which funded Hokulani Aikau and Karla Erickson's preliminary work as research assistants on the project) as well as a Humanities Institute Fellowship, which provided her with a course release for one semester to write.

Throughout the writing process, we have benefited from the careful attention and counsel of audiences attending panels on feminist theory at the American Sociological Association and the Mid-America American Studies Association, where we presented papers on our thinking about feminist waves and feminist generations. We appreciate our external reviewers for the University of Minnesota Press, Arlene Kaplan Daniels and Lynn Weber, who provided thoughtful and detailed comments for improving the introduction and the volume in its entirety. We also thank Richard Morrison, acquisitions editor at the University of Minnesota Press, for his support and encouragement, and Raphael Allen, now at the University of Michigan Press, who in conversations at meetings for the Berkshire Conference of Women Historians and the American Sociological Association provided inspiration and intellectual guidance. Many thanks to Amy Tyson, who worked tirelessly to polish and format the text for publication. And finally, thanks to Miglena Todorova, who produced the index.

Like many collaborative projects, this one entailed a great deal of time, effort, and innovative thought from all three of us. In the accounting system of the corporate university, coauthored projects, particularly anthologies, often "count less" for promotion and tenure because they are considered less work to produce than sole-authored monographs. As Lisa Disch and Jean O'Brien argue in their essay in this volume, much of the innovative work done by politically committed faculty is accomplished in overtime. Our coedited anthology and coauthored introduction were indeed produced in overtime. Hokulani and Karla both completed their PhDs, went on the job market, and moved to tenure track positions while working on this book, and Jennifer completed her term as director of graduate studies and then later her term as director of the Center for Advanced Feminist Studies. While we are well aware that administrators are unlikely to change their accounting procedures at our behest, we would nevertheless like to acknowledge the work that the three of us did in reading, meeting, discussing, writing, commenting on our contributors' chapters, and preparing the manuscript for final publication. We are enormously grateful to our contributors—Sam Bullington, Susan Cahn, Dawn Rae Davis, Lisa Disch, Sara Evans, Elizabeth Faue, Roderick Ferguson, Peter Hennen, Toni McNaron, Wendy Leo Moore, Jean O'Brien, Felicity Schaeffer-Grabiel, Anne Firor Scott, Janet Spector, Amanda Swarr, and Miglena Todorova—who responded graciously to our many questions and did their own overtime to write their essays.

Our intent in producing this anthology is to shed light on the rich complexity of feminist generations in the academy that have been so central to our lives and work. The same networks of individuals who sustain (and have sustained) us as scholars, teachers, and women have also contributed their wisdom and strength throughout the making of this book. To all of you, we offer our thanks.

Introduction

Feminist Waves, Feminist Generations

Hokulani K. Aikau, Karla A. Erickson,
and Jennifer L. Pierce

*What would feminism look like if we were to adopt a perspective
born of movement and mobile trajectories?*
Kalpala Ram

On a chilly February 2000 day in a small basement classroom at the University of Minnesota, Jennifer Pierce asked the graduate students in her seminar to describe how and when they had developed a feminist consciousness. At first glance, there was nothing atypical
about this room of women (of various ages) being asked about feminism. Looking back, what stands out were the answers these students
gave about their "encounters with feminism." The older women in the
seminar came of age as feminists in the 1970s and spoke of arriving at
academic feminism later in life as a result of personal experiences such
as divorce or their involvement in social movements such as labor organizing outside the university. By contrast, the younger women encountered feminism in the 1990s and described an early exposure to feminist
ideas through their formal education and through exposure to American popular culture including films and television shows. When they arrived at undergraduate institutions, they were prepped to develop feminist politics, and they were able to point to stronger institutional support
for their feminist concerns, including faculty, mentors, peers, texts, and
courses, which they drew from and added to while developing their own
feminist visions.

This seemingly generational distinction amid this small group of
women spurred an ongoing conversation among the three of us—Hokulani Aikau, Karla Erickson, and Jennifer Pierce—about the changing
lives, conceptual frameworks, and politics of feminists in the academy
over the past thirty years. Initially, we were struck by how these stories
seemed to reflect recent generational narratives about feminism that
position the second wave as those who "came of age" during the rise of

social movements in the late 1960s and early 1970s *against* the third wave, or those who first came to feminism in college in the 1990s. One recent account, for instance, conceptualizes generations between feminists as a timeless and universal relationship between mother and daughter. Here, (young) graduate students tell stories of (older) faculty "mothers" who not only fail to empathize and listen but attack their ideas as apprentice scholars, while feminist faculty, on the other hand, lament the thrashing their work receives by this younger generation of "ungrateful women."[1] Yet another narrative assumes a linear, progressive understanding of history in the relations between generations. Here, third wave writers presume that their brand of feminism is more theoretically and politically sophisticated than earlier versions.[2] And still another story asserts that collective struggle is a relic of the past and either celebrates or bemoans third wave feminism's more individualistic forms of political style.[3]

However, as we talked about the feminists in our lives as well as our own experiences, this generational narrative began to break down, and we found ourselves instead talking about the uneven diffusion of feminist teachings across disciplines and within different institutional locations over time. While some graduate students we knew learned about feminism in college courses in the 1990s, others in other institutions and disciplines simply did not have this opportunity. On the other hand, while some faculty received training in feminist theory and methods, others had been involved in social movements, and still others had neither experience. At the same time, we were also aware of continuities between so-called generations with respect to the continuing significance of particular forms of politics, conceptual ideas, and/or experiences. Some graduate students, for instance, strongly identified with and practiced the collective forms of political activism that often characterizes second wave feminism. Generations seemed too rigid a category to fully explain the variety of experiences represented by the lives of our feminist colleagues. How, then, to account for the internal differences we noticed within feminist generations? And how do we explain continuities between them?

To answer these questions, this volume takes up Kalpala Ram's challenge by looking at feminist generations in the academy through the lens of movement and mobile trajectories.[4] To do so, we turn first to the metaphor of waves. Although waves offer the possibility of thinking in terms of fluidity and movement within and between generations, the metaphor has often been used in recent scholarship to cut genera-

tions in two by fixing second and third wave feminists in static opposition. By contrast, our intent is to trouble the static figuring of generations by placing emphasis on how feminism *moves* and develops *over time
and place*. While individuals may belong to generations based on year of
birth, their experiences are also influenced by the ideas, support, and
resources available at a given time and place. Here, we use feminist generations as a reference point for the timing of one's entry into graduate
school, and feminist waves as a metaphor for the movement and relocation of theories, politics, methods, and ways of knowing across time
and place. As we argue in this volume, thinking about feminist waves as
movement highlights the variations within generational groups as well
as continuities between them.

Although there are problems with these terms, which we discuss below, there are good reasons for retaining and redefining them *provision-
ally*. If we are to have any kind of conversation at all about generations
of feminists, and many of us do see ourselves as products of different
generations, we need to begin somewhere. This is not to say that our categories are seamless or innocent; they are, of course, fraught with normative assumptions. At the same time, however, categories also have the
productive power to open up new possibilities for seeing and knowing.
By engaging and critiquing them, our objective is to create productive
trouble for the binary between the second and third waves in feminist
historiography. For example, by rethinking these terms, we draw attention to the critical presence of at least one in-between generation, what
we call the 2.5 generation.

To capture the multiplicity of generations and the fluidity within and
between them, this volume draws upon life stories from contemporary
feminist scholars at various points in their academic careers. Methodologically, life stories (or personal narratives) have the potential to provide
the kind of detail that is often missing in synthetic historical accounts.
They can bring to light new or untapped perspectives on broader historical processes and phenomena that may undermine, refute, or contradict dominant views.[5] The personal narratives in the chapters that follow challenge recent feminist writing about generations in several ways.
First, they move beyond the second and third wave binary to reveal the
multiplicity of feminist generations in the academy. In research university settings, there are graduate students in training as well as junior and
senior faculty trained at distinct historical moments in varied disciplines
and institutions. What this means is that in the contemporary moment

there are at least three, if not more, generations of feminists producing knowledge in any given research institution. Second, while there are obviously some broad similarities within academic cohorts—for example, our contributors who "came of age" in the late 1960s and 1970s all discuss the significance of the women's movement in their lives—the essays in this volume also highlight important differences within generations. Attending graduate school at a particular historical moment does not mean that scholars come to feminism in the same way. Nor does it mean that they work within the same theoretical traditions or with the same analytic categories. By contrast, we argue that waves of feminist thought have been *uneven* in their diffusion and reception in the academy across the United States within disciplines and institutional locations. Finally, while much of the literature on the third wave assumes that each generation breaks definitively from the previous one, many of the essays in this volume emphasize continuities between generations.[6]

We situate the personal narratives collected in the volume within a larger historical context in order to explore the contradictions, tensions, advances, and setbacks of feminism in the academy and then use these life stories from three decades of feminist scholars from the University of Minnesota as a case study of feminist generations more broadly. As such, we use the local to address our broader theoretical and conceptual questions. As one of the premier institutions for feminist scholarship in the country, Minnesota is particularly well situated to pursue our questions about academic generations. Not only does it have a thirty-year history of feminist scholarship, pedagogy, and campus activism, but it also houses the nationally recognized Center for Advanced Feminist Studies and a women's studies department with one of the few PhD programs in the country. Over the years, the center brought together scholars from a wide range of disciplines and academic ranks to foster the development of interdisciplinary research and in the mid-1980s to create a graduate minor in feminist studies for graduate students who were pursuing their doctorates in a variety of disciplines. The establishment of the graduate minor and, later, the PhD program at once represents years of collective work by an active community of feminist scholars and also highlights their focus on training future generations of feminist scholars. By institutionalizing professional training through the transmission of a body of knowledge, rules, practices, and conventions to graduate students, Minnesota leads as one of the few universities in the self-conscious creation of generations of scholars.

Certainly, when compared to the histories of other disciplines and fields, feminism is a much newer influence in the academy. Nevertheless, in the past thirty years, feminism has had a profound impact on disciplines, pedagogy, and even on the demographic face of the academy. The numbers of feminist publications as books and articles, the development of new courses and programs such as women's studies, gender studies, and queer studies, as well as the numbers of women graduate students and faculty have grown exponentially across disciplines since the 1970s.[7] By looking at the University of Minnesota as one particular shore where feminist waves of thought have swelled and ebbed, this volume also contributes to what sociologist Karl Mannheim has called the "sociology of knowledge." In Mannheim's conception of this term, knowledge is not produced by individual "great men" but in and through particular intellectual and political communities within specific social historical contexts.[8] Consequently, we are interested in the conditions that make it possible for individuals to produce feminist scholarship at particular historical moments. As the life stories in this volume reveal, these conditions vary widely across time, disciplines, academic departments, and even within the same institutional location at the same historical moment.

Waves and Generations

The distinction between "second wave" and "third wave" is typically used as a way of organizing the history of American feminism in the post–World War II era as well as identifying the generations of activists and scholars who fall within it. While the second wave refers to the women's movement of the 1960s and early 1970s, as well as its intellectual critiques, and the feminists who came of age within it, the third applies to 1990s feminism and those whose first encounter with feminism came within institutional contexts such as college courses or women's studies programs.[9] We challenge this commonplace usage for several reasons. First, it collapses differences between generations of feminists and their intellectual work, thereby reinforcing the false notion that second wave feminists, for instance, are trapped within second wave frameworks and cannot see beyond the significance of gender in their analytical thinking.[10] In addition, it flattens the details of individual life stories as well as the complexity of theories and concepts produced in particular historical moments. The broadly stroked story of second wave feminism as white and middle-class, for example, omits the stories of women of color and others who do not fit this dominant narrative.[11] Further, this narrative also implies that race as an analytical category did not emerge until recently despite the fact that women of color feminists have always theorized about the intersection of gender, race, and class.[12]

To avoid these conceptual problems, we disentangle these terms, using *feminist waves* as a metaphor for the displacement and movement of theories, methods, and ways of knowing that flow within a given generational cohort as well as across time and space, and *feminist generations* as a reference point for the timing of one's entry into the academic life cycle. As Hokulani Aikau's essay in this volume reminds us, attention to the scientific basis of the wave metaphor allows us to redirect the focus of feminist historiography from the general to the specific. To those of us standing on the shore, waves appear to be distinct entities connected only rhythmically to the one before and the one after. By contrast, scientists find that waves do not exist in isolation but are connected to multiple sets of waves called wave trains. Rather than think about the "second wave" and "third wave" as separate waves that we can count from the shore, Aikau suggests that we look to the horizon for the variety of waves that combine to produce a single wave train in order to understand the "multiplicity central to feminist legacies and trajectories." Such a conceptual move brings more detail into focus by acknowledging the variations that exist within each larger swell, and disrupts the notion that second wave feminism is monolithic, insisting instead that it is comprised of many smaller waves such as third world feminism, liberal feminism, and radical feminism, to name only a few.

Further, the science of waves speaks to how energy is carried forward from a previous force, such as a storm center in the Pacific Ocean, and also how it changes as it encounters islands, shores, and currents. Applying this insight to academic feminism, we can see that at particular historical moments certain ideas and theories gain momentum (for example, the dramatic increase in the number of books and articles that theorize the intersection of gender, race, and class in the 1980s), but their widespread diffusion and reception depend on the particular institutions and disciplines they encounter along the way. In some colleges and universities, this scholarship may become part of an established curriculum in women's studies and other disciplines, and in others it may be marginalized or completely neglected. For example, in the early 1980s the Center for Research on Women at Memphis State University took the feminist intellectual project of race, class, and gender seriously in its curriculum workshops and research, while other institutions in the same historical moment did not.[13] Here, the wave metaphor helps us to understand the uneven diffusion and reception of feminist thought across institutions in the United States.

Institutions, in turn, produce generations of academic feminists through graduate training and professionalization. As the initial entry point into academic careers, graduate school is a professionally formative experience. Not only does it serve as the means for familiarizing students with a body of knowledge, rules, practices, and conventions relevant to particular disciplines and fields, but the process also leads to the collective formation of cohorts who share this experience. In fact, many of the contributors to this volume describe themselves as someone who was trained in the 1970s, the 1980s, and so on. Consequently, rather than taking year of birth as a point of entry into a generation, we consider the year entering graduate school to be significant. Further, the clockwork of academic careers suggests a distinctive time span for separating one cohort from the next. Within roughly a ten-year period, one academic generation may complete coursework and exams, research, write, and defend their dissertations, and ultimately establish themselves in their first tenure track position. Within this ten-year cycle many academics journey from undergraduate training to positions as professors, at which time they, in turn, train the next generation of graduate and undergraduate students.[14]

By focusing on the timing of entry to graduate school, we are not suggesting that other life events are unimportant. As many of our contributors make clear, early life experiences, participation in social movements, or the mentors and courses they encountered in college produced lasting and formative experiences in defining themselves as feminists. In fact, for some, graduate school did not involve any kind of feminist training at all. Regardless of the specific training they receive, for academics, entrance into graduate training often becomes an important social and historical marker. Not only does it mark the point for the creation of distinct cohorts, but it also serves as an organizing principle in how academics narrate the temporal dimension of their careers. Reconceptualizing generations through the clockwork of academic careers disrupts the simplistic binary between generations of feminists from the so-called second and third wave and introduces the possibility of multiple generations. From the late 1960s to the present, one can imagine, for instance, cohorts who were trained in the 1970s, the 1980s, the 1990s, and so on. Further, dispensing with age as the primary determinant of one's generation enables us to avoid the familial and sometimes essentialist assumptions that situate the third generation as oppositional to the second.[15]

This volume focuses on three generations of feminist scholars: those who entered graduate school in the late 1960s and 1970s (the second generation), those who began in the 1980s (the 2.5 generation), and those who began in the 1990s (the third generation).[16] While our thinking about generations as *multiple* disrupts the binary between second and third wave feminism, it is suggestive, nonetheless, of a linear progression of people and their ideas. Certainly, generations taken alone cannot fully describe the complex interplay of forces that come into effect when one encounters feminism, how one receives feminist ideas and politics, and the style and form of feminist politics one subsequently advances. We disrupt the notion that feminist generations are somehow marching inexorably forward in a progressive history of ideas by arguing that feminist generations must be understood in conjunction with feminist waves in particular institutional and disciplinary locations.

Unlike our definition of generations, which privileges time over place, the wave metaphor requires us to pay attention to historical time *and* institutional place. Bringing them together allows us to see how waves of thought are selectively appropriated in specific institutional locations at particular historical moments. In our conceptualization of waves, the University of Minnesota operates as one particular "shore" upon which feminist waves have swelled. However, keeping place constant does not mean that we imagine the University of Minnesota as a static institutional space. We use this one institution to demonstrate how the diffusion and reception of ideas and resources vary over time, space, and even *within* particular institutions. Consequently, thinking about generations through the metaphor of waves becomes useful for describing the variety of experiences, politics, and forms of feminist thought that exist within a single generational cohort.

Feminist Generations at Minnesota, 1964–2000

Feminism of the 1960s developed within a global and national context of intense social and political change. As struggles for independence and liberation went on across the African continent and reverberated

around the world, Mao declared a cultural revolution in China, student protest movements took off in Europe, and the Soviet Union invaded the countries of Eastern Europe. At the same time, within the United States, the environmental movement began to grow, while civil rights protests such as freedom rides and sit-ins and the numbers of participants in the Black Power movement exploded across the country.[17] For members of the New Left, the civil rights movement, Black Power, and the struggles of the Vietnamese against U.S. imperialism—a small third world country unwilling to surrender to the most powerful country in the world—inspired radical action and a politics characterized by "a kind of third-worldism."[18] Indeed, rhetorical claims of third world oppression and liberation were appropriated not only by the New Left in their manifestoes and other publications but by second generation feminists as well as many other activist groups in their writings.[19]

Equipped with an analysis of power often inspired by Marxism within this transformative political climate, numerous radical women's groups began to proliferate in the late 1960s and early 1970s across the United States. A small sampling of some of these groups includes collectives and organizations such as the Black Women's Liberation Group, Bread and Roses, the Chicago Women's Liberation Union, the Combahee River Collective, the National Black Feminist Organization, the Redstockings Collective, WITCH (Women's International Terrorist Conspiracy from Hell), and WARN (Women of All Red Nations).[20] Their analyses of sexual as well as racial and class politics became a wave that swept into the academy as many feminist activists entered graduate and professional programs across the United States.[21]

As on most American colleges and universities in the 1960s, the women's movement, the civil rights movement, and the anti–Vietnam War movement had a profound effect on the University of Minnesota, resulting in the creation of new academic programs and departments as well as in changes in teaching methods and curriculum. Campus activism inspired by the civil rights movement led to the January 1969 occupation of Morrill Hall, the administration building, by African American students who had formed an alliance with community representatives. This demonstration led directly to the creation of the Department of Afro-American and African Studies as well as the programs in American Indian studies later in 1969 and Chicano studies in 1972.[22] In May 1970, after the Nixon administration announced the U.S invasion of Cambodia, students and faculty at Minnesota planned a campuswide protest

against the war and began to hold teach-ins on U.S. foreign policy and the military, the war, and corporate responsibility. Protestors called for the suspension of classes and demanded that the university remove ROTC from its campus, stop war-related research, and sell its stock in companies providing munitions. May 26 and June 30 were designated as "days of reflection" on the "national crisis" for faculty, students, and staff, and class attendance dropped to an all-time low of 10 percent.[23]

This was also a time of intense feminist activity and organizing. As early as 1960, the first Women's Center opened with generous funding from the Carnegie Foundation. According to former director Anne Truax, "It was the first such program in the United States, followed the next year by one at Sarah Lawrence, and then rapidly in subsequent years at most universities."[24] Initially, the center was designed for women who had married in the late 1940s and 1950s, perhaps never finished a college degree, and wanted to reenter the job market. The first head of the Women's Center was Virginia Senders (psychology), who ran counseling, in conjunction with Elizabeth Cless (Continuing Education). Kathryn Scott Randolph, who became the second head of the center in 1965, was succeeded by Anne Truax, who held the position until 1991. Describing her initial arrival to this position in 1969, Truax writes:

The activities of the Center were completely at a stand still. . . . So, I was free to invent the whole program. . . . I hired a counselor, and it was soon apparent that we needed to turn away from re-entry women, and convince traditional students to realize they would be working all their lives. I started teaching a class in Family Social Science called—I hate to think of this title now—"Life Styles of Educated American Women," and it was probably the first college course based on feminist ideas in the U.S. I hired as many sharp women graduate students as the budget would allow, and let them propose activities that they thought would interest other students to help them see how the world was changing, to bring them the ideas of feminism.[25]

The center also started a newsletter, discussion groups for students, and, in conjunction with many requests, a library. In addition, it maintained strong connections with local and national feminist communities through many of Truax's networks such as Minnesota NOW, the Women's Equity Action League, and the national advisory committee for the Project on the Status and Education of Women of the Association of American Colleges, which spearheaded Title IX.

The differential treatment of women and men faculty and administrators also led to other important innovations at the university. In

1969, Truax proposed the first Council on University Women's Progress (CUWP) to Don Smith, then vice president for academic affairs, who welcomed the idea and made the initial appointments that formed the CUWP. The first issue the council tackled was the exclusion of women from university committees and the faculty senate. They also conducted a survey on women faculty affiliated with the Women's Center, and after finding that neither Academic Affairs nor payroll had any records based on sex, they used faculty insurance records "since only insurance cared about the effects of gender."[26] Statistics published by this group in 1971 reveal that approximately 11 percent (125 of 1,400) of tenure track faculty across all ranks and colleges were women. In fact, departments such as anthropology, history, music, psychology, and many others had no women faculty at all. The CUWP also pressed the issue of salary equity for women and men in faculty and administrative positions.[27]

In reflecting upon this time in her life, Truax, who went on to become not only a respected campus leader for feminist institutional change but also a nationally recognized expert on sexual harassment policy, writes:

I had been a Kenwood matron for twenty years, raising five children and doing volunteer work. In 1969 I never expected to be hired as head of the Women's Center; I was still a graduate student, I had no previous paid work experience, I had no idea what was expected of me nor did the people I reported to. . . . Minnesota had just appointed the first vice president of student affairs, a progressive speech-communications faculty member who was making up his job as he went along. He left me free to do the same. I was worried that I might get into trouble, through my tendency to shoot from the hip, and he told me that if anyone complained about my actions, he would cover for me. . . . I am certain that it would not be possible to have the same kind of career today as I had. The advent of feminism served, for me, as a kind of surfboard, lifting me above petty academic snobbery. . . . I came to represent feminism on the Minnesota campus. I, of course, had my mailing/phone list of supporters in the U, locally, and all over the state ready to bring down on the administration's collective head if I needed it. A change in administration policy removed my faculty appointment, and I never had tenure, but I was untouchable. . . . I have been called an iconoclast, but I think the truth was I was less bound by academic protocol than those with academic appointments.[28]

Along with feminist graduate students Nancy Betz, Louise Douce, Elsa Greene, Andrea Hinding, Judy Wanjala, and Susan Phipps-Yonas, Truax helped frame the initial proposal documenting the need for a women's studies program at Minnesota. They also recruited faculty members including Joanne Arnaud (political science), Clarke Chambers (history),

Toni McNaron (English), Carolyn Rose (sociology), and others who supported the project by helping to revise the proposal and shepherd it through the university bureaucracy. The first courses in the program were taught in the 1972–73 academic year, with McNaron as the first co-coordinator, and a consultative committee of twenty-one faculty members and graduate students.[29] Later that same year, temporary assistant professor Shyamala Rajender filed a lawsuit when the chemistry department refused to consider her for a tenure track job. Her allegations of discrimination ultimately led to a class action suit that was filed on behalf of women in faculty and administrative positions at Minnesota. After seven years of litigation, Rajender and the university settled out of court, and the university agreed to operate under a court-ordered consent decree mandating affirmative action goals with a timetable for hiring more women. The Rajender consent decree had a significant impact on the hiring, retention, and promotion of women faculty not only at the University of Minnesota but at colleges and universities across the nation.[30] At Minnesota, for example, the number of women faculty members increased between 1980 and 1997 from 27 percent to 39 percent of assistant professors, from 16 percent to 32 percent of associate professors, and from 6 percent to 15 percent of full professors.[31]

Like many other feminist activists/academics of this time period, the second generation contributors to this volume, Toni McNaron (English), Sara Evans (history), and Janet Spector (anthropology), were hired during a time of economic expansion in the United States and in the academy. During the 1960s and 1970s, colleges and universities across the country were not only hiring greater numbers of faculty in response to the needs of a growing undergraduate and graduate student body nationwide but were expanding campuses to incorporate new classroom buildings, dormitories, and others facilities, as well as new programs and departments.[32] All three attended graduate school in the 1960s or early 1970s and came to the University of Minnesota as junior faculty between 1964 and 1976, where they spent their entire academic careers. These three women were not only feminist "firsts" in their respective departments but were also part of a small group of feminist scholars who launched the women's studies program at the university in the early 1970s and, later, the Center for Advanced Feminist Studies (CAFS) in the early 1980s, which housed collaborative research projects on comparable worth, personal narratives, and many other topics.[33] In fact, each of them served as either chair of Women's Studies or director

of CAFS earlier in their careers. In short, they were among a handful of the most influential second generation feminist faculty in the 1970s who laid the groundwork for building feminist institutional support at the University of Minnesota.

To be sure, they were not the only feminist scholars to do the important work of institution building. The 1970s witnessed the fluorescent development of a small but critical mass of new feminist faculty hires in the College of Liberal Arts.[34] Our contributors' personal narrative essays capture the intellectual energy and vibrancy of this particular historical moment. Spector, for example, contrasts her feelings of uncertainty in graduate school at the University of Wisconsin, Madison (she considered dropping out to continue her political work, which seemed more meaningful at the time) with her enthusiasm about the feminist community at the University of Minnesota. She writes in her essay:

My enthusiasm about feminist archaeology was reinforced significantly by participation in the vibrant and ever-growing community of feminist scholars at Minnesota. We came together in the context of building the Women's Studies Department (established in the 1973–74 year, coincidentally my first year at Minnesota). From the beginning of my academic career, I was intimately involved in all facets of Women's Studies. The feminist intellectual community, not my "home" department, provided the essential support, encouragement, and safe space for pursuing feminist work. . . . Bolstered by the existence of our "real" home department, we formed an active support group to take on departmental affirmative action battles and to organize feminist anthropology colloquia and other events.

Similarly, in her e-mail exchange with three other women's historians of different feminist generations (this volume), Evans reflects, "Wow, what a difference it makes to have been an undergraduate in the 1960s and to enter graduate school when I did." She recognizes the late 1960s and early 1970s as a period when women's history and other feminist concerns were gaining momentum. McNaron writes in her essay about how the formation of ethnic studies and women's studies programs in the early 1970s played a vital role in changing faculty perceptions about what legitimately could be included as subject matter for courses and for research. She writes,

Suddenly, information about our history and culture as well as books by lesbian artists and activists became available as texts we could teach in our classes. Students demanded information about this crucial phase of feminism's long and illustrious history. More and more lesbian faculty working in such programs

gained the courage to come out to their heterosexual colleagues and to hope
these relationships would be maintained after disclosure.

While McNaron's essay begins in 1964 in the pre-Stonewall era by describing her painful feelings of isolation as a closeted lesbian, her narrative, as well as those of the gay and lesbian academics she interviewed
for her book *Poisoned Ivy: Lesbians and Gay Academics Confronting Homophobia,* marks the dramatic shift in the political and intellectual environment of colleges and universities for gay and lesbian academics in
the 1970s.[35]

As the 1970s became the 1980s, Evans's influential book *Personal
Politics: The Roots of Women's Liberation in the Civil Rights Movement and
the New Left* stands out as a bridge that connects feminist activism "on
the streets" to feminist activism on college campuses and in the classroom.[36] (The book traces the origins of second wave feminism to wom-
en's political participation in the civil rights movement and the New
Left—both movements in which Evans herself participated.) Already
feminism had grown to a social movement with a distinct history and a
relationship to other social movements. It had also spawned a growing
number of grassroots organizations. For example, the women's health
movement, made public by the book *Our Bodies, Ourselves,* helped create a growing number of battered women's shelters, rape crisis centers,
community women's centers, bookstores, and coffeehouses across the
country.[37] During the same time period, women's studies courses and
programs across the United States were becoming institutionalized—for
instance, Minnesota's women's studies program became an official academic department in 1979—and fledgling university policies and procedures for sexual harassment grievances were being developed and put
into place.[38] This heady institutional moment also coincided with a demographic shift in graduate programs nationwide when the numbers of
white women and students of color increased in disciplines throughout
the liberal arts. By the end of the 1980s in sociology, for example, 55 percent of graduate students at the doctoral level were women.[39] While feminist pioneers in the social sciences and the humanities have described
their experiences in graduate school as a time of intense isolation, as
the lone woman scholar who faced intellectual uncertainty and professional exclusion, this newer cohort of women found a critical mass of
like-minded graduate students.[40]

Historian Susan Cahn, who was a graduate student in the 1980s, describes this time period as one in which "the fields of women's history and feminist studies were flourishing" (this volume). Not only did second wave scholarship prove to be inspirational for dissertation projects, but new books and articles published by women of color, lesbian feminists, postcolonial theorists, and poststructuralists posed serious challenges to the ethnocentric assumptions of white middle-class, Western feminism. In 1981, for example, two path-breaking books by feminists of color first came out: Gloria Anzaldúa and Cherríe Moraga's anthology *This Bridge Called My Back: Writings by Radical Women of Color,* and Angela Davis's *Women, Race, and Class.* Both identified the problematic assumptions of academic feminism, specifically, how primarily white middle-class feminists had marginalized the experiences of women of color in their writings, implicitly rendering white middle-class feminism the "official" version of feminism. About the same time, Adrienne Rich's influential *Signs* essay, "Compulsory Heterosexuality and Lesbian Existence," launched yet another critique of feminism by arguing that it had situated heterosexual experiences as central, overlooking the particularities of lesbians' lives.[41] By the mid-1980s, scholars such as Gayatri Spivak were challenging reductive representations of third world women.[42] And many poststructuralists, including Spivak, began to use race-based interrogations of the category *woman* to deconstruct its foundational character. In her now classic 1985 book, *Sexual/Textual Politics,* Toril Moi pitted Anglo-American empiricists against French deconstructionists, celebrating French feminist Julia Kristeva as an exemplary figure whose antiessentialist arguments challenged conceptions of a universal womanhood.[43] For many feminists who entered graduate programs in the late 1970s and throughout the 1980s, this newer scholarship served as a generative force in their own work, provoking new feminist critiques and theoretical formulations of power that would eventually become central to third wave scholarship. While earlier formulations were often inspired by Marxism or sociologist Max Weber, more recent scholarship is often influenced by poststructuralism.[44]

Of course, not all 2.5 feminists encountered these intellectual innovations in graduate school. For some in this in-between generation, their first encounter with feminism came in social movement politics; for others, it came through their coursework in women's studies and other disciplines; and still others had neither experience. Consequently, their first encounters with feminist scholarship and activism were quite different than those of the second generation.

Moreover, despite more than a decade of social movement activism and the creation of feminist institutions and organizations, 2.5 feminists worked against a cultural backdrop marked by a dramatic move to the political right. In response to changing demographics and college curricula, conservative scholars and media pundits of the time declared a "culture war" in the academy, vilifying feminists and scholars of color for dismantling the Western canon, undermining standards for excellence, and stifling free speech. At Minnesota the so-called political correctness follies were further fueled by conservative resentment about the new practices created through the Rajender consent decree such as hiring guidelines, gender equity salary adjustments, and programs devoted to improving the campus climate for women. Members of the local affiliate of the National Association of Scholars lambasted the administration and campus feminists for initiating a mandatory sexual-harassment training seminar for faculty and graduate-student teaching assistants and programs that they perceived to be threats against freedom of speech on campus.[45] Meanwhile, in national politics the Reagan and Bush administrations increasingly weakened or reversed gains made by marginalized groups, tightened budgets for social and educational programs, and instituted protections for the rich and big business.[46]

Against this conservative national landscape and a precipitous decline in resources for higher education, our 2.5 feminist generation contributors Susan Cahn, Elizabeth Faue, Lisa Disch, Jean O'Brien, and Jennifer Pierce prepared for qualifying examinations and defended their dissertations in graduate programs across the country and then took their first tenure track positions in the early 1990s. Just as Cahn and Faue were leaving Minnesota's graduate program in history to take tenure track positions at other institutions, Disch, O'Brien, and Pierce arrived at Minnesota as junior faculty. In their essay, Disch and O'Brien describe their academic generation at Minnesota as one between the boom of the late 1960s to mid-1970s, when innovative programs such as Women's Studies, American Indian Studies, and many others were founded, and, on the other side, the hiring boom in the late 1990s, sparked by the rising stock market and by the retirement of the generation that preceded the 1960s and 1970s. As they write,

At the University of Minnesota, 40 percent of the 540 faculty in the College of Liberal Arts were hired between 1998 and 2004; they arrived in cohorts of forty to ninety not only to fill vacancies but to take up newly created assistant professorships in comparative literature, cultural studies, women's studies, American studies, Afro-American studies, Asian studies, American Indian studies, and more. As "the bust" generation in between, we are a cohort so small we are barely visible as such. The year we arrived, 1990, the college made nine hires, only three of them assistant professors.

The smallness of their academic cohort, the broader political climate, and the existence of a vibrant feminist community created multiple contradictions for these three women's positions as junior faculty. Despite the critical mass of feminist scholars across the campus, the existence of CAFS, and a longstanding Department of Women's Studies, they found the reception of feminism in their respective departments to be uneven. While in history O'Brien had a number of prominent and supportive feminist faculty members as colleagues, Disch and Pierce found themselves in departments (political science and sociology, respectively) where feminist colleagues were few and such scholarship was regarded with suspicion and sometimes hostility. They also encountered vastly different norms about self-government within their respective departments. Whereas democratic representation was taken to an extreme in history, where O'Brien, as one of two junior people, served as the junior representative on practically every committee in the department, in political science and sociology governance structures were more hierarchically structured, and junior faculty were expected to be seen but not heard. Of necessity, as assistant professors they formed cohorts and friendships not within departments but across them.

The waves of innovation in the 1970s that created new interdisciplinary departments and centers at the university also facilitated Disch, O'Brien, and Pierce's relationships with feminist scholars across the campus. All three worked with feminist faculty and graduate students in American Indian Studies, Women's Studies, American Studies, and CAFS, and they served together on the *Signs: Journal of Women in Culture and Society* editorial board during its five-year tenure at Minnesota (1990–95). These sites served as important venues for collaboration with senior scholars and graduate students across the campus. At the same time, the size of their academic cohort as well as their rank meant they were too few and too junior to assume the mantle of perpetuating these innovative programs—there just were not enough people to do all the work. State budget cuts, demographic shifts in hiring, the rise of the corporate university, and a conservative backlash all contributed to what Disch and O'Brien describe as the "precarious institutionalization" of these interdisciplinary departments and centers, and that situation, in turn, set up conditions for the uncompensated and overtime labor that is required to keep them running. In contrast to feminist accounts that attribute such tensions and anxieties to a battle for place between second and third generation feminists, Disch and O'Brien blame structural conditions, thereby contradicting the literature that pits third generation feminists against the second in an oedipal battle for supremacy in the academy.

As this conservative backlash against the legal and economic gains of white women and people of color continued into the 1990s, third generation feminists began to enter graduate school at the University of Minnesota. In contrast to second generation feminists, who came to Minnesota during a time when progressive social movement activism catapulted the university into dramatic change, these scholars began their PhD programs when the university, like many other institutions of higher learning across the nation, was being shaped by what has been called the "corporatization of the university."[47] Decreases in state funding for higher education led to demands on administrators, faculty, and staff for increased efficiency, productivity, accountability, and "excellence." This trend became most visible in 1995 when Minnesota's Board of Regents initiated a review of tenure that began a series of debates and protests widely publicized in the national press. As law professor Fred Morrison argued, the battle over the terms of tenure was part of a larger trend of "employee-ization" that situated professors as the regents' employees. Faculty leaders responded with a union drive to protect tenure and their right to academic freedom.[48] Although the union drive was ultimately unsuccessful, the margin between supporters and opponents was a slim one. Ultimately, the Board of Regents backed down and approved a tenure contract that treated faculty as free agents, not as their employees. Nevertheless, corporate-inspired practices such as staff cutbacks, faculty hiring freezes, and small or zero percent raise increases continued through the 1990s.

Despite these more conservative trends, this time period also witnessed several high points for women and for feminism at the University of Minnesota. By the fall of 1998, the university enrolled 52,000 students, 51 percent of whom were women; 11.5 percent, students of color; and 3,000 international students representing 130 different countries.[49] In the same year, the graduate school had approached parity by gender: 48 percent of the 8,000 graduate and professional students across the university were women. As these percentages indicate, gains in demographic representation were not the same for all groups. Inroads for white women continued to outpace access to higher education for women and men of color. In addition, the history of earlier work to institutionalize a diversity of intellectual paradigms had begun to pay off. In 1999, Afro-American and African Studies and American Indian Studies both celebrated their thirtieth anniversaries. Chicano Studies had been institutionalized for over twenty years, Women's Studies for twenty-five years, and CAFS for fifteen. And finally, in 2000, the Schochet Center for Gay, Lesbian, Bisexual, and Transgender Studies (the Schochet Center) first opened its doors.

Inside the academy waves of feminist thought continued to grow. The emergence of postmodern, postcolonial, and queer theories intersected with waves of feminist theorizing to produce new and important intellectual trajectories. For example, early in the 1990s, edited collections such as *Making Face, Making Soul, Haciendo Caras: Creative and Critical Perspectives by Women of Color, Third World Women and the Politics of Feminism, Scattered Hegemonies: Postmodernity and Transnational Feminist Practices*, and *Feminist Genealogies, Colonial Legacies, Democratic Futures* were published.[50] These anthologies along with now canonical essays such as Chela Sandoval's "U.S. Third World Feminism" propelled third generation feminists to think both locally and globally and to harness global technologies as tools for feminist activism.[51] Just as women of color and third world feminists were articulating a politics of feminism that challenged a homogenizing category "woman," the feminist "sex wars" of the 1980s had evolved into the field of queer theory. For example, Judith Butler's *Gender Trouble: Feminism and the Subversion of Identity* and edited collections such as *The Lesbian and Gay Studies Reader* became critical texts in this growing area of inquiry that drew from psychoanalysis, feminist theory, and the postmodern method of deconstruction to call into question normative connections between sex, gender, sexuality, and the body.[52]

In addition to postmodern, postcolonial, and queer theory, third generation feminist scholars also benefited from the increasing canonization of a women's studies curriculum. In addition to a wealth of monographs, previous feminist works had been gathered into a variety of readers that analyzed race, class, and gender simultaneously, including the anthology *Race, Class, and Gender, An Anthology* edited by Margaret Anderson and Patricia Hill Collins (first published in 1992, now in its fifth edition) and *Race, Class, and Gender in the United States* edited by Paula S.

Rothenberg (also first published in 1992 and now in its sixth edition).[53] The availability and wide use of these resources in the classroom meant that third generation feminists were more likely than their predecessors to be exposed to interdisciplinary and intersectional ways of thinking and conducting research.

As these waves of feminist thought swelled within disciplines, departments, and research centers, they also began to move into institutional networks *not* explicitly marked as feminist. In addition to obvious and longstanding sites for the support for feminist scholarship such as CAFS, the MacArthur Interdisciplinary Program on Global Change, Sustainability, and Justice (the MacArthur Program) also became a space that strongly encouraged feminist research. (Established in 1990, the MacArthur Program provides fellowships and research grants to graduate students across disciplines whose research focuses broadly on global studies, sustainability, and social justice.[54]) Consequently, third generation feminists had more institutional resources and networks available to them than previous generations had, providing them with both financial and intellectual support throughout their tenure as graduate students. The availability of these financial and intellectual resources, however, was not the same in every department. While some third generation feminists found themselves in departments and networks that were rich in feminist resources, others struggled to find intellectual spaces within which to work and develop as feminist scholars.

For third generation students in less feminist-friendly departments and disciplines, their graduate training was often a lonely and alienating experience. Peter Hennen and Wendy Leo Moore in the Department of Sociology found few faculty members who supported their research interests. The tenure battle that their adviser, Jennifer Pierce, faced in the mid-1990s reinforced their sense that feminist research was not welcomed in their discipline. For Hennen, the tenure battle was one of many reminders that he was precariously positioned in his institutional "home" department:

It is 1996. I have hit what might euphemistically be referred to as a "bad patch" in my graduate training. My faith in the academy has been severely shaken by what I see happening to Jennifer as she fights for tenure, I am floundering in my attempt to find meaning in my political sociology studies, I am also struggling with grave doubts about my ability to pass the department's qualifying examination, and most of the members of my original cohort have dropped out of the program or transferred to other schools.

The personal narratives by third generation scholars housed in department and networks rich in feminist resources typically recount more positive graduate school experiences. Hokulani Aikau, Karla Erickson, Felicity Schaeffer-Grabiel, and Miglena Todorova all found the Department of American Studies to be a welcoming place to pursue their research. Todorova, for example, describes her transformation in thinking when she found mentors in her department who encouraged her interests:

The intellectuals who helped me find the language and strength to express myself were not the white feminists in the department but an unorthodox historian and the queer scholars. Thanks to David Noble, Roderick Ferguson, and Jennifer Pierce, I finally found an intellectual, postnationalist niche, where I was allowed to question the theories and methods to which I was exposed. I could apply and assess the relevance of these theories to other, non-American and non-Western worlds. I indulged in studying qualitative methods of research, theories of postcolonialism, U.S. third world feminist and queer theories, and U.S. histories challenging American exceptionalism. . . . I could now explore what U.S. history and culture shared with the larger world and how the "backward" culture I came from [Bulgaria] intersected with the "superior" American experience.

Just as Todorova's training brings her into contact with crucial faculty mentors, Aikau, Erickson, and Schaeffer-Grabiel too find their mentors among the faculty in American Studies.

These departmental associations were further strengthened by crosscurrents made up of networks of support provided by interdisciplinary programs such as CAFS. The CAFS network connected nearly all of the feminists in this anthology at one time or another, operating as an extradepartmental institutional site that offered feminists from a wide range of departments across the university a place to come together, share resources, provide support, attend colloquia, workshops, and conferences, and work on collaborative projects. Janet Spector, Sara Evans, Toni McNaron, Jean O'Brien, Jennifer Pierce, Lisa Disch, and Rod Ferguson were all involved in CAFS at one point in their tenure as faculty at the University of Minnesota. In addition, graduate students Sam Bullington, Karla Erickson, and Felicity Schaeffer-Grabiel all received graduate minors in feminist studies through CAFS courses, while Amanda Swarr transferred from the graduate program in anthropology to the feminist studies PhD program once it was available. And finally, Dawn Rae Davis entered Minnesota's feminist landscape in 1998 as part of the first cohort of feminist studies PhD students.

Just as the CAFS network created connections between the contributors to this volume, many were also connected through their work with the MacArthur Program. Graduate students Aikau and Schaeffer-Grabiel, who received MacArthur fellowships, benefited not only from the financial support but from the formal and informal intellectual networks established and nurtured in the program, where they would eventually meet other graduate students such as Bullington and Swarr, who both began their graduate careers in the anthropology department. Each of them participated in MacArthur workshops that introduced them to University of Minnesota faculty, visiting scholars, policy makers, activists, and advocates in a wide variety of fields and areas of expertise. Informal gatherings at brown bag presentations and discussions, and social activities in the MacArthur office over cups of tea or coffee provided them with a feeling of belonging and intellectual camaraderie that went beyond their individual disciplinary departments. For Bullington and Swarr, who found themselves in a less feminist-friendly academic department, the MacArthur program enabled them to find feminist mentors, funding for their research, and "a vibrant intellectual and political community."

The MacArthur Program also operated as a crosscurrent that often brought feminist graduate students together for the first time, as well as building on the strength of existing networks among faculty. For example, faculty members Lisa Disch, Jean O'Brien, and Jennifer Pierce were all affiliated with the MacArthur Program. Further, Disch and Pierce were actively involved in the MacArthur Consortium Gender Network, which brought faculty and students together to workshop grant proposals, dissertation chapters, and other works in progress. Graduate students Aikau, Bullington, Schaeffer-Grabiel, and Swarr all participated in one or more of these workshops.

For third generation scholars fortunate enough to be housed in departments where feminism was deeply rooted, these extradepartmental networks deepened and widened their intellectual resources. Not only did they find themselves more often surrounded by feminists of their own generation, but they were also able to build on and move through the networks built and maintained by previous generations. These institutional networks—whether explicitly marked as feminist or not—were an essential ingredient in the context within which the third generation of feminist scholars began graduate school, received their training, and moved forward into their own careers.

Reconceptualizing Feminist Generations

The personal narratives collected in this volume bring the outlines of the broader history of feminist generations that we have just described into sharper focus. They not only give us a sense of the distinct routes that brought each of our contributors to feminism at different historical moments but underscore what feminist waves of thought look like and how the waves they encountered varied in different institutional and disciplinary contexts. In contrast to the static picture of difference often used to depict feminist generations, the life stories collected here complicate such narratives, compelling us to reimagine difference within and between generations.

"Coming of Age" and Intellectual Trajectories

Recent writing about the "third wave" narrates a particular origin story for this generation. While the "second wave" comes to feminism through social movement activism, the third generation first encounters feminism through the courses they take in college. While most of the essays by our second generation contributors reveal the importance of the women's movement to their intellectual and political development as feminist scholars, the personal narratives by third generation feminists reveal that the routes to "coming of age" are incredibly varied. Karla Erickson, for example, writes of growing up in a white middle-class suburban family in the Midwest and reading books like *Free to Be You and Me* as a young girl. When she began college in 1991, she painfully discovered how the backlash against feminism played out on her small liberal arts college campus but also found the intellectual support and encouragement of three feminist mentors, who nurtured her intellectual growth and feminist vision. By contrast, Roderick Ferguson, who grew up in the rural South, writes about the early influences of "sissies at the picnic," the black men who brought books and music alive to children and adults, men who sauntered and sang but were also admired and respected in the community for their talents before the AIDS crisis of the 1980s. For a young boy who preferred reading books and imagining himself as Wonder Woman to playing sports, these men not only provided important role models for his love of books but for the possibilities of a feminized black masculinity. As he discovered later, in college and graduate school, it is the scholarly work by women of color feminists and queer theorists that provides him with the theoretical tools to make raced, gendered, and queer sense of his life story and his intellectual work.

In another third generation story, which begins in Eastern Europe, Miglena Todorova highlights the importance of place in constructing and shaping her understandings of feminism. In Bulgaria, her first encounter with Western feminism came through American movies, such as *Working Girl,* that equate women's liberation with work in the paid labor force. From her vantage point, the notion that women had to fight for liberation through work seemed hopelessly out of touch with the lives of Bulgarian women in the postsocialist era who had always worked. It was only when she read the writings of women of color feminists and postcolonial critics as a graduate student at the University of Minnesota that she was able to connect her intellectual questions with feminist critiques. Despite the fact that Todorova, Ferguson, and Erickson all began in the same generational cohort, each one came to feminism in different ways. Just as the contours of waves change when they encounter island shores, the narratives collected in this volume reveal how the feminist legacies each person brings with them to graduate school change and shift direction as they encounter new theoretical and methodological paradigms and insights.

Just as the timing of entry into graduate school does not necessarily determine whether one receives training in feminist scholarship, neither does it fix the theoretical focus of one's work. New conceptual and theoretical developments may be transformative for many feminists regardless of generation. For example, while second generation feminist scholar Janet Spector's earliest scholarship is well known for challenging archaeology's androcentric canon, her most recent book, *What This Awl Means,* reflects changes in her thinking about the production of knowledge in her discipline.[55] She writes in her essay (this volume),

There were two major turning points in the project. First, after working without Dakota involvement during the early years of the research, in 1985 I began working collaboratively with two Dakota colleagues whose relatives had lived at the site in the 1830s and 1840s. Second, in February 1986, Renato Rosaldo presented a lecture at Minnesota titled "Where Objectivity Lies: The Rhetoric of Anthropology." Just as the initial click experience about "Man the Hunter" in 1968 provoked a major reassessment of what I had learned so far in anthropology, these two turning points prompted another major phase of "unlearning the discipline." My attention shifted beyond the treatment of women and gender as subjects of study in archaeology to incorporate issues relating to the treatment of Indian people, men included. I also moved from an emphasis on developing a new method for the archaeological study of gender to finding new ways to portray the past we had unearthed and our relationship to it.

Spector's book challenges problematic assumptions in archeology about whose voice counts in the production of knowledge—specifically that archaeologists and not American Indian people know best how to conduct research—and expands its boundaries by insisting upon new forms of narrative influenced by literary criticism and Native American fiction to tell stories about the past. In this way, her second generation narrative marks the moments when she encounters new perspectives that complicate her earlier work.

Not only do feminist projects change over time in response to new scholarship and theoretical formulations, but scholars take up divergent theoretical projects even within the same historical moment. The 2.5 feminists in this volume—Lisa Disch, Jean O'Brien, and Jennifer Pierce—all came from different disciplines and research institutions in the 1980s. Pierce, for example, was influenced by feminist mentors in sociology and anthropology at the University of California at Berkeley such as Nancy Chodorow, Arlie Hochschild, and Nancy Scheper-Hughes. Her first book, *Gender Trials: Emotional Lives in Contemporary Law Firms*, an ethnographic study of the reproduction of gender and class relations in corporate law firms, is informed by feminist psychoanalytic theory, the sociology of emotions, and Marxist studies of the labor process. While Pierce's first project reflects a modernist understanding of the self, Disch's first book, *Hannah Arendt and the Limits of Philosophy*, is a critique of modernism from within. She joins Arendt's concept of storytelling to feminist conceptions of "situated knowledges" for a model of political thinking that is neither abstract and world-transcending nor experience bound. And finally, in yet another example, O'Brien's first book, *Dispossession by Degrees*, a historical study of Indians in colonial America, responds to historiography that erases the existence of Native Americans in this particular time period. Her work not only challenges this scholarship by emphasizing the persistence of native people through time who are dispossessed of their lands by colonists, but importantly brings gender to bear as a category of analysis in this historical process. These divergent projects, in turn, speak to the variety of waves of feminist thought in the 1980s and 1990s such as psychoanalytic feminist theory, poststructuralism, and women of color feminism.[56]

Varying theoretical concerns can also be seen in the scholarship of third generation feminists. While many third generation feminists in this volume assume an intersectional feminist analysis, their personal narratives highlight the many routes through feminism and the resources available along the way. For example, third generation feminists Hokulani Aikau and Felicity Schaeffer-Grabiel write eloquently of finding a place from which to speak when they first encountered the work of women of color feminists, while for Karla Erickson and Wendy Leo Moore, who did not have access to these resources in college, the integration of gender and race theoretically remains an ongoing challenge. These differences mark the advances made by feminist of color critiques as widely varied and uneven with respect to their availability and incorporation across time, institutional location, discipline, and generation. As such, these essays do not support an ever-improving narrative of progress, nor do they irretrievably splinter into a form of "everybody is different" individualism. Conditions and resources at the local and national level intersect with individual goals and trajectories to produce a feminism that is always in flux, up for debate, and challenging.

Reimagining Oedipal Relations

Feminist Waves, Feminist Generations also challenges descriptions of feminist generations that fall back on family metaphors to describe mentoring relationships, specifically that of mother and daughter, by contextualizing them in structural terms.[57] We argue that the institutional context of the academy, specifically the unequal structure of relations between faculty and students within it, the competitiveness of the current academic job market, and the larger conservative backdrop of the backlash against feminism, affirmative action, and the Left all have powerful consequences in shaping relationships between faculty and students. Given these structures of uneven power, privilege, and opportunity, it is not surprising that uneasiness, resentment, or anxiety surface in relationships between faculty and students. In this light, family metaphors also underestimate the unique character of intellectual mentoring. English professor Toni McNaron's essay, for example, reveals the larger complexity contained in the mentoring relationship as she ponders the difficulties her students will face being "out" in the academy. Unlike a parent, she is invested in the politics associated with revealing one's sexual identity, her own ideals of how the academy should be, as well as the professional goals and aspirations of her students.

Even if we accept for the sake of argument that *some* student-teacher relationships are like mother-daughter relationships, these terms are often adopted in a nonreflexive and ahistorical way. The disapproving mother/ungrateful daughter trope these writers construct is particular to white middle-class women in Western industrialized countries at a particular historical moment. It may not apply to women who are not white, Western, or middle class. In fact, the few essays by women of color in these same anthologies indicate that race, not generation, is the central issue in their experiences.[58] Our argument here is not with the concept of generational difference itself (or with oedipal theories, for that matter) but with the essentializing ways these terms have been deployed.

Essentializing relationships between mentors and mentees runs the risk of overlooking professional and institutional power differentials between faculty and students, but also collapses varied experiences into one inflexible familial model. By contrast, the narratives collected here reflect a network of relationships rather than the psychologically intense, one-to-one, hierarchical relationship assumed by the mother-daughter dyad. Third generation feminist Peter Hennen disrupts the primacy of the academic mother-daughter metaphor in his essay where he writes about the legacy of his own mother from his perspective as a queer son. He respects and admires both his mother and the feminist faculty who mentored him, but their roles in his development are profoundly different. Similarly, third generation feminists Roderick Ferguson and Wendy Leo Moore both point to important adults in their early years who shaped how they imagined themselves, their politics, and, subsequently, the sort of people in the academy they sought out as colleagues and mentors. In all these essays, personal and professional relationships crossing time and place are much more varied and complex than the narrative implied by the one-to-one mother-daughter relationship.

Contributors' personal narratives reflect interlocking networks of individuals who influence, direct, and encourage one another. For example, Karla Erickson focuses on the early mentorship from three professors in her undergraduate years, one of whom inspired her eventual return to Minnesota as a graduate student. There, she worked with Jennifer Pierce, who then became a conduit to many other feminists on campus, located in different disciplines but who shared similar politics. Similarly, in their efforts to create the PhD program in women's studies, third generation feminists Sam Bullington and Amanda Swarr worked together with both second and 2.5 generation feminists Helen Longino and Jennifer Pierce. Over the course of one year, the committee surveyed existing doctoral programs, planned curriculum for the new program, wrote and revised numerous proposal drafts, and garnered student, faculty, and institutional support along the way. Their efforts at building networks across the university to support the PhD proposal met with success. As Bullington and Swarr observe, by the end of the year, the faculty successfully presented the committee's case to the administration, and in "fall 1998 a new PhD program in feminist studies was part of the curriculum at the University of Minnesota" (this volume). As these examples suggest, both graduate students and professors decide whether to enter into working or mentoring relationships based on shared politics, prior relations, shared intellectual interests, and the possibilities and limitations due to location in time and place. Consequently, decisions about how and with whom to align themselves during their training is a confluence of graduate students' personalities and commitments along with the presence and approachability of faculty at any given time. Further, mentoring relationships rarely remain one to one but rather expand into networks of affiliation, subsequently affecting how communities of scholars develop. Reimagining these relationships as dynamic networks rather than mother-daughter dyads also leaves room for the relative influence of partners, siblings, students, friends, and previous mentors to influence the course of scholars' training and development.

While the essays in this volume by third generation feminists do not fall back on familial metaphors to describe their relationships with faculty, they do reflect critically upon what they do politically and intellectually in relation to second wave feminism. Rather than defining themselves in opposition to the "second wave mothers" as many writers in third wave anthologies do, their personal narratives instead reveal tensions and continuities across generational cohorts. In her essay, Dawn Rae Davis writes about the University of Minnesota's feminist studies PhD program from her vantage point as a member of its first graduate cohort. Here, she describes a tension between faculty and feminist studies graduate minors who regard women's studies as their "home," a refuge from other, less feminist-friendly departments and disciplines, on the one hand, and the meaning of this program for the new feminist studies PhD students, on the other. While recognizing the historical reasons that women's studies became an intellectual refuge for many scholars, Davis nonetheless cautions us about the danger of such metaphors. As she argues, within the metaphorical field of "home," women's studies becomes a "feminized space of safety" cloistered away from the corruption of masculine academic commerce. "This takes the feminization of the space of feminist and gender studies in an unfortunate direction and reinscribes gendered hierarchies of work and work space within a private/public distinction." Traditional disciplines such as history, political science, and sociology become marked by masculinity, thereby privileging both conventional disciplinary boundaries and the public power of masculine space and knowledge production. In Davis's analysis, this unexamined metaphor lies behind struggles that took place between new PhD students and the feminist studies graduate minors over office space and departmental resources as well as in conversations with second generation faculty about the changing institutional expression of women's studies. While drawing attention to generational differences and tensions, she also sees moments of convergence within the feminist academy. "We are here . . . not to plant our feet but to keep moving—looking both forward and behind to see that generational convergences are themselves a sustaining source of visionary movement and feminist possibility."

Political Sensibilities and Commitments

While Davis characterizes the second generation feminist faculty as somewhat threatened by the possibility of changing the parameters and institutional expression of women's studies, third generation feminists Sam Bullington and Amanda Swarr both see themselves as clearly aligned with second generation feminists in their desire to develop the graduate degree program. Bullington and Swarr imagine the development of a PhD as a continuation of second wave efforts to create a locus of feminist scholarship *and* community in the academy and find themselves in conflict with others in their generational cohort whom they regard as overly concerned with professionalization. Recognizing that feminist studies programs do have a responsibility for preparing graduate students for the job market, they believe that they also have a responsibility to feminist principles of social and economic justice. These debates over professionalization in connection with a doctoral degree in feminist studies and the reorganization of space and resources for graduate students in connection with these historic changes reflect internal differences within generational cohorts, as demonstrated by the disparate concerns reflected in Bullington and Swarr's and Davis's personal narrative essays.

Taken together, their narratives speak to the conflicting impressions of what is at stake in the effort to transform the role of women's studies in the academy.

At the same time that Bullington and Swarr see themselves aligned politically with second generation feminists, they too reflect critically upon second wave feminist thought. Second wave feminism, for example, launched a number of critiques of transsexuals as either antithetical or irrelevant to feminist politics.[59] Transgender activists, on the other hand, have viewed feminism as threatening to trans people, and some have targeted feminists as enemies. In fact, in the past decade, some of the most heated feminist "border wars" have taken place at the Michigan Womyn's Music Festival, where transgender activists have protested Michigan's "womyn-born-womyn only" policy. Both Swarr and Bullington share concerns about creating representational and material "space" within the academy for transgendered experiences; however, rather than seeing themselves in direct opposition to second wave feminism, they recognize the ways they straddle political locations and social categories. In their view, holding multiple positions does not represent a lack of commitment but rather a lack of exclusive commitment. While lack of "exclusive commitment" points to ongoing contradictions and tensions, their essay also reveals their powerful desire to create community and connections between the particular political and intellectual commitments of feminist scholars across generations and other categories of difference.

Bullington and Swarr's emphasis on coalition building also serves to challenge the notion that such feminist practices have been supplanted by more individualized forms of feminism. For example, in *Manifesta: Young Women, Feminism, and the Future,* Jennifer Baumgardner and Amy Richards's examples of third wave activism—from little girls with temporary tattoos at women's World Cup soccer matches to single mothers who organize the babysitting chain on election day—celebrate individual acts. They write, "It's a sign of the times that feminists today are more likely to be individuals quietly (or not so quietly) living self-determined lives than radicals on the ramparts."[60] While we admire Baumgardner and Richards's intent to look in a variety of places for evidence of feminist activity, their emphasis on individualism as a key characteristic of the third wave neglects other forms of activism. While the consciousness-raising groups of the 1960s and 1970s may have disappeared, academic feminists continue to gather and join forces. As the influence and power of feminism in the academy has expanded, so too have the opportunities for collective action. For example, both Felicity Schaeffer-Grabiel and Hokulani Aikau were attracted to the University of Minnesota not only because of the strength of the feminist community on campus, but also because of the presence of Más(s) Color (an acronym for Minnesota American Studies Students of Color), an organization committed to the recruitment and retention of students of color, in which they both became actively involved. Further, the personal narratives here offer a wealth of personal and professional allegiances within institutions, disciplines, and areas of study as well as personal connections that influence ongoing professional and intellectual development. For example, the group of feminists who supported Jennifer Pierce during her tenure battle crisscrossed disciplines and generations across the university but shared a political commitment to protecting a junior feminist scholar.

Another danger of highlighting individual stories is that it detaches personal stories from time and place, obscuring the structural conditions that produce uneven waves of feminism and the varied expressions of politics within each generation. For example, in Leslie Heywood and Jennifer Drake's *Third Wave Agenda,* their attention to the continued influence of individualism mutes the stories of isolation and alienation from community and family told by women of color.[61] Whereas white women in their anthology find community in the ranks of feminist movements, women of color feel alienated from their home communities and on occasion marginalized in feminist circles. Similarly, in *Listen Up: Voices from the Next Feminist Generation,* Veronica Chambers writes in her chapter "Betrayal Feminism" about how the presumed whiteness of feminism created a divide in her political and personal persona.[62] Although her feminist consciousness came out of both feminist studies and black studies, she was shocked and hurt by the racism she experienced from white feminists who claimed to be her sisters.

Chambers's ambivalent relationship to feminism is echoed in many of the personal narratives by women of color in *Feminist Waves, Feminist Generations* who first found feminism at college. Almost without exception, the women of color in this volume express having had feelings of liberation when they first encountered feminism, but their exhilaration was tempered by the separation they felt from their communities and families. Much like Chambers, they drew from a feminist canon that included Barbara Smith, Audre Lorde, June Jordan, Gloria Anzaldúa, and Cherríe Moraga, to name just a few. Unlike their white counter-

parts, these women felt sorrow for the distance feminism created between themselves and their mothers. For example, in her essay, Felicity
Schaeffer-Grabiel vividly describes her sense of guilt for betraying her
Mexican American mother's expectation that she become a traditional
wife and mother. Their relationship changes over time as she begins
to see parallels in the gender and national power differences between
women and men in her study of an international cyber-dating service
matching women from Mexico with Anglo-American men and the asym-
metries in the relationship between her mother and Anglo father. While
embracing feminism initially challenges her connection with her family
and her personal history, eventually, she is able to find a voice that brings
these concerns into concert, creating enough space to imagine herself
as both a feminist academic and as a wife and mother. Similarly, Hokulani Aikau expresses the tensions that emerged while she was in college
because of her newfound feminist politics and the wedge it created between herself and her parents as she raised new questions about gender,
power, and equality. Like Schaeffer-Grabiel, Aikau eventually develops a
research agenda that allows her to critically embrace her Latter-day Saint
and native Hawaiian family history. Her story points to the ability to tolerate complexity and to eventually find a way to honor values of family
while maintaining a commitment to feminist politics. These stories both
reflect the particular personal and structural challenges for feminists of
color in the academy.

Personal Narratives, Feminism, and the Academy

In June 1998, *Time* Magazine posed the rhetorical question, "Is Feminism Dead?" on its cover with a pictorial of four floating heads: Susan B.
Anthony, Betty Friedan, Gloria Steinem, and Fox TV's fictional female
lawyer Ally McBeal. The magazine's cover story mourned the loss of a
serious and politically engaged feminism and lambasted its most recent
iteration (read the third wave) as apolitical, "narcissistic," and "silly."[63] As
feminist scholar Pam Butler observes, to make this argument, the author
compared the political work and activities of actual feminist activists and
scholars such as Betty Friedan, Gloria Steinem, and Simone de Beauvoir to those of fictional characters and pop culture icons including Ally
McBeal, Glenn Close (as portrayed in the play *The Vagina Monologues*),
and Ginger Spice.[64]

Despite its gross oversimplification of differences between feminist generations as well as its conflation of the antics of fictional characters with the politics of actual people, this article helped make public a debate—at once popular and academic—about the state of feminism today. Since about that time, both feminists and antifeminists whether as scholars, politicos, or pop culture pundits have focused on "what's wrong with feminism." While some conclude that feminism is in a state of disarray, others maintain that the newest generation is complacent, lazy, or politically disengaged, and still others argue that feminism is flailing, if not dead.[65] In part, this anthology is shaped by these larger concerns as well as our own theoretical interest in reconceptualizing feminist generations and waves. Our focus, however, is on a particular institutional setting with its own distinctive generational dynamic—the academy—and a method that relies on the life stories of the actual participants themselves.

The logic of the academic life cycle allows us to mark a single academic cohort as those who attended graduate school roughly within the same ten-year period. Consequently, we have organized the remaining chapters by generational cohort, beginning with second generation feminists. Throughout we are attentive to situating when and where women and men first encounter feminism. By using the academic life cycle to delineate feminist cohorts, rather than year of birth, the essays reveal what feminist academics share as a generational cohort, as well as highlighting the variations that exist within them. Their stories not only give us a sense of the distinct routes that brought each of them to the University of Minnesota but underscore the uneven diffusion of feminism in other institutional and disciplinary contexts.

Methodologically, we rely on personal narratives by a variety of feminists—senior faculty, junior faculty, and graduate students—who came to feminism as early as the 1970s and as recently as the 1990s who at some point in their careers worked at the University of Minnesota. Here, we use the term *narrative* purposefully to emphasize the *socially constructed* nature of the material in the essays that follow this chapter. As many feminist scholars have argued, to make sense of our lives and to communicate meaning, we tell stories about ourselves, stories that draw from larger culturally and historically specific discourses that are not of our own making.[66] In this sense, "[n]arration is a cultural practice; in making sense of experience, any narrative draws on and is constrained by the culture in which it is embedded."[67] This is not to say that narratives do not contain individual biographical or idiosyncratic elements but rather to underscore the point that they also draw from broader cultural discourses. As the personal narrative essays in this volume demonstrate, women and men between *and* within feminist generations tell very different stories about their first encounter with feminism, stories that not only reflect their divergent standpoints and personal biographies but also draw from larger cultural narratives about feminism, social justice, "coming of age," "coming out," and professionalization.

In addition, the essays gathered here reflect each contributor's answer to a series of questions we provided with the call for submissions including: When and how did you first encounter feminism? How has feminism influenced your scholarship and teaching? Contributors were directed to situate their stories within a historical and institutional context as well as to be reflective about how their stories were not solely about the individual but connected to longer traditions of feminist theorizing and practice.[68] These personal narratives thus provide a rich terrain for making links between what sociologists call the micro and macro levels of analysis. At the micro level, personal narratives approach the social world from the standpoint of the social actor, providing an opportunity to unpack the meanings of feminism within the institutional context of the academy. Furthermore, examining a life over time adds particular insight into how larger structural events can constrain or enable the choices available to social actors. In this way, personal narratives can shed light on the interplay between biography and larger historical forces.[69]

It is precisely this intersection between personal biography and history that makes personal narratives valuable for our project. Their very particularity can often challenge dominant public narratives (e.g., "what's wrong with feminism?" and "third wave feminists are apolitical") by bringing to light new perspectives on broader historical processes and phenomena. As we have argued, the personal narratives in the chapters that follow create productive trouble for recent feminist writing about generations in several ways. First, they move beyond the second and third wave binary to reveal the multiplicity of feminist generations in the academy. Further, they highlight both similarities and differences within academic generations. And finally, while much of the literature on the third wave assumes that each generation breaks definitively from the previous one, many of the essays in this volume emphasize continuities between generations.

As queer activist Amber Hollibaugh has written, "where our own personal narratives meet with larger historical events often results in a profoundly unique human drama of transformation."[70] The life stories in this volume reveal that feminism has been and continues to be a transformative social movement—each successive wave bringing with it new ideas, political strategies, and life experiences that have reverberated locally, nationally, and globally.

Of course, not all our contributors' stories are celebratory; some are less hopeful about the future than others. Like many other public research universities, feminism at Minnesota remains vulnerable to the whims of administrators and a fiscally conservative state legislature. Most recently, CAFS, one of the central hubs of intellectual vitality for the ever-expanding feminist community at the university, was involved in a battle to stay open. In spring 2004, a committee of faculty, staff, and students involved in CAFS, the Schochet Center, and the Gay, Lesbian, Bisexual, and Transgender Programs Office worked together to create a proposal for a new center combining both CAFS and Schochet in an effort to sustain both their intellectual missions. The proposal was rejected by the College of Liberal Art's Budget Advisory Committee (BAC)—it was deemed too costly—and in the end, the dean of the College of Liberal Arts concurred with BAC's decision.[71] Although the dean declined funding for the infrastructure for the recombined center, he did not officially close CAFS or Schochet.[72] Currently, both CAFS and Schochet are in "hiatus," meaning that they exist in name only with no director, no staff, no office space, and no programming.

What these institutional take-backs will mean for future generations of feminists at University of Minnesota is a story that remains to be told. The personal narratives we have gathered here illuminate how waves of feminist thought hit Minnesota's shores at distinct historical moments and how, in turn, generational cohorts made use of the energy from those waves. Our hope is that these life stories will form the basis for the next chapter of feminism at the university. Despite the contemporary conservative backlash, the rise of corporate practices, and state cutbacks to higher education, the force of feminist waves at Minnesota is now marked by a growing diversity of people, resources, and networks that bring them together. We must remember, as scientific wave theory suggests, waves never cease to move even as they encounter obstacles. Their energy may change shape and form, but they can also be harnessed and put to work in new, lively, and exciting ways.

Notes

1. See Lynda Zwinger, "Dancing through the Mother Field," in *Generations: Academic Feminists in Dialogue,* ed. Devoney Looser and Ann Kaplan (Minneapolis: University of Minnesota Press, 1997); Rebecca Quinn, "An Open Letter to Institutional Mothers," in *Generations,* ed. Looser and Kaplan; and Nancy Miller, "Jason Dreams, Victoria Works Out," in *Generations,* ed. Looser and Kaplan.

2. This assumption is common to most anthologies on third wave feminism. Leslie Heywood and Jennifer Drake, for example, assert that "'third wave' makes things 'messier' [than second wave scholarship] by *embracing* second wave critique as a central definitional thread while emphasizing ways that desires and pleasures subject to critique can be used to rethink and enliven activist work" (7, italics in original). See Leslie Heywood and Jennifer Drake, introduction to *Third Wave Agenda,* ed. Leslie Heywood and Jennifer Drake (Minneapolis: University of Minnesota Press, 1997). Also, see Rebecca Walker, ed., *To Be Real: Telling the Truth and Changing the Face of Feminism* (New York: Anchor Press, 1994); Barbara Findlen, ed., *Listen Up: Voices from the Next Feminist Generation* (Seattle: Seal Press, 1995); Jennifer Baumgardner and Amy Richards, eds., *Manifesta: Young Women, Feminism, and the Future* (New York: Farrar, Strauss, and Giroux, 2000); and Rory Dicker and Alison Piepmeier, eds., *Catching a Wave: Reclaiming Feminism for the Twenty-first Century* (Boston: Northeastern University Press, 2003). Their assertion that using desire and pleasure is a novel theoretical and political move ignores the second wave scholarship on this topic. French feminists in the 1970s and early 1980s were among the first to theorize women's pleasure and desire in their work. See Hélène Cixous, "The Laugh of Medusa," *Signs: Journal of Women in Culture and Society* 1, 4 (summer 1976); and Luce Irigaray, *This Sex Which Is Not One,* trans. Catherine Porter and Carolyn Burke (Ithaca, N.Y.: Cornell University Press, 1985). Second wave feminists in the United States were also writing about pleasure and desire at this time. See Cherríe Moraga and Amber Hollibaugh, "What We're Rollin' Around in Bed With," *Heresies: The Sex Issue* 12 (1981); and the papers from Barnard College's Feminist Conference 1982 that appeared in Carol Vance, ed., *Pleasure and Desire: An Exploration of Female Sexuality* (Boston: Routledge and Kegan Paul, 1984).

3. For one example that celebrates individualism among third wave feminists, see Baumgardner and Richards, eds., *Manifesta.* For another that bemoans the individualism of the third wave, see Ginia Bellafante, "Feminism: It's All about Me!" *Time,* 29 June 1998, 54.

4. Kalpala Ram, "Special Issue Introduction," *International Women's Studies Forum* (1998): 572.

5. M. J. Maynes, Jennifer L. Pierce, and Barbara Laslett make this point about the epistemological advantages of personal narrative analysis in their book *Telling Stories: Personal Narrative Analysis in the Social Sciences and in History* (in progress). For other discussions of the uses of personal narratives, see Personal Narratives Group, *Interpreting Women's Lives* (Bloomington: Indiana University Press, 1989); Ruth Behar, *Translated Woman: Crossing the Border with Esperanza's Story* (Boston: Beacon Press, 1993); and Michelle Mouton and Helena

Pohlandt-McCormick, "Boundary Crossings: Oral History of Nazi Germany and Apartheid South Africa—A Comparative Perspective," *History Workshop Journal* 48 (1999): 41–63.

6. While a number of feminists have pointed to the problems in the ways generations have been conceptualized in third wave feminist writing, particularly the assumption that the third generation definitively breaks from the last, none provides an alternative conceptualization as we do in this volume. For example, both Alice Walker and Angela Davis argue there are continuities between second wave and third wave feminism in their respective "Foreword" and "Afterword" in the first popular anthologies to describe third wave feminism. See their pieces in Walker, ed., *To Be Real.* This argument has also been made in a number of feminist scholarly journals. See Jennifer Drake, "Review Essay: Third Wave Feminisms," *Feminist Studies* 23, 1 (1997); Cathryn Bailey, "Making Waves and Drawing Lines: The Politics of Defining the Vicissitudes of Feminism," *Hypatia* 12, 3 (1997): 17; Catherine Orr, "Charting the Currents of the Third Wave," *Hypatia* 12, 3 (1997): 29; and Lisa Maria Holeland, "Against Generational Thinking: or, Some Things that 'Third Wave' Feminism Isn't," *Women's Studies in Communication* 24, 1 (Spring 2001). And finally, this argument has also been made in a more recent anthology. In *Catching a Wave,* feminist academics Rory Dicker and Alison Piepmeier question the meaning of "third wave," its usefulness as a descriptive category, and the tendency to depict the third wave as oppositional to earlier feminist work. Nonetheless, the contributors in their volume continue to struggle in defining what the third wave is, still seeing it in opposition to a unified and cohesive understanding of a "less advanced" second wave. See Dicker and Piepmeier, eds., *Catching a Wave.*

7. Marilyn Boxer reviews the dramatic explosion of feminist scholarship, curriculum changes, and new programs in her book *When Women Ask the Questions: Creating Women's Studies in America* (Baltimore: John Hopkins University Press, 1998).

8. Karl Mannheim, *Essays in the Sociology of Knowledge* (New York: Oxford University Press, 1952).

9. For some examples of authors who make this distinction between second and third wave, see Boxer, *When Women Ask the Questions*; Ednie Garrison, "U.S. Feminism—Grrl Style: Youth (Sub)Culture and the Technologies of the Third Wave," *Feminist Studies* 26, 1 (Spring 2000); Sara Evans, *Tidal Wave: How Women Changed America at Century's End* (New York: Free Press, 2003). Also, see the volumes listed in note 2.

10. This problem is common to a number of third wave anthologies. See the volumes listed in note 2.

11. Anthologies on third wave feminism tend to uncritically accept the notion that second wave feminism is white and middle-class—even in the most recent publications. For instance, while the contributors in the *Fire This Time* at times recognize continuities between second wave and third wave feminism, they still equate the "second wave" with a single cohesive movement built by and comprised of white middle-class women. See Vivien Labaton and Dawn Lunday

Martin, eds., *The Fire This Time: Young Activists and the New Feminism* (New York: Anchor Books, 2004). It is true that scholarly work on second wave feminism has tended to focus on the experience of white middle-class women. See Jo Freeman, *The Politics of Women's Liberation* (New York: Longman, 1975); Sara Evans, *Personal Politics: The Roots of Women's Liberation in the Civil Rights Movement and the New Left* (New York: Knopf, 1979); Alice Echols, *Daring to Be Bad: Radical Feminism in America, 1967–1975* (Minneapolis: University of Minnesota Press, 1989); and Verta Taylor and Nancy Whittier, "The New Feminist Movement," in *Feminist Frontiers IV*, ed. Laurel Richardson, Verta Taylor, and Nancy Whittier (New York: McGraw-Hill, 1997). However, these narratives have been challenged by a number of historical studies focusing on women of color during the same time period. See Deborah Gray White's discussion of the National Black Feminist Organization founded in the early 1970s by Florynce Kennedy and Margaret Sloan and its two-pronged assault on racism and sexism in her *Too Heavy a Load: Black Women in Defense of Themselves* (New York: Norton, 1992). Also, see Becky Thompson's feminist movement timelines comparing multiracial feminism from 1959–95 with white middle-class feminism in her book *A Promise and a Way of Life: White Antiracist Activism* (Minneapolis: University of Minnesota Press, 2001.)

12. Becky Thompson provides an overview of the contributions women of color made to feminist politics and theory beginning in the 1960s through 1995 in her *A Promise and a Way of Life*. For specific examples of scholarship on race and gender in the 1970s, see Toni Cade Bambara's classic anthology *The Black Woman* (New York: New American Books, 1970). Also, see Frances Beal, "Double Jeopardy: To Be Black and Female"; Black Women's Liberation Group, Mount Vernon N.Y., "Statement on Birth Control"; and Enriqueta Longauex y Vasquez, "The Mexican-American Woman"; all in *Sisterhood Is Powerful*, ed. Robin Morgan (New York: Anchor Books, 1970). Other scholars have argued a feminist legacy can be traced back to the nineteenth century when enslaved black women intimately understood the connections between race and gender. See Angela Davis, *Women, Race, and Class* (New York: Random House, 1981); and Patricia Hill Collins, *Black Feminist Thought* (New York: Routledge, 1990).

13. Lynn Weber, Elizabeth Higginbotham, and Bonnie Thornton Dill, "Sisterhood as Collaboration: Building CROW for Research on Women at the University of Memphis," in *Feminist Sociology: Life Histories of a Movement* (New Brunswick, N.J.: Rutgers University Press, 1997).

14. Our conceptualization draws from sociologists and demographers who define generations as a cohort of individuals who were born in a given period of time. For a recent overview of the different ways this concept is defined and used by sociologists, historians, and demographers, see Jane Edmunds and Bryan Turner, *Generations, Culture, and Society* (Buckingham and Philadelphia: Open University Press, 2002.) Because we focus on the academy and because birth year does not always neatly coincide with the timing of entry into graduate training—some may begin PhD programs immediately after college at age twenty-one, and others may start years later—we define cohorts by the timing of

entry into graduate school. A common problem with cohort analysis is its presumption that members of the same generation share particular historical experiences. Our conceptualization departs from such analyses in that we do not assume that academic cohorts all have the same experience. We recognize the possibility of similarity and difference within cohorts, and we also emphasize the possibility of change over time.

15. This familial model is most explicitly invoked in Rebecca Walker's popular anthology *To Be Real*. Here, Walker and many of her contributors distinguish their version of feminism from the politics of their actual feminist mothers. This generational assumption is also apparent in the other third wave volumes listed in note 2. Although the essays in Looser and Kaplan's academic volume *Generations* do not describe actual mother-daughter relationships, many do draw upon this familial trope to characterize relationships between faculty and graduate students. Susan Fraiman's critique of this volume is similar to our own. See Susan Fraiman, "Feminism Today: Mothers, Daughters, Emerging Sisters," *American Literary History* 11, 3 (Fall 1999): 525–44. For another critique, see Madelyn Detloff, "Mean Spirits: The Politics of Contempt between Feminist Generations," *Hypatia* 12, 3 (1997).

16. Although we have developed an alternative terminology for feminist generations, this usage is not shared by all the contributors in our volume. For example, Lisa Disch and Jean O'Brien prefer the term *bust generation* to describe the cohort that we term 2.5 *feminist*. Like many social scientists who work with personal narratives, we draw upon theoretical terminology from sociology and other disciplines to conceptualize our contributors' experiences. See note 14. This does not mean that we have ignored what our contributors' personal narratives tell us. To the contrary, our use of these concepts is dependent on the connections we have made to what their essays tell us. In the case of Disch and O'Brien, we have paid careful attention to the details of their lives and their self-understanding in order to make connections to our terminology.

17. Luisa Passerini, *Autobiography of a Generation* (Hanover, N.H.: University of New England, 1996); James Miller, *The Passion of Michel Foucault* (New York: Simon and Schuster, 1993); Frances FitzGerald, *Fire in the Lake: The Vietnamese and the Americans in Vietnam* (New York: Vintage Books, 1972); Aldon Morris, "Centuries of Black Protest," in *Race in America,* ed. Herbert Hill and James Jones (Madison: University of Wisconsin Press, 1993); Angela Davis, "Black Nationalism," in *The Angela Davis Reader,* ed. Joy James (Malden, Mass.: Blackwell, 1998); and Robin Kelly, "Stormy Weather: Reconstructing Black (Inter)Nationalism in the Cold War Era," in *Is It Nation Time?* ed. Claude Eddie (Chicago: University of Chicago Press, 2002).

18. Wini Breines, "What's Love Got to Do with It? White Women, Black Women, and Feminism in the Movement Years," *Signs: Journal of Women in Culture and Society* 27, 4 (Summer 2002): 1108.

19. For examples from the women's movement, the gay liberation movement, and Native American activism, see Linda Gordon and Ann Popkin, "Women's Liberation: Let Us Now Emulate Each Other," in *Seasons of Rebellion: Protest*

and Radicalism in Recent America, ed. Joseph Boskin and Robert Rosenstone (New York: Holt, 1972), 304–5; Martin Duberman, *Stonewall* (New York: Dutton, 1993); and Paul Smith and Robert Warrior, *Like a Hurricane* (New York: Norton, 1996).

20. White, *Too Heavy a Load;* Echols, *Daring to Be Bad;* Morgan, ed. *Sisterhood Is Powerful;* Gordon and Popkin, "Women's Liberation"; Margaret Strobel, "Consciousness and Action: Historical Agency in the Chicago Women's Liberation Union," in *Provoking Agents: Theorizing Gender and Agency,* ed. Judith Kegan Gardiner (Urbana: University of Illinois Press, 1995); Duberman, *Stonewall.*

21. For a discussion of the connections between feminist activism and the academy, see Barbara Laslett and Barrie Thorne, eds., *Feminist Sociology: Life Histories of a Movement* (New Brunswick, N.J.: Rutgers University Press, 1997). For a broader historical account of the legal, political, and social changes brought about by second wave feminism, see Evans, *Tidal Wave.*

22. Stanford Lehmberg and Ann M. Pflaum, *The University of Minnesota, 1945–2000* (Minneapolis: University of Minnesota Press, 2001), 116.

23. Lehmberg and Pflaum, *The University of Minnesota,* 118–21.

24. Anne Truax, e-mail communication to Jennifer Pierce, September 5, 2005.

25. Ibid.

26. Ibid.

27. Lehmberg and Pflaum, *The University of Minnesota,* 126.

28. Anne Truax, e-mail communication to Jennifer Pierce, September 5, 2005.

29. Lehmberg and Pflaum, *The University of Minnesota,* 144; Janet Spector, personal communication, September 4, 2005; and Anne Truax, e-mail communication to Jennifer Pierce, September 5, 2005.

30. For a history of Minnesota Plans I and II, see the Web site of the Office of University Women, http://www1.umn.edu/women/history.html; George La Nour and Barbara Lee, *Academics in Court: The Consequences of Faculty Discrimination Litigation* (Ann Arbor: University of Michigan Press, 1987).

31. Lehmberg and Pflaum, *The University of Minnesota,* 188.

32. From 1950 to 1970 the numbers of students enrolled at the University of Minnesota jumped from 22,637 to 50,580. See Lehmberg and Pflaum, "Appendix A-1. Fall Quarter Enrollments for Selected Years," *The University of Minnesota,* 324. For national comparisons, see Craig Calhoun, "The Changing Character of College: Institutional Transformation in American Higher Education," in *The Social Worlds of Higher Education,* ed. Bernice Pescosolido and Ron Aminzade (Thousand Oaks, Calif.: Pine Forge Press, 1999).

33. In 1983, the Center for Advanced Feminist Studies, a research center whose mission is "to foster collaborative interdisciplinary scholarship among feminist scholars," first opened. Over the years, the center has generated a number of innovative projects, including a project on comparable worth; another on personal narratives, which hosted a national conference; a Rockefeller Humanists-in-Residence Program, which brought six internationally known feminist

scholars to the university as fellows; an initiative in feminist global studies called "Ways of Reading," which was funded by the Ford Foundation; a number of conferences, workshops, and colloquia series; and most recently a research initiative and summer institute on "Gender, Migration, and Global Change." These projects ultimately became books and anthologies, including Sara Evans and Barbara Nelson, *Wage Justice: Comparable Worth and the Paradox of Technocratic Reform* (Chicago: University of Chicago Press, 1980); Personal Narratives Group, *Interpreting Women's Lives*; Social Justice Group, Center for Advanced Studies Editorial Collective, *Is Academic Feminism Dead? Theory in Praxis* (New York: New York University Press, 2000); and Mary M. Lay, Janice Monk, and Deborah S. Rosenfelt, eds. *Encompassing Gender: Integrating International Studies and Women's Studies* (New York: Feminist Press at the City University of New York Press, 2002). In 1983, CAFS also created an interdisciplinary minor in graduate feminist studies. In addition, from 1990 to 1995, CAFS housed the prestigious feminist journal *Signs: Journal of Women in Culture and Society* and worked with the Women's Studies Department to launch the PhD program in feminist studies in 1998.

34. Some of these scholars included Susan Geiger (women's studies), Elaine Tyler May (American studies), Shirley Nelson Garner (English), M. J. Maynes (history), Riv-Ellen Prell (anthropology), Naomi Schemen (philosophy), Madelon Sprengnether (English), Ann Waltner (history), and Gayle Graham Yates (women's studies).

35. Toni McNaron, *Poisoned Ivy: Lesbian and Gay Academics Confronting Homophobia* (Philadelphia: Temple University Press, 1997).

36. Evans, *Personal Politics*.

37. Boston Women's Health Collective, *Our Bodies, Ourselves: A Book by and for Women* (New York: Simon and Schuster, 1973). Also see Patricia Yancey Martin and Myra Marx Feree, eds. *Feminist Organizations: Harvest of the Women's Movement* (Philadelphia: Temple University Press, 1995).

38. Catherine Stimpson with Nona Cressner Cobb, *Women's Studies in the United States: Report to the Ford Foundation* (New York: Ford Foundation, 1986); and Boxer, *When Women Ask the Questions*.

39. American Sociology Association, "Survey of Sociology Departments and Divisions: 1991–1992," unpublished paper, American Sociology Association, 1993.

40. See Laslett and Thorne, eds., *Feminist Sociology*; Anne Goetting and Sarah Fenstermaker, eds., *Individual Voices, Collective Visions: Fifty Years of Women in Sociology* (Philadelphia: Temple University Press, 1995); Kathryn Orlans and Ruth Wallace, eds., *Gender and the Academic Experience: Berkeley Women Sociologists* (Lincoln: University of Nebraska Press, 1994); and Gayle Green and Coppelia Kahn, eds., *Changing Subjects: The Making of Feminist Literary Criticism* (New York: Routledge, 1993).

41. Gloria Anzaldúa and Cherríe Moraga, eds., *This Bridge Called My Back: Writings by Radical Women of Color* (San Francisco: Aunt Lute Press, 1981); Davis, *Women, Race, and Class*; and Adrienne Rich, "Compulsory Heterosexuality and Lesbian Existence," *Signs: Journal of Women in Culture and Society*, 1980. For other

critiques by women of color and lesbian feminists, see Moraga and Hollibaugh, "What We're Rollin' Around in Bed With"; bell hooks, *Ain't I a Woman* (New York: St. Martin's Press, 1981); Hazel Carby, "White Woman Listen! Black Feminism and the Boundaries of Sisterhood," in *The Empire Strikes Back*, ed. Centre for Contemporary Cultural Studies (London: Routledge, 1982); and Audre Lorde, *Sister Outsider: Essays and Speeches* (Trumansburg, N.Y.: Crossing Press, 1984).

42. Gayatri Spivak, "Can the Subaltern Speak?" in *Marxism and the Interpretation of Culture*, ed. Cary Nelson and Lawrence Grossberg (Urbana: University of Illinois Press, 1988); Trinh Minh Ha, *Native, Woman, Other: Writing, Postcoloniality, and Feminism* (Bloomington: Indiana University Press, 1989).

43. Toril Moi, *Sexual/Textual Politics* (1985); Toril Moi, ed., *The Kristeva Reader* (New York: Columbia University Press, 1986); and Julia Kristeva, *Powers of Horror: An Essay in Abjection*, trans. Leon S. Roudiez (New York: Columbia University Press, 1982).

44. Thanks to Mimi Schipper for reminding us of this important point.

45. On the changing parameters of higher education, its history, demographics, and the "culture wars," see Derek Bok, *Universities and Marketplaces* (Princeton, N.J.: Princeton University Press, 2004); Bill Readings, *The University in Ruins* (Cambridge, Mass.: Harvard University Press, 1996); Jeanette McVickers, "General Education for the Transnationalized Masses," *Crossings* (1999) 3: 41–55; Craig Calhoun, "The Changing Character of College: Institutional Transformation in American Higher Education," in *The Social Worlds of Higher Education*, ed. Pescosolido and Aminzade; Charles Green and Dean Dorn, "The Changing Classroom: The Meaning of Shifts in Higher Education for Teaching and Learning," in *The Social Worlds of Higher Education*, ed. Pescosolido and Aminzade; and Robert Bellah, "Class Wars and Culture Wars in the University Today," in *The Social Worlds of Higher Education*, ed. Pescosolido and Aminzade. For discussions of the "culture wars" at Minnesota, see John K. Evans, "Minnesota's Latest PC Follies," *Academic Questions* 7 (June 1994): 56; Norman Fruman and John Evans, "Sensitivity Training Offends Faculty," *Minnesota Daily*, 24 November 1992, 7; and John Evans and Norman Fruman, "Academic Freedom under Siege at the U of M," *Minnesota Scholar* 1 (1993): 13–16. For a discussion of the "chilly climate" women faced during this time, see The Commission on Women, "The Minnesota Plan II: 1995–2000: Recommendations to Increase the University Community's Capacity to Improve the Campus Climate for Women," unpublished report, University of Minnesota, 1995.

46. On the backlash against feminism and affirmative action and other social and economic changes during the Reagan era, see Susan Faludi, *Backlash: The Undeclared War against America's Women* (New York: Crown, 1991); Michael Schaller, *Reckoning with Reagan: America and Its President in the 1980s* (New York: Oxford University Press, 1992); Terry Anderson, *The Pursuit of Fairness: A History of Affirmative Action* (Oxford: Oxford University Press, 2004); Lydia Chavez, *The Color Bind* (Berkeley and Los Angeles: University of California Press, 1997).

47. Lehmberg and Pflaum, *The University of Minnesota*, 243.

48. Ibid., 250–51.

49. Ibid., 262.

50. Gloria Anzaldúa, ed., *Making Face, Making Soul, Haciendo Caras: Creative and Critical Perspectives by Women of Color* (San Francisco: Aunt Lute Foundation, 1990); Chandra Mohanty, Anne Russo Talpade, and Lourdes Torres, eds., *Third World Women and the Politics of Feminism* (Bloomington: Indiana University Press, 1991); Inderpal Grewal and Caren Kaplan, eds., *Scattered Hegemonies: Postmodernity and Transnational Feminist Practices* (Minneapolis: University of Minnesota Press, 1994); and M. Jacqui Alexander and Chandra Talpade Mohanty, *Feminist Genealogies, Colonial Legacies, Democratic Futures* (New York: Routledge, 1997).

51. Chela Sandoval, "U.S. Third World Feminism: The Theory and Method of Oppositional Consciousness in the Postmodern World," *Genders* 10 (Spring 1991).

52. Judith Butler, *Gender Trouble: Feminism and the Subversion of Identity* (New York: Routledge, 1990); and Henry Abelove, Michèle Aina Barale, and David Halperin, eds., *The Lesbian and Gay Studies Reader* (New York: Routledge, 1993).

53. Margaret Anderson and Patricia Hill Collins, eds., *Race, Class and Gender, An Anthology*, 5th ed. (Belmont, Calif.: Wadsworth/Thomson Learning, 2004); and Paula Rothenberg, *Race, Class and Gender in the U.S.*, 6th ed. (New York: Worth Publishers, 2004). Rothenberg's volume was published under the title *Racism and Sexism: An Integrated Study* (St Martin's Press) in 1988 and first published as *Race, Class, and Gender in the United States* in 1992.

54. The MacArthur Program "emphasizes study and research on four broad dimensions of world society: global governance and transnational norms; environmental sustainability and social justice; war and peace in historical context; and production, performance and representation of identities." See http://www.icgc.umn.edu/About%20MacArthur.htm.

55. Janet Spector, *What This Awl Means: Feminist Archaeology at a Wahpeton Dakota Village* (St. Paul: Minnesota Historical Society Press, 1993).

56. Jennifer Pierce, *Gender Trials: Emotional Lives in Contemporary Law Firms* (Berkeley and Los Angeles: University of California Press, 1995); Lisa Disch, *Hannah Arendt and the Limits of Philosophy* (Ithaca, N.Y.: Cornell University Press, 1994); and Jean O'Brien, *Dispossession by Degrees: Indian Land and Identity in Natick, Massachusetts, 1650–1790* (New York: Cambridge University Press, 1997).

57. See Lynda Zwinger, "Dancing through the Mother Field," in *Generations*, ed. Looser and Kaplan; and Nancy Miller, "Jason Dreams, Victoria Works Out," in *Generations*, ed. Looser and Kaplan. Also see Susan Gubar, "What Ails Feminist Criticism?" *Critical Inquiry* 24 (Summer 1998); Robin Weigman, "What Ails Feminist Criticism? A Second Opinion," *Critical Inquiry* 25 (Winter 1999); Madelon Sprengnether, "Generational Differences—Reliving Mother Daughter Conflicts," in *Changing the Subject: The Making of Feminist Literary Criticism*, ed. Gayle Greene and Coppelia Kahn (New York: Routledge, 1993); Nancy Miller, "Decades," *South Atlantic Quarterly* 91, 1 (1992): 65–86; Jane Gallop, Marianne Hirsch, and Nancy Miller, "Criticizing Feminist Criticism," in *Conflicts in*

Feminism, ed. Marianne Hirsch and Evelyn Fox Keller (New York: Routledge, 1990); and the third wave volumes listed in note 2.

58. See Heywood and Drake, *Third Wave Agenda.* Also, see Veronica Chambers, "Betrayal Feminism," in *Listen Up,* ed. Findlen.

59. See Janice Raymond, *The Transsexual Empire* (Boston: Beacon Press, 1979).

60. Baumgardner and Richards, eds., *Manifesta,* 36.

61. Heywood and Drake, *Third Wave Agenda.*

62. Chambers, "Betrayal Feminism."

63. Bellafante, "Feminism," 54.

64. Pam Butler, "Contemporary U.S. Feminisms and the Politics of Making Waves, 1994–2004," Directed Reading Paper: Department of American Studies, University of Minnesota, 2004.

65. This focus on "what's wrong with feminism" pre-dated the publication of the *Time* article in a number of books as well as in one televised debate on *Firing Line* titled, "Women's Movement Has Been Disastrous," featuring William Buckley, Elizabeth Fox Genovese, Betty Friedan, Camille Paglia, and others. For accounts that pre-dated the article, see "Women's Movement Has Been Disastrous," *Firing Line* (Columbia, S.C.: ETV, 1994); Christina Hoff Sommers, *Who Stole Feminism? How Women Have Betrayed Women* (New York: Simon and Schuster, 1994); and Elizabeth Fox Genovese, *"How Feminism Is Not the Story of My Life": How Today's Feminist Elite Has Lost Touch with the Real Concerns of Women* (New York: Doubleday, 1996). For two academic responses after the *Time* article, see Social Justice Group, Center for Advanced Feminist Studies editorial collective, *Is Academic Feminism Dead?;* and Ellen Messer-Davidow, *Disciplining Feminism: From Social Activism to Academic Discourse* (Durham, N.C.: Duke University Press, 2002). And for a popular response, see Kristine Rowe-Finkbein, *The F Word: Feminism in Jeopardy* (Emeryville, Calif.: Seal Press, 2004).

66. See Joan Scott, "The Evidence of Experience," *Cultural Critique* 17 (1991); Susan Chase, *Ambiguous Empowerment* (Amherst: University of Massachusetts Press, 1995); and Maynes, Pierce, and Laslett, *Telling Stories.*

67. Chase, *Ambiguous Empowerment,* 7.

68. Initially, we sent out a call for abstracts to graduate students and faculty on four different list-serves at the University of Minnesota: Feminist Studies, the Comparative Women's History Workshop, the MacArthur Interdisciplinary Center for Global Studies, and American Studies. From the initial call, we received nineteen abstracts. We have included all of those papers here with the exception of those authors who did not have time to turn their abstracts into completed papers. We recognize that our contributors do not reflect a representative sample of feminist scholars at the university. Our sample of contributors is most likely skewed by including those who had the time and inclination to write personal narrative essays.

69. Sociologist C. Wright Mills called the link between personal biography and history "the sociological imagination." C. Wright Mills, *The Sociological Imagination* (New York: Oxford University Press, 1959). Our argument here has rel-

evance for a longstanding metatheoretical debate in the social sciences about the problem of theorizing both structure and agency. Basically this problem concerns how to develop an adequate theoretical account that deals simultaneously with macro-structural and micro-processual levels of analysis. Bridging this dualism between deterministic theories and voluntaristic theories of action and developing what British sociologist Anthony Giddens has called the "duality of structure" has become a central theoretical project among a number of prominent social theorists. For examples, see Anthony Giddens, *Central Problems in Social Theory* (Berkeley: University of California Press, 1979); Pierre Bourdieu and Loic Wacquant, *An Invitation to Reflexive Sociology* (Chicago: University of Chicago Press, 1992); James Coleman, "Social Theory, Social Research and a Theory of Action," *American Journal of Sociology* 91, 6 (May 1986): 1309–35; Jürgen Habermas, *The Theory of Communicative Action, Vol. 2: Lifeworld and System: A Critique of Functionalist Reason* (Boston: Beacon Press, 1985).

70. Amber Hollibaugh, introduction to *My Dangerous Desires: A Queer Girl Dreaming Her Way Home* (Chapel Hill, N.C.: Duke University Press, 2000), 8.

71. Ironically, the CAFS/Schochet coalition was also told that they could resubmit the proposal, provided that they asked for less money from the university and could ensure funding through large external grants at the very moment President George W. Bush had chosen to eliminate sexuality as a research topic from federal funding agencies such as NIMH.

72. Kevin Murphy and Jennifer Pierce, personal communication, May 2003.

1. Feminist Archaeology
What This All Means (After All These Years)

Janet D. Spector

Reminiscences

In October 1994, on my fiftieth birthday, my partner and I bought a house from a friend in Albuquerque, New Mexico. We had not been thinking about early retirement or leaving the University of Minnesota, where we had both taught for two decades, until this opportunity arose, but once it did, we found ourselves ready to move on and were able to negotiate early, phased retirements. Some friends and colleagues thought we were foolish to leave our tenured positions; others thought we were brave. We just kept thinking about the place that prompted this unexpected life change. The small house is on a two-thirds-acre lot. It faces a wild bird refuge managed by the nearby Rio Grande Nature Center and State Park. Looking out the front windows, beyond the refuge, we have an unimpeded view of the majestic Sandia Mountains, which turn red as the sun sets. It is an entirely lovely, quiet, tranquil, pace-slowing place.

I moved to Albuquerque in fall 1995, having left the university at what I considered the high point of my career: I had just completed a very challenging and rewarding assignment as Assistant Provost for Academic Affairs with the "charge" to improve the campus climate for women, and had finished a wonderful, long-term archaeological project that culminated in the publication of *What This Awl Means: Feminist Archaeology at a Wahpeton Dakota Village*.[1] During the next three years as I was "phasing" out of academics (I returned each summer to teach), I had idle time for reflection—about what I wanted to do next; about how much of my identity was tied to academic life; about how difficult it was to be idle.

In 1998, I was invited to participate in a small seminar at the School for American Research in Santa Fe on the implications of doing archaeology as a feminist. This provided an opportunity to focus my ruminations. Eight archaeologists, a historian, and a philosopher gathered for five days to consider various facets of doing feminist archaeology guided by key questions framed by the organizers, philosopher Alison Wylie and archaeologist Meg Conkey. Though we were not asked to write reminiscences about our careers as feminist scholars, that format seemed most appropriate to my new circumstances. What follows is a version of the paper I wrote for that seminar.

What it means to be a feminist archaeologist depends on our personal history as both. When, where, and how we became feminists, whether or not we were practicing archaeology at the time, and if so, the kind of archaeology we learned all shape our interests, intentions, questions, and motivations. It matters that I became a feminist while doing graduate work in archaeology in the late 1960s at the University of Wisconsin during an era of optimistic political activism: against the Vietnam War, against racism and sexism, for student power, and for the establishment of black studies, American Indian studies, and women's studies. We believed we could change things. It also matters that I specialized in "historic" rather than "prehistoric" archaeology, of Indian people rather than Euro-Americans, in the U.S. upper Midwest rather than some other region. And it matters that my socialization into the profession occurred during a period of change in the field from the "old" to the "new" archaeology, before the existence of feminist scholarship in any discipline.

I remember my first glimmerings of what feminism could bring to archaeology. It was in 1968, my second year of graduate school, during a conversation with Maria Bode, a student colleague at the University of Wisconsin. At the time some of us were beginning to talk (quietly) about sexism in the anthropology department. We were teaching assistants for the introductory archaeology course. One day Maria and I were discussing the new and very popular "Man the Hunter Theory" of evolution we were teaching in Anthro 101.[2] In the middle of the conversation we had a classic *Ms.* magazine "click" experience. In a sudden and funny epiphany, we realized that the theory was, unbeknownst to its originators and adherents, a projection of mid-twentieth-century suburban-American lifestyles and attitudes back into the remote past. Australopithecine males, like their modern counterparts, left their nuclear families each day to do important work, procuring vital necessities for their dependent children and their dependent wives, who were tethered at home by the immobilizing constraints of childbearing and child rearing.

We laughed because the theory was such a parody, because the men who created it were so unconscious of its political ramifications and of their male arrogance (to think that *all human* characteristics evolved because of early male hunters!), and because it was so seductive. Until our feminist consciousness was awakened, we had not seen the androcentrism or the Eurocentrism in Man the Hunter. Afterward, we saw the connections between the treatment of women within the profession and the treatment of women as subjects of study. And we realized that feminism changes the way one sees things.

The good humor and insight of feminist criticism were further exemplified for me by the 1972 publication of Elaine Morgan's smart and witty book *The Descent of Woman*.[3] Morgan raucously deconstructs what she labels the "Tarzan Theory of Human Evolution." Mincing no words, she exposes the sexism of Desmond Morris, Robert Ardrey, and other popularizers of the theory, carefully illustrating how their theories about the past were embedded in contemporary social thought and politics, and how they rationalized the subordination of women (it was virtually built into the species!). As an alternative, she proposed the ingenious "aquatic theory," which explained (much more convincingly in my opinion) how human posture, tool use, intelligence, language, sexual behavior, and the loss of body hair had evolved because of women's, rather than men's, actions and adaptations.

However flawed "Man the Hunter" is in terms of explaining human evolution, it does explain, in part, the emergence of feminist critiques of archaeology. When I came to the University of Minnesota as an assistant professor in 1973, that theory provided the perfect foil to use in classes and public lectures about the many facets of archaeological androcentrism. At the time, feminist students and community feminists across the country were very interested in archaeology. They had questions and expected answers about women's power and status in the remote past. I remember being asked about the existence of ancient matriarchies and Amazons by feminists eager to have positive and powerful images of women before the rise of patriarchy. I could not answer their questions, but I did puzzle over them and gave lectures about how sexism had shaped archaeological reasoning and research.

My enthusiasm about feminist archaeology was reinforced significantly by participation in the vibrant and ever-growing community of feminist scholars at Minnesota. We came together in the context of building the Women's Studies Department (established in the 1973–74 year, coincidentally my first year at Minnesota). From the beginning of my academic career, I was intimately involved in all facets of Women's Studies. The feminist intellectual community, not my "home" department, provided the essential support, encouragement, and safe space for pursuing feminist work. This was true for the feminist faculty (two of us) and students (many of them) in the Anthropology Department during the 1970s and early 1980s. Bolstered by the existence of our "real" home department, we formed an active support group to take on departmental affirmative action battles and to organize feminist anthropology colloquia and other events.

Women's Studies provided a fertile environment for experimenting with feminist approaches to teaching, mentoring, and research. In spring 1974 I taught my first women's studies course, "Comparative Studies of Women: Anthropological Perspectives," working with one graduate and seven or eight undergraduate teaching assistants. We spent hours every week of the quarter discussing the course content, structure, process, and power dynamics. Each undergraduate teaching assistant led a small discussion/research group that scoured anthropological sources for information on topics like "Ancient Amazons and Matriarchies," "Women and Power," "Women as Gatherers," "Women in Agricultural Societies," "Women in Early States," and so on. There was very little published in feminist anthropology at that time, and we relied heavily on a small pamphlet titled *Women's Liberation: An Anthropological View.*[4] Using that reference as a point of departure, each group created bibliographies and presented reports about their research for the rest of the class. It was a heady time. The experience deepened our feminist critiques of anthropology and suggested a host of new topics for future research.

My first feminist research project began in 1976, when I organized a small group of women students interested in feminist archaeology to work on developing what I called a " task differentiation" framework. Influenced by feminist anthropology's new conceptualizations and insights about gender and by the new approaches in archaeology that focused on people rather than artifacts, we were interested in learning about the material and nonmaterial dimensions of gender. For example, how do various cultures use material things such as tools, clothing, ornaments, or decorations to signify differences between men and women? How do the activities of women, men, girls, and boys affect the physical layout of their work or living spaces and their communities? How do objects reflect and reinforce gender-based differences in power or status? How are they used to socialize children into culturally appropriate male and female roles? By initially studying well-documented groups, we hoped to discover correlations between the social, temporal, spatial, and material dimensions of task performance and the sites people created and used. Ultimately, we wanted to learn enough about the material expressions of gender to study past societies based on the archaeological record alone. Then we might be able to determine more reliably whether or not there had ever been sexually egalitarian groups and to examine how female subordination and male dominance developed, varied, and changed over time and in different cultural settings. We believed archaeology could have an application in the real world of feminist politics.

The first writing I did about feminist archaeology and the task differentiation approach was in a women's studies setting, a 1977 conference for University of Minnesota students and faculty.[5] Because the paper was for a multidisciplinary audience, I felt simultaneously obliged and free to write about the potential contributions of feminist archaeology to women's studies and to the women's movement. There was a stark contrast in tone and language between that essay and a National Science Foundation proposal I wrote at about the same time seeking support for task differentiation research.

I situated the Women's Studies Conference paper in the context of issues raised by the women's movement, noting that many feminists looked to archaeology for explanations about past conditions that might explain contemporary "sexual asymmetry"—the phrase describing male dominance/female subordination in more neutral terms coined by Michelle Rosaldo and Louise Lamphere in *Women, Culture, and Society*.[6] After describing archaeology's pervasive androcentrism, I argued that the field needed to develop new approaches taking into account the complexities of gender arrangements and their potential manifestation at sites. Without this, inferences about the division of labor, male and female power or status, and gender-specific artifacts would remain as speculative and untestable as the popular theories about matriarchies and Amazons so easily dismissed by professional archaeologists. I introduced the task differentiation framework as an example of such an approach.

These early experiences demonstrated the importance, power, and necessity of collaboration in feminist scholarship, though this was not a highly valued work style in the department or college. In feminist studies, there was too much to be done alone. The work was much richer and more fun when done with others. And as an untenured member of an anthropology faculty that had little appreciation for feminist work, collaborating with other feminists provided the positive energy and sup-

port needed to resist pressures to assimilate into the academic mainstream for tenure and promotion purposes.

In today's academic world, some people seem to think of my generation's women's studies teaching, committee service, and advising
as unpaid labor since we were doing the same work in our home departments. I did this work willingly because I knew we were building
something together that could transform the institution. For most of
my contemporaries, women's studies enriched our academic lives: it
was a refuge from pressures of being the one or two women, let alone
feminists, in male-dominated departments; it was the incubator for our
emerging ideas about feminist teaching, research, and institutional
change; and it provided invaluable support for us at the time of merit,
tenure, and promotion reviews. Over the years, I remember watching
some prospective feminist scholars enter the university and refuse to
participate in women's studies "until they got tenure." But by then, they
often had forsaken their feminist work or had been unsuccessful in the
tenure process. I felt well compensated for the extra labor in women's
studies, and I continue to believe that "sheltering" untenured faculty
from active participation in women's studies is, among other things, a
way to depoliticize and isolate them.

My next collaborative project began in 1978, when Meg Conkey
(now professor of anthropology at Berkeley) and I started work on "Archaeology and the Study of Gender."[7] Michael Schiffer brought us together after we each mentioned feminist archaeology (maybe we said
the archaeology of gender) in response to a questionnaire he circulated
soliciting essay ideas for *Advances in Archaeological Method and Theory*.
From 1978 to 1983 we worked long distance, without ever meeting in
person. Our correspondence was intense. Many letters and drafts were
sent back and forth. There were steady expressions of support for and
excitement about each other's ideas, apologies for being overworked
and late in responding, and digressions about academic worries (both
of us were untenured when we started) and about how long it was taking
to get the piece out. The correspondence was a rich mix of the personal,
the political, and the academic, a hallmark of feminist scholarship. And
it was a contrast to my work relationships with nonfeminist archaeology
colleagues (implicitly competitive, compartmentalized, secretive, and
distrustful).

Another important feminist collaboration for me was serving on the
national advisory board for the American Anthropological Association's

"Gender and Anthropology" project. This three-year project (1986–88) was explicitly designed to bring feminist anthropology into introductory textbooks and classroom settings. It culminated with the publication of *Gender and Anthropology: Critical Reviews for Research and Teaching.*[8] All subfields were represented on the board and in the book. As we outlined the format for the essays during board meetings, we had many thought-provoking discussions about how to increase the overall impact of feminist work on the discipline, still a vexing question.

One of the most exciting parts of writing the archaeology essay with Mary Whelan for *Gender and Anthropology* was designing classroom exercises. One of them, "Critically Reading Introductory Texts," subversively asks students to evaluate their introductory textbooks in terms of ethnocentrism and androcentrism. We provided a set of key questions as a guide:

- Does the author give equal attention to the roles, activities, and experiences of women and men in discussing prehistory (we directed their attention to photos and illustrations as well as the text)?
- In what contexts is the author gender-specific, and what are the implications of this in terms of the power and status of men and women?
- What activities, materials, and skills are linked with males versus females? What characteristics are taken to be universal? Of those, which might be culturally specific? How could you know?
- Given specific cases of gender bias in the text, what alternative "scenarios" can you suggest?

The second exercise, "Material Expressions of Gender in the United States: A Case Study in Ethnoarchaeology," encouraged students to think about the *material* cultural construction of gender. We posed a series of questions to help them see how materials and spaces not only reflect but also shape gender roles, power relations, ideology, socialization, and gender attribution processes. We asked them to create archaeological maps of familiar, gender-specific spaces, to exchange the maps with someone else in the class, and then to interpret the sites in terms of U.S. gender arrangements. I knew from experience in my own classes that this exercise convinced students of the importance of gender as an analytical category of analysis.

Among other things, working on the gender and anthropology project reinforced my conviction that archaeological questions can deepen understandings of gender. While it is true that we rely on work done outside of archaeology to conceptualize gender, it is also true that no field is better equipped than archaeology to examine how gender is materially constructed.

I do not know how many people have actually used the book or our article in their classes or texts. I do know that David Hurst Thomas drew on our essay extensively in revising both the second and third editions of his introductory text *Archaeology*. In a recent edition, he discusses different dimensions of gender bias in the field in several parts of the text, and he prominently features the work of women and feminist archaeologists. This text reaches thousands of students a year who might not otherwise have any exposure to feminist scholarship.[9]

Writing Archaeology as a Feminist Political Activity

The Little Rapids project, centered at a nineteenth-century Wahpeton Dakota summer planting village, was the most comprehensive feminist enterprise of my archaeological career.[10] It entailed many facets of feminist archaeology: teaching, fieldwork, research, mentoring, and writing. Launched in 1979 to field test the task differentiation approach, the project evolved in unexpected directions over the next fourteen years to 1993, when *What This Awl Means*, the book based on the research, was published. The awl referred to in the title is a small, delicately inscribed antler leather punch handle that we discovered in the community dump. Deciphering the meaning of those inscriptions proved to be a turning point in the writing of the book.

There were two major turning points in the project. First, after working without Dakota involvement during the early years of the research, in 1985 I began working collaboratively with two Dakota colleagues whose relatives had lived at the site in the 1830s and 1840s. Second, in February 1986, Renato Rosaldo presented a lecture at Minnesota titled "Where Objectivity Lies: The Rhetoric of Anthropology." Just as the initial click experience about "Man the Hunter" in 1968 provoked a major reassessment of what I had learned so far in anthropology, these two turning points prompted another major phase of "unlearning the discipline." My attention shifted beyond the treatment of women and gender as subjects of study in archaeology to incorporate issues relating to the treatment of Indian people, men included. I also moved from an emphasis on developing a new method for the archaeological study of gender to finding new ways to portray the past we had unearthed and our relationship to it.

Archaeologists create public images of the past, and this is a political act. Our writing provides the props and scripts for museums, the media, textbooks, educators, and the general public about human origins, developments, variations, capabilities, and accomplishments—hardly trivial subjects. As Mark Leone pointed out in a 1973 article, a largely unrecognized rationale for archaeology is the substantiation of national mythology.[11] In 1984, Meg Conkey and I adapted his insight to show that archaeology has played an active though unacknowledged role in the substantiation of a specific *gender* mythology, one that elevates males and subordinates females.[12] Indigenous people around the world have made a similar point. The ways archaeologists have treated their sites and site materials and have portrayed their histories and cultures have harmed them. For me, part of writing archaeology as a feminist is to acknowledge the power of our words and to interrupt the perpetuation of damaging gender, race, or class-based stereotypes, stereotypes that celebrate some groups and harm others. To put this in more proactive terms, through our research and writing feminist archaeologists should produce and distribute socially and politically responsible (not "politically correct") images of the past. With respect to writing this involves being intentional about our audience, content, language, writing style(s), tone, and vantage point.

The power and privilege of knowledge production was very much on my mind in writing *What This Awl Means*. Inspired by Rosaldo's call to experiment with new forms of writing anthropology, by my immersion in the site and associated sources, and by my relationships with Dakota people, I was committed to producing an accessible, human-scale portrayal of the nineteenth-century community at Little Rapids. I did not want to employ the distanced, detached, object-centered, objectifying rhetoric common to midwestern archaeology or the equally stultifying and esoteric jargon of some postmodern feminist theory. Most of all I wanted to avoid language that might caricature or otherwise diminish Dakota people, past or present. As part of my feminist agenda, I featured the accomplishments and activities of Dakota women, challenging the politically motivated and distorted images conveyed in most written accounts of the Eastern Dakota as "roving bands of [male] hunters and warriors." They were not.

It was not easy to unlearn standard archaeological writing. I have described elsewhere how the awl narrative happened.[13] I did not set out to write what others have referred to as a "story" about the awl. There is currently great interest in "archaeologists as storytellers" (the title of a popular session at a recent Society of Historical Archaeology conference and the topic of subsequent e-mail discussions). I find myself resistant to this notion. I know at least one Indian person who thinks this kind of "storytelling" is yet another example of Anglos appropriating indigenous cultural forms. I am also disturbed by the trivializing connotation of the word *storytelling*, particularly in academic contexts. Archaeological stories can be construed as fictional, simplistic, or childlike, something made up in contrast to the "serious" or "real" or "true" versions presented in standard archaeologese. I prefer the phrase "narrative" or "creative nonfiction." I do not advocate "making up" stories about sites or artifacts in any writing style. We should be able to empirically "justify" the content and tone of what we write. I can do this more convincingly for the awl narrative than I can for the usual presentation formats used to describe and discuss awls.[14]

In any case, my initial motive in writing the awl narrative was not about creating a story but rather about breaking away from the usual archaeological writing modes. I was searching for ways to present varied voices and perspectives about the Little Rapids Wahpeton community during a turbulent period of their history. I did not pretend or intend to be neutral about the terrible consequences of European colonial policies and practices for Dakota people or about the legacies of that period that continue to taint relationships between Dakota and non-Dakota people, including archaeologists.

The narrative was the first thing I wrote for the book, and it prompted the next piece, a memoir-like introduction, "Archaeology as Empathy." Both of these were easier to write than some other parts. Throughout the writing process I experimented with different formats, some of which never made it into the book. One was an imaginary dialogue between Wahpeton Dakota elders who had lived at Little Rapids in the early 1800s and Theodore Lewis, the first archaeologist to visit the site in 1887. By then the elders were living at the Devil's Lake Reservation in North Dakota. They had ceded the land around Little Rapids to the U.S. government in 1851 and were forcibly removed from Minnesota in 1862. Lewis visited the site in August 1887 to map the earthworks there. He, like many of his (non-Indian) contemporaries, believed that ancient "moundbuilders," not ancient Dakota or any other Indian people, had constructed them. In my imagined dialogue I tried to convey what would have happened if Lewis had asked the Dakota elders at Devil's

Lake about the earthworks. Of course, given the political realities of that period, he would not have thought to ask, and they would not have told him the truth. The point of the dialogue was to present, in nonpolemical terms, something about the long and troubled history of relationships between archaeologists and Dakota people as a backdrop for a discussion of current repatriation issues. Though it did not quite work, it did help me write that part of the book.

I also tried to write another awl story to undermine the notion some readers might have that the one eventually published was yet another "master" narrative. That did not work either. Still, the process of experimenting with different ways of writing eventually freed me from some well-disciplined habits. Since the book was published, I have gotten many inquiries, particularly from graduate students, about how to write narratives. Often they want to know how to get such writing accepted by their examining committees. I am never quite sure how to respond. My writing was informed by more than a decade of research about Little Rapids. I have academic credentials and tenure. Disciplinary norms and values have not been transformed yet, and until they are, students need to be pragmatic about taking risks. One thing I do encourage without hesitation is to use nontraditional sources to ignite their creativity before writing.

What I have learned most clearly about writing feminist archaeology is that sites and artifacts can be tremendously evocative, but to unlock their potential, we need to draw on a much wider repertoire of sources. While rigorous technical analysis is important for some purposes, it cannot tell the whole story about a past community. Part of the transformative potential of feminist archaeology is the incorporation of multiple sources and voices.

Writing *What This Awl Means* stretched my sense of how to use sources and what sources to use. Beyond the usual archaeological, historical, ethnographic, and feminist materials, I drew heavily on Dakota-authored texts and an early edition of the Dakota/English Dictionary.[15] Each word I looked up—menstruation, village, the names for colors, months, tools, clothing, buildings, plants, and animals—helped me see and write about things differently. Until I worked with Chris Cavender and Carrie Schommer, it never occurred to me to use Dakota words or family names in writing. Doing so undermines the anonymity of the archaeological record—one can picture individuals who lived at the site and have a sense of the words they might have spoken there.

Using literary sources was also inspiring. I drew on novelist Toni Morrison's words about "literary" archaeology—the phrase she uses to describe her research process for writing *Beloved*—to introduce the Little Rapids fieldwork and site interpretation:

On the basis of some information and a little bit of guesswork you journey to a site to see what remains were left behind and to reconstruct the world that these remains imply. What makes it fiction is the nature of the imaginative act: my reliance on the image—in the remains—in addition to recollection, to yield up a kind of truth. By "image" . . . I simply mean "picture" and the feelings that accompany the picture.[16]

If I were teaching a course on writing archaeology, I would urge students to read widely outside of the field, to do anything they could to see sites and envision the lives of site residents in new ways. I would require them to read Indian-authored novels, short stories, poems, and essays produced by writers who generously give readers access to Indian cultures from inside rather than outside perspectives. Three culture and time-transporting novels stand out for me: Dakota ethnologist Ella Deloria's *Waterlily*, Chickasaw poet and essayist Linda Hogan's *Solar Storms*, and Ojibway author Louise Erdrich's *Tracks*.[17]

I would also expose students to artifact descriptions by nonarchaeologists. Naturalist, poet, and nature writer Terry Tempest Williams, who spent some time excavating Great Salt Lake flood-endangered cave sites with the Utah state archaeologist, writes eloquently about the evocative quality of site materials. She also shows how years of bird-watching in the area helped her understand symbols on ancient pots. In *Refuge: An Unnatural History of Family and Place*, she writes:

Artifacts are alive. Each has a voice. They remind us what it means to be human—that it is our nature to survive, to create works of beauty, to be resourceful, to be attentive to the world we live in. A necklace of olivella shells worn by a Fremont man or woman celebrates our instinctive desire for adornment, even power and prestige. A polished stone ball, incised bones, and stone tablets court the mysteries of private lives, communal lives, lives rooted in ritual and ceremony.

And sometimes you recognize images from your own experience. I recall looking at a Great Salt Lake gray variant potsherd. A design had been pecked on its surface. It was infinitely familiar, and then it came to me—shorebirds standing in water, long-legged birds, the dazzling light from the lake reflected on feathers. This was a picture I had seen a thousand times on the shores of Great Salt Lake: godwits, curlews, avocets, and stilts—birds the Fremont knew well.[18]

Her insight about the pottery design reminded me of deciphering the inscriptions on the Little Rapids awl handle. There are things we can do to help us find meaning and write about the past more effectively. Experimental archaeology is one route. Learning more about the natural world surrounding sites is another. I would direct people to anthropologist Keith Basso's wonderful book *Wisdom Sits in Places*, about landscape and language among the Western Apache, to break out of stereotypic thinking about archaeological sites.[19] Having established close relationships with Apache elders, Basso was asked by them to make "Apache" maps of their land. In the process, he was told in great detail what places mean to them—how Apache names for and stories about places shape their sense of morality, community, and identity. In a similar vein, Australian archaeologist Shelley Greer wrote a thought-provoking dissertation about what sites mean to Aboriginal people and the ramifications of this for archaeology. Her initial research project was a standard archaeological survey in Northern Cape York, but after becoming well acquainted with local aboriginal community members and learning from them how archaeological sites form a part of contemporary landscapes and identity, she abandoned the survey.[20] Although neither Basso or Greer looked at how gender arrangements can influence women's and men's sense of place or space, they do make us aware of how culture, that of an indigenous population and that of the archaeologist, can affect perceptions of the same site.

Setting Limits and Pushing Boundaries

The parameters of feminist archaeology have changed since my initial glimmerings in 1968.[21] But the fundamental questions and problems propelling the enterprise have not. While the women's movement can claim many successes, female subordination and oppression continue worldwide. Academic feminists have challenged prevailing theories, methods, structures, attitudes, norms, values, and practices that exclude or harm women. There is much more to be done.

Within archaeology we must continue to document and challenge the ways our field discriminates against women—as practitioners and as objects of study. We also need to clarify our vision of a "feminist-transformed" archaeology. We claim that feminist initiatives can significantly change all facets of archaeology: professional demographics, leadership, and reward systems; research, teaching, writing, and publishing norms and priorities; the treatment of archaeological sites and site materials; the ways the past is regarded and presented. But what will each of these look like after the revolution? Without some concrete images, how can we organize effectively or know when or if we have succeeded?

This presumes that a primary target for our efforts is the field of archaeology. Judith Stacey and Barrie Thorne might disagree. They find that their early notion of instigating a "feminist revolution *in* sociology now seems oxymoronic or at least deeply flawed."[22] Their vision of the future is transdisciplinary. Academic fields as we know them will disappear to be replaced by new ones like cultural studies, women's studies, and various ethnic studies. Like some others who responded to their essay, I think a retreat from the disciplines is unrealistic and premature. An exodus of feminists to new and still institutionally marginal interdisciplinary departments will leave the dominant departments and disciplines unchanged. Most of these are alive and well entrenched in our colleges and universities, and they continue to do serious damage to women and others who have been ignored, trivialized, or excluded from them.

This issue reminds me of the early years of Women's Studies at Minnesota. We debated the wisdom of creating an independent department with tenured faculty lines versus an interdisciplinary program drawing on faculty housed in traditional departments. We opted for both, garnering approval for the establishment of a department with several full-time positions tenured and budgeted in Women's Studies to be supplemented in teaching and service by feminist faculty from other departments. This arrangement, though imperfect in its execution, has worked to prevent the ghettoization of Women's Studies while at the same time actively fostering multi- and interdisciplinary feminist studies. Many of us developed our feminist research, teaching, and political strategies in Women's Studies and brought them back to our home departments.

I suspect that the end of archaeology as we know it is much more likely to occur because indigenous people around the world deny us access to their sites and artifacts than because of the challenge of feminist archaeologists. Meanwhile, we have work to do. Though I do not believe there is just one recipe for doing archaeology as a feminist, I do think there are some essential ingredients. First is maintaining a strong connection to the women's movement that inspired it. We still need to change norms, values, practices, and priorities that exclude, oppress, or marginalize women and their contributions. This entails work in the field and in our labs, classrooms, departments, universities, and professional organizations.

In regard to research, doing feminist archaeology means continuing our ever-deepening critique and using it as we focus on women and gender arrangements in all of their complexity and variations. We have hardly begun to rewrite (let alone rename) prehistory; we have not determined what we can and cannot know about gender roles, power relations, or beliefs in the past; we have not probed the depths of the *material* cultural construction of gender; we do not know when or how gender emerged as a meaningful category for differentiating and/or ranking people; and we do not know how many or what kinds of gender categories existed in the past. We have just skimmed the surface. The list of possible topics for feminist archaeological research goes on and on.

The heart of our project is to create and "popularize" new ideas about the past. We need to overturn still prevailing archaeological "myths" about the most important trends in prehistory, about where the most important objects and institutions originated, and about who is responsible for them—myths about gender, race, class, and nationality. And we cannot wait until we know the *real* facts of the matter. The best we can do is raise questions, debunk demeaning and damaging theories or scenarios, and propose better alternatives. Part of this entails making the results of feminist archaeology more accessible. We need to write textbooks and children's books, consult on television specials or other mass media projects, serve on publication and funding review panels, and so on. We also might lobby that these activities be factored more positively into disciplinary and academic reward systems.

While these ingredients set some limiting boundaries for defining an explicitly feminist archaeology, in contrast to an uncritical and uncomplicated "archaeology of gender," there is much room for experimentation and variation depending on specific contexts and individual tastes. What has been especially rewarding for me about feminist work is that it leads in unexpected directions. It pushes boundaries—institutional, disciplinary, and conceptual—in ways we do not anticipate. Most feminist scholars find themselves becoming more interdisciplinary as they study the multiple dimensions and complexities of gender and participate in intellectual networks outside of their fields. Similarly, the conceptual boundaries of gender become more permeable as we explore the intricate links between gender, race, class, nationality, and sexuality and the circumstances under which these multiple dimensions of identity, politics, and social organization become more or less salient.

In the Little Rapids project, I found myself pushing the boundaries of feminist archaeology to incorporate the many ramifications of excluding Indian people—both women and men—from the production of archaeological knowledge. Working with Dakota people forced me to deepen the process of "unlearning" the discipline, this time in ways related to "culture" (race? ethnicity?) rather than gender.[23] I had absorbed many problematic messages in my training about Indian people and their relationship to archaeology, and these created tremendous barriers to working with Indian colleagues. For example, we were taught (explicitly or implicitly) the following:

1. There is little connection between contemporary Indian people and the sites we study—before or after European colonization: too much has happened; too many moves; too much has been lost (so why bother to consult with them?).
2. Contemporary Indian people are interested in archaeological sites and site materials primarily for "political" reasons, not because of cultural, spiritual, or historical ties (in contrast to the completely neutral interests of archaeologists).
3. Sites and site materials "belong" to the state, universities, or museums (not to descendants of the people who made and used them).
4. Archaeologists, not Indian people, know best how to "treat" sites and site materials.

Some of these problematic messages are compounded by the ways anthropology is subdivided. Separating cultural anthropology from archaeology fragments knowledge about Indian and other indigenous people. Typologically defined archaeological "cultures" (e.g., Woodland and Mississippian) are seen as distinct from those known ethnographically (e.g., Anishanabe and Dakota) as if they have no relationship to them. The Eurocentric subfield division of "historic" versus "prehistoric" Indian archaeology, based exclusively on the presence or absence of European texts and artifacts, further disrupts any sense of long-term cultural continuity and obscures the whole process of colonization. Surely, an Indian-centered anthropology/archaeology would resist such compartmentalization.

Working with Dakota colleagues transformed the field school program at Little Rapids, shifted how I viewed the site and the artifacts we found, and shaped how I wrote about the project. These work relation-

ships were different from and more complicated than earlier collaborations with feminist colleagues. Beyond cultural and political differences,
we had different interests and stakes in the project, different expectations, levels of involvement, and investment, and different access to institutional resources and power. While it is true that I have felt marginalized in academics because of my gender and sexuality, relative to my
Dakota colleagues, my privileges on the basis of race and position are
much more conspicuous.

We need to find more nuanced language to describe different types
of relationships between Indian and non-Indian people on archaeological projects. Seeking advice, "consulting," is very different from an active and equal partnership. The word *collaboration* is problematic given
the connotation of the word *collaborator*—one who works for the enemy.
Like many feminist endeavors, complicated issues of power, control, and
authority need to be recognized and negotiated with care.

Moving to Community-based Archaeology

My feminist consciousness and values compelled me to work with Dakota people on the Little Rapids project. This in turn deepened my
appreciation of the defects of "exclusionary" archaeology. On several
occasions Chris Cavender and I talked about organizing a more "community-based" project at Little Rapids, one that would involve more Dakota people as teachers, advisors, and students. We imagined rebuilding
scaffolds and lodges, preparing foods, dancing in the enclosure, working hides, and making the clothing, ornaments, and tools, all in ways
that would have been used there in the early 1800s. Little Rapids would
become a kind of on-site learning center that could include excavations,
hands-on learning, and demonstrations. Various things intervened to
stop us from pursing that dream, but now that I have relocated to New
Mexico and am away from a university, I am increasingly interested in
and committed to the notion of community-based archaeology. Community-based archaeology could shift the balance of power, control, and
authority over sites and site materials as well as the production and distribution of archaeological knowledge.

My ideas about community-based archaeology are still forming. I am
now working without the privileges or the constraints of an academic
base and without the contacts I had in Minnesota. One of my ideas is
to study several archaeology projects in North America, Australia, and

perhaps South Africa that go beyond legally mandated community consultations to see how collaborations between archaeologists and local descendant communities are shifting the nature of the enterprise—a kind of ethnography of archaeology. How are sites and materials viewed and treated? How are the fieldwork, lab work, writing, and publication processes different from the archaeology typically practiced in the area? What questions propel the work? How is the past conceptualized or understood? How are priorities set and decisions made? Throughout I would examine how people work across lines of difference including those based on gender, race, class, and ethnicity. This study could delineate some parameters of community-based archaeology as it is evolving.

A second community-based project I have envisioned involves building a multifaceted curriculum around a site for children (ages thirteen to fifteen) who are underserved by traditional school programs. This could be done at any site where there are complementary written, pictorial, and oral records to supplement those underground.

I drafted a project proposal after spending several months volunteering on the excavation of La Plaza de Señor de San José de Los Ranchos, located on the east side of the Rio Grande several miles north of Old Town Albuquerque. Initially established around 1750, Los Ranchos was one of six Spanish colonial plazas established near the river, north of Old Town. It was continuously occupied by Spanish and, much later, by Anglo residents and frequently flooded by the Rio Grande and then rebuilt. In the 1980s, the farmstead then on part of the remaining site was sold to the present village of Los Ranchos, and all buildings were demolished. It would be an ideal site for experimenting with community-based archaeology.

The project I have in mind would involve small teams of students and adult "coaches"—some archaeologists but others as well: historians, computer and video specialists, naturalists, photographers, children's book authors, community members knowledgeable about traditional arts, sciences, agriculture, architecture, and literature. Liking to work collaboratively and with children would be primary qualifications. The students and some community coaches would be drawn from neighborhoods surrounding the site. The goals of this project are as much about creating new learning environments and community building as they are about archaeology per se. Students would learn how to dig and come to appreciate the value and meaning(s) of sites, but archaeological method and theory, historic preservation, and cultural resource management would not be at the center of the endeavor.

In this idealized and still-hypothetical yearlong program, students would excavate parts of a site, document the experience for a cable TV program to be aired monthly, work with computers to record and map findings, and create a project Web page and newspaper linking them to community organizations and their schools. They would collect oral histories from longtime area residents and descendants of the archaeological community and construct "life histories" of different objects found at the site, tracing how the item was fashioned from the original raw material, how it was manufactured and used, and how it found its way into the archaeological record. They would study all kinds of written sources relating to the site over time, both fiction and nonfiction. They would learn about the past climate and environment and about how people's activities altered the landscape, natural resources, and plant and animal life, often to their own detriment.

As their research progressed, the students would re-create scenes from community life as experienced by people of different genders, ages, classes, occupations, and ethnic groups. They would build rooms using old adobe construction techniques, plant a garden that might have been present at the site, prepare foods and beverages, weave blankets, sew clothes, make tools and ornaments—all in the old ways. Each team member, adult and youth, would establish an empathetic link to the community, imagining and conveying what life would have been like if they had lived there in the past. What would they do each day? How would family and community conflicts be resolved and decisions made? How many people would be counted as family members? Who would live together? How might they travel, and whom would they know outside the boundaries of their community? What games would they play? What music, dances, and songs would they know? What would they daydream about? Fear? Laugh at? Worry about? Celebrate? What major events would mark their life course? What illnesses would plague them, and how would these be cured? What were their joys and challenges? How long could they expect to live, and how were they likely to die?

After completing the research, students would present their findings to their families and community in multiple media. Working with adult coaches, some teams might produce and perform a play; others might do a documentary, photo essay, or mural; some students might write poetry, a mystery, short stories, or technical reports. Replicas of the site and its excavation and reconstruction might be constructed as a traveling exhibit. Hopefully in doing all of this, students would discover and hone their interests, talents, and skills.

At this point, this project is in my computer and my head. I have talked to many people about it but have not yet activated the plan. I need to find community partners to shape it and to build the team, select a community and site, raise the funds, and so on. The logistics are daunting. It is where I have ended up after doing feminist archaeology for three decades. Is the project feminist? Is it archaeology?

Notes

1. Janet Spector, *What This Awl Means: Feminist Archaeology at a Wahpeton Dakota Village* (St. Paul: Minnesota Historical Society Press, 1993).

2. S. Washburn and C. S. Lancaster, "The Evolution of Hunting" in *Man the Hunter*, ed. by R. Lee and I. DeVore (Chicago: Aldine, 1968), 293–303.

3. Elaine Morgan, *The Descent of Woman* (New York: Stein and Day, 1972).

4. M. Borun, M. McLaughlin, G. Oboler, N. Perchonock, and L. Sexton, *Women's Liberation: An Anthropological View* (Pittsburgh: KNOW, 1971).

5. Janet Spector, "Male/Female Task Differentiation: A Model for the Archaeological Investigation of Sex Role Dynamics," unpublished paper presented at the University of Minnesota Women's Studies Conference, Spring Hill Conference Center, 1977.

6. Michelle Rosaldo and Louise Lamphere, *Women, Culture and Society* (Stanford, Calif.: Stanford University Press, 1971).

7. Meg Conkey and Janet Spector, "Archaeology and the Study of Gender," *Advances in Archaeological Method and Theory* 7 (1984): 1–38.

8. Sandra Morgen, ed., *Gender and Anthropology: Critical Reviews for Research and Teaching* (Washington, DC: American Anthropological Association, 1989).

9. David Hurst Thomas, *Archaeology,* 3rd ed. (Fort Worth, Tex.: Harcourt Brace and Co., 1997).

10. Janet Spector, "Collaboration at *Inyan Ceyaka Atonwan* (Village at the Rapids)," *SAA Bulletin* 12, 3 (1994): 8–10

11. Mark Leone, "Archaeology as the Science of Technology: Mormon Town Plans and Fences," in *Research and Theory in Current Archaeology*, ed. by C. L. Redman (New York: John Wiley and Sons, 1971), 125–50.

12. Conkey and Spector, "Archaeology and the Study of Gender," 1.

13. See, for example, Spector, *What This Awl Means;* and Spector, "Doing Feminist Archaeology: What Difference(s) Does It Make?" in *Redefining Archaeology: Feminist Perspectives,* ed. M. Casey, D. Donlon, J. Hope, and S. Welfare (Canberra: ANH Publications, Australian National University, 1998).

14. See "Other Awl Stories," in Spector, *What This Awl Means.*

15. Charles Eastman, *Indian Boyhood* (1902; New York: Dover Publications, 1971); and Black Thunder, E. N. Johnson, L. O'Conner, and M. Pronovost,

Ehanna Woyakapi: History and Culture of the Sisseton-Wahpeton Sioux Tribe of South Dakota (Sisseton, S.Dak.: Sisseton-Wahpeton Tribe, 1975). Seth Riggs, "A Dakota-English Dictionary" in *Contributions to North American Ethnology*, vol. 7 (Washington, DC: Government Printing Office, 1890).

16. Toni Morrison, "Site of Memory" in *Inventing the Truth: The Art and Craft of Memoir*, ed. W. Zinsser (Boston: Houghton Mifflin Company, 1987), 112.

17. Ella Deloria, *Waterlily* (Lincoln: University of Nebraska Press, Bison Books, 1990); Louise Erdrich, *Tracks* (New York: Harper and Row, 1988); Linda Hogan, *Solar Storms* (New York: Scribner, 1995).

18. Terry Williams, *Refuge: An Unnatural History of Family and Place* (New York: Vintage Books, 1992), 189.

19. Keith Basso, *Wisdom Sits in Places* (Albuquerque: University of New Mexico Press, 1996).

20. Shelley Greer, *The Accidental Heritage: Archaeology and Identity in Northern Cape York* (PhD diss., James Cook University of North Queensland, Australia, 1996).

21. See M. Conkey and J. Gero, "Programme to Practice: Gender and Feminism in Archaeology," *Annual Reviews of Anthropology* 26 (1997): 411–37.

22. Judith Stacey and Barrie Thorne, "The Missing Feminist Revolution: Ten Years Later," ASA Theory Section Newsletter, *Perspectives* 18, 3: 1.

23. See Spector, "Collaboration at *Inyan Ceyaka Atonwan*."

2. Poisoned Ivy

Lesbian and Gay Academics from the 1960s
through the 1990s

Toni McNaron

In 1964, when I began to work at the University of Minnesota, there simply were no publicly defined lesbian or gay faculty. Perhaps faculty were able to declare their sexual orientation on a few campuses in California or New York City. In the overwhelming majority of cases, however, such faculty were silent, reluctant to risk credibility and jobs by announcing their sexual identities. This self-monitoring, based on homophobic displays at the national and local levels, as in the political efforts of Senator Joseph McCarthy and the House Un-American Activities Committee and the routine raiding of gay bars, allowed universities and colleges to avoid even thinking about the needs or concerns of lesbian and gay faculty.

At the time of my arrival, the English department employed two unmarried women and one unmarried man. Rumor had it that one of the unmarried women and another woman shared a secluded river house an hour and a half from the university. The unmarried man was elegant and had three or four close friends in other departments who, like him, were officially "single," and who, like him, traveled to England or Europe at least once a year for a more relaxed and open life.

Of the six assistant professors hired that fall into the department, I was one of two women. This fact seemed miraculous to me, since so few women were placed at major research universities. When I asked the other new woman, also unmarried, to have lunch with me at the faculty dining club, she refused, saying, "Oh, I don't want to be seen at lunch with another single woman; I'm hoping to find a husband."

Efforts to make some kind of an alliance with the tenured woman living on the river were equally daunting. Since neither of us was capable of speaking the "L" word, our social moves were opaque at best. Rather than reaching out to me, she seemed somehow threatened by my presence in ways I did not understand. Our offices were located in such a way that it was impossible for her to enter or leave without passing my door.

One Friday afternoon when we both were still at work, she poked her head in my door to ask if I would read a poem given to her by a young male student in her modern poetry class and let her know on Monday what I thought of it. I spent too much of my weekend deciding how to respond and went to work prepared to discuss the merits and weaknesses in that rather tortured lyric, which did, however, possess some effective imagery for the student's feelings about his girlfriend.

When I approached my colleague in her office, she barely looked up from what she was doing to listen to my comments. I tried to offer a mix of praise and suggestions for improvement, calculated to show her the seriousness with which I had taken her request and that I was trying to earn her warmth. When I finished, she leaned back slowly in her chair, poker-faced to the end, and said, "Oh, do you really think so? I found it sophomoric in the extreme."

I felt dismissed and demolished, consigned to some outer realm of cretinous readers. I would only much later comprehend that this woman feared I might encroach on the acceptance that she had won for herself. Her need to establish permanent distance between us may well have been to keep herself inside the functional parameters she had established. The older patriarchs of the department admitted her to their sanctum in large part because she presented herself as "one of the boys," who could drink more than they at extended lunch hours in downtown hotels, curse as vividly, and win regularly at their weekly smoke-filled poker marathons.

Genuine kindness and understanding came my way from the elegant man, though his carefully imposed silence about his own life, together with our shared terror of being "found out" by colleagues, left powerful omissions in our contact. Beside these immediate colleagues, I knew only one other unmarried woman in those early years. She was full professor in another department in the College of Liberal Arts. We met after I was delegated by my chair to serve on a collegewide curriculum committee, and we liked each other from the start. However, she was so intense that she frightened me. One evening when the committee had met later than usual, she invited me to go for a drink. I refused before I knew what I was doing. Instinctively I withdrew from an invitation I was sure was for more than a whiskey sour; this woman, so senior to me professionally, was the subject of ominous rumor. After my rebuff, she never again extended herself, most likely for fear she had mistaken whatever silent cues I had sent out that we might both be lonely lesbians. A few years after I met her, she left the University of Minnesota to become an academic administrator at another midwestern university. A few years after that, she committed suicide.

Aside from these tortuous encounters, I was convinced for some years that there were no other lesbians or gay men at the University of Minnesota. Two decades later, Audre Lorde's *Cancer Journals* resonated deeply in me as she discussed women's hiding of their radical mastectomies behind prosthetic breasts.[1] Like them, none of us working for the university could find each other, because, like them, we were in hiding, making heroic attempts to pass for heterosexual, usually being thought of as pathetically neuter.

Far from being neuter, I came to Minnesota with my lover, a woman who left her established life behind her to make a home with me and to pursue a graduate degree in counseling. Though very much in love, we each occupied a closet of considerable depth. Not even comfortable calling ourselves lesbian, we certainly had no intentions that anyone else do so. Consequently, we seldom saw one another on campus and then only in locations unassociated with either of our official domains. Our commitment to isolation prevented us from making efforts to find any other lesbians.

However, at some point during our second year in Minneapolis, I became aware that my partner's academic advisor had had a somewhat older women companion for many years, thought they both maintained utmost secrecy. They never attended official university functions together or spoke of their shared household or personal lives. If my partner mentioned her summer vacation, her advisor might do likewise, both speaking as if they had traveled alone.

I learned of this relationship primarily through observation. My partner's advisor drove a foreign sedan, unmistakable on a campus where more of us drove Fords or Chevrolets if we were buying American, or Volkswagens or used Volvos if we preferred imports. In the late afternoon, I often parked near the advisor's building, waiting for my lover to emerge from another day of seminars, practicums, and office interviews with faculty. If she were later than 3:30, the moment the university closed the administrative offices where the advisor's companion worked as a high-level administrator, I saw the sleek, dark-colored car glide past me only to pause briefly outside the adjacent building as a gray-haired, well-dressed woman hurriedly got in. Being both a good amateur sleuth and a lesbian desperate for assurances that my partner and I were not the only lesbians on campus, I concluded that these two women were a couple.

The first time I asked my partner if she thought her advisor was "like us," she flatly denied any possibility. But the more she described the conversations she had with her advisor, the surer I became that I was right. I also became sure that the advisor sensed that her advisee was like her and that she was trying to make contact in the most convoluted codes imaginable. Perhaps because my lover was nearly the age of her advisor, perhaps because her advisor found my lover as appealing as I did, perhaps because she had been watching us closely and had seen us together enough to confirm her hunches, this deeply closeted woman eventually invited my partner to tea, adding that she should feel free to "bring a friend." After much debate about whether she should go alone or with me, we decided to make the trip together. Looking back, I see that decision as a tiny coming out on my part. At the time, it felt both dangerous and exciting.

The actual tea was inevitably awkward since no one acknowledged either their own or the other relationship. The two older faculty women hesitated to ask me questions about my work or department; I felt constrained from inquiring about their professional lives because they were so senior to me in academic terms and because they were in fields unfamiliar to me. We chatted haltingly about sports and about visits to Lake Superior. The advisor talked with my lover about possible job opportunities for her as an older woman candidate while the advisor's partner and I remarked on the unusually colorful fall weather outside their sliding patio doors. When we left, I was exhausted from participating in an afternoon full of simultaneous intensity and opacity.

During all the years between that strained afternoon and this advisor's retirement, we were thrown together periodically through committee work. Though she was always cordial, a tense reserve made it impossible for her to be of any assistance to me as a junior faculty member. In the absence of heterosexual senior women and in the unexamined presence of sexism, I had no mentors of either sex or any sexual orientation.

In this context, I became mute as a teacher, a potential scholar, and a colleague. In my literature classes, I avoided texts and topic that might lead to any whisper of homosexuality. My writing was bland and ineffectual. Relationships with colleagues progressed nicely up to a point but then stopped as surely as if we had come up against a solid brick wall. My inability to mention my private life kept our conversations on a fairly superficial, impersonal level. Those who liked me and suspected I was a lesbian were too polite to break the silence. Those who did not like me and suspected I was a lesbian watched closely, hoping to catch me in some glaring mistake. A third group, who ignored me altogether, seemed not to suspect that I had a sexual or emotional life at all, since I was neither married nor interested in dating men. Encased in silence, I nonetheless made my way in the academy, succeeding in the classroom and governance structure, while languishing as a scholar and person.

Design of the Broader Project

This essay comes from my book *Poisoned Ivy: Lesbian and Gay Academics Confronting Homophobia.*[2] In my initial thinking about the book, I had proposed to write a straightforward autobiography, tracing my thirty-year trajectory as a case study for theorizing about the country at large. Very early on, however, I decided such an exclusively personal slant was too insular to reflect the immense variety within the world of gay and lesbian faculty. I decided to augment my own story with narratives from other faculty around the country whose long-term employment gave them a perspective from which to judge change. I knew how to execute this project because previous training as a literary critic had taught me the structures and functions of narrative form.

The more personal narratives I read, the more I wanted to enlarge the portion of my book that did not relate directly to my own experience. I decided to use myself as frame rather than as center: to organize my book around aspects of academic life experienced by anyone working in such an environment. Because I was interested in studying change over time, I decided to focus on those faculty with many years in their field. I sent the questionnaire to faculty who had worked at least fifteen years in a North American college or university. I focused on the impact of being gay or lesbian on three aspects of academic life that seemed to me to determine any faculty member's success and satisfaction. These themes are pedagogical choices, friendships and associations with colleagues, and research or intellectual development.

Whatever limitations there may be in Freud's theories, he was correct in asserting that happiness and fulfillment depend in large part on our ability to find satisfaction in the realms of love and work. Institutions of higher learning in the United States usually emphasize the pursuit of knowledge as well as the development of all its citizens' full potential. The presence of lesbians and gay men on college and university campuses has long been undeniable and considerable, among students, staff, and faculty. Unmasking what it has been and is like to make our way in this context seemed to me especially important because I knew from my own story the difficulty of integrating love and work. If others in similar situations could share their academic histories, surely we would have a compelling and revealing story.

I was encouraged in such hypothesizing by a letter I received early in the questionnaire collection phase. It came from a much younger colleague who had seen the call for volunteers on the Internet, had been disappointed that her years in the academy fell short of my fifteen-year minimum, yet was eager to encourage me to tell some of the complex truth about our experiences as scholars and teachers:

I personally believe that academe is one of the most difficult places to be out because though we are often enveloped by a (supposedly) liberal environment, heterosexism has an insidious way of permeating that seeming accepting exterior and striking at people's deepest fears.

The ironies expressed in this brief condemnation are everywhere apparent. Higher education, like its K-12 counterpart, all too often preserves and even endorses the prejudices of its surrounding culture. Simultaneously colleges and universities are seen as guardians of truth and sources of new knowledge. Formal studies of gay and lesbian history and issues, like those of racism and sexism, are either tolerated around the edges or disallowed altogether. This colleague at the beginning of her career helped convince me that I was on the right track.

Theoretical Foundation

My theoretical position concerning memory and memoir is that remembering one's past, if that past involves oppressive elements, constitutes radical political action. For those of us who have been told, overtly or subtly, that our existence is not quite valid, insisting on having and shaping memories into coherent form constitute disobedience on a personal level and dissonance or destabilization on a cultural level. Certainly lesbians and gay men wishing to pursue careers in academe have been among such groups. Some report that younger scholar-teachers have a much better situation in the present. Although this may be true for those who are fortunate enough to be hired at institutions that at least tolerate research and teaching on gay and lesbian issues, I know that many still must downplay, if not completely efface, sexual identity in pursuit of scarce tenure track positions.

Just recently, I had the unhappy job advising a new PhD in drama to wait until she had a job offer in hand before declaring her lesbian research and pedagogical interests. As in most of the humanities disciplines, new positions in drama have become significantly reduced, a reality that has meant that this young scholar did not have a full-time position two years after receiving her degree. A state university eager to bring her to campus is located in the rural Midwest, where her truest intellectual concerns are likely to be highly suspect because of their lesbian/gay cast.

It would have been irresponsible for me to assure this woman that things were categorically better today than they were when I was being interviewed in 1963. I certainly do not wish to dampen individual or collective celebrations of gains on some campuses and within many professional associations. But the stories offered in this essay are a reminder of the reality of homophobia, which still demands serious attention. My hope is that all those who continue to struggle with persistent and lingering degrees of invisibility within departments and institutions will be heartened by reading what follows and that we all discover new ideas to use in overcoming the limiting conditions within which we continue to work.

The Risks Involved in Change

Many scholars and artists currently speak about the devastating impact of not having a language for who one is. Lesbian and gay faculty in the 1960s struggled with silence as we attempted both to protect ourselves and to find others like us. Yet we simultaneously joined many of the cultural movements for change sweeping the country. We protested the Vietnam War on and off our campuses; we participated in sit-ins and demonstrations for the civil rights of other oppressed groups; we often worked vigorously to help form the ethnic and women's studies programs springing up across the academic landscape.

Though we were vocal and active on behalf of political causes, most of us remained quiet and passive in the face of discrimination against us. I myself was unable to make simple social contact with women and men who shared my particular outsider status. For instance, I refused for years to go to the nicest gay bar in town, located quite near campus. Even though it advertised a "ladies' night," I was terrified that someone from school would see me. Irrationally, I envisioned a place full of heterosexual monitors poised to spot deviants who darkened the doors. I could not grasp that, more likely, people in the bar would be equally nervous about being seen there and were unlikely informants. By staying away I denied myself the possibility of meeting potential friends, since at that time there were not safe alternative spaces for doing so.

Responses from other long-term faculty showed that many experienced those early years as I did. As one participant who teaches philosophy at a liberal university put it so profoundly:

When I began teaching (in 1966), no one even said those words ["lesbian" or "gay"] out loud. One heard rumors about certain faculty, but no one was open about being lesbian or gay. The card catalog listed only hostile materials, mostly by psychologists, nothing by self-identified lesbian or gay authors, and it didn't list much. There was no women's studies, no mention of the possibility of studying "homosexuality" as anything but a perversion.

If the narratives I collected and my own history are representative, this negative climate began to change on many campuses during the 1970s. Faculty who began their academic lives after 1975 report much less invisibility surrounding their being gay or lesbian than was the case for those of us working at most institutions of higher learning prior to that time. Several factors contributed to such changes. The formation of ethnic and women's studies programs played a vital role in changing faculty perception of what legitimately could be included as subject matter in our curricula and as topics of our research.

For middle-aged and older lesbians in this study, alignment with women's studies programs is most often cited as the chief external prompt for change. Suddenly information about our history and culture as well as books by lesbian artists and activists became available as texts we could teach in our own classes. Students demanded information about this crucial phase of feminism's long and illustrious history. More and more lesbian faculty working in such programs gained the courage to come out to their heterosexual colleagues and to hope these relationships would be maintained after disclosure. We were not always right in our assumptions, but even in cases where conflict erupted, there was great value for all who endured scathing and excrutiatingly long meetings.

Even when losses and rejections occurred, the lesbians involved came away stronger and clearer about who we were and how we intended to teach and carry out research in the future.

For gay men on faculties across the country, the absence of any organized intellectual movement like feminism has meant a delay in the formation of specifically gay studies courses and programs until quite recently. As male scholars and teachers, gay men often stand to lose much more than lesbians by coming out academically. Many of them are leading researchers in their fields with decades of publication and reputation-building at stake. Even those not yet prominent in their fields sense that by being public about their sexuality, they will lose possibility for preeminence. Many of the gay academics in my study said they do experience loss of credibility when they make their sexual orientation public. They speak of this loss in terms of student interaction and of career opportunities, specifically that they are passed over for high-level administrative positions, as one gay respondent wrote:

I believe my movement upward into an administrative position such as department head or associate dean is blocked permanently because I am gay. This is a conservative university, and while they tolerate and sometimes even support my openness, they would never go so far as to appoint me to such positions. They would get too much flak from alumni.

This state of affairs figures in the words of a professor emeritus at a large midwestern research university:

In the mid-6os, I was interviewed for a prestigious professorship at my old undergraduate college in New England. I spent a weekend there, gave a public lecture, and was warmly entertained by the president and the faculty, some of whom had been my teachers. The interview went extremely well, and while I was being driven to the airport afterwards, the chair of the department told me that I would be receiving a very lucrative offer within 48 hours. No offer came, and I was understandably puzzled. After two weeks the president of the college phoned to say that a delicate problem had arisen which could only be discussed face-to-face in New York, and offered to pay my full expenses to this second interview. I knew immediately what the "problem" was. As an undergraduate I had had an affair with one of the young professors (fired after my graduation for questionable relationships with gay students), and we had remained close friends over the years. When my name was presented to the faculty for approval, one of the older professors (a closeted gay, but married, who had known of my relationship with the fired professor) objected to my appointment. He was obviously afraid that I would expose him as a closeted gay.

When I met with the president of the college in New York, he said that he was very embarrassed to question me about being gay, but felt he had an obligation to the trustees of the all-male college. If I would simply deny the charge, he would hire me on the spot at a very attractive salary. Without actually denying the charge, I angrily demanded to have the name of my anonymous denouncer in writing together with a written apology from this person, and was ready to walk out of the hotel room in high dudgeon. The president promised to have the accuser write me an apology immediately. He then wrote out a letter of appointment. I later got the apology but declined the offer since I thought the climate had been so poisoned against me, that I would always feel uncomfortable there.

Because gay men on faculties have been able to gain advantages that are unfairly afforded to men in general, they have been more reluctant to be public about their true identities than lesbians have. Some gay men will continue to have difficulty incorporating their sexual orientation into their academic lives. Lesbians often see ourselves as having less to lose professionally, because unfairness based on gender persists at many colleges and universities.

In 1993, at a small liberal arts college in the East, an on-campus search for a new dean had been narrowed to two candidates. One was a white gay man, the other an African American lesbian; both were highly respected and supported by colleagues across the campus. The white gay man, described to me by a colleague as "not 'in' and not exactly 'out,'" was seen at campus events with his partner, a social presence that could be interpreted in a variety of ways. On the other hand, the black lesbian candidate had maintained a much higher profile as an out lesbian who clearly expected her partner to be invited to official functions.

After being encouraged to stand for the post by faculty and administrators, these two candidates made vastly different decisions. The white gay man refused to run, saying that the college was not "ready" nor would it be "well-served" by having a gay man in such a visible position. Specifically, he felt his ability as a fund-raiser—an important element of his administrative duties—would be seriously hampered by the fact of his sexual orientation. The black lesbian stood for election and was widely supported. Now that she has the position, she is successfully raising funds and performing her other duties with skill.

Some of the factors influencing such disparate decisions by people facing the same potential prejudices hinge on gender and race bias within academic culture. The woman in this anecdote may have had more at stake and less to lose by accepting this new challenge than did her white gay colleague. This story suggests how the academy simultaneously allows for new, more open stances by some of its citizens while remaining far too risky a place for others to step out of established expectations and patterns. Campuses reflect momentum for change countered by an undertow for the status quo.

How Change Occurs

In addition to the growth of ethnic and women's studies programs, faculty respondents affirm additional factors as having played a major role in the changes they see on their campuses. In 1973, the American Psychological Association removed homosexuality from its catalog of diseases, reducing its classification from psychosis to neurosis. Especially prominent since the 1980s, student activists ask ever more insistently for inclusion of lesbian and gay material in relevant courses, for space and support services for gay/lesbian/bisexual student activities and issues, and for coherent clusters of courses, if not full-fledged programs, focusing on gay and lesbian topics. Studies show that during the 1980s and early 1990s, lesbians and gays had the ambiguous distinction of being the only group not to lose previously hard-won civil rights. Some speculate that this sad fact has depended on the inability even of a conservative Republican administration to ignore the threat of AIDS.

Faculty who participated in my study also noted the importance of those few administrators who are beginning to advocate on behalf of lesbian and gay faculty, staff, and students. Scholars inside and outside the academy are quickly generating new knowledge through gay and lesbian research. The concomitant presentation of such research at conferences held by virtually every professional academic discipline fosters a growing context within which faculty members may feel freer to teach courses and conduct scholarship with a clear focus on gay and lesbian issues.

The burgeoning of queer theory in the 1990s has undoubtedly been helpful to some younger gay men and lesbians entering colleges and universities in the United States. Since much queer theory argues against identity politics as being too solipsistic and narrow to be helpful in understanding a postmodern world, it has become possible for a faculty member to conduct and publish research about gayness or lesbianism without necessarily being gay or lesbian. To the extent that this new field of inquiry provides a protective umbrella for some faculty who might otherwise refrain from integrating their sexual orientation into their work, it can only benefit students and faculty alike. To the extent that it runs counter to the ideas of an older generation or academic era, those who continue to advocate for greater visibility in asserting the existence of intimate and unavoidable connections between the personal and the intellectual, queer theory runs the risk of diluting gains made at great risk to individual faculty members.

Such a rift can be avoided if all concerned are willing to discuss similarities and differences and to value contributions made by members of each group. In the absence of such dialogue and mutual respect, however, queer theory stands to splinter the gay and lesbian community, once again allowing internecine disagreements to divide a vulnerable population. Such division, I believe, plays directly into the hands of faculty members who continue to wish that lesbian and gay colleagues would stay closeted, personally detached from their intellectual pursuits.

Ironically, the legal recognition of sexual orientation as a potential target for bias and its attendant verbal and physical harassment together with the recent upsurge in hate speech on campuses are forcing some top-level administrators to come to grips with the virulence of homophobic attitudes, even in supposedly accepting environments. This change agent may be particularly galling to those who object to a more tolerant attitude toward gays and lesbians but is consistent with academic rhetoric that promises an open exchange of ideas as a centerpiece of academic discourse.

Probably the single factor rated most pivotal for change is the vocal and visible presence of out faculty on campus. Such individuals and small groups are credited with articulating both by their being and doing the sheer existence of persons within a category that was often allowed to remain faceless in the past. Invisibility is one of the mainstays in preserving prejudice and injustice—as long as I think I do not know anyone who fits some category I find abstractly offensive, I can keep my prejudices intact. If I actually know and work with another person who is part of a group previously defined as offensive, I have several options: I can reject someone who I admired, liked, and easily associated with moments before; I can view the person as an exception who does not fit stereotyped definitions of the group to which she or he belongs; I can extend my definition of acceptability to include a few representatives of the offending group; or I can begin a slow and usually unsettling process of redefining my own sense of acceptability in human behavior.

To demonstrate how central such a person or persons can be, I offer two accounts from faculty members who participated in my study and a story of my own. In the first, a lesbian professor of education working in the Midwest describes an incident in which a closeted colleague died of AIDS, after which faculty held a memorial service. This professor writes as follows:

I thought maybe we'd change then, since our new president seemed so much more tolerant than his predecessor. But that's not enough—you need overt leadership—you need folks who will pick up the flag. I am going to try to pick up the flag—at least in some ways. I may not have done that if: (1) I hadn't witnessed discrimination that was overt; (2) gay/lesbian students hadn't expressed need to be supported. So my interest is/was "others" oriented—I didn't seem to feel the need to do anything for myself.

The second account comes from a member of the science faculty at a southern university. After saying that he has never discussed his sexuality with any colleagues in his department, though most of them know he is gay and have socialized with him and his companion, he goes on to describe a campus event:

I came out on the floor of the faculty senate when the president of our university took the words "sexual orientation" out of the antidiscrimination regulations, and then asked the senate for endorsement. Two homophobic professors (one a classic closet case) took the floor in support of the president, saying that there was no need for this sort of language because gays and lesbians are not subject to discrimination on our campus. I came out right then and there in a twenty minute speech which outlined for the senate the real problems that exist for gay and lesbian faculty and students. I convinced the senate to vote against the president (first time in ten years). In short, being gay and able to relate the experiences of gay people to others proved to be essential for changing the outcome of this situation.

On my own campus, a handful of faculty and staff began lobbying for greater visibility in the early 1990s. I had been asked to write an essay exploring some ways campuses could assist their lesbian students for a book being published by the American Council on Education titled *What Women Students Want*. Our president at the time was a man who enjoyed being in the academic vanguard. Capitalizing on this fact, I sent him an advance copy of my essay, accompanied by a note suggesting that Minnesota might be the first major research university to include sexual orientation in its nondiscrimination policy. Within weeks, he had established a task force charged with drafting a resolution that would include lesbian and gay faculty, staff, and students in the university's nondiscrimination statement. That group worked efficiently, consulting with the three or four out faculty members on campus about the relative merits of phrases like "sexual preference," "affectional preference," and "sexual orientation." We chose the latter, finding it the most precise and inclusive.

The president endorsed the resolution and took to the board of regents a phrase prohibiting discrimination on the basis of sexual orientation at all levels of the university, making Minnesota one of the first large public institutions to have such protections. Since that regents meeting, where, I was told, not a single word was uttered of inquiry, support, or objection before a unanimous vote was recorded, tangible changes have been painful and infuriatingly slow. It is as if the heterosexual establishment exhausted itself in this initial verbal gesture and has resisted harnessing additional energy or will to move forward.

Passive resistance and neglect reflect the depth of self-delusion at work on today's campuses. Administrators, seeing themselves as benign liberals, do not define their current behavior as discriminatory to gay and lesbian faculty. Therefore, when they add "sexual orientation" to antidiscrimination statements, they do not imagine that such an action will have any tangible impact on educational or personnel policies. When faculty, staff, and students pressure them for delivery of services and changed attitudes based on the promised protection, such administrators are genuinely surprised and often defensive.

Pressure at the University of Minnesota and scores of other campuses has remained constant, however, usually led by gay and lesbian faculty and supported by invaluable heterosexual allies and by ever-stronger coalitions defined by race or disability. Because all this work is so important and administrative inertia so deeply engrained, a relay team approach has proven most effective. As one or another of us has reached the limits of our energy, someone else has stepped in to carry the baton. If fewer of us had been vigorous in our dealings with the administration, it is possible that no changes might have occurred. This reality suggests that the greater the number of faculty members able to be public advocates for gay and lesbian interests and rights, the more rapid progress will be on a given campus.

A relatively small group of faculty and staff at the University of Minnesota convinced our former president to set up a blue ribbon committee reporting directly to him with recommendations for warming the campus climate for lesbians and gays. He was finally galvanized by evidence of hate speech in dorms, restrooms, and even on university committees. He could not longer deny the reality of such violence against a significant number of his staff and student body.

At one point, the committee took voluntary testimony from lesbian and gay faculty, staff, and students, closeted and out. The resulting narratives were among the most convincing elements of the committee's presentations of its recommendations. Administrators who had hidden behind budget crunches, federal restrictions, and other external barriers suddenly saw the faces behind the issues. Professors and staff members they knew and worked with made them listen to the frustration and pain at being made invisible over and over again. Ironically, testimony also was given about the painful discrimination suffered by those faculty whose very visibility made them easy targets for discriminatory behavior and hate speech from some colleagues. Students told repeated stories of humiliating classroom jokes or innuendos originating from their teachers as often as their classmates.

As a result, the University of Minnesota now has an office for gay/lesbian/bisexual/transgender concerns, headed by a full-time staff member with training in psychology and with experience as a community activist. Faculty members may register domestic partners, who then are eligible for tuition and recreational sports membership benefits and who may use library facilities on the same basis as married spouses. In addition, a university employee in domestic partnership may receive medical and bereavement leave and may be reimbursed a set amount to cover health insurance for his or her partner. As of this writing, there is still no direct coverage of domestic partners for health insurance, but the same group of lesbian and gay faculty continues to press the administration for this crucial benefit, arguing that until it is in place, the equal treatment of gays and lesbians is only rhetoric.

One objection put forth by insuring agencies is that the actual number of such faculty who claim benefits for a formally registered domestic partner is too small to make it economically feasible for them to extend coverage. On my campus, most of the faculty who have declared their partnerships are lesbian, raising the gender question. Not only may gay men feel more pressure to remain closeted than do most lesbians, but they are also more likely to have partners in a work situation that guarantees them good health benefits in their own name. Like women in general, lesbians are more likely to hold part-time jobs that provide no health coverage. Finally, like most women in academia, lesbians are often paid less than their male counterparts and therefore less able to help their partners purchase private health insurance.

A single voice or the voices of a very small group have been pivotal in gaining recognition and affecting change. The burden of this role is expressed by a gay faculty member:

Being one of the only two openly gay or lesbian faculty members makes me the "official gay." I do not like being tagged as a gay faculty member; I would prefer being known for my research and teaching abilities, which are formidable but being ignored in the glare of my sexuality. In addition, all the calls to lecture or participate on panels, etc. are time-consuming. Finally, my companion and I have to act as role models for the gay and lesbian students, and frankly, it is exhausting. I love these kids, but sometimes I just want to be left alone. There are many times I wish I were back in the closet—not for lack of pride, but because of overexposure.

Faculty like this will continue serving as models for students on our campus, but we must be allowed space to voice our occasional frustration at the demands that go along with being public. Such faculty also know that our own private and professional lives would be greatly enhanced if more of our colleagues felt sufficient support from administrators and coworkers to allow them to come out of their closets and stand among those already open about sexual orientation.

Support and Hostility

In my broader study, I asked faculty to tell me some of the primary sources of support for and hostility toward lesbian and gay members of their academic communities. The response surprised me. I expected to read that individual colleagues and students as well as members of the religious Right were vocal opponents of any supportive environment for lesbians and gays. I did not expect that faculty members would cite as the primary source of hostility their colleagues on the faculty who remained closeted. This unexpected finding forced me to think more closely about my own experiences and to discuss the topic with lesbian and nonlesbian friends on campus. Old resentments surfaced. Some closeted faculty still resent associates whose coming out has occasioned a certain distancing and an accompanying sense of loss of the ability of the closeted person to preserve his or her position. Some out faculty still feel pain over withdrawn personal support and also anger over the lack of support for efforts to gain greater equity from administrators.

The worst part of this scenario in my own case is that these feelings make it very hard to build even informal networks among lesbian faculty. I believe lesbian colleagues and I need a facilitated retreat at which everyone could say what she feels about her colleagues who are situated differently on a continuum of "outness." Even if such an exchange took place and was successful, all of us would still have to work within the prevailing environment. Before many of my colleagues can teach and conduct research informed by their knowledge of and perspectives on gay history, culture, and politics, that surrounding climate must be warmed considerably. Making that happen will require leadership from the president and others in positions of academic power, together with a change of heart at the grassroots level.

As faculty on campuses across the country wait and work for this ideal world, we form what alliances seem possible in the world we have. Some of the faculty members in my study describe having groups of lesbian and gay faculty and staff who meet regularly to socialize and to work on strategies for convincing administrators to recognize them more positively. In keying such responses to the size and type of institution, I find that in most cases the closest associations are located on campuses having relatively few gay and lesbian faculty and staff. Such groups realize all too well what a vulnerable minority they are, choosing to suppress whatever internal differences may exist to meet the more urgent needs and goals of the group as a whole.

By contrast, institutions that boast larger numbers of lesbian and gay personnel may think (erroneously, I believe) that they can afford to indulge internecine conflicts. The usual debate in such settings turns around whether to have a campus organization that includes faculty and staff or a separate group exclusively for faculty. Some lesbian and gay faculty are reluctant to join with logical allies because we cannot get past a seeming refusal to see ourselves as employees of the institutions that pay our salaries and organize our working conditions to ever-greater extents.

Smaller campuses and campuses where gay or lesbian are still dangerous markers succeed better at forming social alliances among academic and support staff. A professor at a large midwestern research university with an active feminist community, many of whom are lesbians, has written at length on this tangled topic:

I would like to share an odd kind of hostility I felt as an "out" professor on this campus. Although there are other "out" professors, there are many who are not as "out" or not "out" at all. Because the community among the outs is virtually nonexistent and because the ins often seem to turn away from publicly supporting or giving energy to lesbian (and gay) issues, I often feel very lonely. I find this a hostile and painful aspect of campus climate. Sometimes, I really don't know how I survive, except perhaps for the rewards of teaching. I am hoping through Lesbian Area Studies to bring lesbian faculty and graduate students together, but so far no other faculty member has appeared at our meetings. My interactions with lesbian grad students are always guarded and defined by professional parameters. My alliances with other lesbian faculty members are fragile and unreliable.

Where are we, the lesbian faculty members? We had a lesbian supper group that dissolved (allegedly) because of class issues, because of lesbian faculty not wanting to associate with lesbian staff. The lesbian faculty members have not seen each other as a formal/informal lesbian group for over a year. The lack of community, or the ill-wishes toward such a community, I find frustrating, contributing to my sense of going to work on thin ice with nobody else out there with me. Now that I write this, I realize how stressful this is for me.

This story makes patently clear that as long as groups historically shunned and hated by a dominant culture shy away from internal conflicts, no lasting community can be forged. This situation slows the rate of significant systemic change by blunting the voices of those who must advocate for it.

How Being Gay or Lesbian Matters

Regardless of whether lesbian and gay faculty are "in" or "out" of the closet, almost all of my respondents see the fact of being gay or lesbian as having a profound impact on how they conduct their business as teachers and scholars. One of the most interesting questions I asked turned out to be: "Has being gay or lesbian had an impact on your teaching and/or research?" Although approximately 18.5 percent said their sexual orientation had no effect on their teaching or research, the vast majority felt it played a significant role in their academic development and mental/intellectual health. Here are some of the roles they noted: designing new courses, or units in existing courses, that focus on lesbian or gay subject matter; gradually incorporating gay or lesbian issues into conference presentations and eventually into formal research; deciding to sponsor gay/lesbian/bisexual student organizations on campus, regardless of the possible criticism this might incur; ordering books and other resources for use by faculty and students in the campus libraries; and advising advanced undergraduate and graduate students who wish to study gay and lesbian topics for honors or senior papers, graduate papers, or doctoral dissertations.

In addition to these perhaps predictable effects, faculty spoke eloquently of less direct impacts on their thinking and behavior: a heightened awareness of and sensitivity to other oppressed groups, and knowledge of who has been historically suppressed, ignored, or trivialized by academic communities and the larger culture. These comments are representative:

- I teach family law. Being gay has had the indirect effect of making me more sensitive to difference, attentive to the "other."
- I do not teach specific courses in g/l studies nor have I done research in the area. But I do include the experiences of gay and lesbian people in my general history courses. I would like to think I would do that even if I were not gay—as I include the experience of people of color and women even though I am a white man. I do believe that my sexual orientation has heightened my sensitivity to other oppressed groups.
- As a teacher and administrator I believe being gay helps me be more empathic. In particular, I think that being openly gay disrupts a lot of traditional gender tensions, power plays, etc. This is an area I really think might be worth examination in structures other than academic institutions.
- I have always been more inclusive in a variety of perspectives in my teaching. I think this comes more easily because of my own experiences of exclusion in course material I studied.
- I believe that I have always viewed the world from the outside because I am a Jew. Lesbianism continued this outside viewpoint, which aided my critical attitudes, my detachment from accepted norms. As a result, I was one of the first in my department to teach black literature and to accept a multicultural perspective, even though I was among the older teachers.
- I'm not sure being a lesbian has had the impact it should have on my teaching or research save for advising students. It did, however, have a major impact on my sensitivity to issues of discrimination, affecting my research and even more a temporary career choice to serve as Director of Equal Opportunity.

These accomplishments are important and may be significant over time, but it is also true that 18.5 percent note little or no carryover into academic pursuits. I thought about this issue further. Some of their language is emphatic (e.g., "Being gay has had absolutely NO impact on my reaching or research"; "Of course not, I've had great success."). When I showed these responses to friends in psychology, several remarked that some faculty may have interpreted my question defensively. It may be similar to a woman being asked on a questionnaire about realizing career goals, "Has being a woman had any impact on your success?" For some, the "right" answer involves asserting their own ability to rise above their seeming disadvantage. In this case, some lesbian and gay faculty may be showing pride in their ability to put aside whatever discrimination may have been felt or to cover some self-doubt. Of course, simple denial may lie behind these statements.

In addition, some gay and lesbian faculty who have been working in the academy for fifteen years or longer view sexual orientation as having meaning only in terms of their sexual lives. Such individuals do not connect their personal lives with their work, whereas others see sexual identity as inextricable from intellectual perspectives on knowledge and research and thus integral to a fully realized academic career.

The narratives collected for *Poisoned Ivy* trace many journeys, the recounting of which casts light on lesbian and gay history. This tracing also reflects the history of higher education in the United States as it has impacted and continues to impact gay and lesbian faculty who work within it.

Notes

1. Audre Lorde, *The Cancer Journals* (Argyle, N.Y.: Spinsters Ink, 1980).
2. Toni McNaron, *Poisoned Ivy: Lesbian and Gay Academics Confronting Homophobia* (Philadelphia: Temple University Press, 1997).

3. Women's History in the New Millennium

A Conversation across Three "Generations"

Anne Firor Scott, Sara Evans,
Susan Cahn, and Elizabeth Faue

THIS chapter was originally conceived by Leila Rupp, then editor of the *Journal of Women's History*, in anticipation of the year 2000. She saw an opportunity "to reflect on where the field of women's history has been and where it might be headed." The result was an e-mail conversation across three generations of historians: Sara Evans; her teacher, Anne Firor Scott; and two of Sara's former Minnesota graduate students, Susan Cahn and Elizabeth Faue. They discussed shifts and changes in the academy during the past thirty years in personal and intellectual terms, with attention to the tensions and contradictions that created openings for feminist historians to research and write women's history. This chapter is an excerpt from Part I of a two-part conversation published in the *Journal of Women's History* in the spring and summer of 1999.

Date: Wed., 25 March 1998
From: A. Scott <ascott2@e-mail.unc.edu>
Subject: Re: Women's History in the New Millennium

Dear Friends,

I was startled to learn that my message has disappeared into cyberspace—and so I will try to reconstruct. If I understand what Leila [a reference to Leila Rupp, editor of this particular issue of the *Journal of Women's History (JWH)*] had in mind, it was that we would use e-mail to talk informally with the notion that only whatever turned out to be significant would be preserved and the rest would disappear. . . . So one doesn't have to try to be profound but can just engage in free association and hope to stimulate all the others. . . .

So here goes. As readers of the *JWH* know, I tend to trace the beginnings of any considerable interest in the history of women in this country to the early nineteenth century when the first outspoken proponents of women's rights encouraged reference to the past as a way of attracting women to their way of thinking The first vaguely academic interest in the subject appeared in the teens with Mary Beard's *Women's Work in the Municipality* and later with her contributions to the *Rise of American Civilization*, still said to be the most widely read book dealing with American history. Then came Elizabeth Anthony Dexter, Mary Benson, Virginia Gearhart in the 1920s; Guion Johnson and Julia Spruill in the 1930s (along with a raft of MA theses at the University of Texas—why there?); A. Elizabeth Taylor's work on southern suffrage in the 1940s; and Eleanor Flexner in 1958. Then the floodgates opened. Why then, and not sooner? . . . What do you see as the significant moments when the conceptual framework broadened, when useful theoretical formulations appeared? Maybe that's enough to start the conversation. I hope this one doesn't get lost.

Yrs faithfully, Anne Scott

Date: Mon., 20 April 1998
From: Sara M. Evans <s-evan@maroon.tc.umn.edu>
Subject: Millennium

Dear Anne, Liz, and Susan,

As I read Anne's note, I find myself wondering how we each came to women's history as the life-absorbing passion it has clearly become for us. The oral historian in me wants to ask for the personal stories that we can try to place in the broader intellectual history that Anne begins to lay out. One way to think about this is to ask ourselves where we got our questions. Why we thought history—particularly the history of women—was important and for what? And how did each of us change as we encountered the existing historiography and ever-changing community of scholars that developed in the 1970s and 1980s? I know, for example, that Anne's journey into academia took her through the League of Women Voters (LWV). I'd like you to tell us that story, Anne, and then talk some about what the field was like when you came into it. Having done that, I'm interested in knowing what it was in life from your vantage point to see the field of women's history explored into being. What I imagine is that we can start by sketching our stories, and then asking each other questions or point out differences of perception or experiences that may be generationally linked. . . .

I'll make a start here by laying out the beginning of my story—which is the middle generation in this conversation. . . .

Where to start: One place would be Anne Scott's classroom in my sophomore year at Duke University, 1963–64. Anne was famous among Duke undergraduates for her Socratic method (I think today we would call it "active learning"). She announced on the first day that lectures became obsolete with the invention of the printing press and that we would come prepared to discuss (which she ensured by calling out "Miss Evans?" as soon as I stared at the floor). I have no idea why I chose a women's history topic for the research paper we were assigned, but I remember finding a Civil War diary of a young woman who visited Andersonville Prison on a picnic outing. My paper basically struggled to make sense of this blithe young woman's account, which was more focused on courtship than on the horrors my secondary reading confirmed she must have seen. I was utterly unaware of Eleanor Flexner, or Julia Cherry Spruill, or any of those writers. But Anne had assigned us to read Alice Felt Tyler's *Freedom's Ferment,* and I remember Anne talking about the article she had just published about women and Southern Progressivism.

Before I went to Duke, however, as a white southern woman, I knew something about the importance of history. I love telling my students that I first encountered historiographic debate on a playground in Columbia, South Carolina, where we had raging arguments over who should have won "the war." I was alone on that one, as I didn't know anyone besides my parents who would argue that the North should have won or that the Civil War was fought over slavery rather than states' rights. It matters here again that my father is a Methodist minister and that my mother is a radical egalitarian in her bones.

In order to keep this conversational, I'm going to stop and send this off. Is this a useful way to proceed? Does it spark stories you are willing to tell? Do you have questions you want to ask the rest of us?

Warmly, Sara

Date: Tues., 21 April 1998
From: A. Scott <ascott2@e-mail.unc.edu>
Subject: Re: Women's History in the New Millennium

As an undergraduate in the 1930s, my heroines were Dorothy Thompson, Anne O'Hare McCormick, and Eleanor Roosevelt. I thought I would grow up to be a journalist, and wrote a paper on a book called *Ladies of the Press.* I also looked for women's autobiographies, and I particularly remember one by Edna Ferber in which she wrote, "I have seen the man I would marry and the man who would marry me but they were never the same man. . . ." I thought at the time her fate would probably be mine. My first after-college job was in the office of the Dean of Women at Syracuse University, where I had a remarkable woman boss, Mary Gilmore Smith. She used her maiden name (Gilmore) in the office, and she and her husband took a great interest in me. My next job, by contrast, was in a situation where men ruled the roost: the Atlanta office of International Business Corporation . . . a job I got because so many men were being drafted. I don't find much to encourage feminism in my record of that twelve months nor in the ensuing year as a graduate student at Northwestern University, when I got very much interested in political philosophy. The next stop, as an "intern," was also one in which the fact that men had gone to war gave women a great deal of opportunity. I wound up working for a congressman from California, one of the New Deal stars, Jerry Voorhis. He certainly gave me as much responsibility as I could carry and maybe a bit more. Then came the League of Women Voters, where I met or corresponded with giants of the suffrage movement (Carrie Chapman Catt, Katherine Ludington, Mary Morrison, Maud Wood Park) and worked for the legitimate heirs: Anna Lord Strauss, Katherine Stone, and Percy Maxim Lee, among others. Again, due to the war and the snatching by the State Department of the seasoned senior staff, three of us in our twenties had responsibilities we would never have had in peacetime. After this experience I never doubted the ability of women to do most anything, nor did I think I would settle into the kind of domestic life I had known growing up. My first memory of any idea of writing women's history is from 1944, when I came home from seeing Greer Garson in *Madame Curie* and fantasized about writing "a history of women from the beginning to now." Nothing came of it. Or at least not for years. Is that a good start to answering Sara's questions?

Anne Scott

Date: Tues., 21 April 1998
From: EFaue <EFaue@aol.com>
Subject: Women's History in the New Millennium

Anne, Sara, Susan,

I read with interest the past two letters, mostly because it is times like these I am reminded how a story's content and message takes shape the moment we decide where to begin. Do I begin with fomenting rebellion over doing the dishes and organizing my first strike (my brother didn't have to do them), talk about writing an editorial on the ERA (Equal Rights Amendment) for sophomore English, start with walking the streets of Athens, or with Adrienne Rich? I usually begin my origin story with the incredible confusion that followed my college degree about what to do with my life. I wrote poetry, worked on a novel, and read political autobiography and theory. I recall Sylvia Plath's image in *The Bell Jar* of the pomegranate tree. As she saw each of the fruits lush and full before her, she had no clue which to pick. I felt similarly torn. In my last two years in college, I had taken feminist courses in literature, but I had never had a history course that was more than about great men, treaties, and treatises. My history instructors (almost all men) treated history and culture as disembodied and disconnected, an ethereal realm in which "no women allowed" was written on the door, even if I was, for that sign, a resistant reader. Soon after, I ran headlong into my passion for women's history. But how does something that today in my mind is so coherent and understandable arise from what seems in retrospect unfocused rebellion (Emma Goldman and Emily Dickinson were my heroes) and discontent?

I might say that we find things when we need them. At that point in my life, I needed some sense that it was possible to act positively in the world, to be an agent, to be "the hero of my own life" (to paraphrase Charles Dickens), to recover and reclaim the history of women and of family and community. I do not know if I would have articulated it in that way, but I know the poetry of Adrienne Rich resonated with me. Her long poem "From an Old House in America" powerfully conveys the history of women, echoing the call for a social history, for a women's history. . . . The poem refers to other evidences of women's lives—toys and cars and "three good fuses," which suggest the humble tenacity of things. "There is an invisible palm print on a door frame" and the "dried, dim ink" of signatures. In the poem, Rich cautions against living too individually. She speaks of a women's history in which "most of the time, in her sex, she was alone" and warns against "Isolation, the dream of the frontier woman," which "still snares our pride—a suicidal leaf." Rich concludes, "Any woman's death diminishes me."

In the fall of 1978, I took Sara Evans's undergraduate class at the suggestion of a friend. I had no idea when I walked in that room what would happen; I expected nothing more than a course of study. I found in both Sara's social historical approach, informed by a belief in the power of human agency, and by political passion the intellectual and political direction for which I had been looking. (I still wonder, after many years, whether it was the right pomegranate or another thing entirely.) By the end of the year, I had applied to graduate school in women's history.

This is where I stop, having gone on too long for a first take. It sounds like a different place entirely. I await more stories and thoughts.

Best, Liz

Date: Thurs., 30 April 1998
From: Susan Cahn <scahn1@leland.stanford.edu>

Dear Anne, Sara, and Liz,

I guess I am the laggard in getting this discussion going. I kept puzzling over the responses until I realized that Sara had sent one that I never received, asking the biographical question. She re-sent it, and now I've got all the pieces. I was really fascinated to hear your stories. Mine is quite different since my involvement in women's history came on the heels of participating in a well-established women's studies program and feminist community.

I first got involved in feminism, and with it feminist scholarship, in Berkeley in 1973. I had moved there as a seventeen-year-old, basically to come out as a lesbian. I read books on lesbian culture, with their little bit of history, and remember reading a couple of early books on women's history, *Herstory* by June Sochen and *We Were There* by Barbara Mayer Wertheimer. The next year I started college at the University of California in Santa Cruz as a committed feminist and women's studies major. Through my undergraduate years, I took a sampling of history courses along with other humanities and social science courses taught by some of the first generation of second wave scholars—Barrie Thorne, Nancy Chodorow, Bettina Aptheker, Ellen DuBois, and Barbara Epstein. By the end of college I realized that history was the subject that I found most compelling, and I was repeatedly drawn toward. I hastily added a history major to my women's studies degree with only the vaguest idea of going to graduate school. I thought, in a classic garbling of feminist thought and practice, that middle-class, feminist lesbians ought to reject privileged white-collar work and take up a trade. Lacking both aptitude and drive, I worked for a couple of years at a combination of jobs—women's basketball coach, janitor, groundskeeper for softball fields, and worker in the local recreation department. I got tan but very bored.

In the meantime, Marge Franz, an influential teacher/mentor from college, had invited me to volunteer as a T.A. for her women's history course. I had also attended a graduation speech by Marge in which she encouraged students to take their skills and passions and use them to "make a contribution" to the world. A longtime radical and inspiring teacher, Marge offered me an opportunity and reason to pursue women's history. This is where things started to click for me. My intellectual pursuit of feminism/history had always been passionate, but not channeled. I guess the most honest way of putting it is that a combination of my political beliefs, intellectual loves, and job dissatisfaction—and hoped-for job opportunity—led me to graduate school and a more focused commitment to women's history.

It seems significant to me that courses on women's history and other fields of feminist scholarship were already in place. I could pick and choose, think across disciplines, and model myself on the teachers I respected. I could ask people for advice on graduate school and advisors—which is how I ended up at Minnesota studying with Sara and with students like Liz to talk to.

Now I'm wondering how our various entry points into the profession of history and the study of women's history influenced us as thinkers. What were our frameworks, and how were they taken from our larger worlds of work and political experience and/or from internal dynamics of history and feminism? This gets back to Anne's original question. I'm wondering if her interest and awareness of women's political history isn't bound to her experience in politics and with the League of Women Voters. And Sara's early exploration of Civil War diaries and even earlier defense of "the Union" in schoolyard arguments could easily connect to her later experience in the civil rights movement, to feminism and *Personal Politics*. And Liz, did your heroes, earlier experiences in family and school, and the political environment in the late 1970s shape your understanding or interests?

I don't want to be too biographical or simple-minded, but rather to think about the frameworks within which we began to work, and, then, how we as individuals, as "representatives" of a generation, and then members of a common discipline or field have moved from these initial experiences.

That's enough for now. I hope this gets to everybody. (One thing

that may be typical of all three of our cohorts is a technological tenta-
tiveness.)

Best, Susan

Date: Thurs., 30 April 1998
From: EFaue <EFaue@aol.com>
Subject: Second Millennium

Anne, Sara, Susan,

I am speaking out of turn, as I just got Susan's message, and I decided
to write while inspired. I assure you I probably won't answer again until
another round has passed.

The first thing I have noticed among our stories is not only a generational difference but the question of how politics played a role in all
our stories. I do think that our paths were guided by political involvement that ranged from the League of Women Voters and the civil rights
movement to lesbian feminism, and for me the politics of culture. I have
always thought it a tad backwards in terms of organized politics or social
movements; my involvement began after I had already become a feminist for both personal and poetic reasons. First, I read and wrote feminist
poetry; then I went on marches and participated in protests.

Complicating that story is another one. Much as I internally rebel
at identity politics, I can't tell the story without admitting that I grew up
working-class and in a union household and without a role model for
feminist activism on any scale, except for being difficult or rebellious. I
rebelled first and foremost against being a girl, which was hard on my
parents, who liked my long and curly hair to stay that way. I rebelled
against boredom, which usually led me and my younger sisters in to the
kind of misdemeanors that earns punishment without martyrdom. That
is, we dug up the backyard, reordered the house, and I personally had
difficulty being silent in church. And I had imagination, which constitutes treason in a household of very practical people. They thought a
wild imagination would get me in trouble. It had the effect of making
me prefer school to home.

For reasons that are idiosyncratic, I grew up in one of the last remaining Victorian families in the United States. That alone might require an
explanation, but family loyalty and devotion to duty, combined with class
and working my way through college put politics on the backburner. I
sometimes wished I could become a hippie, join the civil rights move-

ment, or a major demonstration against anything. Much of that was gone by the time I went to the University of Minnesota in the fall of 1974. Rebellion was then constituted, or so I thought, by wearing jeans, flannel shirts, boots, and an old army surplus jacket. I took Russian, drank strong bad coffee in the old student union, and tried to smoke. It didn't work. Reading Fyodor Dostoyevsky and Albert Camus didn't either.

Three years later, having abandoned my Russian major, I spent two summers in Greece, with lots of experience being sexually harassed as a woman in public places and discovering whole new aspects of myself. I read with growing awareness a good part of the misogynist Western canon; I still worked on my poetry, trying to figure out what, if anything, I had to say. . . . Being a woman, a young woman, that being so long denied a subject position in literature and history and denied the writer's authority, I was constantly torn up inside.

That was when I encountered Toni McNaron, a feminist writer/ teacher in the English department. When I went to talk to her about doing an honors thesis on Emily Dickinson and the romantic tradition, she openly scoffed. What I remember (inaccurately, I am sure) is her yelling at me that Dickinson was a woman first, and maybe there was something to be learned by that. Reading Dickinson, writing on her use of peripheral imagery and thought, and taking courses from McNaron, initially on Virginia Woolf and later on contemporary American woman poets, first awakened me into what feminism was and how it might affect my scholarship, my writing, my life, and the politics in all three. I took the suggestions that my being a woman might have something to do with me rather seriously. A revolution in thought and lots of wrestling ensued.

History came both before and after. I had loved it as a child, but I had put it away as a guy thing. (Like science, in our household history was masculine in gender.) But Adrienne Rich's poetry convinced me that in order to understand literature, I had to understand history. This is where the leap of faith was to be made. I think I am a historian in part by a "multivehicular accident of thought." I didn't give up writing poetry or creative prose, but I did choose to study, write, and teach history. The main reason I left literature as an area of study and chose to devote my career to women's history was, I think, because it seemed more practical and infinitely more political. . . . As the daughter of a working-class family, I could, however, study working-class women's history and connect up to a working-class politics through that history. Perhaps it was a compromise I had to make between my wild imagination and the practical bent of my family heritage. I couldn't be a dreamer; I had to be an intellectual "mechanic," an artisan—not an artist. At the time, I knew few women from the working-class who had even gone to college, let alone graduate school. Taking Sara's course was the year I discovered these many things, and Sara's insistence that the personal was political and that good history made good politics allowed me the way out of my contradictory desires both to be a writer and continue to be the daughter of my socioeconomic class.

I don't know if that does answer Susan's questions, but I am eager to hear what others have to say about their own connections and lives.

Best, Liz

Date: Sat., 2 May 1998
From: A. Scott <ascott2@e-mail.unc.edu>
Subject: Second Millennium?

As I read it, it strikes me how very different life was for my generation than for yours. . . . Or maybe it would be more accurate to say how very different my youthful experience was from yours. Susan asks how our entry points into the discipline affected us as thinkers. (I wonder if I can qualify as a thinker, but never mind that.) Certainly, by backing into women's history as I did, I became a social historian without knowing there was such a thing. I remember making an impassioned statement at some scholarly panel, possibly at the Organization of American Historians, but I'm not sure, for attention to all the historical actors who had been overlooked—when the prevailing view of history was still pretty much the old political one. I was like Molière's *Gentilhomme,* who had been speaking prose all his life. Theory as such has always intimidated me, yet when I reread even the early stuff, I can see a lot of unexamined theoretical underpinning, which I might not have been able to articulate at the time.

Liz's latest message discussing the possible consequences of a working-class background set me thinking, what *was* my class background? My family, from 1929 until the end of World War II was always very hard-pressed, sometimes desperately so—as during 1933 when the state of Georgia was bankrupt and no salaries were paid at the university. My father had grown up on a farm and all his life considered himself a farmer even though he became a college professor and chaired a department, which he had organized. My mother was descended from Leading Citizens, members of the slaveholding planter class, but for some reason (maybe because we were poor or maybe because she didn't feel at ease even with women she had gone to school with), she pretty much opted out of the world of the social leaders of our small town. To complicate the matter further, my parents placed an extremely high value on education, so of the four children two earned a PhD, one an MD, and the fourth a master's degree, although he spent a good many years after that farming. So, what *was* our class position? And how did it affect my thoughts about history, women's history, career, etc.? Aha. This will take a while to figure out. Do the rest of you feel as mixed up about the answer to that question as I do?

Anne

Date: Thurs., 7 May 1998
From: Sara M. Evans <s-evan@maroon.tc.umn.edu>
Subject: Second Millennium?

Dear Anne, Liz, and Susan,

Wow, what a difference it makes to have been an undergraduate in the 1960s, and to enter graduate school when I did. I started graduate school in 1969 at the University of North Carolina in Chapel Hill, propelled there by involvement in the women's liberation movement. I believed that a movement that told women they could and should make history had to have a history to stand on and build from. It was the movement that provided the questions—and the sense of political mission.

I became an activist as an undergraduate at Duke University. My parents taught me that segregation was wrong. The civil rights movement made it possible to act on that belief. My first radical language was existential theology—and I soaked it up on the fringes of the Methodist Student Movement in high school (my father was a campus chaplain) and then in study groups at the Methodist Student Center. The Methodist Student Center was also the center of civil rights activism on the Duke campus in the years before a CORE (Congress on Racial Equality) chapter was formed. There were some extraordinary women leaders on campus who inspired me to do things like sign up for Operation Crossroads African in the summer after my sophomore year. Being in Africa was a life-changing experience. I laid bricks in Malawi with an integrated group of American students (my first experience of integration) in 1964 and read in African newspapers about the Mississippi Freedom

Summer, the nomination of Barry Goldwater, and the Harlem riot. In Africa, while arguing with my own comrades about the viability of non-violence and the role of the United States in the world, I also remember debating with at least one of the men whether women could have a family if they also pursued a career. The authority I cited for my view that women could do it all was Betty Friedan, whose book I had just read—on the suggestion of Anne Scott.

From that point on both in the classroom and outside, I was seeking ways to explore and act upon my new perceptions. I took courses in international relations and African history and ended up writing an honors thesis on a Kenyan politician, Tom Mboya. Charlotte Bunch and I pushed the campus YWCA (Young Women's Christian Association) on issues of internationalism, race, and poverty. We also suggested that the Y-cabinet read *The Feminine Mystique* for its fall 1964 retreat. By the spring of 1965, I joined my first antiwar picket line, attended the march on Montgomery, and began to see myself as an activist. While completing a master's degree in international relations in 1966–67, I was deeply involved in union support work with African American employees at Duke and textile mill workers in Greensboro, North Carolina.

To respond to Anne's question about class, it was the work in the labor movement that made the issue of class real for me. My family, too, was financially pressed (we lived on a Methodist minister's salary), but there is no doubt that we were middle class and fundamentally secure. Both my grandmothers went to college, and one of them was a frustrated intellectual her whole life. . . . My activism led me to read and think about the intersection of race and class in the South—the unique shape of class within the African American community and the complex realities of poor whites—and to look to populism in its brief interracial moment as a hopeful sign from the past. . . .

I returned to graduate school in 1969 to study women's history after being involved in the women's liberation movement in 1967–68 in Chicago and spending another year in Durham working in community and labor organizing and at the same time bringing women's liberation to North Carolina with missionary zeal. I had no idea that I was part of a large and wonderful cohort of women driven to do the same thing. They were not visible to me until I went to my first Berkshire Conference in 1974.

OK, I'll stop for the moment and let another round begin.

Sara

Date: Mon., 11 May 1998
From: Susan Cahn <scahn1@leland.stanford.edu>

Hi Anne, Sara, and Liz,

Your last responses gave me lots to mull over. I've been trying to think of how to connect our biographical histories with the field of women's history as it has developed and will keep developing. I was struck immediately in our discussion of class how our personal concerns and experiences resonated with early historiography. Liz's lack of working-class models of feminist womanhood and her restless academic and literary search for a bigger world and vocabulary to live within resonates within a lot of early work on working-class women and their struggles as laborers and community/family members. It seems that much work in the 1970s was concerned with tracing this history, finding inspiring stories of women's strikes or experiences of community (like the Massachusetts Lowell mill girls), and implicitly linking it to contemporary images of liberation. . . . And, then, by contrast, all the early work on domesticity and "the private sphere" in the nineteenth century seems to flow right from Friedan—choices between work or family, what kinds of work, and the "female complaints" that led to early activism.

In considering where our questions come from, it feels like in one way or another we all might have been searching for a usable past and pursuing the "revolutions in thought" (Liz's term) that inspired us. Clearly, questions came from the women's movement and from our particular experiences and entry points. I'm struck by Anne's interest in "invisibility" and "unheard voices"—certainly the history of women in the profession and women's history prior to the 1970s. Sara's gut instinct that a movement of women making history had to have a history to stand on turned into a book about the history of that movement in which she provided both some history to stand on and an analysis of how her contemporaries made history. It seems like one of the constant threads in Sara's work is situating feminist politics in relation to other social movements and broader political context.

I began my scholarly work with a focus on the history of sexuality and sexual politics, an interest that certainly grew out of my own identity and politics. But also my undergraduate and (limited) activism had given me a deep interest in broad structures of oppression, big picture "isms" like capitalism, sexism, racism, and heterosexism. I wanted to know where each came from, and how they related to each other, and how they prevented "us" from coming together in one big movement that would surely revolutionize the world if we could come to understand our own and others' oppression.

Where did our answers come from and our inquiries lead us?

Some brief thoughts. . . .

By the 1980s, when Liz and I were in graduate school, the fields of women's history and feminist studies were flourishing and beginning to generate some of their own intellectual momentum, yet still always touched by questions from the larger political world. I'm thinking about the anthropological and theoretical work that tried to figure out the origins of women's oppression, the relationship of capitalism or class structures to patriarchy and gender arrangements, and the ongoing efforts to tease out the ideological and empirical relations between public and private. For me, socialist feminist theory was particularly illuminating at the time. So was work that tried to answer the question: "What is political?" Feminism raises this in a fundamental way with the notion of "personal politics," and this question seemed especially important in understanding the history of sexuality—an issue deemed "private" that I experienced as core to my persona, social, and political life (not to mention academic career). The question of the nature of "the political" got debated in some of the early disputes over the politics of women's culture and whether a term like "domestic feminism" was an oxymoron or an important explanatory concept.

Where have our questions continued to come from? And how have we answered them (changing methods, topics, theories, and frameworks)?

Feel free to take up these questions or shift the conversation in another direction if this doesn't seem useful.

Best, Susan

Date: Mon., 11 May 1998
From: EFaue <EFaue@aol.com>
Subject: Third Wave

Anne, Sara, Susan,

The round of discussion keeps bringing up and bringing along new ideas, which was after all the plan. The major difficulty is the speed with which we are moving. I am back telling stories about how I got to women's history, and Susan is describing the syllabus of the study group on socialist feminism that we organized her first year in graduate school and where she went from there. Sara and Anne each have the story of their generations in hand, and so we go by revolutions around each other's ideas and lives.

For me, engaging in women's history in the first few years of graduate school was a heady experience. It wasn't that I hadn't read socialist-feminist theory before. It was just made more real for me when we collectively shared with one's office mates, one's peers, among the seminar students, and with faculty, in a wild cacophony. New words, new ideas, and new experiences jumbled together in a long conversation about how to get to a more equitable society, one more just in terms of gender, racial, class, and sexual equality, but also more open debate, not frozen in time. The feminist revolution in academia, for that is what it was, opened up new horizons that started with something as singular as hearing Sara lecture on the "manly-hearted woman" of the Native Americans. It was repeated through debates about race (sharing stories with black and white graduate students from around the country), about sexual politics among graduate students, and about class, a touchy subject in a divided academic community.

Class remains a difficult topic, largely due to the legacy of a male-inflected class theory. Class analysis remains one area in which neither postmodernism nor cultural studies (at least in the United States) has made much of a dent in core beliefs on the Left. It is hard, as Anne says, to know to what class one belongs or owes allegiance to, or how class affects or shapes one's intellectual development and perspectives. I was more intellectually peripatetic than most college students, in large part because my family didn't have that kind of intellectual tradition, and I did not have a sense that roving was bad. The content of what I wrote about history was in part determined by my class background, but only because I chose to puzzle it out. Ironically, the poetry I write probably has few class markers in language or subject matter; and that has to do with choice, too. Being between classes, or being transclass (part of both classes), makes a stronger mark on me than if I had somehow mystically retained my membership in a working class that these days is hard to define.

This leads to one conclusion that seems to emerge from the jostling of my memory about why I chose to pursue women's history. The details missing have to do with the stories of woman as subjects, agents, and as political actors, which permeated Sara's undergraduate lecture course in women's history. I remember once her lecturing about women as agents of change; at the time, I didn't realize its implications. But now, remembering, I believe it is that movement—from woman as passive to woman as active, from woman as object of history to woman as subject of history, from woman as nonpolitical to woman as political agent—that was the core of what the early women's history courses did and perhaps still have to do. In an age when heroism and subjectivity are under assault from one political position or another, the idea that one can be an acting subject in the world has lost some its cachet but not its power. In all our recent ramblings on postmodernism and poststructuralism, and the willing acceptance that the subject really is dead, we have forgotten that one real goal of feminism (as with civil rights and gay and lesbian rights movements) was collectively to make possible for ourselves to "be a person," subjects capable of acting in the world.

The centrality of the effort to restore "female subjectivity" in history determined many of our questions—at least through the mid to late 1980s. Even as women's historians took on the challenge of how to make a more inclusive, more equitable, more comprehensive women's history, one that respected equality and difference among women (and, by extension, among men), we retained, I think rightly, the importance of understanding, analyzing, and restoring female subjectivity. Even when we distance ourselves by calling them "subject positions," that core idea haunts women's history. Why, after all, would women's history be important, (a) if women's history were not, in some aspect, different from men's and shared among women (caveats to differences among women), and (b) if women were not to be the subjects of history? That has existed, even as we analyze and apply our understandings of other systems of oppression, and even as we work to integrate different perspectives and to understand our older perspectives. Even the best discursive analysis in women's history has to do with understanding how women keep disappearing as subjects in history. Over the past decade, as we have struggled with the challenges of "difference" among women, we still have the question of women's agency at the heart of debates in our field.

Best, Liz

Date: 12 May 1998
From: Leila Rupp <rupp.1@osu.edu>

I hope you don't mind if I interject a question here, but I've been following your conversation, and this is something I would really like to know. How do you think your entries into women's history have been affected by the state of the development of the field (i.e., almost totally unplowed versus extremely well-cultivated)? I ask this because I often wonder what it is like for students to come to a field that now has a long history of changing conceptual frameworks, a massive literature, multiple approaches, etc. . . .

Just curious—feel free to ignore, and pardon the intrusion.

Best, Leila

Date: Wed., 13 May 1998
From: A. Scott <ascott2@e-mail.unc.edu>
Subject: Re: message from Leila Rupp

To respond quickly to Leila's interesting question: there must be a vast difference coming into the field—it wasn't even a field—in the late 1950s and in the 1970s and thereafter. At some time in the 1960s, a colleague asked me to write a chapter for a biographical volume designed for teachers in high school, and as I remember all the sources I could list were old memoirs, HWS, and the like. Only an article or two represented new research at that point. Certainly during the years I was writing *The Southern Lady,* there was very little. . . . I remember being charmed by the serendipitous appearance of Gerda Lerner's *Grimke Sisters* in my mail one day when I was working on Sarah Grimke's book! As for theory, as I said earlier, what I worked on was implicit not explicit and probably not even recognized by me or many other people as theory at all. I was then, and probably am still, what E. J. Hobsbawm calls "an old fashioned artisan" of a historian—even though I understand the perils of believing that one can, in fact, find out how things really were, and sometimes have claimed to be a moderate postmodernist. . . . No postmodernist has yet risen up to smite me but neither has any come along to embrace me! I liked and still like to turn up manuscripts, memoirs, and articles that I can ponder and use to try to understand a different era, women with conditioning so different from my own. And to answer a question Liz or Susan raised: as a result of my years working for the League of Women Voters, when I began to find women using their organizations to get things done that were otherwise not possible, I was prepared to recognize the phenomenon. League members in my day (1944–47; 1951–53) tended to feel superior to "club women" or "temperance women," but having known League women, I recognized the type when she turned up in clubs or the WCTU (Women's Christian Temperance Union), and especially in missionary societies. The latter were clear to me from family experience and a perfectly splendid in-house history (*Crown of Service* by Noreen Dean Tatum). The author was telling a story; it was unlikely that she would have interpreted her story exactly the way I did. (You may be amused to hear that when I discovered the book, I soon had my mother's Sunday school class reading it to learn about their past!) The use southern women made of their own associations led me on to the larger picture, which I tried to analyze in *Natural Allies.*

Back to Leila's question: In 1959, I went to the UNC library looking for books on women, and there were two shelves, most of them written in the nineteenth and early twentieth centuries. A few were published in England. Now, of course, that section of the library requires a whole stack of its own, and there are a number of different call numbers, so one would spend quite a lot of time just casting an eye at everything in the library on the subject. Not to mention the bibliographies, encyclopedias, *Notable American Women,* etc., etc. Also, of course, there are parallel outpourings in England, in Europe, etc. "Keeping up" would be a full-time job. I read so much for three years worth of the Kelly Committee as to suffer intense mental indigestion. . . . Quite a contrast from the early 1960s when I knew every single thing that was appearing in print. How to handle the present situation? Please advise!

Anne Scott

Date: Wed., 27 May 1998
From: Sara M. Evans <s-evan@maroon.tc.umn.edu>
Subject: Response to Leila's query

I must apologize for holding this up. . . .

In response to Leila's query about the effect of the state of the field from when we were in graduate school, I realized that when I started graduate school in 1969, I set out to learn about women's history in quite a piecemeal way. It hadn't really occurred to me to be systematic about exploring the field. In fact, in keeping with the general hubris of my generation, I probably did not think there was a "field" to explore (and it never occurred to me that there would be a prelim question on women). In every class, I wrote a paper on women or something related to women. That took me into literature on the colonial family for one paper, a field that had just produced a string of fascinating community studies. I remember enjoying Demos's *A Little Commonwealth: Family Life in Plymouth Colony* but lambasting Philip J. Greven Jr. for writing a book on the "family" (*Four Generations: Population, Land, and Family in Colonial Andover, Massachusetts*) that was only about fathers and sons. I wrote papers on the Richmond Bread Riot during the Civil War, the strike in Elizabethton, Tennessee, in 1939, and something on abolition. Clearly, I had a strong interest in collective action, and I remember thinking of such events as moments of public visibility when we could learn something about women who were otherwise inaccessible in the historical record. It was a sociology class on collective behavior that gave me some theoretical concepts and methodological tools to use in this quest.

In my various research projects, I discovered that there were monographs—some quite old—on many topics I had assumed might not have been touched by historians, but there was very little recent historiography in the traditions of the "new social history," which was rapidly opening up fields like family history, labor history, and African American history. Gerda's *Grimke Sisters* stood almost alone in the late 1960s. I also loved reading Eleanor Flexner because of her broad definition of women's struggle and her attention to labor history. The overview that shaped my thinking most, however, was probably the one Mari Jo Buhle, Nancy Schrom Dye, and Linda Gordon published in *Radical America*. This, I suppose, was the first time I really felt that I was in a generation of historians and that we shared a mission. That perception was fed by the excitement of new work that suddenly began to appear at every turn. Anne's *Southern Lady*, Gerda's "The Lady and the Mill Girl," the collection from the first Berkshire Conference edited by Mary Hartmann. By the time I joined two other graduate students and Peter Filene to teach the first women's history course at Chapel Hill in 1974, something new and exciting was appearing almost every day.

As a member of this in-between generation, I felt both encouraged and also on my own. I actually did have mentors who were already writing women's history: Peter Filene at Chapel Hill; Bill Chafe and Anne Scott at Duke. And yet, not only were there no courses on women's history, there were no women on the faculty in U.S. history at Chapel Hill (until Jackie Hall was hired as I was finishing). So I looked to several other graduate students for intellectual support, and with even more intensity I participated in a dissertation group made up of members of a socialist-feminist group in Chapel Hill. While my graduate coursework in history had little or no focus on theory, I was very involved in debates about class and gender in the socialist-feminist part of the feminist movement, as were many members of my cohort that I had yet to meet (I think here of the Berks panel I was on in 1974 where I met Mary Ryan, Ellen DuBois, and Mari Jo Buhle—all of us writing dissertations out of similar intellectual and theoretical impulses).

I better stop or this will languish again waiting for the opportunity to spill out the other stories that are crowding into my head.

Sara

Date: Fri., 29 May 1998
From: A. Scott <ascott2@e-mail.unc.edu>
Subject: Re: Response to Leila's query

Reading Sara's latest, I decided to make an outline of our correspondence to date to see if any general statements might emerge. Perhaps there are a few:

1. If one defines intellectual history as what people who like to think are thinking about and the questions they are asking at any given moment, then it makes a huge difference when an individual tunes in, so to speak. Going to college in the South in 1937, the only thing approaching "radical thought" was found in the Methodist young people's summer programs. The faculty, for the most part, were stuck in the "southern way of life," which meant keep your head down and if you must ask questions, confine yourself to the nineteenth century. . . . I was pretty much involved in various religious activities and had my first thoughts about civil rights in that context, but I didn't think much about the rights of women, taking for granted that anything men could do I could do better. Politically, I was intently interested in international affairs, in some New Deal Programs, in Eleanor Roosevelt. . . . I got involved trying to raise money for the Spanish Republicans. . . . Then came the war, and when I went to Washington, I encountered students from other parts of the country, and we were at least intellectually committed to the labor movement, but we did not focus at all on race. Wartime offered women all kinds of opportunity, so I was being reinforced in my assurance that the world was my oyster. I remember being stunned when a philosophy professor at Northwestern (where I went for an MA in 1943) told me that there had never been any women geniuses! I countered of course with Madame Curie but was hard put to come up with others. Then I went to

work for the League of Women Voters and brushed up against those old wonderful suffragists. . . .

Contrast this with the world Sara grew up in, and going to college in the 1960s in the South with the civil rights movement boiling all around. . . . Charlotte Bunch went missing from class for two weeks, and when I asked, with some asperity, where in the world have you been? She calmly remarked that she had been organizing housing in Selma, Alabama. Or the 1970s when Susan went to Berkeley after the free speech movement, the antiwar movement, and feminism everywhere.

2. Gerda and I used to talk about what we called the "laying on of hands"—e.g., Susan B. Anthony choosing and mentoring Carrie Chapman Catt, Catt picking Maud Wood Park and Marguerite Wells; Wells picking the women who ran the League when I arrived . . . and so to me. Now in this exchange I find Sara in my undergraduate class, and both Susan and Liz in Sara's classes. . . . So, you can trace your intellectual ancestry right back to Susan B. Anthony! (I hope you like that.)

3. In a situation of rapid social change, the younger scholars influence the older scholars probably more than the traditional way. Certainly, I was continually having to cope with undergraduates like Sara and Charlotte, and with young women whose dissertations I was involved in (Ellen DuBois, Mary Jo Buhle, Suzanne Lebsock, and Dolores Janiewski, for example).

4. Individuals find their inspiration in different aspects of their experience. So I think being southern was important to the way I have developed, just as Liz thinks being working-class or Susan thinks being lesbian has shaped thinking. I perceive Sara as about equally influenced by Christian socialism and southernness . . . is that right? This bears more thought in relation to conceptual frameworks and even to theoretical issues.

Leila wanted us to think about the future, but I find myself running against a wall when I try to ask where women's history should or might go from here. I do worry about the overspecialization of historians of women and sometimes am thankful for having studied in the old days first—so I do know a good deal of both European and American history as it was understood in the first half of this century; not a bad takeoff point when one tries to place women in context. . . .

At some point, do we need to try to bring this exercise to some sort of grand conclusion? . . . Or is that not possible? Nobody has sent me any advice about keeping on top of the outpouring of scholarship, good, bad, and indifferent, that threatens to bury me. Please do.

Cheers, Anne

Date: Fri., 29 May 1998
From: A. Scott <ascott2@e-mail.unc.edu>
Subject: Re: Response to Leila's query

Just as I signed off I realized it is premature to talk about conclusions before we tackle the question of the future, but I confess I don't know where to begin. Could anybody say where the field is at this moment, or is it too diverse, chaotic, growing, etc.? Because that seems to me to be the place we have to start if we talk about what's next. What theoretical structures continue to be useful? What about the so-called gender studies, which I confess baffles me a little. I will be much interested in what you all think.

Anne

4. Traveling from Feminism to Mainstream Sociology and Back

One Woman's Tale of Tenure and the Politics of Backlash

Jennifer L. Pierce

FEMINIST scholars like myself who "came of age" in the 1980s found ourselves in a contradictory historical moment. On the one hand, more than a decade of feminist social movement activism brought about sweeping legal, social, and institutional changes across the United States and within the academy. Not only did we witness the proliferation of new organizations and institutions such as battered women's shelters and the emergence of legal remedies for discrimination against women in employment and education, but the numbers of new scholarly publications inspired by feminist thought had exploded. At the same time, however, we also worked against a cultural backdrop marked by a dramatic move to the political right. In response to changing demographics and college curricula, conservative scholars and media pundits of the time declared a "culture war" in the academy, vilifying feminists and scholars of color for dismantling the Western canon and undermining standards for excellence. Feminist calls for improving the "chilly climate" in the classroom or ending hate speech on campus were castigated as fascist impositions of "political correctness." Meanwhile, at the level of national politics, the so-called Reagan revolution increasingly weakened or reversed gains made by marginalized groups, tightened budgets for social and educational programs, and instituted greater protections for the rich and big business.[1]

The social, political, and historical particularities of our experiences are absent in contemporary narratives about feminist generations. As described in the introduction to this volume, the second wave is typically regarded as the generation of women who rode the swell of late 1960s and early 1970s social movement activism, while those who "came of age" in the 1990s within institutional contexts such as college courses are understood to be the third wave. This chapter challenges this generational binary by introducing the term "2.5 feminist" to conceptualize my generation as one that neither belongs entirely to the second wave nor fits comfortably in the third. As I will demonstrate, my in-between positioning as a 2.5 and queer feminist brought with it a rewarding intellectual legacy but also carried a host of painful contradictions. Further, I suggest that these contradictions arose as a consequence of the uneven diffusion and reception of feminist scholarship, particularly feminist ethnography, within institutions and academic departments across the country from the 1980s through the 1990s. This essay, then, is a personal narrative of my political and intellectual trajectory from graduate school to the present, grounded in particular historical times and places. At the same time, it also tells a part of a larger story about the emergence of backlash against feminism in the academy and its consequences for my "in-between" generation.

Keeping the broader intellectual and historical backdrop in mind, my intent throughout is to capture shifts in perceptions about feminism and feminist scholarship as I traveled over time and place from feminism to the sociological mainstream and back again in my movement from graduate school at the University of California at Berkeley to my position as a junior faculty member in the Department of Sociology at the University of Minnesota, and, finally, to my current position as an associate professor in the Department of American Studies. As feminist scholar Maria Lugones has argued in her essay "Playfulness, 'World' Traveling, and Loving Perception," traveling from place to place, geographically, or even imaginatively, can yield new experiences but can also alter our taken-for-granted assumptions, perceptions, and understandings of the world.[2]

When I first came to the University of Minnesota in 1993 as an assistant professor of sociology, I had many taken-for-granted assumptions about the place of feminism in the academy, the kinds of research and teaching that I planned to do, and the kinds of colleagues that I would have. These unstated assumptions had much to do with where I had gone to graduate school, the kind of training I had received, as well as my personal biography. To fill out this story, my essay opens in my intellectually formative years as a graduate student in sociology at Berkeley, an intense intellectual, political, and professional socialization experience. From there, I move to consider my position in the *mainstream* in the sociology department at Minnesota, where I encountered what feminist philosopher Marilyn Frye terms the "arrogant perception" of faculty who were unable to identify with someone different from themselves.[3] The section that follows relies on a variety of documents, which I detail below, as well as personal experiences to describe my tenure battle and the politics of backlash in that department. Finally, I conclude with the movement of my tenure line to the Department of American Studies. My essay, then, is a travel narrative of sorts, and, as I suggest, it is in my movement across the country from a graduate program on the West Coast to a sociology department in the upper Midwest and finally to American studies that I discover some of the pleasures invoked by traveling, but I should add that mine is a cautionary traveler's tale. My encounters with "natives" were not always friendly ones.

A Note on Writing Personal Narratives

This essay draws on my personal experiences as well as official and unofficial documents that were created before, during, and after my tenure battle in the Department of Sociology. Unlike many colleges and universities, the University of Minnesota has an open-files policy in tenure and promotion cases. This means I had access to *all* of the documents in my tenure dossier. The two sections of this essay on the University of Minnesota draw on excerpts from many of these documents to highlight the incidents and events at each stage in the process that led up to my promotion to associate professor and, ultimately, the transfer of my tenure line from sociology to the Department of American Studies. Some documents are from the department chair, others are from university administrators such as deans and provosts, and still others are from graduate students. To further complicate this multilayered pastiche, I have added excerpts from my "Notes on Departmental Problems" that describe meetings and incidents that occurred inside the department itself.[4]

Each of these documents tells a different piece of the story about my tenure case and its aftermath. As public records, letters from department chairs and college deans marshal the best possible arguments about the quality of a candidate's scholarship, teaching, and service, and in doing so they implicitly reveal assumptions within academic debates about "standards" for tenure and promotion. Documents from students are sometimes public, such as letters of recommendation to administrators, and at other times intended for private or backstage audiences. Although they do not carry the same weight as letters from administrators, they provide insights into students' viewpoints. My departmental notes, on the other hand, which document the day-to-day harassment I experienced in the sociology department, were initially written with a legal audience in mind. (In lawsuits, such notes are used to document patterns of harassment and discrimination.) In writing this essay, my notes also served as a form of field notes about this workplace, jogging my memory with descriptions of conversations, meetings, personal interactions, and other details. Unlike the official tenure dossier, these notes lend some insight into what is going on behind the "reasoned" arguments of the public record and help to make sense of some of the seeming irrationality of the process.[5]

Together these documents tell a larger story about the nature of academic debate and argumentation in tenure decisions, particularly those that revolve around feminist scholarship, the development of strong partisanship among colleagues over these decisions, and some of the problems with the policies and procedures designed to protect junior faculty. In writing it as a personal narrative, I have at times told it in a passionate voice, at others in a more analytical tone, and at still others with the documents standing in for a number of institutional voices. Like all personal narratives, this one is a socially constructed and "partial" account, mediated not only by my personal biography, the existing archival record, and my own memories but also through larger cultural and historical discourses.[6]

Graduate Training: Berkeley in the 1980s

Feminist pioneers in sociology have described their experiences in graduate school as a time of intense isolation, as the lone woman scholar who faced intellectual uncertainty and professional exclusion.[7] By the time I entered graduate school in early 1980s, the number of women graduate students had increased dramatically—half of my entering cohort of twenty students were women, and two of them were women of color. Although there were only two women on the faculty when I entered the program, Arlie Hochschild, who was then an associate professor, and Victoria Bonnell, who was still junior, by the time I left in 1991, there were six women among the twenty-four faculty members, including prominent feminist scholars such as Nancy Chodorow and Kristin Luker. In fact, by fall 1991, the majority of graduate students in sociology across the United States were women. Fifty-nine percent were at the master's level, and 55 percent were at the doctoral level. At the same time, only one in four full-time tenured faculty were women, and the mentors available in graduate departments were overwhelmingly male.[8] The fact that I had already had women mentors in the mid-1980s suggests that Berkeley was slightly ahead of the rest of the country, in terms of both the number of women on the faculty and the number among its graduate students. Far from feeling isolated, I was an active participant in many feminist study groups, on the editorial board of a student-run journal, on department search committees for new faculty, and in the graduate student union that organized teaching assistants in the 1980s.

The Berkeley Department of Sociology was, and still is, an intense, intellectually engaged, leftist, and feminist department that encouraged its students to do theoretically informed, interdisciplinary scholarship. It is well known for its strength in qualitative methods, particularly ethnography and historical sociology.[9] As a young feminist scholar, I was trained not only in social theory, particularly psychoanalytic sociology, but also in ethnographic research methods. I read extensively in contemporary labor studies, particularly in the area of gender and work, and in feminist theory and scholarship in related disciplines. My dissertation, a feminist ethnography on the dynamics of gender, occupation, and emotional labor among paralegals and trial lawyers in two northern California law firms, reflected these interests.

In addition, I was trained to be an active department citizen. Like faculty, graduate students were expected to attend and participate in weekly colloquiums given by visiting scholars as well as in job talks and other scholarly events across the campus. Because no scholar—whether as a job candidate or a visiting scholar—is excused from the difficult, analytical questions posed by students and faculty, Berkeley has acquired a reputation as a tough place to give a talk. If the audience had criticisms about a scholar's work, he or she would find out immediately in the question and answer period. Quite simply, intellectual rigor and debate were the departmental norms. These skills became one more "lethal weapon" that I carried with me in my intellectual arsenal to other institutions.[10]

Although I began my graduate career—as I suspect many graduate students do—uncertain of my intellectual abilities, the mentoring I received from feminist scholars such as Nancy Chodorow, Arlie Hochschild, and Nancy Scheper-Hughes, as well as from supportive male professors such as Tomás Almaguer, Robert Bellah, Michael Burawoy, and Eli Sagan, helped me to develop confidence in my analytical skills. I was "taken seriously," in Adrienne Rich's sense of the term, and I began to take myself seriously as a young feminist scholar.[11] By the end of my graduate career, I had received many awards for my research, including one from the American Sociological Association for my dissertation, and several fellowships and grants. As I suggest in the following section, the intellectual rewards and the confidence I had gained over the years were my precious legacy from Berkeley, but it was, at times, also perceived as "contentiousness." And, as I was to learn, being considered contentious is not always a good thing.

Mainstream Sociology

I came to the University of Minnesota in the Department of Sociology to fill a junior position in gender and qualitative research methods in fall 1993.[12] Although I was not completely won over by the department during my job interview—there were a few senior scholars who seemed hostile to ethnographic methods—I was delighted to have the opportunity to come to Minnesota. In the early 1990s, the academic job market was still tight—hiring freezes and fiscal budget crises at research universities across the nation meant that there were very few jobs available. So, I felt incredibly fortunate to have a position at a well-regarded research university when I knew many graduate students across the country were having difficulties obtaining academic employment.[13]

Most important, Minnesota had an excellent reputation for feminist scholarship. Not only did it house the Center for Advanced Feminist Studies (CAFS), but it also employed a number of influential feminist scholars across campus.[14] Not long after I arrived, Shirley Garner invited me to join CAFS, and Barbara Laslett invited me to join the editorial board for *Signs: Journal of Women and Culture and Society* for a three-year term. CAFS and *Signs* were not only important to me as centers of intellectual debate and rigor but also as venues for developing professional friendship networks across the campus with senior and junior feminist scholars. Early on, I met two assistant professors, Lisa Disch (political science) and Jeani O'Brien (history), who also worked in the tall, ugly, red brick social science tower on the West Bank of the Mississippi River, and we began to meet weekly for coffee and, later, worked together in a writing group on our first books. It was, and still is, a lively and engaging community of feminist scholars.

By contrast, my tenure home, the Department of Sociology, became a source of great disappointment. At the time, the majority of the faculty were associate or full professors, and 80 percent were white men. There were two other assistant professors (both male), and one of them later married a senior faculty member in the department. Almost one-third of the faculty were men in their sixties, associate or full professors, who were at best indifferent, or at worst hostile, to feminism and to my methodological expertise in ethnography. I learned, for instance, over coffee with one of these senior men, who belonged to the National Association of Scholars, that he had just written an article for their journal titled "Salem at Minnesota." In this article, he castigated feminist graduate students for making allegedly false claims about sexual harassment to get rid of "politically incorrect" professors in the Scandinavian studies program, where he had a brief stint as director. In a reversal of the original narrative, he likened these male professors to the falsely accused, and the graduate students to those who persecuted them. Other faculty members responded in more friendly but distant ways. After several pleasant hallway conversations with one kindly professor, I invited him to lunch. He declined, explaining somewhat apologetically that his wife did not approve of such activities. And after lunch with another shy senior member of the faculty, I learned that he had been brought up on sexual harassment charges some time in the 1980s. Given how reserved this man was, I found the story difficult to believe, but it made me feel uncomfortable enough to avoid meeting with him alone.[15]

There were five women faculty in the department, besides myself, who, though friendly and well intentioned, knew very little about feminist ethnographic research or expressed suspicion about its validity. One senior woman admitted to me that she thought "*that kind* of research was not very rigorous." (Since I actually did *that kind* of research, I wondered why I had even been hired in the first place.) The one exception, of course, was Barbara Laslett, an influential and award-winning feminist sociologist, who came to Minnesota in the mid-1980s and coedited *Signs* with Ruth-Ellen Joeres at Minnesota from 1990 to 1995. From my vantage point in the department, things did not seem to be going a whole lot better for Barbara—and she was a full professor.[16] Most of the senior faculty appeared to be taken aback by her blunt intellectual style and acerbic wit. When she spoke out in faculty meetings, they refrained from engaging with her political and intellectual arguments. To make matters worse, a graduate student told me that these same timid men who were afraid to argue with her publicly referred to her as a "bull dyke" behind her back. As the only queer faculty member in the department, I could only wonder what they said about me.

In addition to the number of women on the faculty, the demographics for people of color were even more dismal. There were *no* faculty of color at either the junior or senior level, and *no* faculty who worked in the area of race relations, one of the oldest and most influential fields in sociology. Rose Brewer, an African American sociologist, had been in the department before I arrived, but decided to move her tenure line to African American studies after an unpleasant tenure battle in the 1980s. Before I knew of the details of her departure, I made the mistake of mentioning to Professor X, the chair at the time, that she and I were working together on a feminist anthology. Before I could get another word out of my mouth, he began lecturing me about her so-called lack of qualifications, defending his decision to deny her tenure in the department. Given Rose's considerable reputation in race relations in sociology—I had read some of her work in graduate school and admired it—I was completely taken aback by his argument and his sense of personal outrage.[17]

What began to emerge from these early interactions was a perception of the place of feminism in sociology that was different from my own. For the most part, my male colleagues were either dismissive of feminist scholarship or not interested in it. And most of my women colleagues, though more open to me socially, were no different. This "unfriendly-to-feminism" intellectual climate was further complicated by a normative principle that regulated face-to-face disagreement. As I was to learn, my early encounters with malicious backbiting comments were not unusual but rather pieces of a larger climate of conflict avoidance that pushed tensions and disagreements beneath the surface.[18]

In addition to confronting an unfriendly climate for feminism, women, and people of color, I also faced the disciplinary constraints of mainstream sociology. Although there is a widely recognized split between competing epistemologies in sociology between those who favor positivist, quantitative methods and those who prefer interpretive, qualitative approaches, the dominant paradigm in the discipline is positivism. And as the histories of the department reveal, Minnesota has had a long mainstream tradition.[19] Although I had been trained to regard these competing epistemological and methodological approaches as different ways to conceptualize problems and conduct research, I soon discovered that many of my new colleagues firmly believed that there was *only one way* to do sociological research. Although Barbara Laslett and Ron Aminzade, as historical sociologists, were important exceptions to this way of thinking, the majority of the senior members of the faculty were not. One demographer, for instance, snidely remarked during a faculty meeting that ethnography was "not *real* sociology." And in my participation on search committees for new faculty, I learned that job descriptions that read "open" to all methodologies were, in practice, open to those who employed quantitative approaches.

This mainstream vision carried over into discussions about the meaning and use of appropriate sociological theory in the graduate seminars I taught. An associate professor, after perusing my syllabus on contemporary sociological theory, wondered aloud why I had not included James Coleman or any articles on rational choice theory, strongly encouraging me to do so. And another asked, "Why do you have all these European theorists? Some of these scholars [a reference to Michel Foucault] aren't even sociologists. And what is 'queer' about theory? [a reference to readings by Judith Butler] Is this supposed to be some kind of a joke?" After launching into a serious discussion of my choices, we ended up in a heated debate arguing about the merits of feminist theory.

The worst came during my fourth-year annual review. As required by department policy, I met with Professor X, the chair at the time, to discuss the faculty's departmental meeting review of my scholarship. At the time, I had a book contract with University of California Press, several articles, and a file of excellent teaching evaluations. Surprisingly, the review was lukewarm to weak in tone, suggesting that my file might not be strong enough for tenure. When I inquired about the tone of the review, the chair told me that the department was being especially "hard-nosed" in the fourth year to make clear to candidates what was needed for a strong tenure case. I said that I had already been told by a number of faculty members that a book with California constituted a strong case. He glibly remarked that "a book counts like attendance—if you don't come every day, it counts against you, and if you do come every day that's good—but it's not enough to get tenure. What's important is moving beyond the dissertation." I pointed out that I had already moved beyond the dissertation and had published a number of articles on topics unrelated to my dissertation. He said that was not clear from my record, adding that my "identity" was not clear to the department either. "My identity?" I queried.

Professor X said that I needed to have an identity in *sociology*. Because "qualitative work was a new area [sic] in the department, and faculty didn't know a lot about it," it was, therefore, my responsibility to educate people about the kind of work that qualitative sociologists do.[20]

He also cautioned me about my involvement with *Signs* and the Center for Advanced Feminist Studies, suggesting that some might view this as "disloyal" to the department. "You'll have to decide whether you are a feminist or a sociologist," he told me sternly. As I continued to contradict him, he became increasingly angry and in a final blow told me "most of the faculty think feminists are flakes."

After this series of unpleasant interactions, I began to realize how deeply held these different perceptions about feminism and sociology were. After my meeting with the chair, and at the advice of friends and colleagues, I started keeping a written record of all my interactions with him as well as anyone else who participated in these kinds of exchanges. I also wrote a response, as university guidelines allowed, to the chair's review. I then went to talk to Professor Y, the associate chair, about my annual review and the response I had drafted to the chair's letter. To my surprise, she was not at all sympathetic and, further, told me that Professor X had told her that he had written a *response* to my response to the annual appraisal report, adding that it was "not favorable to me." She thought it was "highly unusual" for junior faculty to write responses to their annual appraisals. In her view, my submission of such a document could only be perceived as confrontational, escalating conflict between the chair and me. Further, she felt that in a year when we were having an external review of the department, it presented a risk for the department's receiving a favorable review. I replied that I did not see my response as confrontational—it was a very tempered and polite memo raising points of clarification for the annual appraisal. She agreed that the response was tempered but thought that submitting it to the dean would "escalate the situation." She added that if I agreed to withdraw my response, the chair would also withdraw his.

Over the next several days, I received phone calls at home from the associate chair and her partner, who was also a faculty member, as well as a visit in my office encouraging me to withdraw my response. I could not understand why they were so adamant about what my political allies saw as an even-handed response. Nor did I understand why the very procedures designed to protect junior faculty such as written responses to annual reviews were being used against me. Finally, at the end of the day, the administrative assistant and secretary to the chair of the department told me that I still had time to withdraw my response if I wanted to do so. While she hovered over me, I wavered back and forth and finally told her to go ahead and take *my* response out of the file. Then she said,

"It's my understanding that this [the chair's response to mine] doesn't go over to the dean's office." I nodded, and then she took *his response* to my response out of the file folder as well. As I rode the bus home, I felt like I had been the victim of an elaborate con scheme.

When I got home, I called Janet Spector, a feminist colleague in anthropology, who was also head of the University's Commission on Women. She thought that I had been pressured unfairly to withdraw my response to my annual appraisal and characterized this as an instance of harassment, among other things. She accompanied me, several days later, to see the associate dean of faculty affairs for the College of Liberal Arts. The associate dean advised me to resubmit the response so that there would be a written record of the chair's mistake in the college record. She and Janet also advised me to continue keeping written accounts of any future incidents.

In the aftermath, I tried to make the best of a bad situation. Barbara Laslett and Ron Aminzade, two of my political allies and friends in the senior tier, advised me to keep my head down, avoid future disagreements with the chair, keep my mouth shut, and just do my work. "After tenure, you can do whatever you want," one of them explained. But I was still puzzled. Why had the chair gotten so angry? Why didn't the associate chair support me? In exasperation, I once asked another political ally what he thought about what had happened. He observed that it had to do with a clash of personalities—"the chair has a bad temper and blows off steam from time to time." While most of the faculty avoided confrontations with him, I had stood up for myself. According to him, my assertiveness had "pissed the chair off." He too advised me to keep my head down and "not to make a big deal out of it." As for the associate chair and some of the other women on the faculty, he told me, in what I now imagine he construed as a helpful remark, that they perceived me as "contentious." "Because I like to argue about intellectual ideas, they think I'm contentious?" He tried to reassure me, telling me he thought "being contentious" was a good thing.

As I look back now at these stories, I am struck by how my narrative individualizes what are, in fact, workplace dynamics. Rather than thinking about these issues as a matter of hostile climate or aspects of a top-heavy, predominantly white and male departmental structure—the very themes I developed in my first book on the dynamics of gender and status in contemporary law firms—I wondered what I was doing wrong. Yet, my political allies who were also sociologists responded in similar ways. Ron and Barbara provided strategies for individual success: "Keep your head down"; "Do your work." And my other colleague's explanation for the chair's behavior was entirely psychological: "The chair has a bad temper." But as time went on, particularly after the incident with the chair, I realized that it was not just me and my intellectual style that irked people but rather a combination of things—the dynamics of gender in the department, its top-heavy demographics, and my rank as assistant professor. Within this gendered context, I was not deferential to senior male scholars, as some expected I should be, but treated them as equals in intellectual debate. Nor was I the nurturing female type who bolstered their egos by flattering them and telling them how clever they were. I did not prepare elaborate dinners for them at my home or fuss over them, as one of my female colleagues did. I also suspect my intense intellectual queries became a source of annoyance, even discomfort, for some. I brought to light scholarship they were unfamiliar with, reminding them, albeit unwittingly, of what they did not know. And academics *hate* not knowing things. But most important of all, I was a young woman *and* a queer feminist who brought these facts to their attention.

For the next year and a half, I followed Ron and Barbara's advice: I kept my head down, stayed away from the department chair, finished my book, wrote grant proposals, and taught my graduate and undergraduate courses. I was also invited to several universities to give talks about my new book, and I accepted each opportunity to do so. In short, I was a very *good girl*. At some point, one of my male colleagues commended me for taking the "high road" in "my conflict with the chair." I remember thinking that if taking the "high road" meant being silent and uncomplaining, then I preferred being considered "contentious." Maybe that was not a good thing at Minnesota, but at least it was honest. Meanwhile, the swarm of harassment continued to buzz around me.

In 1996, I went up for tenure. By this point, I had published my first book, seven journal articles, three invited book chapters, one invited essay, and several book reviews. My teaching record was considered "exemplary." I had made service contributions throughout the College of Liberal Arts in American Studies, CAFS, the MacArthur Program on Interdisciplinary Global Studies, and Women's Studies. My external letters from prominent senior scholars in my field were stellar, and my book had already received a number of favorable reviews. Based on this dossier, the department's Promotion and Tenure Committee recommended unanimously that I be promoted to associate professor. Despite these facts, I worried about how the politics of the department would affect the faculty vote. I knew Professor X still harbored bad feelings about me, and though he was no longer department chair, he wielded influence with some of the senior men. Ron and Barbara were confident that the strength of my record would override any political considerations. And MJ Maynes, one of my colleagues in the Department of History, thought that even if the department did not vote on my behalf, given the strength of my record, a negative departmental recommendation would be overturned at the next level in the tenure review process for the university. Still, I was not optimistic.

As if to confirm my doubts, I received an anonymous memo in my faculty mailbox a week or so before the tenure vote. One side of the paper had excerpted quotes from my book *Gender Trials*, and next to these quotes someone had handwritten "Rambo litigator" and "feminized emotional labor." On the back of the page was a xeroxed passage from an unknown source that was taped to the piece of paper. It was about "Negroes" and "pickaninnies," something about "Negroes taking care of their pickaninnies." It was obviously intended to offend me.

Just before Thanksgiving, the department voted on my tenure and promotion case. As I later learned from my supporters, it was a divisive and contentious meeting. The resulting vote among the senior faculty for my tenure and promotion was seven to twelve. Seven voted for tenure and promotion, while twelve voted against it. The majority submitted a report to the chair, as did the minority. The departmental vote was but one step in a series, requiring that the dossier go forward for review to the College of Liberal Arts' Promotion and Tenure Committee. The purpose of the college committee review is to ensure that the department followed university guidelines in the tenure review process. After their review, the file was forwarded to the dean of the College of Liberal Arts, the provost of the university, and, finally, to the Board of Regents. The following section details my experiences through the steps in this process and its aftermath.

The Tenure Debacle

The night in November 1996 when I got the phone call from the department chair to deliver the news about the department vote, I was sitting in Lisa Disch's living room with my friends Mary Jo Kane and Jeani

O'Brien. "The vote is seven to twelve," I told them. I had to repeat it twice. They assumed, as I initially had, that it was seven against, *not* seven in support of my tenure case. Of course, I was devastated, but given the climate of the department and all that had transpired before the vote, I was not completely surprised. Mary Jo, being Mary Jo, immediately went into political strategy mode. In the meantime, Barbara Laslett, Ron Aminzade, and MJ Maynes all called to offer their support. Barbara was so upset she finally came over to hang out with us, commiserate, and plot strategy.

My political allies in sociology and my feminist colleagues in CAFS rallied on my behalf and wrote numerous letters of support to the dean's office in protest. Mary Jo Kane held a meeting for me at her house to plan my written response, and seven CAFS faculty members attended to offer support. Over the Thanksgiving weekend, Jeani O'Brien and Ann Waltner from the history department helped me revise and polish what Ann termed "the most important document in my tenure file—its purpose to explain to the College Committee why there are such disparate interpretations of your work." Friends from the East Coast sent me a care package of lox and bagels, an old friend from graduate school sent me a box of brownies and other assorted goodies, and other friends from Berkeley called to commiserate and offer strategic advice.

Jeani, Ann, and I spent the rest of Thanksgiving weekend working on my response, while eating lox, bagels, and brownies. At the time, I was alternately livid with rage and then completely depressed, but as Jeani and Ann kept reminding me, the tone of the response had to be professional. For my father, who was not an academic, the tenure vote made absolutely no sense. "Why don't professors just take an exam like lawyers and doctors do, and then be done with it?"

The Majority Report's argument dated November 16, 1996

[T]he book lacked a testable hypothesis, did not use valid and reliable measures, and constituted descriptive research that could not be replicated. One faculty member stated that the book posed unclear questions, contained only one table, used a flawed random sampling method, did not provide an interview guide, and presented research that could not be replicated. Another faculty member stated that the bitterness expressed in the methodological appendix made him/her question Professor Pierce's credibility as a field researcher. . . . [And another] faculty member noted lack of publications in major sociology journals, despite prior annual reviews urging her to publish there.

Graduate Students' Letter to the Department Chair and to the Associate Dean of Faculty Affairs in the College of Liberal Arts on Professor Pierce's Teaching dated November 22, 1995

During the short time she has been here, Jennifer has been instrumental in guiding many students through the process of professional conference presentations and publication. Though too numerous to list, some of the student accomplishments Jennifer supported include a host of presentations at both the ASA and PSA conferences, an ASA section graduate student paper award, and publications through such prestigious qualitative journals such as *Qualitative Sociology* and an upcoming publication in a JAI Press volume. Her involvement in both the CAFS and the MacArthur program also attests to her commitment to students. Also, it is our understanding that Jennifer serves on an unusually high number of student committees . . . acting on many of these committees as the required methodologist. This reflects not only the large number of students in our department who are doing qualitative work, but also the great need in our department for Jennifer's expertise.

The Minority Report's response dated November 26, 1996

Several faculty argued that Professor Pierce's research record was of very high quality. One faculty member stated that Professor Pierce's record is comparable to tenured ethnographers at other research universities and that the research reflects a clear scholarly agenda that has produced high quality work, as is indicted by all of the outside review letters. . . . One faculty member argued that disagreements about Professor Pierce's research reflected larger epistemological disagreements in the department and in the broader discipline, which were evident during the two years we had searched for an ethnographer. S/he stated that the criticisms of the book say more about the type of book others would have liked her to write than about what Professor Pierce actually wrote and reveal an extremely narrow view of what constitutes sociological theory. . . . One faculty member asked if there is only one type of sociology done in this department. . . .

The Department Chair's Recommendation dated November 25, 1996

Professor Pierce's research record is insufficient in terms of quantity and quality for promotion to associate professor. Professor Pierce's major piece of scholarship since 1991 is her book. . . . I was troubled by the book's theoretical narrowness, its neglect of a substantial empirical literature on gender and work, as well as Professor Pierce's failure to employ scientific objectivity throughout the manuscript. Professor Pierce also gives the reader no information regarding the representativeness of the cases she cites. . . . Since 1991 she has coauthored one article in a respected journal. Her post-1991 productivity raises questions about her potential level of productivity. Further, her scholarly record shows insignifi-cant evidence of a future research agenda. Her dossier contains only a seven-page proposal outlining a new project on marginality in Utah. (W. Brustein)

Jennifer L. Pierce's Response to the Chair and to the College Committee dated November 28, 1996

The chair states in his letter that he "was troubled by the book's theoretical nar-rowness and underdevelopment, its neglect of substantial empirical literature on gender and work, as well as Professor Pierce's failure to employ scientific objectivity throughout the manuscript." This assessment stands in stark contrast to the external letters, the internal letters, the PT&S report, the minority report, the book reviews, and his own recent assessment of the same book in *his* nomina-tion of me for the McKnight Land Grant Professorship dated October 19, 1995:

> In her book, Pierce uses a multi leveled theoretical approach along with participant observation and extensive interviewing to expose and analyze the gendered nature of large bureaucratically organized law firms. The work clearly makes a significant contribution to our under-standing of the dynamic interaction between organizational structure and gender identity in the concrete behaviors of individuals. I suspect that her book will generate tremendous scholarly attention and will be a candidate for a number of book awards in our discipline.

Professor Brustein's assertion that I lack a consistent publication record reflects an inaccurate reading of my file. My consistent record of publication is noted in *his* letter of nomination of me for the McKnight Land Grant Professorship:

> Professor Pierce has already accumulated an impressive publication re-cord in her brief academic career. As a graduate student she authored or co-authored four articles in refereed journals, one review essay, and three book reviews. One of her co-authored articles appeared in the *American Sociological Review,* which is generally considered the number one journal in sociology. Since receiving her PhD in 1991 Professor Pierce has: completed her major book-length monograph which will appear with the University of California Press early in 1996; published two co-authored articles in refereed scholarly journals; authored or co-authored five book chapters in edited volumes; and published three book reviews. She has a number of projects that are currently under review including a co-edited volume entitled *Social Justice, Feminism and the Politics of Location.* Also, Professor Pierce has been invited to present her research at the most important regional and national meetings of sociologists and has maintained an exceptionally high level of profes-sional activity. . . . In short, Professor Pierce's publication record and professional activities exhibit the highest quality scholarship and are

consistent with the norms of scholarship existing by the most prestigious graduate Departments of Sociology.

Meanwhile back in the department after the negative tenure vote, the social dynamics were uncomfortable, to say the least. The "magnificent seven" were supportive and kind, and since they had all identified themselves to me, I knew who voted for me and, equally important, *who* had voted against me. Given the department's norm of conflict avoidance, it is probably not surprising that most of the dirty dozen *acted as if* they had actually supported me. In fact, Professor "Why don't you have rational choice theory on your syllabus?" actually sent me a Christmas card with a note saying how sorry he was that I was "going through a difficult time, just now." Ditto for the associate chair and her boyfriend. At the time, I could not understand why anyone who voted against me would do such a thing. "They must know that *I know* they voted against me," I said to several friends, "Why all the pretense?" In retrospect, I can see how these kinds of gestures reveal the discomfort and guilt of the participants in the negative vote or, perhaps, their unwillingness to take responsibility for their decisions. Further, such actions served to reinforce a climate of denial and silence about my tenure case.

The graduate students as well as my friends on staff were also upset by what had transpired but remained supportive. On her breaks, Marie Milsten-Fiedler, one of the secretaries, would stand outside the social science tower with me in the below-zero Minnesota winter, smoking cigarettes and listening to my complaints. And, for a while, it seemed that every other week another graduate student would appear in my office either crying about the fact that I might leave Minnesota to take a position elsewhere or ranting about the latest thing that one of the dirty dozen had said or done. Professor Z, for example, told graduate students in one of the required seminars that my feminist scholarship did not meet the bar for departmental standards of methodological rigor. And another professor used my book as an example of how *not* to do ethnography on criminal populations in his seminar. He also distributed a handout with quotes taken from my book that turned out to be the same one that had appeared in my mailbox just before the tenure vote. And in a final gesture of self-importance, he reported to a graduate student that the reason I was "in trouble" was because "I had followed Ron and Barbara's advice, and not his."

The graduate students rallied back, and in a very touching and

humorous holiday note in December, they sent me a "top ten" list, which
I excerpt here:

TOP TEN REASONS WHY JENNIFER SHOULD GET TENURE:
1. Jennifer is a snappy dresser.
   Let's face it; we're not exactly the best-dressed department on campus, or
   even in the social sciences for that matter. Jennifer's impeccable sense of
   style and adventurous clothing choices will make her a welcome addition to
   our shabby department. Her ability to accessorize is without equal this side
   of the Mississippi. Furthermore, Jennifer's fashion skills extend to an area
   sure to be in great demand in the future: she is one of those rare academics
   able to wear leather convincingly. . . .
2. Jennifer pisses off all the right people.
   Here is a talent we especially admire. Moreover, this is a talent that will only
   increase in value over the next few years. During this period it will be very
   important to get certain faculty to consider early retirement. Jennifer will
   not only help immeasurably in this regard, she may actually cause the offending faculty members to age faster. This uncanny ability reminds us, of
   course, of the *Sound of Music*. Remember that great scene where all those
   crabby old nuns are singing about how irritated they get around Maria?
   God, we love that scene. . . . Not since Maria Von Trapp has one woman
   demonstrated such an extraordinary ability to piss off all the right people
   for the right reasons!

I began to rally too. I had already been talking with the chair of American Studies, Dave Roediger, about transferring my tenure line, an idea
that he and the faculty in his department supported. And I had heard
through the college grapevine that the College of Liberal Arts' committee was incensed by my treatment by sociology and had reversed the
department's decision in a ten to zero vote. Then on February 21, my
thirty-ninth birthday, I got a phone call from a friend who had just heard
through "official sources" that I got tenure. I was with Barbara Laslett at
the time, and she drove me to the campus to get the official news. The
chair had already gone for the day, but the administrative assistant told
me the good news and gave me a big hug. When I ran back to the car to
tell Barbara, Dave Roediger was there. We all hooted and hollered, and
Dave said, "Now, you can move to American Studies."

*From the College Promotion and Tenure Committee's Report,
February 3, 1997*

There is nothing negative in the dossier except the departmental report. The
department has not developed its case. It was noted that the department's Pro-

motion and Tenure Committee voted unanimously in favor of Pierce's promotion and tenure. CLA's P & T Committee members agreed that the outside letters cannot be dismissed nor can the recommendation of the department's own committee. The Committee is disturbed that the chair states that he discounts letters solicited under Minnesota's open-files law. Committee members expressed concern that the department is now defining the discipline very narrowly. The department implies that Professor Pierce's research methodology is flawed. The CLA P & T committee disagreed.

Committee members agreed that no case against the candidate was presented in the dossier. Counter-arguments to each point of the majority report are in the dossier. It was also noted that only a brief synopsis of the departmental meeting was included in the file.

The two principal areas in which the department expressed criticism, methodology and theoretical contributions, are explicitly praised by the external reviewers selected by the department. It was noted that a favorable review of Pierce's book appeared in one of the major journals in which she was instructed by her department to publish.

It was noted that other departments on campus have praised Pierce and that she has a great support from the graduate students.

CLA's P & T Committee members were unanimous in their strong support for Pierce and expressed a willingness to meet with the Dean as a committee to discuss this case. (C. Kendall)

From the Dean of the College of Liberal Arts dated February 21, 1997

The record before us reveals an apparent disjunction between the department's obligation to review the *quality* of the candidate's work, and the desire of some in the department to raise a different question, concerning the *kind* of work she should be pursuing. The time to exclude a certain kind of work from the department's repertoire, were that desirable, was at the time of hiring, not now. The question to ask now is whether the candidate does her kind of work well. The evidence shows that she does. (S. Rosenstone, emphasis in original)

The following Monday when I went into campus, I knew that university guidelines required that I meet with the chair to discuss my tenure and promotion case. So, after careful consultation with the fashion police, I went in dressed to kill. Appropriate to the occasion, I dressed in black— a black leather miniskirt, black tights, tall black boots that zipped up the front, a black turtleneck, and a black blazer. For accessories, I wore a pair of earrings that one of my graduate students had given me. One earring was a tiny martini glass with the word *bad* embossed on it, and the other was a tiny bra with the word *girl*. After giving me a quick once-over, especially after he saw the length of my skirt, the chair started the meeting by congratulating me on getting tenure. He told me that he was very sorry about what had happened and hoped that we could put this behind us for now. He also promised to do everything in his power to support me in the department in the future. In a parting comment, he commended me on my professionalism throughout this process. (I felt particularly *professional* sitting in his office in a thigh-high miniskirt and tall black boots!) As I stood up to leave, he moved forward as if to shake my hand. Then he looked embarrassed for a moment and said, "Can I have a hug?" As I stood there dumbfounded, saying "uh," he leaned in and hugged me.

Although I think that the chair was genuinely sorry—and to his credit, he was the only faculty member who voted against me who apologized for doing so—his request for a hug transformed a meeting about a professional matter into a strangely personal, almost intimate moment: one inappropriate not only for a professional relationship but also in light of his own role in my tenure debacle. In the moment, I felt like a mother whose small child has come home, wanting to be forgiven for a bad deed, hoping that she will make everything okay again. From his vantage point, it is possible he interpreted the hug as a demonstration of his sincerity, or maybe as a gesture of future friendship. (Or perhaps it was the black leather I was wearing!) Whatever his actual motives, his behavior was reminiscent of my Christmas card–sending colleagues; it suggested that, like them, he wanted to gloss over the conflict and pretend that everything was fine.

From the Provost dated March 31, 1997

I have reviewed the attached documentation in support of the tenure and promotion of Dr. Jennifer L. Pierce of the Department of Sociology from assistant professor to associate professor with tenure effective on the starting date of her 1997–98 contract. I fully concur with the recommendation. Letters from external reviewers praise her energy and creativity. Her book on law firms has been called a "path breaking" study. Such comments speak well for her continued success in the profession. (W. Shively)

From the Board of Regents at the University of Minnesota dated May 9, 1997

I am pleased to inform you that the Board of Regents, at its meeting on May 9, 1997, approved the following change in your appointment from assistant professor to associate professor. This change will become effective with the beginning of your appointment terms for the 1997–1998. The Regents join with me in extending congratulations upon your achievements. (S. Bossier)

But things did not get better in the department. In fact, once I received the dean's letter, the harassment escalated. First, one of my opponents lashed out at me in a graduate awards committee meeting, baiting me with comments such as, "And what do you think as the *minority* on this faculty?" (She spat the word *minority* out as if it were a racial epithet.) I reported her behavior to the chair. Then, I discovered that she and another one of my opponents had gone to the chair in an attempt to convince him to go with them to the dean's office and protest the tenure reversal. When he refused to do so, one of them yelled at him in a public departmental space. Later, a *New York Times* article about a study of amorous pygmy chimpanzees and their female-dominated social organizations appeared *anonymously* in my department mailbox, complete with black-and-white photos of the chimps. When I told the chair, he asked me to document the incident in writing—which I did—but he never followed up on it. Meanwhile, the faces of the rest of the dirty dozen were completely blank. They acted as if nothing had ever happened. As if to reinscribe this silence, the department chair never publicly announced that the Board of Regents had approved my promotion for associate professor in May.

During this time, I had numerous meetings with the department chair, an administrator in the university's EEOC Office, the associate dean of faculty affairs for the college, and others about the escalation of harassment in the department. The college-level administrators were supportive and helpful in offering potential strategies and solutions—one suggestion, for example, involved an EEOC investigation of the department. But it was also clear from talking to several attorneys about this possibility, that while I had carefully documented my case, I had to consider that if I launched such an investigation—whatever its outcome—I would most likely encounter further antagonism along the way and be labeled a "troublemaker." In other words, marshaling the very policies designed to protect me against harassment and discrimination could also, once again, be used against me.

Finally, at the end of May, I met with the chair yet again to discuss continuing problems and my dissatisfaction with his efforts to do anything about it. I also told him that I wanted to move my tenure line to

American Studies. Though he agreed with me about the problem in the department, he urged me to stay and help make a change—"with all the retirements in the next five years, the department will be a different place." I told him that I intended to submit my request to the dean, and that if he wanted to support me, as he promised me he would in February, then he would assist me in making the transfer as amicable as possible.

Over the 1997–98 academic year, the backbiting continued. While Professor Z was cordial and polite to me in face-to-face interactions, he publicly denounced my qualifications as a candidate for tenure as well as the dean's decision to reverse the department's vote in a collegewide meeting that several of my colleagues from around the campus had attended. In the fall, when I met with the chair to discuss this event and related problems, he told me that "many people were victimized by my tenure decision" and suggested that Professor Z "felt that the dean has challenged his judgment." He recommended that I not take the public remark personally. At the same time, discussions about my request to transfer to American Studies went on behind closed doors. The chair submitted my request to the department's Executive Committee and later told me that they refused and that there was nothing he could do about it. Since he offered no explanation for their decision, and I doubted he had actually supported my request, I wrote the committee a formal letter asking for an explanation. I received a written response from the committee on March 9, informing me that the chair was supposed to communicate their response to me directly.

Two weeks after I had submitted my formal request, I discovered that someone had scrawled the word *bitch* on a flyer announcing one of my public presentations on my office door. I immediately reported it to the chair. About a week after that, I went to the campus parking garage at the end of the day and discovered that my car had a flat tire. A nail had been hammered into its sidewall, suggesting this was an intentional act. According to the parking lot attendant, I had been the only one to report a flat tire that day, and it could have been a prank done by anyone who had access to the garage. Whatever the reason, my car, a Japanese economy model, had been singled out.

Finally, near the end of the academic year and in response to these incidents, the chair set up a meeting with administrative staff from Human Resources (HR). The purpose of the meeting, as I understood it, was to enlist their help in devising departmental solutions to these problems. After I reported the events of the past two years, one of the staff from HR suggested that I try to get to know the faculty better, "maybe have lunch with them." "As a counselor, I find that these kinds of interactions often engender empathy," he added. I told him that this was not an individual problem but rather one of departmental climate. One of the department's staff members who also attended the meeting supported my argument, while the chair sat by my side silently. The HR person quickly backpedaled and apologized.

Before moving on in my narrative, I want to pause here to highlight several themes that emerge from this story about the nature of academic debate in tenure decisions, the development of partisanship surrounding these decisions, and some of the problems with policies designed to protect junior faculty. First, the academic arguments about "standards" for my tenure case did not revolve around the *quality* of my scholarship, as university guidelines for promotion and tenure suggest they should, but rather the *kind* of scholarship I did. The majority report, for instance, did not question whether I did feminist ethnography well, but the epistemological assumptions underlying feminist interpretive sociology. The good news is that by underscoring appropriate procedures and the majority report's narrow understanding of sociology, the university not only ensured my tenure and promotion but protected my academic freedom as a feminist scholar.

However, once the department's decision was reversed at higher levels, the harassment escalated, and here, I suspect individual motivations, academic partisanship, and departmental dynamics worked together in complex ways. Some probably did feel threatened that their judgment had been challenged by the dean. And others with a strong investment in positivism may have felt their very understanding of sociology was under attack. And still others just did not want a "contentious" woman in the department. As a consequence, I became a floating signifier for their collective angst: for some I signified the threat of a female-dominated social organization (i.e., the pygmy chimpanzee article); for others, a disruptive "*minority*" among a majority of positivists; and for still others, a "bitch." Further, given the norm for conflict avoidance, most of the harassment took the form of anonymous communications or backbiting. The fact that this kind of harassment continued unabated and that the chair did little about it demonstrates not only how a climate of conflict avoidance can be sustained and reproduced, but how such a climate can exacerbate tensions and problems that already exist.

Finally, by advising me not to take slanderous remarks "personally" and by encouraging me "to have lunch with my colleagues," the chair and the Human Resources counselor individualized a problem of climate, rendering me responsible for "fixing" things, thereby denying larger structural issues. While college-level administrators who spoke with me seemed to recognize these larger issues, it was also the case that some of the strategies proposed to help me could also create more antagonism.

Moving to American Studies

In August 1998, and less than a week before I left for sabbatical, Dave Roediger called to tell me that the dean had just agreed to move my tenure line out of the sociology department and to American Studies. Though I was pleased by the news, at that point I just wanted to get out of town, go to California, and get on with my life. I was emotionally exhausted. And when I went on sabbatical, I finally collapsed for the first time in the two years. As it turned out, my sabbatical in Berkeley was restful and regenerative. I spent time with friends hiking along the Pacific Coast, attending talks at the university, and reading. Most important of all, I began to reevaluate my priorities. "If this is what being an academic is like," I once told a close friend, "then I would rather clean toilets." If American Studies did not work out as I hoped it would, then I would leave the academy altogether to become a full-time writer.

At the same time, I also began to reevaluate my intellectual trajectory. The marginality project in Utah no longer held my interest. (The forty oral histories sat for my sabbatical year in a box, untouched.) What did capture my interest was the backlash against affirmative action. The research for my first book opened up some possibilities for exploration in this direction: one of the sites for the study, a large corporation with a legal department, had a federally mandated affirmative action program. My old field notes contained a daily record of negative comments and bad jokes about affirmative action. Further, the backlash spoke not only to my own experiences as an assistant professor but also to larger trends nationwide. While on leave, I began the arduous process of locating the lawyers who had worked there in the late 1980s and then reinterviewing them. The interviews with the African American lawyers blew me away—their experiences in law firms were hauntingly similar to my own. The professional exclusion, the harassment, the myriad of small acts of discrimination—it was all there. So, at the end of year, I returned to Minnesota and my new academic home in American Studies with thirty-three interview transcripts, a new book project, notes for a conference paper, and a box filled with books.

In writing about his years as a professor in the Department of American Studies at Minnesota, historian George Lipsitz paints a political and intellectual portrait of its faculty and students, as well as its research and curricular agenda, that is reminiscent of my days as a graduate student at Berkeley. "The courses we taught and the research we conducted and supervised was shaped by 1960s efforts to diversify the curriculum, the faculty, and the student body, to include women, people of color, and other unrepresented or under-represented groups in both the curriculum and the classroom."[21]

In transferring to American Studies, I was fortunate to discover firsthand that this department, while in some ways similar to the sociology department at Berkeley, was absolutely nothing like the sociology department at Minnesota. American Studies is a progressive, feminist, antiracist, and queer-friendly space. It is also one of the few institutional spaces that is actually multicultural in its curriculum as well as the composition of its faculty and graduate students. Of the ten core faculty members in 2002, two are American Indian, one is Asian American, one is African American, and two, including myself, are queer. Thirty-two percent of our graduate students are students of color, and the most recent cohort is forty-six percent. Of course, like every academic department, American Studies is not without disagreement or conflict. Nevertheless, these numbers stand as impressive achievements in a time of declining federal and state resources for public education, an ongoing backlash against affirmative action, and a conservative administration in our nation's White House.

Once I moved to American Studies, a friend of mine who teaches at Berkeley teased me about becoming a "traitor to the discipline." His claim about my "disloyalty to the discipline" is particularly ironic given that my training at Berkeley in sociology was always interdisciplinary and feminist. While it continues to be true that I "think" like a sociologist, as a consequence of being in American Studies, I have also learned to think like a historian as well as a postnationalist American studies scholar.[22] In interdisciplinary exchanges with David Noble and Jeani O'Brien, I have learned much about the importance of history and historical thinking, and in my collaborative project with MJ Maynes and Barbara Laslett

I have rethought the value of personal narratives in interdisciplinary research.[23]

These productive exchanges continue with my graduate students. These bright, energetic young scholars work on a wide range of important projects, and their enthusiasm and their research interests have had a synergistic effect on my own. In fact, this volume has its origins in a graduate seminar when Karla Erickson, Marie Milsten-Fiedler, and Deb Smith discussed the importance of feminist scholarship and activism to their own generation. In addition, their intellectual engagement has often sustained me during difficult times, particularly in my years in mainstream sociology. They have always cared deeply about the project of feminist scholarship, and their enthusiasm, passion, commitment, and concern carried me through the low moments in my career.

Conclusion

This personal narrative essay has explored my intellectual and political trajectory as a 2.5 feminist, one that brought with it a rich intellectual legacy but also carried with it a host of painful contradictions. As a 2.5 feminist, I began in feminism in Berkeley's Department of Sociology in the 1980s. At that time, half of the members of my cohort were women, and the number of women graduate students in sociology and the number of women sociology faculty were increasing there as well as among students and faculty across the nation. However, the 1980s were a politically conservative time, and as many have argued, a backlash against feminism, affirmative action, multiculturalism, the welfare state, and immigrants was well under way. During this time, feminist scholarship proliferated in the academy across the United States, but its reception varied from place to place and within institutions. This uneven reception is evident at the University of Minnesota. On the one hand, the university has an excellent reputation for the production of feminist scholarship. The Department of History is an excellent example of this point. On the other, with the exceptions of Ron Aminzade and Barbara Laslett, the reception and support of such scholarship in the Department of Sociology was nonexistent in the 1980s and early 1990s.

While feminist pioneers in sociology have described their graduate school years as a time of isolation, intellectual uncertainty, and professional exclusion, as a 2.5 feminist, I experienced my graduate training in quite different ways. I did not encounter isolation, and I emerged from graduate school intellectually confident and certain of my analytical abilities. Once I left graduate school, however, much like the feminist pioneers, I experienced professional exclusion, hostility, and indifference. The emotional and psychological costs of such professional exclusion are difficult to measure. There is no doubt that it was stressful. Mainstream sociology at Minnesota was not a safe place to conduct the kind of research I was trained to do. To survive, I developed a heavy coat of armor to protect myself from daily assaults on my dignity and self-worth. In doing so, I also shifted and changed my disciplinary location, my intellectual trajectory, my perceptions about the academy, and my priorities. I have in Maria Lugones's sense of the term "traveled." Throughout my travels, feminism and feminist communities have served as a legacy, a guide, a resource, and, at times, an anchor. I imagine that I will always be a feminist ethnographer, but I can travel many places to do that.

Upon reflection on my own experiences, then, it appears that while many things have changed for the better for feminists in the academy, some things have remained very much the same. Positivist sociologists who regard feminist interpretive research as threatening to their view of science, personal antagonisms toward women and lesbians in academic departments, and partisan debates about "standards" all highlight the micro processes through which the backlash to feminism in the academy operates.[24] In this case, participating in partisan debates behind closed doors, avoiding conflict, harassing a junior colleague through anonymous communications, and failing to be accountable for these actions were not simply the actions of aberrant individuals but collective practices that created a working environment that was at best indifferent to my experiences as a feminist ethnographer and at worst hostile. Further, when a department such as this one fails to disrupt such practices, it implicitly suggests, as I have argued elsewhere, that this kind of behavior is acceptable, "a 'normal,' taken-for-granted feature of the workplace."[25] In this case, it appears that part of the majority's inability to squarely face the reversal of my tenure decision and take responsibility for their own decisions, decisions that were probably difficult to justify even to themselves, lies in the normalization of a climate, one in which an antifeminist stance, a narrow understanding of sociology, and conflict avoidance prevailed.

This is, of course, my story of one department in a particular historical time and place. Sociology departments across the country vary widely in their intellectual emphases: some top departments are well-known for ethnographic and historical research, while others have reputations for rigorous statistical training. Despite its positivist core, American sociology as a discipline has diverse interpretive, qualitative, and theoretical traditions. Consequently, departments too are uneven in the extent to which they embrace positivism and other epistemological frameworks. Moreover, departments also change over time. The composition of the faculty at Minnesota, for instance, is not the same since I left in 1998. With a greater number of junior faculty, new senior hires, and recently tenured faculty, its intellectual center may be in transition.[26]

Still, with these painful lessons behind me, I would like to think in my travels from feminism to the mainstream and back that things have gotten better. Certainly, this is true of my experiences in American Studies, and it appears to be so for many of my graduate students as well. As part of the third feminist generation, they expect feminist scholarship to be taken seriously. They are confident and smart, and they stand up for themselves and for others when it really matters. They are, in short, truly wonderful people and scholars. What remains to be seen is what will happen to this generation as they leave graduate school and begin their own tenure track positions. Will they face professional exclusion? Will they find obscenities scrawled on their office doors? Or will they win awards for their books and be welcomed by their senior colleagues? As we say in my discipline of origin, "the data are not in yet." "It's too soon to tell." My hope is that they will find departments and institutions where they are valued for who they are and the kind of scholarship they do and encouraged to share their feminist visions with their colleagues and students. In short, I hope the "natives" will be friendly.

Notes

This chapter has benefited from the careful readings by many people, particularly Robert Zussman and Arlene Kaplan Daniels, but also Hokulani Aikau, Ron Aminzade, Rose Brewer, Karla Erickson, Doug Hartmann, Barbara Laslett, MJ Maynes, and Dave Roediger. Finally, special thanks to the members of the SABLE seminar, Jean Allman, Anne Carter, Anna Clark, Lisa Disch, Kirsten Fischer, and Jeani O'Brien.

1. For a more detailed discussion of these social, historical, and intellectual shifts, see the introduction to this volume.

2. Maria Lugones, "Playfulness, 'World' Traveling, and Loving Perception," *Hypatia* 2, 2 (1987): 3–19.

3. Marilyn Frye, *The Politics of Reality* (Trumanburg, N.Y.: Crossing Press, 1983).

4. The documents I rely on to reconstruct this account include: S. Bossier, "Letter from the University of Minnesota Board of Regents regarding the tenure and promotion of Jennifer L. Pierce," May 9, 1997; W. Brustein, "McKnight Nomination Letter for Jennifer L. Pierce," October 19, 1995; W. Brustein, "Chair's letter of recommendation for Jennifer L. Pierce's tenure and promotion," November 26, 1996; C. Kendall, "College Promotion and Tenure Committee's Report on the Promotion and Tenure of Jennifer L. Pierce," February 3, 1997; Majority Report on the Tenure Case of Jennifer L. Pierce, Department of Sociology, University of Minnesota, Minneapolis, Minn., November 16, 1996; Minority Report on the Tenure Case of Jennifer L. Pierce, Department of Sociology, University of Minnesota, Minneapolis, Minn., November 26, 1996; Jennifer L. Pierce, "Notes on Departmental Problems," January 1995–August 1998; Jennifer L. Pierce, "Response to Annual Appraisal," January 1995; Jennifer L. Pierce, "Response to Chair and Departmental Recommendation," November 28, 1996; Jennifer L. Pierce, "Internal Memo to W. Brustein," May 1, 1997; Jennifer L. Pierce, "Internal Memo to Members of Sociology's Department's Executive Committee," March 2, 1998; S. Rosenstone, "Dean's Recommendation for the Tenure and Promotion of Jennifer L. Pierce," February 21, 1997; and D. Ward, "Response to Pierce's Response to Her Annual Appraisal," January 1995. All documents are on file with the author.

5. I have used actual names as they appear in these public documents or when individuals have given me permission to do so.

6. See Joan Scott, "The Evidence of Experience" *Critical Inquiry* 17, 4 (1991): 773–97; Susan Chase, "American Culture, Professional Work, and Inequality," in *Ambiguous Empowerment: The Work Narratives of Women's School Superintendents* (Amherst: University of Massachusetts Press, 1995); James Clifford, introduction to *Writing Culture: The Poetics and Politics of Ethnography*, ed. James Clifford and George E. Marcus (Berkeley: University of California Press, 1986).

7. Barbara Laslett and Barrie Thorne, eds., *Feminist Sociology: Life Histories of a Movement* (New Brunswick, N.J.: Rutgers University Press, 1997); Kathryn P. Meadow Orlans and Ruth A. Wallace, eds., *Gender and the Academic Experience* (Lincoln: University of Nebraska Press, 1994); and Anne Goetting and Sarah Fenstermaker, eds., *Individual Voices, Collective Visions: Fifty Years of Women in Sociology* (Philadelphia: Temple University Press, 1995).

8. American Sociological Association, "Survey of Sociology Departments and Divisions: 1991–1992," unpublished paper, 1993.

9. See Gloria Cuadraz and Jennifer L. Pierce, "From Scholarship Girls to Scholarship Women: Surviving the Contradictions of Race and Class in Graduate Education," *Explorations in Ethnic Studies* 17, 1 (January 1994): 21–44; and Troy Duster, "Graduate Education at Berkeley," *American Sociologist* 22 (Spring 1987): 83–87.

10. For a humorous discussion of "lethal weapons" in my ethnographic research, see Jennifer L. Pierce, "Lawyers, Lethal Weapons, and Ethnographic Authority," in *Qualitative Research and the Researcher Experience*, ed. Susan Moch and Marie Gates (Thousand Oaks, Calif.: Sage Publications, 2000).

11. Adrienne Rich, "On Taking Women Students Seriously," in *Lies, Secrets, and Silences* (New York: Norton Press, 1979).

12. In 1991, I began my first assistant professor appointment in the departments of women's studies and sociology at the University of Utah in Salt Lake City. Given that I was there only for a short time, I have not included a narrative of those experiences here.

13. These broader shifts and changes in the academic job market are also reflected in the changing numbers of faculty hired from 1993 to 2004 at the University of Minnesota. When I arrived in 1993, the number of junior faculty hired in the entire College of Liberal Arts was 8. By 1998, the academic job market had begun to turn around with increasing retirements at Minnesota, and new faculty members have been arriving in the College of Liberal Arts since that time in cohorts of *40* to *90*. Currently, 40 percent of the 540 faculty in the College of Liberal Arts were hired between 1998 and 2004. This trend is apparent in academic departments. By 2002 there were 9 new junior faculty and 2 new senior faculty in the Department of Sociology. These new hires constituted approximately 40 percent of the department's faculty.

14. See the introduction to this volume for a listing of these feminist scholars.

15. For a discussion of the history of sexual politics in the Department of Sociology, see Dan Martindale, *The Romance of a Profession: A Case History in the Sociology of Sociology*, Social Science Series, No. 3. (St. Paul, Minn.: Windflower Publishing, 1976).

16. Before coming to Minnesota in 1982, Barbara Laslett had been an associate professor of sociology at the University of Southern California. She retired from the University of Minnesota in 2002.

17. For the collection Brewer and I worked on, see Social Justice Group, Center for Advanced Feminist Studies Editorial Collective, *Is Academic Feminism Dead? Theory in Practice* (New York: New York University Press, 2000). Also, see Lisa Albrecht and Rose Brewer, eds., *Bridges of Power: Women's Multicultural Alliances* (Philadelphia: New Society Publishers, 1990).

18. Kent Sandstrom suggests that predominantly Scandinavian American communities in states such as Iowa and Minnesota place a premium on the values of hard work, stoic endurance, *conflict avoidance,* and humility. By implication, the climate of Minnesota's Department of Sociology simply reflected the values of the broader community. Others have suggested, however, that conflict avoidance is typical of many academic departments. See Kent Sandstrom, "Embracing Modest Hopes: Lessons from the Beginning of a Teaching Journey," in *The Social Worlds of Higher Education,* ed. Bernice Pescosolido and Ron Aminzade (Newbury, Calif.: Pine Forge Press, 1997).

19. See Gary Alan Fine, "Great Men, Hard Times: Sociology at the University of Minnesota," *Sociological Quarterly* 6 (Spring 1985); Martindale, *The Romance of a Profession.*

20. Actually, the department had employed a number of qualitative sociologists in previous years including Greg Stone and Gary Alan Fine. Lucy Fischer

and Rose Brewer also taught there, but Fischer left when she did not get tenure, and Brewer moved her tenure line to African American Studies.

21. George Lipsitz, *American Studies in a Moment of Danger* (Minneapolis: University of Minnesota Press, 2001), xv.

22. Scholarship in postnationalist American studies stands as a challenge to an earlier body of work that focused on the "exceptionalism" of the United States. Rather than conceptualizing the United States within the confines of a bounded nation-state, this newer scholarship attempts to rethink what "America" means in dynamic relation to other countries. See John Carlos Rowe, ed., introduction to *Post-nationalist American Studies* (Berkeley: University of California Press, 1999); David Noble, *Death of a Nation* (Minneapolis: University of Minnesota Press, 2002); and Lipsitz, *American Studies in a Moment of Danger.*

23. MJ Maynes, Jennifer L. Pierce, and Barbara Laslett, *Telling Stories: Personal Narrative Analysis in the Social Sciences and in History* (book manuscript, in progress).

24. Since I first published this essay in 2003, I have received numerous e-mails from feminist graduate students and junior faculty in sociology departments across the country thanking me for writing about my "tenure trials." Many of these communications also included detailed descriptions of similar problems and dynamics in their own departments. Their responses, of course, do not constitute a representative sample. Nevertheless, they do suggest that the problems I describe resonate with other feminist sociologists whose scholarship stands outside the positivist norms of their mainstream departments.

25. Jennifer L. Pierce, *Gender Trials: Emotional Lives in Contemporary Law Firms* (Berkeley and Los Angeles: University of California Press, 1995), 183.

26. See note 13.

5. Innovation Is Overtime

An Ethical Analysis of "Politically Committed"
Academic Labor

Lisa J. Disch and Jean M. O'Brien

Hyde Park, Chicago, Spring, 1989

A professor strides rapidly out of the Joseph R. Regenstein Library. She crosses Fifty-seventh Street, steps onto the quad, and turns her mind toward class. She is a high-powered academic, famously overworked, but one who appears poised at all times. For this, she is venerated.

How does she do it? She finds time for just about everything she is asked to do—and as a woman academic she is asked to do a lot. The University of Chicago in 1989 is at least ten years behind the times, if "the times" in this context can be defined by its response to feminism. It has yet to create a feminist, gender, or women's studies program and counts few women among its tenured and tenure-track faculty, despite the fact that nearly half of its undergraduate students are women. Under such conditions, a scholar who happens to be a woman is called on to represent women no matter what her research specialization. She has landed a job in a context that makes her an exception.

This means that she will be expected to participate in a unique category of service, service that presents itself as political, over and above that which she is asked to perform for her department. Five or six times a year, administrators tap her to serve on collegewide or university-wide committees as a kind of insurance policy. It doesn't look good to have all-male committees speaking for the faculty as a whole. She nearly always agrees, taking it as her calling to speak for this university's systematically underrepresented. This is a self-imposed duty ("If I don't do it, no one else will do it *well*.") that strikes a familiar chord in so many of us who invest our academic careers with political meaning.

This is how women (and other "exceptional") faculty become role models for more than their scholarship: We are models of how not to say "no" in the face of what presents itself as breaking new ground. We are the ones you count on. To take it on. And pull it off. Seemingly effortlessly.

Jeani O'Brien was crossing the quad that afternoon, just as this high-powered woman was making her way toward class. She was ABD, and she had great news: she had just been hired to fill a one-year replacement slot as an American Indian historian at the University of Minnesota. An exchange took place.

THE PROFESSOR: How are you?
JEANI: So busy. Frantically busy. I can't wait to get to this job because then things will finally slow down.
THE PROFESSOR: *Laughs. Says nothing more.*

Introduction

"Innovation is overtime." That is really how we thought of our lives as feminists. Paying with our weekends for the privilege—and it truly was one—of being able to work on academic initiatives that meant something to us. Wasn't this what Jeani was meant to take away from that accidental encounter with one of the women professors she had looked up to? Isn't this what her silence meant to say? "You think you're working hard now but just wait until you start your job: you'll be one of the ones they count on not just to get things done but to make a difference."

It was 2002. We had both held tenure for about five years. And we had both learned, to our dismay, that earning tenure puts you on the fast track for administrative service. Jeani did a three-year stint as chair of American Studies and Lisa Disch served a term as director of the Center for Advanced Feminist Studies.

We both took on these assignments pretty much the same way we had taken on our feminism—as something you did without question. That's one of the peculiarities of being neither of the "second" nor of the "third" wave. People were burning bras before we were even *wearing* them. We grew up as feminists, but we were too young to be part of the struggle. We didn't need college professors to introduce us to feminism. And good thing, too, because feminism was not something you studied in the mid-1970s, except at the few places (like Minnesota) that were way ahead of the curve.

This was true for each of us even in graduate school, for different reasons. Jeani chose a field, history, where feminist studies were flourishing but went to a school, University of Chicago, that was (as we have noted) well behind the times. Lisa went to Rutgers, a feminist hotbed, where Catherine Stimson (a founding editor of *Signs*) was a dean, and departments like history and English were blazing new trails. But she did a degree in political philosophy in the political science department, which had few women faculty and hired its first feminist theorist only as Lisa was on her way out the door in 1987.[1]

We did not have feminist mentors. We barely had women professors. But the few we knew were famously overworked. Now we were too. That is how we came to reduce our lives as feminists in academia to a motto: *Innovation Is Overtime.*

Of course, at the time Jeani could never have formulated such a dictum to describe the life of the venerated professor. Nor could she have anticipated how closely her own academic life would subscribe to it. We started this essay hoping to figure out how she—that is, we both—got there.

Our goal changed over the course of the writing. We discovered that what we were calling "innovation is overtime" is already widely recognized as something that impairs academic advancement, especially for women and members of minority groups.[2] Why bother writing to testify to the truth of an already well-documented phenomenon? How much more interesting it would be to analyze what made us susceptible to this message in the first place. As highly privileged professionals, we were neither coerced into overwork by the mechanized pace of a factory line nor compelled to take on multiple jobs by low wages and poor benefits. Even before tenure, we enjoyed a flexibility that any other worker would kill for (epitomized by the sabbaticals).

Could it be that we were not just exhausted but also *empowered* by the pace of our lives? This suggestion opened up a whole new set of questions for us: How did we come to identify as politically committed academics? How did we get sold on the idea that the university can be a force for progressive political change, and that we should count our politically committed academic labors as overtime? By what institutional rhythms had we come to take pleasure in working to exhaustion?[3]

The result of our writing is that we no longer regard "innovation is overtime" as a simple fact of academic life. We think of it as a subsidy—ethical not financial—that funds programs that are necessary to the university's public mission but that do not materially enhance its profit margins. What we experienced as "innovation" is part of a larger story of the way that corporate funding and corporate logics are restructuring public universities in a time of state budget cuts to higher education.[4] We observe that the University of Minnesota has been reluctant to sacrifice all the programs that are vestiges of its land-grant public mission (at least *so far*). Yet because such programs are not good prospects for corporate sponsorship, their funding needs to come from elsewhere. This is where the labors of faculty and, just as crucially, staff who can be mobilized to work "overtime" come in. Our thesis is that the University of Minnesota counts on the labor that is motivated by the ideal of "innovation" and the commitment to "overtime,"[5] even as those of us who perform it imagine ourselves to be engaged in more or less radical acts of resistance against canonical curricula, traditional pedagogy, and the intrusion of market rationalities into the academy.

We present this not as a generalizable thesis but as a provocation. We recognize that academic reward structures and work loads vary widely. This is true even within the same institution, let alone among liberal arts colleges, research universities, and community colleges, or between public and private schools. We do not claim to be representative. Instead, we hope that our own reflections will prompt faculty, staff, and graduate students to reflect in turn about how their institutions work, and about the inequities that their work habits perpetuate.

Is the University in Ruins?

We begin by considering the structural context in which we acquired our work habits: the transformation of the university by neoliberal privatization.[6] We both started at the University of Minnesota around 1990, which was a moment of multiple contradictions. There was an economic downturn. Academic jobs were scarce, yet innovative and politically radical programs were beginning to have their own tenure lines. In the popular media and on talk radio, there raged a political backlash against "academic radicalism." By this time, liberal had become the "L" word, and students had stopped protesting the military-industrial complex to take on (in their words) the "political correctness" of the campus radicals who were their professors. Conservatism gained momentum outside the academy, yet political critique was being institutionalized within.

We are of "the bust" generation, hired in the trough between two anomalous periods of unprecedented academic growth. On one side, there was the boom of the late 1960s to mid-1970s, a period at the University of Minnesota when political activists-turned-academics found jobs and carried their political commitments with them. Minnesota was among the first wave of institutions to create such innovative programs as women's studies, African American studies, American Indian studies, and more. On the other side, there was a hiring spike in the mid-1990s that was funded by the astronomical stock market of that time. At the University of Minnesota, 40 percent of the 540 faculty in the College of Liberal Arts were hired between 1998 and 2004; they arrived in cohorts of 40 to 90 not only to fill vacancies but to take up newly created assistant professorships in comparative literature, cultural studies, women's studies, American studies, Afro-American studies, Asian studies, American Indian studies, and more. As "the bust" generation in between, we are a cohort so small we are barely visible as such. The year we arrived, 1990, the college made 9 hires, only 3 of them assistant professors.

Being hired in a recession taught us an important lesson in academic demographics: the vicissitudes of state budgets and political agendas take a toll on department cultures and program innovation. We were among very few untenured faculty in our respective departments—history and political science—for almost a decade. The two-year pay freeze and hiring freeze that followed immediately upon our arrival locked that demographic into place throughout the College of Liberal Arts. Hiring had been so rare that departments had few—if any—systems in place for mentoring newcomers. Sometimes we did not learn that there were protocols, from the very simple (such as how to order books or arrange for xeroxing) to the very significant (such as how to assemble materials for annual review) until we set someone off by violating them. Lacking in-rank comrades, we formed cohorts not within departments but across them. For our first years here, we could name practically every assistant professor. Especially the women, the American Indians, African Americans, and other "targets of opportunity"—hires made to redress social inequalities—who kept turning up in predictable roles on college- and university-wide committees. And we turned up a lot because the ratio of bodies to committees meant that our services were frequently in demand.

In that tight job market, we considered ourselves lucky to have been hired and especially fortunate to have landed jobs at a place that housed so many cutting-edge academic initiatives. But there was a downside. We benefited by that tide of innovation but were too few to assume the mantle of perpetuating it.

Neoliberalism, which has prompted deep cuts in public spending on such social investments as education, health, and welfare, can be made to explain the squeeze on universities, especially state-funded ones. This is Bill Readings's brilliantly provocative thesis: "The University is not just *like* a corporation: it is a corporation."[7] For Readings, the emergence of the corporate university marks the end of the nineteenth-century idea of the university as model public, a market enclave that was to provide both an escape from and critical vantage point on competitive capitalism. Its foremost task was to turn students from self-interested individuals into public-minded citizens.[8] Readings argues that the advent of transnational capitalism evacuated this idea of a university in service to public values in favor of a business model organized by "the empty notion of excellence."[9]

What makes our experience at the University of Minnesota so surprising is that the wave of hiring that began around 1995 went *against* neoliberal trends. During this period, the university did invest millions of dollars—many of them corporate-sponsored—in fields capable of generating "potentially profitable information" for a restructuring economy.[10] But this pattern of expenditure did not come at the cost of investing in the liberal arts. The university allocated funds both to shore up traditional liberal disciplines and to create new initiatives such as an Asian American studies program and a women's studies PhD, which are unlikely to bring in multimillion dollar grants or to generate marketable knowledge. If Readings were absolutely right, those initiatives should not have happened. Was Minnesota an enlightened exception or an amendment to the transformation Readings describes?

The Minnesota example suggests that even the "corporate" university cannot afford to altogether abandon its identity as "model public." In fact, the ideological work it has always done for the nation-state may even intensify in a global economy. As Samuel Weber has observed, the drive to global competitiveness generates political and social costs (i.e., "negative externalities") for which profitability simply cannot compensate. There are "important functions left for nation-states, related to the organization of unprofitable but necessary social tasks, as well as to the solution of long-range problems whose temporal dimensions exceed the perspectives imposed upon corporations."[11] Foremost among these "unprofitable but necessary social tasks" will be that to which the university has traditionally been assigned: perpetuating faith in representative democracy. In the global economy, this will mean creating citizens for a multinational, multiethnic, multicultural worldwide public.

The university of the late twentieth century accomplishes this task, in part, by means of such hiring and curricular initiatives as founding African studies, women's studies, or GLBT studies programs, redesigning philosophy and literature surveys to incorporate an "international perspective," and introducing U.S. and international cultural pluralism requirements into graduate or undergraduate programs. The advantage of such initiatives is that whereas they can be couched to potential funders and administrators in the recuperative language of "diversity," "public service," and "critical thinking," they can be put into practice in ways that work political transformation from within the university. They *can* be radical enclaves provided that faculty, staff, and graduate students are willing to work overtime to keep them going.

What we have observed at Minnesota is that although corporatization does not put an end to such "model public" initiatives, it changes the way they are institutionalized: on unequal terms with new fields that can promise marketable or market-oriented knowledges. The latter will be promoted for "donations or contracts emanating from the private, corporate sector."[12] Those who work on corporate-funded university initiatives enjoy disproportionately high salaries, reduced teaching loads, commodious facilities, and—crucially—generous staffing that spares them costly administrative labor. New fields and programs that cannot be sold to private and corporate donors will not be eliminated as simple market rationality would dictate. They will be subsidized by faculty and staff time instead of by corporate dollars. The result: the creation of a "public sector" within the corporate university.[13]

This rings true with Michael Hardt's observations regarding the dominant position of "affective labor" in the global capitalist economy.[14] Extending the logic of Hardt's analysis, instrumental rationality will not colonize all relations in the corporate university. On the contrary, there will be an increased emphasis on sociability, on community building, networking, mentoring, and the like, all of which produce feelings of purpose, engagement, and passion that translate directly into value for the university. In short, the university's public sector runs on affective labor.

All this is to say that at the University of Minnesota the nineteenth-century ideal of the university is not "in ruins." Our administrators sustain an investment in programs that incarnate the ideal of the university as model public at the same time as they launch initiatives in response to market logics. In fact, they count on the former—the nonmarketable innovations of faculty who practice critical pedagogies in the classroom, who revise their syllabi in light of new critical debates, or who found an intellectual initiative that takes its bearings from a political movement—

just as much as they do the latter. This does not make the University of Minnesota an enlightened exception to Readings's thesis. Quite the opposite. Whereas administrators count on these labors that do not produce commodifiable knowledge, they get away without having to fully *account* for them in the operating costs and reward system of the corporate university. These programs succeed because their costs are offset by the exertions of faculty and staff who invest their academic jobs with political meaning and, so, accept them as an "add-on" to their work load.

In this context, "innovation is overtime" no longer strikes us as a self-evident fact of academic life. It is the ethic that lends inevitability to this practice of subsidy, calls the "politically committed" academic and staff member into being, and lends the university's public sector an aura of resistance.

Work Ethics

It was a real turning point for us to conceive of "innovation is overtime" as an ethic instead of as the phrase that summed up the truth of our lives. Truths can only be testified to; ethics can be analyzed. An "ethic" as we understand it is not a principle. Instead, it is a way of thinking, perceiving, and reacting that takes hold through the "actual tangible procedures" that we perform everyday.[15] Ethical analysis is clearly different from the exercises that pass for ethical thinking in "The Ethicist" column in the *New York Times* Sunday magazine. The idea is not to apply principles to the dilemmas that arise out of everyday life but, rather, to call attention to the habits of thinking and perception that create the "everyday" from which those dilemmas seem to issue.[16] Such an understanding of ethical analysis calls for a break with the *New York Times* format: "Here is my situation, what should I do?" The alternative: "How did I get here?" and "What would it take to see this otherwise?"

As for the labors that we two innovators have taken on, we are reluctant to explain them by recourse to the Protestant "work ethic." No doubt laboring overtime to innovate is a habit of living that we take up as *individuals*. We imagine it variously as voluntary, as a duty, as a means to self-perfection or to political transformation. Our priorities become imbued with the arrogance of the very busy ("Is this the best use of my time?"). We hire people to do our shopping, clean our houses, do our laundry, cut our lawns, run our errands, raise our children—or we impose these labors on our mates—to find time for the work that only we can perform. But an ethical analysis that takes the modern individual as its starting point (as does Weber's) obscures what it should seek to explain, which is precisely how we subjects are formed *as* individuals in the first place. If we want to break from this, we need to ask what habits of thinking, seeing, and doing go into forming the citizen-producer of the modern, capitalist, democratic nation-state: that "docile body" who identifies with liberty but lives industriously (whatever the objective—wage earning, professional achievement, exercise, housework).[17]

Schools stand at the forefront of the institutions that form this distinctively modern individual. But they have been analyzed one-sidedly, focusing on how *students* are examined, ranked, and rendered productive through standardized tests, seating charts, graduation requirements, and more. This focus on students makes it is easy to fall back into an instrumental way of thinking, to cast faculty as figures who "wield" power in the university setting, and thereby to overlook the many ways that a university faculty is itself a docile body. Remember that "docile" bodies are neither passive or inert. Quite the opposite. They are vigorously active in reproducing the "ordering of [a] field of action" by coming to identify its standards of performance as "*the consummation of their productive powers*."[18] At the University of Minnesota (and—we wager—elsewhere), "innovation is overtime" is one such standard.

Our question is: What made us susceptible to an ethos of productivity that we took to demand not mere efficiency but an *inspired* commitment to work of all kinds—service, teaching, research—that we could not put down until we had made our mark (until the book was published, the program established, the student graduated)? How exactly were we persuaded to conceive the University of Minnesota as an incubator of progressive political change, when universities generally have been so convincingly theorized as apparatuses of social reproduction?[19] (Are we dupes?) In short, by what practices, procedures, and principles did our academic lives call us to understand ourselves not simply as scholars and teachers but as *agents of political and social change who work against the university from within* in order to produce it?

Question: How do we come to imbue our academic positions with political meaning in the first place?
Answer: Professionalism.
The "politically committed" academic is a professional just like any other. Thinking about this brought us back a second time to the Pro-

gressive Era ideal of the university as model public. That ideal set up the professions (the three most notable being lawyer, doctor, and teacher or professor) to serve as a brake on the rapid social and economic changes wrought by industrialization. To be a professional, then, meant not only to be a master of a specialized field of knowledge but to regard oneself as "incommensurable," which is to say valuable in ways that cannot be sold for something so crude as an hourly wage.[20] The professional is a specialist who—as distinct from both a wage worker and a businessman— "seeks to define his service as exclusively determined by public need, and hence, as predominantly a *use-value,* not an exchange-value."[21]

Clearly "innovation is overtime" draws on the legacy of professionalism, specifically from the notion of incommensurability. How better to explain the peculiar appeal of the "pitch" that we so often heard as part of a service request: that there are tasks that we simply have to take on because only we can do them (if we care that they be done well). From incommensurability also derives the belief that our workplace, the university's "public" sector, eschews market logics and that our labor escapes market imperatives. We are willing to do what "needs doing" rather than to stop at what we are "paid for."

All this means that for the salaried professional, there is no equivalent of working "to rule," that is, to the letter of the job description and to the stroke of the minute hand. This also means that, strictly speaking, a professional cannot work overtime. Why, then, does "overtime" figure so prominently in our thinking? We wondered whether even though, as salaried professionals, we do not literally *work* overtime, we *identify* with overtime labor as the sign of our independence from the coercions of the market. Overtime is at once impossible for us because we are salaried and do not quantify our hours, and defining of who we are because it marks us as unique, indispensable, and free from the market (free to work as long as it takes).

There is a complex narcissism at work in the life of *any* tenure track faculty member that is compounded for us innovators. We identify doubly with overtime: once as specialists and then once again as heroes who defy professional convention. The two of us have gone out of our way to flaunt traditionalist hierarchal models of academic professionalism—by the way we dress (often jeans, never suits), the way we teach (participatory—and we learn our students' names, damn it!), the way we construct our syllabi (shoot the canon), and the conferences we choose to attend (no place where you can network yourself upwards into an Ivy League job). Yet it is precisely this heroism that *mimics* professionalism: it testifies to our indispensability and inexhaustible dedication.

How were we socialized into professionalism as tenure track faculty? By two distinct but interrelated forces: the tenure clock and the department meeting.

Keeping Time/Doing Time

What we remember most vividly when we think about our first years holding tenure track positions is how hard we worked to acquire the arts of time "management." We remember calculating how many hours it should take to write a paragraph, produce a recommendation letter, read a book: let no minor activity take more than it should. A syllabus is the product of such calculations ("How many days should I give to Marx? To Frederick Jackson Turner?") We could call this academic Taylorization—the articulation of time to task to maximize productivity.[22]

A tenure track job at a top research university is a professional gift. We found ourselves endowed with travel money to present papers, we taught graduate students, we invited speakers, and we devised conferences. The gift, however, came with a tax. We found ourselves performing a range of tasks that in an actual corporation (as opposed to a privatizing university) would be delegated to others. We were not just professors but agents (literary *and* travel), grant writers, accountants, and even fund-raisers. To manage such a menagerie of obligations, the most ambitious of us developed "to-do" lists that were as incongruous as Borges's imagined Chinese Encyclopedia:

1. publish bk; 2. write paper assgt for POL 1001; 3. convene overworked colleagues to spearhead cutting-edge interdisciplinary program; 4. buy plane tix for conf; 5a. read diss chapt; 5b. find thesis of diss chapt and tell student what it is; 6. estab nat'l reputation.

List-making and other such time management strategies follow from Einstein's revolutionary claim: light is a constant but time is not. Time varies in relation to speed. To us this meant that the more finely calibrated, the more precisely accounted for, the more labor-intensive time could become. The trouble is that Einstein was only half-right. It was revolutionary to hold that time is not a constant. But this is precisely why, as Norbert Elias points out, it makes little sense to speak of time, as Einstein did, as being able "under certain circumstances [to] contract or expand."[23] Nor does it make sense to imagine—as we did—that time could be more or less "full," more or less productive, by virtue of how well we kept track of it—as if by paying attention to time, we could effect an infinite acceleration of labor.

What does this mean, exactly, paying attention *to time*? Is time a force or a being or an event that can exert a claim on our attention? Elias calls such "linguistic habits" a "word-fetishism" that "constantly reinforce the myth of time as something that in some sense exists and as such can be determined or measured even if it cannot be perceived by the senses."[24] Elias identifies in time the paradox that is typical of all fetishization. Time calls for such compulsive strategies only because human societies have invented an "increasingly close and regular mesh of . . . timing devices" so as to standardize and calibrate it with neurotic precision.[25] Societies constitute time not only through clocks and longitude but also narrative history, the thirty-five-hour work week, the curriculum vita, and the ideas of progress and accomplishment that come along with them. The paradox is that the more human-made time becomes, the more it confronts us as a force out of our hands.

Unlike comparable professionals who have a ready measure of hourly worth (the lawyer who is subject to "billable" hours, or the doctor whom managed care subjects to a fee schedule), salaried academics learn to figure time through the "tenure clock." The question is how does the tenure clock, which "strikes" roughly every seven years, become something to reckon with every day? What does it mean to be "on" the tenure clock?

At the University of Minnesota, assistant professors are called "probationary faculty." Each year on probation we are subjected to an annual spectacle of productivity termed "probationary review" (this is like coming up before the parole board except that you hope for the opposite outcome: *more* years at the institution, not less). Probationary review is governed by the principles of the "7.12 Statement," a departmental document that defines the relative weights attached to research, teaching, and service. Although it is the responsibility of each department at the university to craft its own 7.12 Statement, the gist is always the same: publication counts the most; service counts practically not at all; you must teach, but it will never get you tenure—and there is no gauge for innovation.[26]

How not? Faculty make promotion, merit, and tenure decisions by proxy. Not to say colleagues do not read one another's work, but no one is a specialist in everything, and everyone wants to be fair. Disciplines turn out to supply relatively straightforward measures of significance: Did it come out in a top-tier journal or press? Was it refereed (or invited by a friend . . .)? How were the reviews, especially those in top-tier journals? And last but not least: How much is there? How many books? How many articles? How many pages? How many footnotes? How many hits in the Social Science Citation Index?

Our point? Evaluation creates a conservative bias. Score the credential with the *American Historical Review*, the *American Political Science Review*, or whatever counts the most in the mainstream. And then do the work you really love—regardless whether it is publishable or merely public. The result? We come to believe that *Innovation Is Overtime.*

How did we live by the 7.12 Statement? Not just with guilt and anxiety ("Can I take time for coffee?" "Why am I putting so many comments on this paper?"). Or by living perpetually on the run. But also by kvetching about our workloads.

We thought we were blowing off steam (and we were), but we were also carrying the cardinal principle of probationary review into our everyday lives. We were ventriloquists for the 7.12, so accustomed to putting our work on display that even a simple question was likely to provoke the most tiresome list ("Coffee? No way. Can't stop. Before I sleep tonight, I have to grade ten papers, then finish copy edits for that article that just got accepted, then do a conference call with my coauthor . . ."). The rubrics governing scholarly productivity being at once amorphous and grandiose ("publish path-breaking book" or "become nationally visible"), we academics have a hard time knowing when we have put in a good day's work. Broadcasting to others how much we had done (or had yet to do) and how little sleep we allowed ourselves was not the call to solidarity that we imagined it to be: it helped to define for ourselves and others just what counted as enough (When can I stop? Not before you do).

We each have an archive from this period: our appointment books from day one. Well, not quite from day one because Jeani did not *have* an appointment book at first (remember, she thought a job would give her a break from the frantically busy pace of finishing the dissertation). Jeani started out at the University of Minnesota thinking she would keep her appointments in her head, a practice that had always served her well. Two weeks into her career teaching at the university and several missed appointments later, she realized that documentation would be important. She turned to a "month-at-a-glance" format, the paperback provided by the bookstore, free of charge. By the end of that first quarter, Jeani had broken time into still smaller units. She adopted the week-at-a-glance spiral-bound calendar, laminated to survive wear and tear, and small enough to carry with her. By our third year at Minnesota, Jeani's calendar was no longer portable. She reverted to the monthly format, but it was no longer conveniently purse-sized. It had colonized most of her desktop. And no wonder. From the very beginning, her service responsibilities spanned three departments—most notably involving a search committee for a joint position in American Studies and American Indian Studies—and the organizing committee for the history department's international conference on "Matrilineality and Patrilineality in Historical and Comparative Perspective." Jeani's calendar was shaping up to be that of an associate professor even though she was barely an assistant professor (remember: she was hired ABD).

Over time, as Jeani's date books got bigger, Lisa's actually got smaller, as if in denial of the accelerating pace of our lives. Hilarious in its own way was her practice of "whiting out" changes in order to accommodate her appointments in the midget labor minder. She kept track of meetings in the week-at-a-glance, but she charted writing at home, on the Frank Lloyd Wright wall calendar that was an annual Christmas gift from her mom—an aesthetic and symbolic tie to her Chicago roots. The year Lisa finished her first book, 1993, bears a mark for every morning she wrote for three hours: there is a mark on every day from January to mid-April. For years after that period, she had so internalized the practice that she no longer needed to make the marks; she just wrote, minimum three hours a day, every day, including weekends. So the wall calendar tracked the work that really counted, the *productive* labor that resulted in publication in top-ranked venues.

The date books are one record of those early years. Our physiology was another. Throughout that period, we regarded the following conditions as normal. *Jeani:* Chronic sinus infections that resist the antibiotics she is always on, and yet persistent heavy smoking—even after the university instituted an indoor no-smoking policy. There is a persistent knot in her upper back . . . she is constantly reaching back, grabbing, and massaging the pressure point . . . twitching, wriggling, and self-chiropracting . . . working out the tension on the back of a chair. *Lisa:* Cannot turn her head to the left without the rest of her body swiveling with it. Permanently listing rightward (which decidedly does *not* match her political proclivities). We incorporate these anatomical irregularities into our daily routine. Lisa's swiveling. Jeani's smoking and twitching. And neither one of us thinks anything of it.

These are stress-related symptoms to be sure: What do they mean? Perhaps this was how our bodies acted out the tension of the compromises we repeatedly imposed on ourselves to negotiate the gap between how we were instructed to allocate our time by the 7.12 Statement (which would determine whether or not we would keep our jobs), and what we felt drawn to do for colleagues, for students, and with friends. Living with a disjuncture between doing what counted and responding to those who counted on us made self-questioning a daily ritual.[27] Faculty members "on probation" become suspect to themselves.

Probationary Suspects/Departmental Citizens

Life on tenure track would have been unbearable if we had defined ourselves exclusively in terms of the 7.12 Statement. Fortunately, there was a second face to our professional identities, one to which we were drawn precisely because it provided relief from the abject position of "probationary suspect." This was "departmental citizenship." Each of our departments appealed to us to conceive of ourselves as participants in a "democratic" experiment—yet they each defined that ideal quite differently.

We discovered this at Café Noir on October 13, 1992—a full eighteen months after we had first met. How could it have taken us eighteen months to make it to coffee? To appreciate what frustrates academic friendships on the Twin Cities campus, you have to know something about the Social Sciences Building, the monstrosity that houses both of our departments.

Social Sciences is a fourteen-story red brick tower, a monument to late 1960s institutional architecture (an oxymoron to be sure). It is a structure defined—quite literally—by its elevators and bathrooms. The plumbing and the elevator shaft run up the very center of the narrow tower; faculty and departmental offices wrap around them. Imagine concentric squares: physical plant at the core; offices on the outer ring; a strip of hallway runs between them. And such a hallway! The corridor that separates the physical plant from the offices is so narrow that two people cannot walk down it side by side. In fact, it is barely wide enough for two people to stand facing each other—most conversations occur with one of the parties standing in their office doorway. A building more inimical to public space could not possibly be designed, which explains the unnatural importance of its elevators.

The elevators of the Social Sciences Building are legendary. Much is said there (and overheard) because of that peculiar illusion of privacy that comes in some kinds of anonymous public enclosures. Elevator friendships are sustained on the strength of the one to three minute exchanges you have every semester with the people who happen to share your teaching schedule, your smoking schedule, and/or your caffeine regimen. After countless occasions of running into each other on our vertical commute, spending five floors in a chat frenzy, and mouthing "let's get together!" as the doors closed, we had finally made a date for coffee. Subsequent dates would involve stronger libations.

*CAFÉ NOIR 1001: Introduction to (Departmental) Political Cultures
History as Participatory Democracy: "Service Is Socialization"*

Lisa to Jeani, about what she remembers: I listened in shock as you recounted the tremendous amount of responsibility that you had been shouldering. You were always in meetings. To begin with, you were hired as an American Indian historian. Take all three words seriously—and separately. You served on the Graduate Studies Committee in American studies, served on a language search committee for American Indian studies, and participated in the College of Liberal Arts Assembly.

And you performed these extradepartmental labors not *instead* of but in addition to your service responsibilities for the history department, which were considerable because of the department's remarkable interpretation of democracy. Your department was a participatory democracy. It coupled the ethos of active citizenship—where citizens learn by doing and are empowered by it—with a literal notion of representation that called for the composition of its elected committees (there were three of these) to *resemble* the membership of the department faculty by rank. Taken together, these produced a lethal brew: a free pass on service for the most established members of your department subsidized by a service overload among associate and (especially) assistant faculty.

How so? Let's do the math. Forty-six faculty in all. Three elected committees with slots for perhaps twenty members. This means that more than half the faculty will escape election altogether. What is the likelihood that untenured professors will be among them? Enumerate the faculty. Two assistant professors. Half-a-dozen associates. Nearly forty fulls. (Remember: we were the "bust" generation.) Factor in descriptive representation together with the department's motto: "Service Is Socialization." Untenured faculty members were virtually guaranteed election to one of the committees, and quite possibly more than one. Who would escape unburdened by elected service? Mostly full professors. Why? Not only were they presumed to be socialized already (actually, the savvy ones had made themselves ineligible through ineptitude), but the numbers were on their side.

How did you fare under this system? In your second year, the department voted you onto two out of the three elected committees—Promotion, Merit, and Tenure, plus Academic Freedom and Responsibility—and appointed you to screen graduate applications in U.S. history (there were about one hundred that year). This would have been a load for any second-year faculty member. But for Jeani, there was a special bonus: between that year and the next, your colleagues elected you to serve on every committee that would be charged to resolve a serious grievance concerning the *only other* assistant professor in your department.

What choice did they have? Departmental norms (and even departmental ballots) invited them to ensure that the untenured ranks were represented on these committees, and given the rarity of hiring at the time, that had to be Jeani (because no department would expect a faculty member to prosecute a grievance against him or herself). To be fair, the chair did recognize the position she was in and offered her the opportunity to resign. She felt no pressure to continue, but decide to continue she foolishly did. What was she thinking? ("What would my colleagues really think if I got myself out of the work?") Jeani was already fully socialized into the departmental ethos of service democracy. She was damned if she would not do her part.

Turns out, she was damned because she did. Her time was consumed by meetings. She helped to solicit and review the evidence, helped articulate the principles for this pretty much unprecedented decision, helped negotiate a solution that they hoped would preserve this colleague's dignity. And in the end she found herself disenfranchised.

How? This is where the department reveals its radical roots. Literally. The Department of History at Minnesota is populated by more than a few bona fide 1960s radicals who have no patience with guilds. And they are truly to be applauded for this. In that spirit of defiance, they have instituted a departmental-level version of a sunshine law: Assistant and associate faculty participate in *both* probationary and merit review of all of their colleagues, including those at and above their rank. The problem is that this departmental ethos conflicts with college rules, which dictate that faculty can vote only on promotion decisions that involve colleagues below them in rank. Ever defiant in the face of authority, the department devised a balloting rule to get around this. Personnel votes, especially promotion decisions, are taken by secret ballot but *they must be identified by rank to ensure that assistant (and sometimes associate) professor votes are not reported to the college.*

It was by such complex maneuverings that Jeani came to identify with her department as one who resists authority, to imagine herself empowered as part of a community of tenured radicals—even before she had tenure. Yet she was, at the same time, excruciatingly visible by her lack of power, as the grievance vote demonstrated: with only two untenured professors in the cohort, there could be no secrecy for the lone assistant professor who was eligible to vote on the grievances against the only other one.

Did Jeani's colleagues really believe they could share power with her by entrusting her with the responsibilities of a peer, as if by *treating* her as a peer, they could empower her as an equal? She was a peer but structurally she was not an equal, and no amount of collegial treatment would enable her to cross that divide. It would, however, persuade her to identify herself as one of them. By paying her the compliment of their trust—and this was truly a compliment—Jeani's colleagues offered her "time off" the suspect position of being "on probation," but they did so at the cost of time-consuming and traumatic labor that no one at her rank should have shouldered. The department's belief in the power of participation seemed to blind them to the power of structure.

Political Science: Democratic Feudalism, "Untenured Faculty Should Be Seen (at Every Meeting) but Not Heard (Ever!)"

Jeani to Lisa about what she remembers: Next to what I had been through, there is a way that your life could have seemed serene and tame. The political science department made few service demands on untenured faculty. True to the liberal pluralism that defines the mainstream of the discipline, your department was no utopian community but an aggregate of self-interested rational individuals who learned that they could shirk "face time" so long as they taught well and delivered the goods on publication.

What were the goods? You might have learned by serving on the Promotion, Merit, and Tenure (PMT) committee—your department's sole elected committee—on which it was thought to be a good idea that each assistant professor serve a term. In a difference that speaks volumes about how variously "democracy" can be construed, your department had no rule to ensure representation across ranks. Untenured faculty found themselves faced with being shut out of power. They reacted as good pluralists will, by forming an interest group. They quietly organized themselves as a voting bloc to ensure that each untenured faculty member would get a turn on PMT, in order of seniority.

Could these departmental cultures have been more different? History was blind to structure in its utopian desire to abolish rank; political science reified rank to a degree that was almost laughable. As for sunshine laws, political science operated under the wartime principle of information blackout. Case in point: "The Departmental Norms Memo."

This text was occasioned by an unexpected outcome on a tenure vote that (as such votes will) generated unusually widespread gossiping across rank. This gossiping, though consistent with a pluralist commitment to fair competition among organized interests, offended a competing set of republican departmental sensibilities regarding the sanctity of deliberation for determining the common good. Hence, the norms memo. Personally typewritten by the chair, it reaffirmed what it deemed to be the department's central principle: Thou Shalt Not Pass Information Across Ranks. And it communicated this principle in the form of a memorandum.

There is something undeniably self-defeating about publishing norms—even more so through a medium so mundane as an office memo. But there it was:

TO: Faculty; RE: Departmental Norms.

A workaday document posing as sacred doctrine. No kidding. It was all in the typography. It had five paragraphs. The first one—flush left—told a state of nature story. There had occurred a breakdown of order: the "leaking" or (the tone escalated) "hemorraging" [sic] of confidential information across ranks. This breakdown occasioned the need for a reaffirmation of Departmental Norms.

The next two paragraphs were indented, as in the manner of a block quote drawn from a published text. (A treatise perhaps: "On the Departmental Social Contract.")[28] They spelled out the consequences of leaking:

it greatly complicates the often sensitive task of communicating and implementing departmental decisions in a coherent way. . . . "leaking" also has a chilling effect on faculty discussion . . . confidentiality is a necessary condition for honest expressions of differences.

The final two paragraphs, flush left again, delivered the moral: "leaking" was a threat to the political science department's "unusually open" practices of collective decision making. Absent a renewed commitment to confidentiality, the memo regretted that the department might have to move toward a more "closed system."

Fancy that. A memo chastising "leaking" in the name of openness—there is a speech act that undoes itself in the saying (a performative contradiction if there ever was one). What a remarkable contrast to the ideal of transparency that governs the history department's discussions.

Two departments. Two vastly different departmental cultures. Yet these departments share a discourse of "citizenship" that—even if practiced quite differently—communicates a similar message: A department is not a business. It is an ethical community. Its ethic: *We are self-governing*. This ideal persuades us to exalt meetings—a prodigious waste if one calculated their worth as a ratio of words spoken to problems solved—as a form of popular sovereignty.

The department meeting, the departmental committee, faculty assembly: these are cumbersome ways of making decisions, but we consent to give them our time because we believe that they distinguish the university as an institution from a for-profit corporation. We also believe that they distinguish us as academics from members of other salaried professions and, of course, from workers in the wage-labor market. The key here is that these labors are cast not as above and beyond our officially sanctioned workload but as *radical* and *within* the university structure. As academic citizens we are not just voters but creative actors. This ethos of active citizenship only intensifies once we are granted tenure—the academic equivalent of promotion from green card (i.e., resident alien) to naturalized citizen status.

"Tenure. Isn't That Where Ideas Go to Die?"

On probation, there is only one real priority, and, hence, there is no choice: You write all the time you are not teaching, in a meeting, sleeping (not very much), eating (on the run and generally pretty poorly), or running (because Lisa insists on that).[29] Working overtime is a fact of life during this period, albeit a fact socially constructed by the tenure clock, which sets strict parameters within which certain key items on the to-do list must be achieved. Faculty on the tenure clock cannot afford much time for innovation. And, so, precisely because it violates or at least compromises the terms of our probation, innovation is alluring. For Lisa especially, whose terms of appointment did not carry any expectation of allegiance to units beyond political science, serving on the admissions committee for the feminist studies minor, and serving on the editorial board of *Signs* (which both she and Jeani did), teaching a feminist studies seminar afforded the pleasure of transgression: she imagined that she was "stealing time" from political science.

As untenured faculty, we assumed that earning tenure would mean that we had paid our dues. Imagine our surprise at the following: Tenure brings service. You have to fight/For the right/To write.

So, service. There's the service that you are asked to do out of fairness because you were protected as an assistant professor (*Lisa.* Jeani wonders what that would have been like). There is also the service you are asked to do because you are known for saying "yes," having been socialized in the utopian philosophy of a service democracy (*Jeani*). There is the service you take on to pay back the people who bailed you out for tenure (*Lisa*).

Note well: The studiously inept are never tapped for departmental offices. The conscientious overworkers (who pursue their scholarship evenings and weekends when energy permits) have too much pride to do service deliberately badly. That is another way service takes hold: it finds the competent. ("Do you have to be selfish to be a productive scholar?")

Most important for the purposes of this essay is the service you want to do in service of innovation. This is what you do out of your principled commitments to the intellectual initiatives that you believe in, and in the belief that they must be run on overtime (*Lisa and Jeani*).

It is in response to some combination of all of these that, almost immediately upon returning from our post-tenure sabbaticals, we found ourselves running the show. Or running the *sideshow,* we should say.

Both of us took on hefty administrative responsibilities outside our departments for innovative programs that we believed in, Lisa in CAFS and Jeani in American Studies. Neither one of us had ever directed or chaired anything before. We were "promoted" to these responsibilities because there was really no one else who had not already done their turn and more (remember the academic demography of the "bust" generation).

As so many feminist analyses of academia have made clear, this kind of work creates a complicated relationship with the so-called tenure home. We had taken on positions of leadership that we would not *yet* have been asked to assume in our own departments. Did this raise our credibility or compromise us in the eyes of those colleagues? Our sense is that it has done neither: the evolution of our leadership skills has gone unnoticed by our departments. The social costs are difficult to quantify. What price do you pay for simply not being around so much?

Bottom Line: Think back to the model of the famously overworked academic, in Hyde Park, Chicago, circa 1990. Our lives were beginning to follow suit. That we could take it on—and pull it off—surprised even ourselves. Yet something made us uncomfortable.

To be apprenticed to a profession is to have its rhythms drummed into you. Time, which presents itself as a scarce resource, is more like a beat. It is a driving force that forms us as professionals, docile bodies who take a delicious pleasure in a day that propels us through a diverse range of activities (to which we are, of course, indispensable) and delivers us to the brink of exhaustion. We are inspired by John Mowitt (2002) to be aware of the power and pleasure it gives us to work to a beat, and to use this insight to explain the persistence of impulse to labor overtime *after* tenure. Tenure is not (as it can be misunderstood by those who would abolish it) a lifting of the obligation to work but, rather, a grant that effects a release from a "drop dead" deadline. Universities can afford to grant tenure because it is so often the case that by the time we faculty have earned it, we have become not just habituated but addicted to the probationary beat. The ethical question that we might ask each other as one tenured friend to another is (certainly) not "you have tenure, why are you still working?" but "you have tenure, why are you still *rushing*?"

Why Does Innovation Remain Overtime—Over Time?

Programs like women's studies, African American studies, and American Indian studies could not have been established without heroic overtime

162   Lisa J. Disch and Jean M. O'Brien

labors by their founders. This is a fact of historical record that it would
be disrespectful to deny. The important question is: What happens next?
What happens as these initiatives become institutionalized as bona fide
departments, generating undergraduate tuition dollars, sometimes establishing PhD programs, and initiating professional journals and conferences of their own? One common story is that at the point where innovation takes hold, such programs begin to go begging for labor. Some
have blamed this crisis on institutionalization itself, which is said to rob
these programs of the urgency that made people willing to work overtime to get them going.[30] Whether true or not, this explanation strikes
us as somewhat beside the point.

If these programs are institutionalized, why should overtime labor
continue to sustain them? Should it not strike us as out of joint when innovation remains overtime—over time?

It is important not to forget that innovative initiatives produce conventional assets. They generate tuition revenues, help recruit talented
faculty, enhance the academic reputation of the university, and, not
least, produce cultural capital for the university as a twenty-first-century
model public.

Students and faculty of color (and to a lesser extent, white women
faculty members) are selling points at public universities—especially
midwestern ones. At Minnesota they become poster children; their images feature prominently in recruitment brochures and on the front
covers of alumni publications, albeit with a frequency that is well out of
proportion to their numbers on campus. The point is that as innovative programs become institutionalized, they begin to count in terms
that even a 7.12 statement, university accountant, or development of-
ficer can recognize. Why is it, then, that they still cost us—faculty and
staff—extra?

We have tried to account for this phenomenon in light of the drive
for competitiveness. This transformation has meant that administrators
do not cut nonmarketable innovations but rather attempt to external-
ize their costs by cleaving the university into "public" and "corporate"
sectors. We observe that public sector programs tend to be precariously
institutionalized.

The precariousness is due, first, to their size. Ethnic studies, women's
studies, and other such programs tend to have lower undergraduate enrollments, smaller faculty, smaller alumni pools, and fewer staff members. But they have the same number of departmental offices as their

larger counterparts. This means more service work but fewer faculty members and staff to share it. Thus, even as they institutionalize, these programs do not generate less work but, rather, more, because institutionalizing means taking on more tasks. When such departments petition the administration for more funds to take the pressure off overtime, deans make the resources contingent on assuming still more tasks.

Lacking tuition-based and donation-driven sources of funding, precariously institutionalized programs tend to be inordinately dependent on deans and provosts for resources. This means that they are always at risk for budget cuts in an economic downturn. They are not usually at risk of closure, however, because few deans would risk the symbolic politics of seeming to come out "against" women's studies or ethnic studies. Rather than cut them outright, administrators count on these programs to persist *below cost.* And they can make this a reality by imposing high workloads on their faculty and staff, principally by speeding up the service labor through short staffing. [31]

We maintain that precariously institutionalized programs survive because they are subsidized by the exertions of faculty and staff who take satisfaction from working for them because they are persuaded that such programs provide an ethical counterweight to and political critique of neoliberal globalization. This makes them innovative and justifies the overtime. Are we who take pleasure in such labors deceived, manipulated, hoodwinked? No. This is empowerment, albeit within the "particular yet restricted mode of production" of academic labor under global capitalism.[32] These are often risky and exciting ventures that can create networks of faculty and students who speak out against local and global transformations that present themselves as inevitable.[33] We are not trying to discount or debunk them.

But we are trying to prompt each other to think about what we are doing when we permit these labors to be defined as "overtime" in perpetuity. It strikes us that in the name of modeling resistance to the intrusion of instrumental rationalities into the "market enclave" of the university, we have actually been cooperating with the way that global capital has taken hold at the University of Minnesota. We affirm by our actions an ideology to which we would never sign on: that private generosity can compensate for underfunding the public sector.

Does this mean we should stop? That was not the kind of ethical analysis we meant to write: send in a problem, see the answer in print. That said, we have been thinking about the call of overtime and imagining ways to interrupt the broadcast. There is the classic, "I did my turn, now you do yours." What difference would it make to wonder out loud: "I did my turn, how come your turn looks so much like mine did?" The next time we get asked to work "off the clock," we hope to behave un-professionally. We have been practicing the phrase, "let me get back to you when I figure out what I will not do instead." For regular meetings that are "conveniently" scheduled over lunch, we plan to bring loud food and eat it with gusto. For those that routinely extend past five, we imagine exit lines: "My kid will be hitchhiking from daycare." "My dog's bladder expires at six." "I haven't finished my homework." And we have taken a pledge: instead of monitoring ourselves *by* kvetching, we are going to start monitoring ourselves *for* kvetching.

It occurs to us that "Innovation Is Overtime" is an expensive motto. It is not just anyone who can manage to write off its costs. We who subsi-dize the university with our time may be no less an elite than the corpo-rate and private donors who subsidize it with money. This has changed our thinking about the famously overworked academic. It occurs to us now to call her a rate-buster.[34] Nobody reveres a rate-buster. She makes everyone work longer and earn less. The next time we see a rate-buster (and she is likely to be staring back at us from the mirror), we will try saying to ourselves: "Step away from this woman! She's out to steal your weekend."

Notes

We thank Anne Carter, Anna Clark, Kirsten Fischer, Jennifer Pierce, and Ga-briella Tsurutani for excellent feedback on multiple drafts; David Roediger and Robert Warrior, for helpful comments; Tom Roach and John Conley, for conver-sations that sparked critical rethinkings; and Steven Gerencser, for an exception-ally close and insightful reading.

1. This was Linda Zerilli, who would revitalize the political theory program at Rutgers by making it one of "the" places to do feminist theory. This meant that she, too, would be famously overworked.

2. Robert J. Menges and William H. Exum write that because of their "high visibility, women and minorities may be offered more such 'opportunities' [for teaching, advising, committee work, and community service] than are white males. In particular, they may be expected to appear when the institution's pol-icy toward women and minorities requires public affirmation or to serve on com-mittees to guarantee representation of their group" (131). This article also notes that joint appointments are quite common among such faculty and documents the same problem with meeting overload to which the calendars of Jeani's first years on the job bear witness. Robert J. Menges and William H. Exum, "Barriers

to the Progress of Women and Minority Faculty," *Journal of Higher Education* 54, 2 (March-April 1983): 123–44. See also "Advise and Resent," *Chronicle of Higher Education,* 19 December 2003.

3. For the eloquent and remarkable argument that subjects are hailed into being not only by images and slogans but also by rhythm, see John Mowitt, *Percussion: Drumming, Beating, Striking* (Durham, N.C.: Duke University Press, 2002).

4. State funding for the University of Minnesota accounted for 26 percent of the budget in fiscal year 2004, according to the University News Service. The College of Liberal Arts ends up with about 7 percent of its budget derived from state funding in the end.

5. By "the University of Minnesota," we mean university administrators, students, faculty colleagues, the "public" in light of which a land-grant university formulates its mission, corporate and foundation funders, and the state legislature—all of whom exercise some power over the conditions of academic labor through the discourse of "accountability." Bill Readings, *The University in Ruins* (Cambridge, Mass.: Harvard University Press, 1996).

6. We aim here to contribute to the path-breaking analyses by Readings as well as by Samuel Weber, *Institution and Interpretation,* expanded ed. (Stanford, Calif.: Stanford University Press, 2001) by extending their work in a direction that they solicit but do not pursue: analyzing practices of everyday life.

7. Readings, *The University in Ruins,* 40

8. Weber, *Institution and Interpretation,* 226.

9. Readings, *The University in Ruins,* 39. This is not to say that he believed the university ever lived up to that ideal. Rather, as Weber emphasizes, Readings traced a "shift in the nature of [its] subordination" (Weber, *Institution and Interpretation,* 228). The university, which once served to legitimate the idealization of the nation-state as the epitome of enlightened reason, increasingly saw public rationality give way to economic incentives, its budget slashed by neoliberal fiscal policy, and its intellectual agendas shaped by the demands of the market.

10. Over the past decade, the University of Minnesota has created an expansive new complex to house its business school, renovated its law school, inaugurated a new bioethics facility, and built a new facility for the study of plant genomics. Alongside these obviously market-driven initiatives, it has also built a new art museum (designed by Frank Gehry) and inaugurated an "Arts Quarter" with brand-new spaces for studio arts and for dance.

11. Weber, *Institution and Interpretation,* 229.

12. Ibid.

13. This is what Weber calls the "internal differentiation" of the university. The "internal differentiation" thesis counters Readings's claim that in the context of neoliberalism the university is remade *as* a corporation (Weber, *Institution and Interpretation,* 229). We think both that it is a more accurate description of what we have experienced at Minnesota, and that it discloses a more subtle and insidious process of transformation than a simple assimilation of universities to a corporate model would be.

14. Michael Hardt, "Affective Labor," *boundary* 2 26, 2 (1999): 89–100.

15. John Rachjman, *Michel Foucault: The Freedom of Philosophy* (New York: Columbia University Press), 86.

16. We are inspired in this by Michel Foucault, who presents ethical analysis as an experiment in "knowing if one can think differently than one thinks, and *perceive* differently than one sees." The goal of such an experiment would be to defy the everyday. But the insight that follows from Foucault's emphasis on thought and perception is that defying the everyday is not all that hard *provided you have a grip on it in the first place*. Getting a grip on the everyday, taking notice of what we are in the habit of thinking and of how we are accustomed to perceive—that is the real challenge. See Michel Foucault, *The Use of Pleasure*, trans. Robert Hurley (New York: Vintage, 1990), 8.

17. This fusion of liberty and industry is a fruitful way to think of Foucault's concept "docile bodies," which is all too often misread as a form of passivity or simple submission, an interpretation that reduces this term to the very liberal calculus of power (as the opposite of liberty) that Foucault is attempting to complicate. John Mowitt renders the concept perfectly in accordance with Foucault's critique of liberalism when he characterizes docile bodies as "agents who see in their submission to the minute and fully reticulated ordering of the field of action (be it labor or desire) the consummation of their productive powers." John Mowitt, *Text: The Genealogy of an Antidisciplinary Object* (Durham, N.C.: Duke University Press, 2002), 33.

18. See Mowitt , *Percussion,* 33; emphasis added.

19. See Louis Althusser, "Ideological State Apparatuses," in *Lenin and Philosophy,* trans. Ben Brewster (New York: Monthly Review Press, 1971), 127–88; Pierre Bourdieu, *Homo Academicus,* trans. Peter Collier (Stanford, Calif.: Stanford University Press, 1988); Michel Foucault, *Discipline and Punish,* trans. Alan Sheridan (New York: Vintage Press, 1979).

20. Weber, *Institution and Interpretation,* 26.

21. Ibid., 26–27.

22. Of course, we are not unusual in this. Making the best of time is the religion of the notoriously "overworked American." Juliet Schor, *The Overworked American: The Unexpected Decline of Leisure* (New York: Basic Books, 1991).

23. Norbert Elias, *Time: An Essay,* trans. Edmund Jephcott (Oxford: Basil Blackwell, 1992), 44.

24. Ibid., 43–44.

25. Ibid., 84.

26. This from the 7.12 Statement of the Department of Political Science: "All members of the Political Science Department faculty are expected to engage in research, to make periodic published contributions to scholarship, to fulfill obligations as teachers, and to share in service necessary for the successful functioning of the Department." Whereas "participation in the governance of institution and other services to the University and service to the academic unit may be taken into consideration, [they] are not in themselves bases for awarding tenure."

27. It is noteworthy that neither one of us chose to parent in our pre-tenure

years, and that we have both remained childless, because this has given both of us a break on the pressures that some of our peers have faced. According to the basic measures recommended by a researcher at the University of California at Berkeley, the University of Minnesota lacks the infrastructure—reasonable parental leave policy, on-site affordable child care, and partner hire—to provide equitable work conditions for faculty members who parent. With its six-week post-birth leave, its one-year-plus waiting list to gain access to university child care, and its case-by-case approach to partner hires, the University of Minnesota lags behind in all of these. Faculty members who parent at this university, particularly those who do so before tenure and especially those who do so as sole heads of households, pay significant costs for the inequities of this workplace. See "Motherload," *Chronicle of Higher Education*, 5 December 2003.

28. Of course, no such text exists. The memo canonizes its own words by its typography. Such (as Derrida has argued) are the effects of citation. Goes to show you, even pluralists know their poststructuralism.

29. Thank you to our colleague Roderick Ferguson for the felicitously phrased question used as the heading for this section.

30. Leora Auslander, "Do Women's + Feminist + Men's + Lesbian and Gay + Queer Studies = Gender Studies?" *differences* 9, 3 (1997): 19; Ellen Messer-Davidow, *Disciplining Feminism: From Social Activism to Academic Discourse* (Durham, N.C.: Duke University Press, 2002).

31. It is worth noting (and warrants an essay in its own right) that staff bear some of the most insidious effects of the ethic of "innovation is overtime." Staff members in innovative programs typically bear more responsibility and must gain proficiency in a broader range of tasks than do their counterparts in the same job classifications in larger, established departments. They are also more crucial to the transmission of institutional memory in these programs, which tend to have a more fluid cast of characters than do more established ones. Precariously institutionalized programs often draw their departmental officers from outside their ranks in order to spare their core faculty from having to trade off major administrative offices every other year. It falls to staff to train the newcomers. The centrality of staff to sustaining the integrity of precariously institutionalized programs makes these programs even more precarious because they can be devastated by personnel turnover. Yet, thanks to the ethic of "innovation is overtime," staff loyalty to such programs often matches or exceeds that of faculty. This is their gift to "radical" academic politics—to labor more intensely and with less security than their counterparts in conventional departments.

32. Mowitt, *Percussion*, 33.

33. Students in the MacArthur Program organized a two-month series of teach-ins after September 11 in response to the demonization of Islam and the reduction of foreign policy to national security. In fall 2003, faculty who knew each other from working in American studies, comparative literature, women's studies, and other such programs organized in support of a clerical workers' strike.

34. We owe this shift of perspective to our colleague Barbara Laslett.

6. Getting My Story Straight

Masculinity through a Feminist Lens

Peter Hennen

DEAR reader, if every story has to start at the beginning, I think we are both in trouble. I cannot say with any confidence where the story of my engagement with feminism begins. So let me begin with a concept, one that is dear to patriarchy—the concept of legacy. Legacy has traditionally meant male power being transferred from fathers to sons. In this essay I would like to offer a few, brief highlights from my experiences with feminism to talk about a different kind of legacy.

Several years ago I had a phone conversation with my then seventy-five-year-old father. Since the death of my mother in 1997 he had begun calling me for no apparent reason—something he never did while my mother was alive—just to talk. On this occasion, however, he has something to get off his chest. He told me that a couple of days earlier he had hosted a group of his card-playing buddies at his house. At one point in the evening one of his guests complained that my father had only provided root beer to drink. This complaint obviously stuck in Dad's craw, as I had already heard the anecdote secondhand from my older sister. He was apparently repeating it to anyone who cared to listen. "These guys have got to understand," he said. "I don't have a wife to go out shopping for me." As you can see, my attempts to raise my father's consciousness over the years have been largely unsuccessful. On this occasion I settled for gentle chiding, attempting a light-hearted tone. "Dad, you're a twenty-first-century man now—get with the program!" But the words rang hollow, even as they escaped my lips.

My father, a veteran of World War II who has never spoken of the war, a faithful provider for seven children who has rarely mentioned his work, my father will never feel at home in the twenty-first century. My oldest sister loves to tell a story she first heard from my mother. Before she was married, my mother held a full-time job as a telephone operator for eleven years. On the day they returned from their honeymoon, as they settled into the upper floor of the duplex that would be their first home, my father turned to my mother and announced "Honey, you'll never work another day in your life."

That was 1950. By 1961 my mother, in her spare time, had given birth to seven children. I arrived in 1959. From the beginning I was a needy child, with constant cravings for both attention and food. When I was four, I found a way to combine both of my interests with another one I could not quite name. One rainy afternoon I became fascinated by two city workers laying pipe for a new sewer line on our corner. After watching them for half an hour, I stole a box of graham crackers from the kitchen and ran down the block to introduce myself. I thought they looked hungry. They were, and thanked me with broad smiles and hearty laughs for the food. I loved being near those guys. I also loved school, once I realized it was another way to attract attention. On the first day of kindergarten I zipped through my busy box activities like a seasoned professional—zipper, snaps, clips, buttons—no problem. I couldn't wait to start reading.

Schooldaze and Genderblur

There is a peculiar connection in my life history between my first year of grade school and my first year of graduate study. In 1994, during my first year of graduate school, I encountered Barrie Thorne's work on gender socialization in elementary schools—a work that lent tremendous clarity to some of my own early experiences.[1] My reaction to Thorne's work was immediate and visceral. Reading it brought back memories both traumatic and exhilarating, most of them centered on my first experiences with gender transgression at the Catholic elementary school I began attending in 1965. By this time my parents had moved from the Milwaukee duplex to a modest bungalow in the almost exclusively white, middle-class suburb of Wauwatosa. My "nonworking" mother had by this time given birth to all seven of her children; I was the sixth.

My journey through the contested terrain of gender begins with a rather mundane physical detail. I have often wondered how my gender history might have been altered were it not for the fact that I was born with an unsightly, but otherwise harmless, birthmark on my scalp. Roughly the size of a quarter, this small, scaly red patch had a profound effect on my gender socialization. Before I had it surgically removed in 1990, this mark (dermatologically speaking, a *nevus*) sparked a host of questions. These ranged from the impertinent ("Hey, Hennen, is that your *brain* leaking out?") to the dramatic ("Is it . . . cancer?") to the exotic ("Is that where your Siamese twin was attached?"). During summer 1964, "the mark" began to demonstrate its awesome power. It compelled my otherwise conservative parents to let my hair grow out. By September I was ready to enroll in the first grade with enough hair to cover the imperfection.

It was autumn 1964. LBJ was in the White House, Congress had just passed the Gulf of Tonkin Resolution, segregation had just been "officially" abolished, and I had bangs. My parents undoubtedly sought to "unmark" me so that I would not be teased. Thus, I began my primary education as the only boy at St. Pius X Catholic Grade School who did not have a crew cut, utterly unprepared for the lesson in unintended consequences I was about to receive.

And a powerful lesson it was! It just so happened that 1964 also marked the beginning of the "British invasion," that explosion in pop music that began with the release of the Beatles' first album in January of that year, and their subsequent appearance on the *Ed Sullivan Show*. I knew very little about the Beatles' music beyond what I heard from my older sisters, but I soon learned that we shared the same hairstyle. My hair elicited an immediate, almost frenzied response from the girls. Together, these brave little Amazons in their Peter Pan collars and patent-leather shoes intrepidly demonstrated the awesome power of collective action. At recess, they locked arms in a sisterhood powerful even at that tender age and boldly went where good Wauwatosa Catholic girls had never gone before—to the boys' side of the playground! Worse, as they marched in lockstep together, it became obvious that *I* had somehow inspired their campaign. As they made their relentless advance, the little tartan plaid army sang:

> We hate you, Peter,
> Oh yes we do!
> We hate you, Peter, we do!
> Oh Peter, we hate you!

To my great relief, the boys in my class were understanding, some even supportive. While they were clearly uncomfortable with the visiting troops, they wondered aloud at my ability to inspire so much disgust in the girls. "Hey, Hennen, way to go!" But my fate was sealed, my life forever changed, and the first rip in the fabric of my gendered universe appeared on that unforgettable day when the invading Sirens sang a different song:

> We love you, Peter,
> Oh yes we do!
> We love you, Peter, we do!
> Oh Peter, we love you!

A pall hung over the boys' side of the playground. Things deteriorated quickly when some of the girls broke rank, started to chase me, and dragged me back to the girls' side of the playground. Held hostage near the St. Vincent de Paul box, I doubted I would ever recover. I knew only that it would take me a long, long time to get back to the boys' side of the playground. Perhaps I would never make it back. Part of me was traumatized, part of me intrigued . . .

Fast forward three years. I am in the fourth grade, and Laura Zeganhauer is gasping in disgust. For some unknown reason she has fished a crumpled piece of paper out of the wastebasket at the back of our classroom. Her countenance pale, she immediately brings the offensive document to the attention of our teacher. Sr. Mary Celeste is a woman of angular proportions who seems to be all elbows, with a grave demeanor that does nothing to endear her to any of us (with the possible exception of Laura Zeganhauer). Although the rendering is crude, the paper clearly features an obscene drawing of Sr. Mary Celeste riding a bicycle, naked but for her black veil and wimple. At the end of the day, Sr. Mary Celeste dismisses the girls and keeps all of the boys after class, waiting patiently for the young pornographer among us to confess his crime. I remember thinking, "How does she know it wasn't a girl?" Beginning with the first-grade kidnapping episode, I had by this time established a rather unconventional gender profile. Girls always seemed to relate to me with less of the artifice that informed their interactions with the other boys. Because of this, I knew that there were at least a half-dozen girls in our class who were perfectly capable of producing this kind of delightful vulgarity. As we sat there, held captive by Sr. Mary Celeste's malignant gaze, I kept wondering, "How does she *know* it was a boy?" We are finally let go after another boy, Billy Gummerman, threatened to take back the clock radio that the class had given Sr. Mary Celeste for Christmas.

Another year passes. In Mrs. Parlemutter's fifth-grade art class we are making silhouettes of ourselves. If I were to run into her today, I would probably describe Mrs. Parlemutter as "dykey." By 1968 standards she would probably be considered "mannish." She is a large-framed woman who always wears her hair in a sort of wilted, half-hearted bouffant. She has a low gravelly voice, cat-eye glasses, and a powerful set of lungs. We take turns sitting very still in front of a photographer's lamp that casts a shadow on the large piece of black paper on the wall beside us. As we sit, Mrs. Parlemutter carefully traces our profile on the black paper. After she finishes each tracing, we cut out our silhouettes and paste them onto white paper. We put our names on the back of the finished product and lay them on the table to let the paste dry. Afterwards, we proceed to Mr. Tyson's room for geography class.

I realize now that perhaps it was because Mrs. Parlemutter herself was not conventionally feminine (and perhaps because she realized that there was a price to be paid for flouting convention) that she embarked on a relentless campaign of gender surveillance among her young charges. At the time she simply intimidated me, and on this particular occasion, tried to humiliate me. Back in geography class Mr. Tyson is at the blackboard. He has barely finished a rudimentary outline of our home state of Wisconsin when Mrs. Parlemutter enters the room. She is carrying my silhouette. She shows it to Mr. Tyson and whispers something in his ear. He seems not to understand. More whispering, and then Mrs. Parlemutter displays her legendary lung capacity as she wrests control of the class from the bewildered Mr. Tyson. "All right class, I thought it might be fun to play a little guessing game!" she bellows. I feel the urge to run but remain frozen at my desk. I realize that because of my long hair, the silhouette Mrs. Parlemutter is about to reveal to the class makes me look like a girl. Mrs. Parlemutter holds up the little black-and-white oddity for my classmates to examine. She gleefully collects several enthusiastic guesses. "I know! . . . Is it Jeannie Rodemeyer?" "Kelly Lopinski?" "Wait a minute . . . is it Elise Figeuroa?" Nope, na-uh, nope.

Eventually, a consensus emerges. It *has* to be Patty Corbinette, a high-spirited but somewhat plain-looking girl who is well liked despite what everyone still remembers about an unfortunate first-grade pants-wetting episode. Her sadistic little survey completed, Mrs. Parlemutter grins a menacing grin. "Patty Corbinette, eh?" She pauses for effect, then begins chuckling sardonically like a wizened old sailor. Her husky cigarette voice eventually rolls into a full-bodied guffaw as she exclaims, "You're wrong—it's *Hennen!*"

The moment that followed exists outside of time for me. There was a collective gasp, then laughter. Curiously, I felt alienated but not particularly ashamed. I distinctly remember thinking—So? So what? What difference does it make if you think I look like Patty Corbinette on some crappy silhouette? Why is *that* important? Why is *that* so funny? I realized I was more curious than angry.

I Pledge Allegiance to the Fags

Two more years pass—it is 1970. I am eleven years old, sitting in the kitchen, languidly munching Fig Newtons and watching the local news on a small black-and-white television that my father bought for my mother so she could watch TV—while she was "not working" in the kitchen. Right now she is "not working" on an enormous pile of laundry. The news report features a local activist enthusiastically calling for something called "gay liberation." "Mom," I ask idly as I reach for another Fig Newton, "What's gay liberation?" A palpable sense of panic settles on the room. I momentarily lose interest in both the Fig Newton and the television as I watch my mother puff nervously on her cigarette. Eventually she parks it in the ashtray and pretends to be thoroughly absorbed in folding a dish towel: "That's just . . . That's just something for people who think you should be able to do anything you want!"

"Hmmm," I think to myself, "Anything you want . . . I like the sound of that." As I stuff the last Fig Newton into my mouth, I swear a lifelong allegiance to the cause of gay liberation. Over the ensuing years the childish appeal of that initial promise rang hollow. Being gay, as it turned out, did not really mean being able to do anything you wanted. But if my political convictions in those early years were weak, the flesh proved remarkably willing. In any event, this early acquaintance with gay liberation allowed me to name something I was just beginning to feel. This, coupled with my "gender troubles" at school, meant that my socialization into masculinity proceeded problematically. I had an acute awareness of what I would later come to know from Pierre Bourdieu's work as the "rules of the game," even as I was learning them, as I was struggling to consign them to "taken-for-granted" status. Yes, gender was a game, a serious game with *a lot* of rules, but this was an insight apparently not shared by any of the other boys my age. At least it was an insight they were not willing to share with me. Perhaps that was another rule? As I look back on these years, I imagine myself glossing over what must have been a very painful and alienating time by invoking an image of All-American boyhood. I imagine myself like Superman with X-ray vision. Unlike the other boys, I can actually *see* gender.

Getting Personal, Getting Political

It is summer 1977, and I have just walked into my first gay bar. My well-rehearsed entrance is made at a bar called The Red Baron, a disco dance bar in downtown Milwaukee not far from the lakefront. I am eighteen years old, frightened beyond imagining, but determined to make an impression. I tell myself this is all about sex. I am not interested in having a *relationship* with a man. I sidle up to the bar just as I imagine a regular patron would. I pull out a ten dollar bill and order a Smith and Kearns. The harried bartender looks annoyed. "A what now?" I feign impatience as I carefully explain to the bartender how to make my drink. The guy next to me strikes up a conversation with me. I exhale.

I eventually relaxed into the Milwaukee bar scene but never enough to truly enjoy the famed sexual carnival that so many gay writers have touted as *the* defining characteristic of those last heady years between Stonewall and the advent of the AIDS pandemic. Oh, I had my adventures, but nothing like some I have heard and read about. That summer I simply wanted to see and experience as much as I could before beginning college on a scholarship from a small liberal arts college in Iowa. In 1977 I knew that there were no gay men in Iowa. In 1978 I found out I was wrong.

January 1982. I am in the 7-Eleven a block from campus on First Avenue in Cedar Rapids, Iowa, with my friend Lauren. Lauren has an acid wit, a wicked sense of irony, and plans on graduating summa cum laude. She wears a cape and speaks with a British accent, even though she is from a small town in Iowa. Most people think she is weird. I think she is wonderful. Just now she is taken aback by something she has pulled off the magazine rack. "Have you seen this?" she asks me. Her usual sardonic tone has lost its playful edge. Without another word she hands me the current issue of *Rolling Stone*. The cover includes a teaser about a mysterious new disease that's killing gay men in San Francisco and New York, an illness that promises "to make herpes look like a cold sore." I have just recently signed on for an off-campus study opportunity. In two weeks I will leave for a semester of fine arts in New York. In addition to interning at an off-Broadway theater and sampling some of the best of the city's visual and performing arts, the spring of 1982 is about to yield a powerful lesson in ambiguity. I am about to leave the Midwest for the first time in my life and fly to a mysterious territory somewhere between desire and fear.

At this point, no one in New York seems to understand why so many gay men are getting sick. Responding to a vague sense of dread, the men I am meeting seem to be redoubling their efforts to have a good time. No one is talking about "it," but "it" is on everyone's mind. I worry, but not a lot. I am too busy attending to my expanding ego. I have discovered Uncle Charlie's, a midtown gay bar not far from my hotel. Unlike the Milwaukee and Iowa gay circuits, there seem to be no "regulars" here. The crowd is different every night. I find myself flourishing amid the anonymity the scene provides. My experimentation is mostly social—I am surprised to find that I am actually *less* intimidated by the crowd here, less shy, less insecure than I was in Milwaukee or Cedar Rapids. I am feeling unexpectedly strong. One particular night stands in my memory as emblematic of the overall atmosphere in New York that spring. On this night my ego project has advanced to the point where I am ready to attempt a one-night stand, New York–style. I submit to the aggressive advances of a brusque young stud, who surprises me by telling me he is a flight attendant. After some terse negotiations and a short walk back to his apartment, I find myself standing in his bedroom. But not for long. He is a take-charge kind of guy, all business. He instructs me with the same clipped efficiency that I imagine he must use when he is explaining preflight safety procedures. With a speed that surprises even me, I am beneath him. He is a prodigious but mechanical lover; unceremonious with the initial entry, he quickly establishes a reliable but uninspiring rhythm. And to my surprise, he is chatty. The heavy breathing does not prevent his regaling me with a disturbing story from a recent flight.

"We lost 15,000 feet in something like forty-five seconds. I mean at one point it was like the nose of the plane was pointing straight down. I locked myself in the bathroom. I told my friend that if I was going to die, I wanted a private room. All the passengers were screaming: there was nothing we could do. I've never been so scared in my life. We all thought we were going to die." He came, withdrew, and announced that he had to walk the dog. Could I find my way out? It was on that night that I began to think seriously about the complicated connections between death and desire, intimacy and masculinity, and, much later, how all of these elements figured into the erotic logic of penetration.

These kinds of ruminations developed in ways that I considered trivial at the time, but that I later realized were central to the feminist project of theorizing from lived experience. I noticed, for example, when in the mid-1980s it became fashionable once again to invest in an exclusive sexual identity (i.e., as a submissive "bottom" or a dominating "top"). During the late 1970s and early 1980s it seemed positively retrograde to identify one's self as a bottom or top; versatility and the freedom from roles were understood by many as a fundamental part of what gay liberation was about. But slowly I began to notice an increasing insistence that one must *choose* between the active and passive roles. This raised questions about identity construction and the powerful role that sexuality played in the process, and by extension raised questions about the centrality of anal intercourse in most gay men's erotic universe. It seemed to me as well that during the 1980s I was witnessing a slow but unmistakable reinvestment in traditional masculinity (or hypermasculinity), less playfulness, and more stigmatization of the effeminate gay man. Later, in the early 1990s and before the emergence of protease inhibitors, it seemed clear to me that despite the mounting death toll from AIDS and all the attendant horrors, the return to "unsafe" sex practices stood as a testament to the power of gender in complex ways. I became fascinated by the links between risk, masculinity, and *eros*, by the enduring and powerful appeal of submission, specifically submission to the phallus. What was going on? It seemed clear to me that whatever the trend was, gender was heavily implicated, and that gender clearly played a part in the experience of physical sensation, of pleasure in sex. Of course, at this point I had no way to think clearly about any of this. I lacked a language. Eventually, I found that feminism's strategy of linking the personal to the political could be extended even to the most intimate aspects of my lived experience.

Crash Course—Getting in Touch with My Academic Side

It is 1987. After college and a brief move to Colorado, I end up working for the Twin Cities office of a major Wall Street brokerage firm. I stay for seven years and eventually work as an equities trader in their institutional sales department. I work with two highly paid sales associates, the senior member of the team having enjoyed a brief career as a professional football player in his younger days. From my first day working with this man, it becomes clear to me that power and privilege are a taken-for-granted part of his existence. It is also clear that he is completely bewildered by his junior sales associate. She is an ambitious young woman, smart and capable, who refuses to demonstrate sufficient deference. She does not last long. I have recast this unpleasant period of my life as an extended participant observation, a kind of prerequisite training ground for my return to the academy and my work as an ethnographer. By the age of thirty-five, financial security is within reach, and my future with the company seems secure. I am also miserable. In 1994 I apply and am accepted by University of Minnesota Graduate School with a fellowship. I leave the house of money and power to pursue a doctorate in sociology.

My first significant encounter with academic feminism occurred via Jane MacLeod, who taught one of the required research methods seminars during my first year of training. I vividly remember the seminar's first meeting: the way MacLeod made direct eye contact with each student in the room, smiling warmly as she learned more about our individual interests. At the time I professed an interest in political sociology, but something was about to happen as a part of my work in that seminar that would radically alter my course of study. MacLeod, responding to a perceived lack of communication between first-year grad students and faculty, asked each of us to interview a faculty member of our choosing. I chose to interview Barbara Laslett, primarily because I had heard that she had done quite a bit of quantitative analysis early in her career and was now doing almost exclusively qualitative work. This piqued my interest. We had just finished reading Shulamit Reinharz's withering critique of survey research, and I was already beginning to suspect that political sociology was not a good fit.[2] Another reason was my vague sense that this interview would be a challenge for me personally. As a prospective graduate student, I had attended the department's annual Sociological Research Institute banquet the previous spring. I was impressed and a little intimidated by Barbara's personal style. During the entertainment at the banquet there were numerous references to her "tough love" policy, which further intrigued me. I developed the impression that she was someone who strongly identified with her role as a teacher, and that she could be very demanding. These impressions, combined with what little I knew of her academic interests, piqued my interest. Although I had no explicit indication, my sense was that Barbara's presence reflected the interests of a group of graduate students who were very active in challenging the status quo within the department, but I was not at all sure of what to make of this.

These were my thoughts at the time I made my selection, and in retrospect they seem to reflect essentially pragmatic concerns. Focus quickly shifted when I encountered Barbara's work. In preparing for the interview I read an early piece she did on collaborative interviewing techniques, an *American Sociological Review* article on the role of theory in quantitative historical research, two articles on her Los Angeles family studies, and three pieces from her biographical narrative study of William Fielding Ogburn.[3] I was thoroughly impressed by the breadth of knowledge they demonstrated, but I was particularly struck by the Ogburn pieces.

In these pieces, Laslett uses a biographical narrative technique to document the career of Ogburn, a major American sociologist associated with the rise of statistical analysis in the discipline. Ogburn believed that emotion was inimical to the aims of science and explicitly advocated its exclusion from all scientific pursuits. Laslett uses her narrative to explore "the relationship of gender, personal life, and emotion to the social construction of scientific knowledge,"[4] and makes some astonishing observations along the way. She sees Ogburn as representative of the gendered development of the field of sociology, which during the first half of the twentieth century sought to distinguish itself from the field of social work, which was seen as nurturing work and therefore within the feminine domain. This distinction was made on both the personal and structural levels, according to the research, and an understanding of the role of statistical analysis is seen as crucial to an appreciation of the role of gender in the discipline.

Laslett's work marked my first encounter with the feminist critique of objectivity in the social sciences, situated knowledge, and a careful consideration of the relationship between knowledge and knower. Thus, I was primed for my first encounter with Jennifer Pierce when I enrolled in her Contemporary Theory seminar during my second year of graduate school (1995). It was in that seminar that my understanding of the feminist critique of knowledge crystallized around the concept of the Archimedean point—that place of perfect value freedom, untainted by subjective experience of any sort, from which all truly valid and reliable knowledge of the social world should come. "In other words," I remember Jennifer retorting dryly as she quoted Thomas Nagel, "the view from nowhere." It was during discussions like these that I began to realize both the impossibility and the inadvisability of pursuing disembodied social truths. It was also during Jennifer's seminar that I first encountered the work of Pierre Bourdieu, and in the rich feminist context in which that work was presented, I began to think immediately about the various connections between gender socialization and Bourdieu's concept of *habitus,* a connection that informed my dissertation research and continues to fascinate me.[5]

It is 1996. I have hit what might euphemistically be referred to as "a bad patch" in my graduate training. My faith in the academy has been severely shaken by what I see happening to Jennifer as she fights for tenure, I am floundering in my attempt to find meaning in my political sociology studies, I am also struggling with grave doubts about my ability to pass the department's qualifying examination, and most of the members of my original cohort have dropped out of the program or transferred to other schools. I have made up my mind that I will leave graduate school and pursue other work after I complete an MA. I am bitterly disappointed but still interested in teaching, so I send out letters of application to all of the area colleges and universities, letting them know I am available for adjunct teaching. As fate decrees, two weeks after my mother's passing I receive a frantic call from the department chair at the University of Wisconsin, Eau Claire. A faculty member has just left on short notice—would I possibly be available to teach social theory in the fall?

Would I? I gleefully accept the offer, and although my initial teaching experience at UWEC gets off to a rocky start, by January my confidence is sufficiently bolstered, and I am considering a return to Minnesota to pursue my doctorate.

Teach Your Children Well

Putting my feminist convictions into practice in the classroom during my early teaching career resulted in moments of frustration and oppression, times when I felt overwhelmed and inadequate but, paradoxically, grateful for the perceptions that led to the anguish.

It is February 2000—barely a month into the new millennium. It is the first meeting of my Sociology of Sex and Gender class at a small private college not far from the Twin Cities. This college admits only women, but it maintains a very close relationship with a nearby all-male university three miles down the road, which includes the cross-listing of all classes. Teaching this course in an institution that is so thoroughly structured by gender presents a unique set of challenges and opportunities. I am particularly pleased at the composition of the class—slightly over half of those enrolled are men. I find out later that many of the men in my class live on the same dorm room floor and have made a group decision to enroll en masse. I ask for first impressions of the word *feminism*. As expected, a rather awkward silence follows. Eyes scan the floor intently; I cannot make eye contact with anyone in the room. Except for Stacey, who seems willing to take a chance. "Well," she begins, "I'm here at this expensive private college. I grew up in the suburbs. I have my own car. I'm white. I mean, I don't *feel* oppressed." Relief registers on the faces of several students, especially some of the male students. "Oh, thank God," they seem to be saying. "At least we won't have to talk about *oppression!*" Other students, both men and women, simply nod in cheerful support of Stacey's statement. Something tells me it is too early to show my hand. I let it go. "What else do you think of when you hear the word *feminism?*" I wait, for a very long time. To no avail. There are no more responses.

At least not until later. After I dismiss the class, a woman in her forties, the only "nontraditional" student in the class, springs from her chair and asks to speak to me. She tells me she is absolutely shocked by the level of complacency in the class. She angrily recounts several examples of sexism in her workplace. She tells me about the teasing her youngest daughter faces at school because of her strong interest in sports. I tell her how much I think the rest of the class would benefit from hearing these stories. I tell her that her voice is important. She tells me she does not feel comfortable speaking out about this in class. "These kids won't listen—they don't know anything yet." The next day another student from the same class, a young woman in her early twenties visits my office. She tells me she is absolutely shocked by the level of complacency in the class. She launches into a passionate indictment of the low level of political consciousness on campus, the lack of diversity, the middle-class mindset. She seems strangely surprised when I ask her why she herself did not feel comfortable challenging Stacey. She suddenly seems flustered, unsure of herself. "I'm just . . . I'm just not good in those kinds of situations . . . I'm just . . . I don't know, I just can't."

Some months later I am back on campus at the University of Minnesota, this time teaching social theory. It is near the end of spring semester, the warm perfumed breezes blow gently just outside my classroom window, but inside there is a nasty storm brewing. To augment our study of postmodern perspectives on feminism, I have just shown the class a videotaped excerpt of *The Man Show,* a cable comedy show featuring scantily clad "juggy girls," two unapologetically sexist male hosts egged on by a rowdy and predominantly male audience, lots and lots of sketches that resurrect the worst gender stereotypes of both men and women, and, occasionally, an absolutely hilarious fart joke. I invite the class to see the show as an example of a postmodern "open" text. Should the show, I ask, be read as a dangerous deployment of patriarchal backlash humor, a powerful recuperative move masquerading as entertainment, or is the show's humor so broad that its gender politics can actually be read as progressive—by reminding men that only boors and buffoons revel in this kind of piggy behavior? How does the show facilitate each of these readings? Or both? Or are there other readings?

Despite my invitation to consider the show with cool detachment, two students have been drawn into a heated argument. "The truth is," begins Sara, "the truth is that women suffer because of shows like this." Across the room Brad, a devoted fan of *The Man Show,* is having none of this. They engage in a spirited debate about the cultural representation of women on television, and how this affects women's lives. Sara is articulate, strong, well-informed, and unrelenting as she catalogs the harms women suffer by way of their representation on popular television shows. In frustration, Brad nervously adjusts the brim of his baseball cap, smirks, then plays his ace card. "Oh yeah? What about Oprah Winfrey?" Laughter, then a few whispered comments of support. "Yeah, what about Oprah?" Amazingly, Sara seems crestfallen. She seems stunned not so much by the response but by the context in which her remarks have been understood. Sara is not playing a game. She was not keeping score. Now she has nothing more to say.

More recently, in another classroom . . . This time I think I am ready. I have assigned an article critiquing the Promise Keepers' movement from a feminist perspective. The author presents an argument that I am sure is familiar to many readers—that the Promise Keepers, a Christian men's movement ostensibly dedicated to the promotion of marital responsibility and sexual fidelity, represents a religious apology for patriarchy, one that takes on added strength as a result of the all-male rituals that its members participate in during their stadium rallies. This emphasis on the power of ritual makes it an excellent complement to some material I have recently presented to the class on Durkheim and his study of religion. I have ascertained that one of my students, Charlie, is a former member of the Promise Keepers, and I am anticipating a lively defense on his part. What I am not prepared for is Alice. Alice is a returning student, in her late thirties, intelligent but reserved; she is one of my best students. To my surprise, Charlie remains silent as I try to draw the class out with a few introductory questions. No bites. I do notice, however, that Alice looks like she is about to cry. I make eye contact, hoping she will feel encouraged to speak. Nothing. I ask a few more lame questions, and then finally my curiosity gets the better of me. I turn to Alice and suggest gently, "Alice, you look like you have something to say." She begins quietly, stammers, searches for the words, begins again. She does not agree with the author's critique. I ask if she wants to say more. Again she struggles to find her words. "I just . . . , I can't . . . I don't know." A pause. "It's almost like the author, like she's a *feminist*." I assure her that the author is in fact a feminist. Now she finds her voice. "My first husband was a jerk. He never went to church with me—he never even went to work! He never took care of our son. My second husband is a Promise Keeper, and he helps around the house, with my son, with everything." She goes on to relate that she is very glad that her husband has taken charge of the marriage and grateful to the Promise Keepers for making him a better man. I ask her if she agrees with the Promise Keepers' idea that a woman's subordinate position in marriage is divinely ordained. She nods quietly in assent, but she looks into my eyes so earnestly. There is a lingering sadness in her gaze, a somber resignation. "After all," she says, "*he* has to answer to God."

Now *I* feel like crying.

But with such anguished moments comes the occasional golden opportunity. For example, with respect to the Stacey incident, despite our inauspicious beginning I was eventually able to turn things around. After checking with the two students involved and agreeing not to identify them by name, I began our second class by recounting their conversations about feeling silenced in the classroom. A number of students seemed genuinely shocked that not everyone in class felt comfortable speaking. Some even wondered aloud *how this could happen*. I asked my students in that class to keep journals throughout the semester, and I was pleasantly surprised by some of the men's efforts. Although some of these entries adopted the kind of defensive tone I was expecting, far more common were entries confessing ignorance, longing for a way out of oppressive gender relations, and what seemed to me a genuine openness toward revising traditional power relations, particularly with respect to the domestic division of labor and child care. Another topic that struck a responsive chord with them was Title IX. I included an expanded treatment of this topic in the course in response to several sharply barbed comments I had received from some of the male athletes in class. I wondered how they would respond to the extensive data I had that indicated, despite the inflammatory rhetoric blaming women's sports and Title IX for cutbacks in men's athletics, that these moves could be directly traced to the refusal of many universities and colleges to cut some of the fat from their bloated football programs. Again I was pleasantly surprised by some of the responses this material generated. For some of these men, I think it marked the first time that they allowed themselves to see the strength and depth of sexism at the institutional level. Finally, I was pleased to learn that the men's university affiliated with the college had several years previously launched a concerted effort to address sexism and homophobia on their campus. A series of speakers, seminars, and films on issues related to masculinity, gender, and sexism were apparently beginning to show some impressive results. During the term I taught there, the men's university nominated both an openly gay professor of English and a female sociology professor to deliver the graduation address at their annual senior banquet. A first on both counts for this university. These nominations are determined by student vote and have traditionally been taken very seriously. Experiences like these leave me occasionally hopeful but always grateful for what has been accomplished by those who have gone before me in the academy.

Opening the Oyster—Out in the World

Taking my dissertation research on the road with my job search proved to be alternately enlightening, enlivening, and enraging. Perhaps the most remarkable aspect of the whole process is that self-censoring was not a significant issue. When (during a festive meeting of our dissertation group) we hosted a jovial Arlene Kaplan Daniels as our "visiting scholar," she responded to my interest in queer studies with a twinkle in her eye. "My dear," she explained, "the world is your oyster."

In spring 2002 I hit the road auditioning for an academic position in sociology with a job talk that included mention of drag, various subcultures within the larger gay male community (Radical Faeries, Bears, Leathermen), the gendering of sexual cultures, phallocentric logic, poststructuralist theory, even (gasp!) Judith Butler. It also included a frank self-identification of myself as an out gay/queer man.

I never considered not including this material, because I knew that on some level, Arlene was right. Studies in these areas have become legitimized in no small part through the pioneering work of all the academic feminists who had gone before me. While I realized there would be those who discounted my research by virtue of my being "too involved" with the object of study, I was not without a response—one infused throughout by feminist epistemology.

Armed with the knowledge that there *had* to be a place for me, one that would be receptive to the work I was trying to do in examining how gender shapes experiences of sexual pleasure, I was able to adopt a rather Zen attitude toward my job search. If they don't like me, I thought, fine. It was much more important that I be candid about my research interests than to play games trying to win favor. Since I was convinced that more doors would open to me if my first-year job search did not pan out, I was far less willing to edit out the more controversial aspects of my research. But I hasten to add that this would not have been the case were I not the beneficiary of a rich legacy of struggle on the same contested terrain upon which I now moved so freely, and the work of the many feminist scholars who were compelled by practicality to be far more careful than I needed to be.

While many second generation academic feminists struggled, and continue to struggle to be taken seriously, I have proceeded throughout my graduate career largely unencumbered by these concerns. Yes, I am privileged by my whiteness, my maleness, and my training. But I have been fortunate as well.

Patricia Hill Collins writes of "the outsider within," one who inhabits the mainstream centers of power without losing a sense of "otherness." The outsider within "can produce distinctive oppositional knowledges that embrace multiplicity yet remain cognizant of power," something that is definitely true of my current position as an assistant professor at one of Ohio State's regional campuses.[6] However, I find that Collins's idea is not specific enough to describe the particular tensions informing my situation. While Collins tells us that outsiders are often able to acquire hidden or elite knowledge, they are also often unable to lay authoritative claim to the full power granted to members of the "inside" group." In my case, I am consistently reminded in subtle but important ways that I *can* claim the knowledge and possess the full power accorded to incoming faculty. The multiple dimensions of privilege that I bring to my position are immediately acknowledged, taken for granted, and,

I suspect, incorporated into a wider set of conventional assumptions about me that make my access to power relatively unproblematic. My likeness to and liking for the status quo is assumed, and it is only through my own conscious decision to be open about both my queerness and my feminist convictions, to be "out" in the classroom and in discussions of my research, that I am perceived as an outsider.

In this sense I sometimes feel like an "insider without"—inside by virtue of the many privileges I enjoy but without the means to fully explain to my colleagues this very conscious decision I have made, without the means to help my students find their words, and occasionally without the capacity to find my own words. My decision, of course, has everything to do with the feminist training I received at the University of Minnesota, and the vision of a future less oppressed, less terrorized by gender. A world where everyone can breathe, and everyone can find their words, can loudly pronounce what too often seems impossible to say. And as I, like my students, struggle to find my own voice, as I too stammer, reach for words that are not yet there, I, too, think, "I don't know . . . I just . . . I can't." But even as I make these painful attempts, even in that anguish I find moments of deep gratitude: gratitude for what my feminist training has allowed me to see and for what is so clearly still possible.

I would like to back up a bit and conclude with a personal moment. It is July 1997. I am at my father's house as I gather with my family for a party of sorts. Along with my father, my three brothers are there. My three sisters are also there. Two of my nieces, aged sixteen and fourteen, are there as well. My mother is not there. She is gone now. We gather in my father's house to put the sterility of the hospital behind us, to begin the grieving, to begin life without her, to celebrate her life. My father mixes me one of his famous martinis. I settle into my mother's chair. From across the room I hear my nieces. "Who's going to tell the story? We want to hear the story!" My sisters come in from the kitchen. They turn to me. "You tell them, Peter. Tell them the story." I realize that this is a moment of enormous privilege as I begin the story of my mother's final words, to try to convey something of her courage, her strength, her irrepressible humor to her granddaughters. The story goes like this.

At the nurse's urging we have called in a priest. He turns out to be a rather peculiar fellow, with a pronounced flair for the dramatic. As he calls forth a final blessing by gesticulating wildly over my mother's failing body, we join hands to encircle her hospital bed. My mother regards the priest warily. She slyly lifts an eyebrow. Even in her delirium, his eccentricities do not escape her notice. As we notice her noticing, we imagine what she might say if speaking were not such an effort. The eyebrow speaks eloquently. "That's just about enough of that now," it says, or "*(sigh)* Honestly!" The priest finishes and hastily begins to pack up his things. "Mom," I say, pressing lightly on her arm, "is there anything you want to ask the priest before he leaves?" The room falls silent as she considers the question. She struggles to speak, "I don't know . . . not now . . . maybe later." Our hearts sink. Faces fall. She does not seem to understand that there is no later.

Again the situation does not escape her notice. She regards the sullen faces of her children. Unable to tolerate being misunderstood even now, she draws herself up into a childlike shrug, and with one last effort puts all our doubts to rest. "I never died before!" she exclaims loudly. We laugh. She laughs, letting the laughter gently rock her exhausted frame. After a few moments, even the startled priest laughs.

I finish telling the story to my nieces, and we all laugh once again. "Don't ever forget that." I tell them. "That's where you come from. That's the kind of strength you inherited." And, of course, it is not until this moment that I realize that I too have a legacy to claim here. I am my mother's son. Without feminism I might not have recognized this moment. I cannot help but wonder how many other men in similar situations have wasted such treasure. Like an enormous bank of unclaimed assets, our ignorance leaves a different kind of legacy unclaimed. I am grateful for mine and plan to use it to fuel a career as a feminist researcher and teacher. So in closing I would like to acknowledge my debts. For this legacy I thank feminism and the brave work of so many who have gone before me.

Notes

1. Barrie Thorne, *Gender Play: Girls and Boys in School* (Piscataway, N.J.: Rutgers University Press, 1993).

2. Shulamit Reinharz, *On Becoming a Social Scientist* (Somerset: N.J.: Transaction, 1984).

3. Barbara Laslett, "Unfeeling Knowledge: Emotion and Objectivity in the History of Sociology" *Sociological Forum* 5 (1990): 413–33; Barbara Laslett, "Biography as Historical Sociology: The Case of William Fielding Ogburn," *Theory and Society* 20 (1991): 511–38; and Barbara Laslett, "Gender in/and Social Science History," *Social Science History* 16, 2 (1992): 177–95.

4. Laslett, "Unfeeling Knowledge," 413.

5. Pierre Bourdieu, *An Outline of a Theory of Practice* (Cambridge: Cambridge University Press, 2002).

6. Patricia Hill Collins, *Fighting Words: Black Women and the Search for Justice* (Minneapolis: University of Minnesota Press, 1998), 8.

7. Sissies at the Picnic

The Subjugated Knowledges of a Black Rural Queer

Roderick A. Ferguson

THE idea that white people can be queer is sometimes an adjustment for me. My first memories of queerness are not of the Castro or of the Village but are of the black sissies that peopled my world as a child. They were the men with permed hair who pressed their love into piano keys come Sunday morning. They were the erudite teachers with accents acquired somewhere between the departure from home and the return to old landmarks, guides who made Shakespeare and *Beowulf* seem as familiar as the hymns of slaves. The history of these men is too hazy to be transparent, opaque enough that it will not yield to the scholar's techniques of visibility. But historiography is not beholden to transparency. There is reason to seize the bits and pieces of this history as they flash up in the randomness of memory. There is a history jeopardized by prevalent understandings of queer identities and tired notions about black communities, images discarded by hegemonic formations as trifling and unimportant. Since the hegemonic narrative of modern homosexuality is figured around cosmopolitanism, whiteness, and normative gender practices, that narrative can only approach a discrepant history like mine by suppressing it. I will tell this tale as a way to illuminate the heterogeneous makeup of the black communities that I knew in west-central Georgia, a configuration that confused the precincts of past and present, man and woman, heterosexual and queer. This is a narrative whose properties exceed the personal and whose aim will be to catch hold of memories in order to expose moments of danger.

I was a little sissy among older—more seasoned—ones, in a world that now seems like a curious mix of past and present. This was rural Georgia during the 1970s. The small town called Manchester was full of fixtures and languages that the rest of the world had consigned to the archives of history. I remember once I asked my paternal grandfather, Granddaddy Willie Marvin, about the history of our church, Concord Baptist, and its relationship to the Ferguson family. Granddaddy, who in my mind stood like a tree, leaned toward me and told me the story of the bush arbor and how we "came 'cross from slavery." Granddaddy said that the slaves, who had no formal church to claim, would go out and find a clearing in the woods and build a screen made of twigs and leaves. This screen they called the bush arbor and used it to shield their backs from an unsparing sun. There they would have their meetings out of the reach of master and lash. The intimacy with which Granddaddy spoke about slavery convinced me of its recency. It was not until college that I learned to think of segregation and slavery as periods that did not border on the 1970s. It was also in my awakening adulthood that I discovered that the story of the bush arbor was not my family's personal history but a subject to which historians of slavery had devoted considerable interest.

As slavery seemed proximate, it looked to me like segregation ran on the heels of the late 1970s as well. Years after the civil rights movement, public facilities in Manchester adhered to the racial boundaries that characterized the "earlier" era. The medical office that Dr. Smith and Dr. Collins ran jointly had one side for white folks and the other for blacks, and it remained that way at least until I had gone to college. The local YMCA had an unspoken rule of "no blacks allowed" until the school system bought the building when I was in high school.

Further complicating the presumably neat divisions between then and now was my first-grade teacher, Mrs. Rosa Little. Mrs. Little was my older brother's teacher at Meriwether County Training School, the school for black children before the questionable dawn of integration. This was my mother's alma mater as well, as it served generations of black people before the courts mandated the end of legalized segregation due to the pressures brought on them by the civil rights movement. In my eyes, Mrs. Little bridged the gap between segregation and integration, carrying with her the feverish zeal of teachers from a bygone era, a zeal justified in the name of the race and expressed oftentimes in violent devotion. Her reputation as a teacher was legendary. The grown folks talked about how she could teach the most miserable simpleton to read with grace and enthusiasm. And in Mrs. Little's mind teaching us to do just that was proof enough of black people's fitness for American civilization. Transporting the ideals suggested in the name "Meriwether County Training School" to its integrated counterpart, Manchester Elementary, Mrs. Little not only emphasized reading, writing, and arithmetic but deportment as well. For the slightest infraction—a split verb or a fart after mealtime—Mrs. Little would call us to her desk and paddle the palms of our hands with a wooden ruler. It was not long before my cousin Devins observed that Mrs. Little was more severe with us black kids. It was also not lost to us that we were beaten in the name of progress.

My most prized possession during first grade was a shiny red patent leather book bag. I selected it over the black one because red would have been the color that Wonder Woman would have picked. During that time, she was my favorite superhero. To tell you the truth, she kind of still is. I sat enrapt during every episode, wondering what her own history on Paradise Island must have been like. What motivated her mother to found the island of the Amazons? How did they go from being ordinary human beings to immortal superwomen? By what genius did they realize that the feminum on Paradise Island could be used to make their magic bracelets from which bullets bounced? The images that Wonder Woman supplied to me about female agency coincided with what I already believed about the black women around me. In those days, Mama was a seamstress for International Playtex. These were the days before day care was routine. Confronted with the difficulty of working a nine-to-five job at the plant, Mama organized other black working mothers, and together they started the Manchester Day Care Center. My brother and I were among the first graduates, and years later I would watch my nieces and nephews graduate from that same day care started by black women who simply needed some place they could leave their babies.

My memories of childhood are filled with images of Mama's mother, Grandmama Willie Mae. Grandmama had a talent at laughter; she could squeeze humor into the most mundane and taken-for-granted things. Recognizing how smart she was, her grandfather Grandpa Dan offered to send her to school at Savannah State so that she could come back and run his plantation, encouraging her to take this option rather than take the conventional route of marriage. Instead she chose to marry Bo Mulholland, the boy she met while picking cotton. Grandmama was a religious woman, but Christianity took on unfamiliar hues in her hands. On Friday nights, Grandmama would meet with other black women and a sprinkling of black men and gather in the room that adjoined Evangelist Walker's beauty parlor. When Mama took me and my brother to those Friday night services, it felt like we had retreated to some secret society of women to which only a few in Manchester were privy. How many, after all, knew that in the nighttime there were women who prayed and preached without restriction, older and younger sisters who spent their days at a sewing machine, behind a vacuum, in a kitchen, or over a blow-dryer? Next to these women the heterosexual men that I knew seemed ordinary and uninteresting. Understanding agency in terms of womanhood, one day I got one of Daddy's red T-shirts, one big enough that it stopped just above my knees. I tied one of his big leather belts around my waist, jumped into the front yard, and imagined I was Wonder Woman. I whirled around the way that Wonder Woman did whenever she transformed from Yeoman Diana Prince into her superself and stopped in midturn because the contempt in Daddy's eyes had locked me into place. And so began my tutelage into gender normativity.

It was Wonder Woman that made me want to be a reader. I was determined to discover the history of the Amazons. So I had Mama take me to the regional library, and together we got a library card. Soon thereafter, I would walk to the library and check out this large hard-cover book about Greek mythology. There I learned of the Amazon queen Hippolyta and her tragic love for the demigod Heracles. I didn't rest until I had consumed the whole book, learning of ancient mysteries and godlike failures. It was my fascination with books and the things they held inside that marked me as different from the other boys. Soon my brothers and the other boys in my neighborhood noticed that I was spending more time reading indoors than playing baseball and football outside. As I developed skills as a reader, my abilities to catch an oncoming ball plummeted miserably. My reputation as a sissy became a knot that could not be untied, and I was banished from the world of boys.

But even as "sissy" was a stigma akin to the mark of Cain, the men whom folks referred to as sissies had qualities that everybody deemed attractive. One such person was Edward Larue. Edward was the one that our mamas sent us to as Easter approached. Every day after school the kids from around the neighborhood were to convene at the Sanctified Church across the street from my house and practice for the Easter Sunday service. There we would receive the poems that we were to recite come Easter Sunday morning. There we practiced the song that so many black kids during that era knew by heart: "He arose. Yes he rose. He arose. Yes he rose. He arose from the dead. And the Lord shall bear my spirit on." And there we sat, fifty or so loud and snotty-nosed children, finally out of the jurisdiction of cries like "Chile, if you don't get over here you better" or the more ominous "Don't let me tell you another time." Away from our mamas and daddies, we had no intention of minding. And then in walked Edward. He was what Mama and other black women referred to as a "pretty man." He strode down the aisle, limp-wristed with designer sunglasses, fur coat, and two-toned wing-tipped shoes. All of us knew he was "funny"; we had heard our parents say it, but that didn't seem to matter much. For they had entrusted him to teach us to talk proper and sing on key. Back then, they seemed to understand that funny or not, he and men like him were part of us—little pieces in the mosaic that made up the neighborhood. He walked down the aisle, reached the altar, whirled around, and clapped his hands so that they struck like lightning. The sharp-tongued and the unruly came to attention. "It's time to start," he said. The other sissy men had a similar function, distributing their services and talents throughout black working-class neighborhoods.

The Easter practice around 1981, though, signaled a change that was an omen for things to come. The week before Easter Sunday all of us kids gathered at the Sanctified Church, just like we had the year before. Many of us had presented our Easter speeches the year before and had come to consider ourselves veterans. We had the same old butterflies about getting up in front of a church full of folk in our Easter Sunday suits and dresses, but we took comfort in the fact that we had gone this round before. I remember looking for Edward to make his entrance, but no one came through the front doors of the church. And then Evangelist Walker's daughter Jack appeared and took charge of the practice. Bewildered, I looked around, expecting to see Edward at any moment. And then I noticed some strange figure sitting in the front pew, some unshaven man whose hair was hardly combed and who wore a dingy black cardigan with holes in it. It was not only Edward's physical appearance that was different, but something deep inside had flown away from him. And the usual gaiety of the Easter practice slid into melancholy with the fall of this mighty sissy. And soon thereafter Edward passed.

In my mind, Edward's death marked a crucial juncture in Manchester and the way we regarded sissies in black communities. With the advent of AIDS and the white evangelical movements popping up all over Georgia, sissies ceased to be peculiar men whose services we relied on and became pariahs who had to be identified and excluded. The same men whom our parents had lauded for being great teachers of music, literature, and oratory had become these fiends that they had to protect us against. The loss of sissies like Edward and the knowledges they held seemed like the progressive triumph of integration and right-wing Christianity and the advent of a new kind of time.

It is not only the Christian right that threatens the subjugated knowledge of black sissies. Modern homosexuality threatens formations like this as well. In his argument about the Bakla, Filipino queer men who engage effeminacy, transvestism, and homosexuality as part of their self-construction, Martin Manalansan suggests the ways in which modern homosexuality alienates non-Western queer formations. He states,

By privileging Western definitions of same-sex sexual practices, non-Western practices are marginalized and cast as "pre-modern" or unliberated. Practices that do not conform with Western narratives of the development of individual political subjects are dismissed as unliberated or coded as "homophobic." I suggest, by contrast, that we must conceive of "gay" practices as a broad category of analysis, and as multiply determined by national culture, history, religion, class, and region, in and across various cultural and political locations and even within a single group.[1]

We may include black rural sissies within the umbrella of non-Western queer formations. We can do that because of the ways in which sissies of this type arise out of social settings characterized by temporal heterogeneity. This temporal heterogeneity annexes other modes of difference. The sissies that I knew ran the gamut of gender styles; some, like Edward, were limp-wristed and sashayed as they walked; others, like my literature instructor, were straight-laced and masculine; still others, like the pianists and choir directors, had a fondness for perms and relaxers. This gender heterogeneity actually strikes against the ways in which modern homosexuality compels a gender uniformity and presumes a cosmopolitan bias. The time of the Bakla and the time of the sissies run counter to the time of modern homosexuality. As modern homosexuality enforces gender, regional, and racial uniformity, it must do so against the gender, regional, and racial heterogeneity suggested by those "backward" and primitive formations like the Bakla and the sissy. In opposition to this heterogeneity, modern homosexuality suppresses these formations as it privileges its own temporal narrative.

Only now am I beginning to appreciate the generality of the sissy formation and the ways in which it emerges in different cultural sites and achieves specificity because of those locations. In Craig Womack's *Drowning in Fire*, we can see the ways in which sissy formations illustrate temporal heterogeneity, doing so against the universalizing tendencies of narratives of progress.

Lord of the losers that summer, I lived inside my imagination and often felt myself floating away, as others talked, into my private world of dreams. But not when Grandpa launched into his stories, which demanded some kind of listening akin to physical participation, and he cast his voice in such a way that drew you into the presences his words created. Bored on the boat with no place to go, bored with staring at my bobber ride up one hill of waves and down the slippery slope of another, bored with trying to will a fish into hunger for my minnow or dangling night crawler, Grandpa's stories were a welcome, if strange respite. And if I wasn't fishing with him, my grandma would send me over to my cousins to "play with boys your own age instead of being locked up in that room with those books of yours."[2]

Like me, Josh assumes the position of narrator, the one who engages techniques of historical and cultural narration. In my relationship with Granddaddy and in Josh's relationship with his grandfather, the sissy is the one who bears witness to social heterogeneity—a diversity marked in the intersecting relations of temporality, sexuality, gender, and race. For us sissies, history and culture are terrains of the imagination, terrains that offer what official narratives withhold. Sissies suggest temporal arrangements that run counter to the ways in which authoritative histories apprehend and deploy time.

In "Theses on the Philosophy of History," Walter Benjamin warns us about the dangers of progress and the violent enforcement of its own version of time. He writes,

A Klee painting named "Angelus Novus" shows an angel looking as though he is about to move away from something he is fixedly contemplating. His eyes staring, his mouth is open, his wings are spread. This is how one pictures the angel of history. His face is turned toward the past. Where we perceive a chain of events, he sees one single catastrophe which keeps piling wreckage upon wreckage and hurls it in front of his feet. The angel would like to stay, awaken the dead, and make whole what has been smashed. But a storm is blowing from Paradise: it has got caught in his wings with such violence that the angel can no longer close them. This storm irresistibly propels him into the future to which his back is turned, while the pile of debris before him grows skyward. The storm is what we call progress.[3]

To remember the past, we must act against the storm of progress. We who look to history critically and queerly do so by reckoning with the mighty winds of progress in whatever forms they may come—civil rights, the Christian Right, modern homosexuality. Others may see these movements as entirely separate, but all of them throw piles of debris at our feet, heaping that wreckage in the varied names of progress. It is important to recognize that this wreckage is actually made up of the bones of people like Edward Larue. And if we allow ourselves to be carried away from those remains, we do so to our own end. Commenting on the subjugated labor performed by black sissies and the way that modern homosexuality refutes the temporal heterogeneity that they suggest, black queer writer Reginald T. Jackson argues,

It pains me . . . that so many of my fellow brothers look down on me for being a "Queen," snapping my fingers, and adding a "Girlfriend" to the end of my sentences. These brothers suffer from selective amnesia, it would seem. You see, it was queens, in high heels and chiffon, who fought cops for Stonewall; sissies who had bottles and billy clubs wailed at and on them as they marched down city streets for "our" rights. It was drag queens who patrolled the docks and piers with straight razors, fighting and dying at the hands of joyriding homophobes. . . .

Yes, we shimmer in the glitter of expensive fashions, but we also get down and dirty for the cause, allowing our other brothers—who aren't ready to make "the statement" yet, or who can't be identified as queer "Uptown"—to lead reasonably comfortable lives enjoying gay rights, the pride parades, the bars, parks, baths, and movies.[4]

This selective amnesia has compelled us to forget the critical heterogeneity that constituted and still constitutes queer communities. This critical heterogeneity can only be apprehended through an understanding of time that is not uniform but differentiated.

For me, being a black rural queer denotes an alienation from narratives of progress and the ways that those narratives banish certain formations in the name of the modern. I have tried to disseminate that alienation in my life as a teacher and writer in the American academy. The academy is a domain comprised of the time of the now, the time of the once was, and the time of the yet to be. As a teacher this means educating students about the ways in which the legacy of Enlightenment modernity is expressed through discourses of race, gender, sexuality, and class that have their genesis in that "by-gone" moment and their effect in the present-day. Being a sissy means that I cannot take comfort in the university's narrative of progress as it boasts about its own ability to accommodate that which it formerly excluded, as it claims to have integrated the radical critiques of race, gender, class, and sexuality. As we observe the past and its entanglement with the present, being a sissy means encouraging critical formations that can yield different futures.

Notes

1. Martin Manalansan IV, "In the Shadows of Stonewall: Examining Gay Transnational Politics and the Diasporic Dilemma," in *The Politics of Culture in*

the Shadow of Capital, ed. Lisa Lowe and David Lloyd (Durham, N.C.: Duke University Press, 1997), 486.

2. Craig Womack, *Drowning in Fire* (Tucson: University of Arizona Press, 2001), 28.

3. Walter Benjamin, *Illuminations,* ed. Hannah Arendt, trans. Harry Zohn (New York: Schocken, 1969).

4. Reginald T. Jackson, "The Absence of Fear: An Open Letter to a Brother," in *Brother to Brother: New Writings by Black Gay Men,* ed. Essex Hemphill and Joseph Beam (Boston: Alyson Publications, 1991).

8. I May Not Know My "Color," But I Do Know My Politics

"East"/"West" Feminist Encounters

Miglena Todorova

I am a migrant who travels across East and West, and across nation-states. I negotiate between cultures, languages, and ideologies and cannot settle over one final truth. Perhaps that is why I resist classifying myself in terms of "color." In communist Bulgaria, where I was born and grew up, I learned that I was "white," "Bulgarian," and "European." When I came to the United States in 1993 to pursue higher education, my stable identities were challenged. To a clerk at the University of Minnesota, who was helping me with admission forms, I looked "Hispanic." She wondered which box under "race" to mark. To a Latino man in Las Vegas, with whom my company entered into a dispute over a table in a restaurant, I was "a fucking foreigner." A cashier in a Target store asked me if I was an "Arab girl." She knew someone from Palestine and wondered if I knew her, too. Yet a colleague of mine, at the university store where I worked part-time as a student, declared me "white" after carefully examining my skull, facial features, and body hair. "A bit tanned," he said, "but white."

White, nonwhite, or in-between, I identify with U.S. third world feminism, or "feminism of color." My associations with this brand of feminism are not racial, ethnic, national, or cultural but political. Like feminists of color in the United States, I seek large political alliances across nation-states, capable of countering dominant social hierarchies of class, gender, race, sexuality, and nationality. U.S. third world feminist theory and practice thus cross physical and imagined borders "to create a new feminist consciousness and location; not just the third world in the first world, but a new internationalist consciousness and terrain that challenges the distinctions of nation-states." This is the consciousness of "inclusive communities," resting not on biological or cultural threads but "on the political links (women) choose to make among and between struggles."[1] Thus women of all colors and all worlds can align themselves and participate in these nonessentialist but political communities of resistance to systematic forms of oppression and domination. The politics of U.S. third world feminism push even further the boundaries of such imagined communities to include not just women but any subject, regardless of race, gender, and location.[2] And like these feminists, I do not see "globalization" as some benevolent power spreading "democracy" around the world but as a mode of colonization, which closes opportunities for alternative political imaginations.

This powerful postnational and postcolonial feminist imagination gives me a language and conceptual frameworks that allow me to see myself and the world. It empowers me to express and analyze the oppressive forces that designate me and others to "peripheral" worlds, peopled by "unhistorical" backward objects of history made in the West. Feminism of color liberates my imagination to embrace other ways of knowing and being. The knowledges of the non-American, the nonwhite, the queer, and the woman of color enable me to question and to counter the Western dominant epistemologies in which I am educated.

I first called myself a "feminist" less than a year ago. My arrival at this intellectual and political location at the age of thirty-six was the end of a journey that began in communist Eastern Europe, continued throughout migration to the United States, coping with a foreign language, confusion, torturing self-explorations, and a ten-year walk of the corridors of American academia, as I pursued an undergraduate degree in American studies, graduate studies in political science, and a PhD in American studies, all at the University of Minnesota.

I was born in 1965 in communist Bulgaria. The word *feminism* was unknown to me until the early 1980s, when I became vaguely aware of some American feminism. My awareness did not come from school or family discussions on the topic but from the American movies that penetrated the communist censorship. I associated American feminism with women struggling to be able to work outside the home. My associations came from films, such as *Working Girl* (1985), starring Melanie Griffith, which some film critic on Bulgarian television called "a feminist movie." Such pronouncements were possible back then only in the context of the communist rhetoric about the "capitalist enemy," who was criticizing "us" for violation of human rights, while his women struggled for such basic rights as the right to work. I remember being very impressed with Melanie Griffith's character strength and her plight to prove that a great business idea was stolen from her. Yet, she was aided by handsome

Harrison Ford, which indicated to me that U.S. feminism relied on men for achieving its agenda.

I felt, however, that Griffith's character was exceptional against the backdrop of other American movies that reached my generation. I do not remember specific films, but I remember thinking about the happy housewives appearing in these films. There were so many of them that I wondered what was wrong with America. How could a woman just stay home, cook, clean, and rear children . . . many children? You see, in communist Bulgaria in the 1980s, I did not know a single woman who did not work outside the home. In fact, it was so natural for Bulgarian women to work outside the home that I never thought of this issue in terms of "rights," "equal opportunities," or gender discrimination. Child care in the communist state was free and readily available. If a woman did not work outside the home under these conditions, I believed, she ought to be either lazy or crazy.

I also remember being stunned by a newspaper article describing American women's plight over legalizing abortions. Abortions in communist Bulgaria had been legal for a long time, and I did not remember this ever being a public issue. Abortions were also free and available in any hospital. I believed at that time that free and legal abortions allowed Bulgarian women to effectively control the number of their children, which, I also believed, should not exceed two. I had heard many times from my mother, other women, friends, and the popular discourses that to have more than two children was "unmodern" and "peasantlike."

I thought of American housewives with three, four, and even five children in the movies as backward. American feminist struggle over abortions and work outside the home represented to me battles that were won in Bulgaria a long time ago. Therefore, I never associated with these feminist plights and causes. How could I? In the mid-1980s, my thoughts were engaged with a totalitarian communist state, which, I believed, had to be abolished. In 1986, a cloud from Chernobyl, Russia, poured its deadly radiation over Bulgaria. While we were breathing the contaminated air and eating radiated food, the communist elite, which never warned us about the danger, fled to their exclusive villas in the mountains and had their bread made with mineral water. My friends and I believed that this was a genocide committed against Bulgarians by their own government. We committed to the anticommunist movement, which crushed the Bulgarian communist regime in 1989. In light of this struggle, the American feminist plight over abortions and gender inequality seemed insignificant to me.

By 1991, I was jobless and could no longer take the shortages of food and energy and the lack of sensible political discourse in the postcommunist state. I decided to pursue my longtime dream of getting higher education. And I was determined to study in the United States because I wanted to experience the world that, I believed, embodied freedom and democracy. I studied English with a friend for two years, and in summer 1993 my dream came true. Full of energy, I arrived at the University of Minnesota as an undergraduate student at the age of twenty-six.

My arrival marked the beginning of what I now jokingly call my experience of "the great confusion." Nothing in the United States felt, smelled, or looked as I expected. My cultural shock was intensified by my discovery of an America I did not know. I remember my first history course in the Department of American Studies. I had no idea at the time what "American studies" was about, but the course met pre-major credit requirements, and its description sounded interesting. It was in this course that I first learned about racial, social, and gender injustice in the United States, the country I had imagined as the embodiment of "Democracy." My ideas were now challenged by American history of brutal racism, discrimination, and oppression. Yet, I desperately continued to search for the things in U.S. history that would allow me to retain my vision of the United States as a place where democracy and freedom were truly practiced. Disillusioned with communism, I needed to hold on to my dream of a "free" world beyond the communist state. Perhaps that was why I chose to major in American studies.

I was also drawn to the discipline because in American studies courses I was introduced to concepts of "culture" and "social construction" that opened new horizons in the ways I perceived the world. I became strongly aware of the power of cultural production in constructing and perpetuating the notions of race and the values of individualism and materialism that I came to believe drove life in the United States. The undergraduate courses in American studies I took also forced me to see the links between culture and politics—two realms I had imagined as distinct and separated.

It was in American studies that I learned a bit more about American feminism. In fact, my exposure to feminist writings as an undergraduate student consisted of a few readings: Elaine Tyler May's book *Homeward Bound*, and two essays by Sara Evans and bell hooks in William Chafe and

Harvard Sitkoff's collection *A History of Our Time*.[3] A third essay in this collection that impressed me was about antifeminist women by Rebecca Klatch.[4] Based on these works, I left my undergraduate studies with the following map of feminism in mind. The initiators and leaders of the feminist movement in the United States were white middle-class women, also intellectuals. Their agenda, as I had imagined back in Bulgaria, was indeed about job opportunities, gender equality in the workplace, and abortions. These women were discriminated against by both white and black men, I learned from Sara Evans. Black feminists, like bell hooks, implicated racial discrimination in the gender hierarchies, yet these feminists were smaller in number and power and therefore strived to be included in the white women's movement. Klatch condemned "feminism" and spoke on behalf of the "happy housewives" I knew from the movies, whom I began to despise back in Bulgaria.

I still did not associate with this feminism. I experienced it as a patronizing discourse, which prescribed shared behaviors and values to all women. I remember at my senior undergraduate seminar a discussion of May's *Homeward Bound*, which told the stories of married women during the cold war. A female student commented on the mindless ways the women depicted in the book submitted to housework, cooking, and child rearing—the roles assigned to them by a cold war culture of "containment," as May argued. "But I cook for my husband!" I said. "You cook for your husband," the female student replied, "Honey, what time is it?" Suddenly, I felt ashamed and angry, as the class was laughing at me. You see, I did the cooking at home not because my husband demanded it, but because I loved cooking.

My attempts to bring these questions to the next class session were quickly paralyzed as I was told that nothing in women's lives is a matter of choice, but our fates are completely predetermined by a society dominated by men. After class, the same female student told me that my lack of understanding of "feminism" was due to my being from a "backward" country, where we did not understand how we were oppressed by men. These remarks single-handedly killed my desire to explore the "feminism" that was introduced and discussed in my undergraduate courses. My attitude was bolstered by another encounter with "feminism" a few months later.

That summer, my husband and I were invited to drive across the United States with a couple of friends. The friends, Sandy and Chris, were lesbians I had befriended at my part-time student job. As we were driving, we encountered road construction. A female construction worker was holding a sign and directing the traffic, while the male crew was working on the road. "What the hell is this?" Sandy exclaimed. "Why is she holding the sign? She is smart and strong enough to operate this huge machine." Sandy then turned to me and said: "See this? This is what women here fight against." "Fine," I thought, "but why does not it occur to you that this female construction worker may have chosen to hold the sign instead of operating the big machines? Maybe she thinks that holding the sign is an easier and cleaner job that saves her energy she needs elsewhere."

I did not dare to vocalize my thoughts and to confront Sandy with my ideas. I realized that I was afraid I would be perceived again as "backward" and not knowing "female freedom." Curled on the back seat of the car, I started thinking about the housewives I despised. By despising them, I felt I was doing exactly what "feminism" was trying to do to me: deny me any agency in making choices. To choose to hold the road sign at the job or to be a housewife and raise babies is as feminist as to choose the opposite. If feminism did not allow for these choices, it was an ideology much like communism, which prescribed views, ideals, and behaviors. The "women's liberation movement" in America, I concluded, was as oppressive as the gender oppression and discrimination it was fighting. I would not allow this "movement" to tell me how to live my life as a woman. If I wanted to cook for my husband, I would cook. If I wanted to be a housewife, I would be.

Moreover, I believed, this feminism cared about women outside of the United States only in terms of "educating" them on how to struggle for their rights. In summer 1999, I traveled to Bulgaria and happened to meet a woman who was running the first "hot line" for domestic abuse in Bulgaria. Fascinated, I asked to visit the organization's office and to interview a member of the staff. I learned from the interview that the office was organized and funded by an American feminist organization in alliance with a similar organization in the Netherlands. The brochures in the office lobby were translations from English calling upon Bulgarian women to finally learn their rights and to fight gender oppression in postcommunism. Thus, they could become part of the "sisterhood" in the enlightened West.

Yet, my conversations with female friends and relatives about new "feminist" organizations popping up throughout Bulgaria revealed resentment and anger toward "Western," and "English-speaking" feminism, which, like the European Union, the International Monetary Fund, the World Bank, and other experts from the West, was coming to Bulgaria to "teach" Bulgarians how to structure the economy, politics, and society. From the perspective of Bulgarian women, all of the above spoke in a patronizing manner, assuming to "civilize" and "liberate" Bulgarians from their own pre-modern backwardness. But like me, these women felt already "liberated." As a friend of mine put it, "Before 1989, the big Soviet brother was telling [her] how and for what socialism to fight. Now a big American sister comes to tell [her] how and for what womanhood to fight. How do they think communism collapsed if I did not know my causes and how to fight for them?" my friend asked.

Like my friend, I felt I knew freedom and how to fight for it despite the fact that I came from a "backward" communist country. My sense of being "free" was rooted in experiences that profoundly influenced my life. As a child in communist Bulgaria, I dreamt of becoming a teacher and traveling the world. My working-class parents encouraged my dreams. They taught me to read at the age of three and filled my world with books. When I was about sixteen, in one of these books I encountered the following statement: "Freedom is a state of the mind." I immediately interpreted these words in terms of the communist regime that my father openly criticized at the dinner table. My body could be imprisoned and tortured, as were the bodies of those imprisoned by the state for speaking against the communists, but nobody could imprison my mind. In my mind, I could be whatever I wanted. I could go wherever I wished to go, despite a communist state that forbade us to travel abroad and despite its empty slogans of "equality." We were not equal but an elite of self-proclaimed communists enjoyed privileges, rights, and lifestyles that were denied to the rest of us. In my mind, I could map, assess, criticize, and resist this regime and its ideologies. And, for that matter, I could assess and resist young, undergraduate, white "feminists" who designated me to a "backward" world that did not know freedom. Little did I know at the time that my "foreignness" and "backwardness" would mark the rest of my experience in the American academy.

As a graduate student in political science, I shared my early ideas of U.S. feminism in a graduate seminar on the history of the U.S. Constitution. A female colleague in the class defined my understanding of the feminist agenda as rather "simplistic" and felt somewhat offended by my "reductionist" views. She felt compelled to explain to me that feminism was much more than equality in the workplace and abortions.

"Feminism struggles for the equality of blacks and immigrants," she declared, "and as a woman of color, you should know better!"

At that moment, I exploded. "Stop putting me in categories of color!" I replied. "I am not 'of color' because I do not have the experiences of women of color in this country or elsewhere. I do not know what it is to struggle against brutal racism! I do not know what it means to live with a past of slavery or colonization." But I was not talking to the class. My explosion was in my mind because I feared that denying being "of color" would make me look like someone who was an "Oreo," a concept discussed in one of my undergraduate classes—a black behaving as a "white" and imagining to be "white." However, in the United States, I did not feel "white" either because I aligned politically with the oppressed and marginalized. I also shared their visions of social justice and equality. I had not learned these politics in the United States but carried them from my communist past, where the struggle against the communist state was not informed solely by the rhetoric of Western liberal democracy, as Western observers tend to believe, but also by socialist ideas of equality and justice, which many of my generation felt the communists were preaching but not practicing.

I knew that for most of my American friends and acquaintances, including fellow graduate students and professors in political science and American studies, I was not "white." My "swarthy" looks and foreign accent were perceived by both white and nonwhite Americans as racial signs that put me immediately in the category of U.S. "racial minorities" of immigrant background. Hence, Americans expected me to think and behave as a member of a "racial minority." When "race" or the "plight of immigrants" in the United States was discussed in my graduate courses, my fellows expected me to express opinions as if I were some "expert" on these issues. Being "of color" but also a "woman" made me in their eyes a "woman of color," who should certainly associate with "feminism of color," of which I actually knew next to nothing.

It never occurred to my colleagues that I grew up and was socialized as "white," or that I was struggling with my own racism and prejudice acquired through years of education in communist Bulgaria. The idea that the worldviews I brought from home might be closer to those of the "whites" in the United States never crossed their minds. The communist state was not a racially innocent state. To be "Bulgarian" in this state was to be "modern" and "European," hence "white" and culturally superior to "nonwhites" at home, mainly Gypsies, and "blacks" around the world.

I was "unlearning" these "truths" about myself and others as a student in courses on African American, Chicano, and Asian American cultures and histories. There, as I was trying to articulate my understanding of racism and discrimination in the United States, I was confronting and dismantling racialized ways of knowing that were deeply ingrained in my mind by my socialist education and upbringing.

Neither was I the "immigrant" my American friends imagined. I came to the United States on a student visa to study. Sheltered in the diverse and friendly academic community, benefiting from the services provided by the university to international students, I did not really experience the hardship of the "new immigrant." Moreover, Americans often assumed that I was in the United States to escape communist totalitarianism and pursue the "American dream," as "immigrants" do. I was supposed to tremble with admiration for "America" that was the safe heaven for the poor and the tortured. Many times I was invited to Thanksgiving dinners and asked to thank "America" for my good fortune. Yet many times I stood frozen and did not know what to say, because I did not feel thankful.

I was in the United States not to pursue the American dream but my own dreams. I was paying for my education and did not feel that I should thank "America" for giving me the opportunity to obtain higher education. I gave myself this opportunity by studying hard and working hard to pay for it.

Nor was I trembling with admiration for U.S. democracy and culture, because I realized throughout my studies that the ideologies of capitalism are as oppressive as those of communism. For two years, as I was pursuing a master's degree in political science, I sat in classes where the U.S. political system was celebrated as the "best" and as the end of history. I realized that this science of politics is an "American science" full of theories and assumptions rooted in notions of the United States as the center of the world and the embodiment of true "democracy." Yet I could not help but counter these claims with the U.S. history of racism and oppression I knew from American studies.

In political science, I also realized that I cherished a communist past marked by ideas of community and spirituality, and of social benefits of free health care and education. I constantly assessed those against the individualism and materialism of American culture, which I resented. Indeed, simultaneously I appreciated certain aspects of the U.S. social and political system but maintained a critical distance that allowed me to fantasize about a society that embodies the best of socialism and capitalism. But the political science I encountered denies such a possibility of "mixing" by designating socialism and communism as the totalitarian antipode of U.S. democracy. Only through such polarization can the United States emerge as a "superior" and truly "democratic" state, whose superiority is proven by science.

Yet every time I tried to apply the "science" in order to understand the operations of the communist state, for instance, the theories failed. My concerns over these limitations of political science were dismissed in the classes I attended, and I was told again that I "did not get it" because I was from a place where people did not know and did not practice "democracy." Perhaps Professor Steven Smith, a distinguished political scientist in the department, put it well when he told me in class that "foreigners" like me (meaning foreign students who pay for their education) were in the department to enable it to pay for the PhD students, most of whom were Americans.

Hence, I deducted, I was not in the department to contribute to political science but only to absorb its "truths." I was not "an important" student since I was seen only as a "foreign" financial tool contributing to the education of the Americans. In fact, I was clearly so insignificant that nobody in the department bothered to tell me that I had a mail box or to give me keys for the computer lab in the department. I learned about my entitlement to such "privileges" two months before my graduation. Thus, I, the former communist subject from an "underdeveloped country," as political science classified Eastern Europe and the rest of the non-Western world, was supposed to learn the U.S. democratic ways, to return to Bulgaria, and to teach people there how to practice this "polished" U.S. democracy.

And this "democracy" could be expressed in truly "scientific" ways, such as numbers, graphs, charts, and diagrams. In political science, concepts such as "culture" were dismissed as "unreliable," "meaningless," and "unscientific." Therefore, Professor Smith saw in the positivist methodology "the most exciting" political science. I saw in this political science a U.S.-centered discipline that arrogantly claimed to explain the experiences of all peoples and all countries. I also sensed in this political science embedded visions of the "American" as superior to other peoples, which allowed my marginalization in the classroom and in the discipline as "underdeveloped." I resented this "science's" attempts to express in numbers and formulas complex human lives that were guided by feelings, emotions, and imaginations that defied mathematical logic.

In the year 2000, resenting the positivism and U.S. centrism of political science, I took refuge in American Studies, where I pursued a PhD like the "important" American students whom Professor Smith praised. I knew from my undergraduate experience that American studies allowed for a critique of history and culture that I was now eager to express. Also in these courses, teachers encouraged me to freely articulate my visions and understanding of American culture and history, despite the fact that I was "foreign." However, I quickly became aware of the nationalist impulses of American studies as I was experiencing the field at the graduate level. Like political science, American studies imagined the "American" as exceptional and superior. Committed to the struggles of the marginalized and racialized minorities in the United States, including women, American studies envisioned these struggles as improving and expanding U.S. democracy, thus making the "best" even better. It perceived these minorities as agents of radical history happening in the United States. The rest of the "backward" peripheral world could learn from these American struggles.

But I kept asking myself if I should commit my scholarship *only* to the struggles of minorities in the United States. Who is committed to the struggles of oppressed in Eastern Europe, Africa, Latin America, and Asia? Is there not anything we can learn from the struggles of these non-Americans? Moreover, the more I learned about U.S. history and culture, the more I became aware that the American experience was not unique but was related to and intersected with the histories and experiences of other peoples and places. The communist state, for instance, formed and shaped its ideology against the Western capitalist state. The ideology of the former reacted to and depended on the ideology of the latter. Yet the cold war was not the only force that connected us. Past colonization and ongoing globalization of culture and capital also connected the "American" to the rest of the world. Why then keep perpetuating the idea of the "American" as "exceptional" and bound to the territory and history of the U.S. nation-state? Most of my fellow students and some of my professors were not ready for these questions. Again, my ideas were resented and often dismissed in graduate seminars. Again, I felt lonely and marginalized.

The intellectuals who helped me find the language and strength to express myself were not the white feminists in the department but an unorthodox historian and the queer scholars. Thanks to David Noble, Roderick Ferguson, and Jennifer Pierce, I finally found an intellectual, postnationalist niche, where I was allowed to question the theories and methods to which I was exposed. I could apply and assess the relevance of these theories to other, non-American and non-Western worlds. I indulged in studying qualitative methods of research, theories of postcolonialism, U.S. third world feminist and queer theories, and U.S. histories challenging American exceptionalism. In this intellectual space, I did not have to apologize for not committing my scholarship solely to the marginalized in the United States but could openly strive for intellectual politics and scholarship concerned with the struggles of oppressed around the world. Most of all, I could now explore what U.S. history and culture shared with the larger world and how the "backward" culture I came from intersected with the "superior" American experience.

My explorations of an interconnected world and alternative knowledges were especially empowered by U.S. third world feminism. In spring 2002, my mentor, friend, and brilliant social theorist Roderick Ferguson introduced me to the works of Chandra Mohanty, Audre Lorde, Chela Sandoval, Angela Davis, and Gayatri Spivak, among others. In the works of these feminists of color, I found an intellectual community where I did not have to define myself in either/or categories of race, nationality, or culture but could accept the fact that I traveled between countries, languages, and ideologies, claiming none of them as the sole foundation of my identities. As Mohanty put it, to be from the "third world" yet in the "first world" is to exist at "borderlands," where "consciousness is born of the historical collusion of . . . cultures and frames of reference."[5] In my case, this was the "collusion" of my ideas and experiences of socialism and capitalism, of "Western" and "Eastern," of "white" and "nonwhite" that I now accepted as shaping who I was.

Sandoval and Mohanty confirmed my sense that our world "is definable only in *relational* terms,"[6] because culture, identities, and struggles crossed "national" boundaries and were shaped by the larger projects of modernity, colonialism, imperialism, and even communism, much like the ongoing globalization of capital that "crosses all borders," and "colonizes and subjectifies all citizens" regardless of gender and location.[7] Spivak introduced me to "the greatest gift of deconstruction: to question the authority of the investigating subject," and the authority of the "universal," "great narratives," in which I was educated.[8] Spivak's work encouraged me to think of "what is left out" in the construction of the grand Western theories that I encountered in my studies.[9] And what was left out was the knowledges of the non-Western, the queer, the woman of color, and the so-called underdeveloped subject from the "third world," who, like me, felt imprisoned in the Western "Master's House." To break free, Davis and Lorde taught me, one should not rely on the "master's tools" or on the Western ideals that make up the "house."[10] Instead, one should learn "about coalition work" beyond race and gender and should learn "how to make common cause with those others identified as outside the structures in order to define and seek a world in which we can all flourish."[11]

I learned and embraced the "coalitional" politics of this feminism that did not draw boundaries around itself. I flourished within this inclusive feminism that did not care about my nationality, immigrant status, color, or gender. I shared U.S. third world feminist politics committed to transforming a world dominated by Euro-American ideologies and epistemologies that claimed to be the knowledges of all peoples. I also shared these feminists' concern with the liberation not just of women but of all oppressed humans, regardless of nationality, culture, race, or gender. Hence, one year ago, I called myself "a feminist."

However, even within U.S. third world feminism, I remain conscious of the inherent inequality between women in the United States from third world countries and women and men in the third world. Like me, "feminists of color" in the United States benefit from global markets, where the first world enjoys lifestyles and privileges at the expense of the exploited and poor in the "underdeveloped" world. And, like me, U.S. third world feminism is mobile, speaks two or three languages, and has access to intellectual and material resources that are denied to someone in postcommunist Bulgaria, for instance. The large political coalitions that we seek, then, will be possible only if we recognize that we have not been simply marginalized and oppressed as women or unhistorical, backward peoples, but that we live with and enjoy some of the privileges of the oppressor.

Hence, when I go back to Bulgaria, I do not preach the politics of my feminism but listen carefully about the issues and oppression men and women there face. I then try to incorporate these issues in my scholarship so that it may empower and aid struggles for social justice in both Bulgaria and the United States and in both "first" and "third" worlds. In this, I see the power of feminist politics that are now democratized, globalized, and self-critical.

Notes

1. Such politics are exemplified by Chela Sandoval, *Methodology of the Oppressed* (Minneapolis: University of Minnesota Press, 2000).

2. Chandra Mohanty, introduction to *Third World Women and the Politics of Feminism*, ed. Chandra Talpade Mohanty, Anna Russo, and Lourdes Torres (Bloomington: Indiana University Press, 1991), 4.

3. Elaine Tyler May, *Homeward Bound: American Families in the Cold War Era* (New York: Basic Books, 1999); Sara Evans, "Women's Consciousness and the Southern Black Movement," in *A History of Our Time: Readings on Postwar America*, 5th ed., ed. William H. Chafe and Harvard Sitkoff (Oxford: Oxford University Press, 1999); and bell hooks, "Black Women: Shaping Feminist Theory," in *A History of Our Time*, ed. Chafe and Sitkoff.

4. Rebecca Klatch, "Women Against Feminism," in *A History of Our Time*, ed. Chafe and Sitkoff.

5. Mohanty, introduction to *Third World Women and the Politics of Feminism*, ed. Mohanty, Russo, and Torres, 36.

6. Ibid., 2

7. Sandoval, *Methodology of the Oppressed*, 8.

8. Gayatri Spivak, "Subaltern Studies: Deconstructing Historiography" in *Selected Subaltern Studies*, ed. Gayatri Spivak and Ranajit Guha (New York: Oxford University Press, 1988), 9.

9. Gayatri Spivak, "The Post-Modern Condition: The End of Politics," in *The Post-colonial Studies Reader*, ed. Bill Ashcroft, Gareth Griffiths, and Helen Triffin (New York: Routledge, 1995), 18.

10. Audre Lorde, "The Master's Tools Will Never Dismantle the Master's House," in *Sister Outsider* (New York: Quality Paperback Book Club, 1993); Angela Davis, "Reflections on Race, Class, and Gender in the USA," interview with Lisa Lowe in *The Angela Y. Davis Reader* (Cambridge, Mass.: Blackwell Publishers, 1998).

11. Lorde, *Sister Outsider*, 112.

9. Mixed Race and Third Wave Feminism

Felicity Schaeffer-Grabiel

We were not born women of color, but became women of color here.
Jacqui Alexander and Chandra Mohanty

THE personal is not "naturally" political but became political in the university where I learned to connect personal oppression with larger webs of power. I chose the above quote because it speaks to my own experience of becoming a woman of color *here*—here meaning in multiple places and time periods: in the United States, the university, during the 1990s multiracial hip-hop explosion, and, I would add, in a U.S. immigrant family context. In this chapter, I weave in and out of my family genealogy and academic journey from the early 1990s to the present to demonstrate how my entrance into feminism has been a transformation that shifts, stretches, and moves between and across periods of time and space.

As a mixed race Chicana of the third feminist generation, I was provided the foundation for my political feminist consciousness by women of color feminists of the 1980s. This was as much a personal revolution as a radical questioning of histories, academic textual canons, theoretical paradigms, and political struggles. I entered feminism through various queer Xicana writers such as Gloria Anzaldúa and Cherríe Moraga as well as Ana Castillo.[1] This academic trajectory begins with my exposure to women of color writers in the early 1990s and continues with transnational feminism in 2003. I also make the case that *mestizaje,* or living between cultural contexts, and borderlands theories set the stage for current transnational feminist politics and interdisciplinary scholarship. The dominant trajectory of second wave feminism tells the story of women who brought struggles of gender and class (and sometimes race) to the streets and then fought to institutionalize this political consciousness in the academy during the late 1960s and early 1970s. Like many of us who grew up in the conservative climate of Reaganism, I developed a mestiza feminist consciousness in the 1990s in the context of the university, a wary place that worked to exclude and erase our experiences and histories, yet was also the place of liberation.

My understanding of feminism has come from many places but, most memorably, from within my family; it then became a conscious part of my world at the university. Like so many of us, I live in a body, places, and contexts crisscrossed by multiple histories, racial backgrounds, and disciplinary locations. I have always lived between multiple worlds, especially the different regions and countries my parents brought into the same home. My parents embodied the most extreme opposites between oppressor and oppressed. As an undergraduate in English at San Diego State University during the early 1990s, the vision I had of myself in relation to my parents' tumultuous interracial union changed while reading about the conquest of Mexico in Anzaldúa's *Borderlands/La Frontera*. Anzaldúa mythologized the conquest through the story of the Spanish conquistador Hernán Cortés and the Indian slave woman Doña Marina, who served as his translator and concubine. I realized that my body represented the modern tale of conquest between my Anglo father and Mexican mother.

I grew up in a home and city (Los Angeles) of racial conflict and many contradictions. My parents met in Los Angeles, across different sides of the track. My mother's family migrated to San Antonio, Texas, from Mexico during the Mexican revolution of 1910. Her parents raised ten kids, hustling odd jobs such as working in the fields, opening a small grocery store, fixing worn-out tires, and selling secondhand goods in my grandmother's thrift store. Her mother was both *indigena* and *española*; her father, *mexicano* and *alemán*/German. As a Mexican family struggling to survive during the 1950s and 1960s—when Anglos barred Mexicans from entering certain stores, public places (such as swimming pools and restaurants), institutions of higher education, and many professions—my mother and most of her brothers and sisters learned to survive by attempting to assimilate into the dominant Anglo society around them. While my mother was a young elementary and junior high student, the schools sponsored assimilation through Americanization programs where Euro-American teachers would reprimand them for speaking Spanish in the hallways and in the cafeteria. While they were less discriminated against because of their German last name, my mother continues to bare the scars of being made to feel inferior to her Euro-American classmates in San Antonio, a city pregnant with racism against both African Americans and Mexicans. Yet, being Mexican was a source of pride for my grandmother, who would not let her children, especially her daughters, stray from the rigid codes of correct behavior delineated by the Catholic Church. To escape the heavy racist climate in Texas (as well as her mother's strong-willed demeanor), my mother left for California in the 1960s—"Vamos a Califas," they would say—in hopes of a more open and liberating place to develop as a young woman.

My father's family comes from many generations of Lutheran German immigrants who fled persecution by the Catholics and wealthy aristocrats in Bavaria. Similar to the blacks in the South, Lutheran Germans were treated like second-class citizens in Germany, excluded from the best schools and jobs. Yet, their search for a better life in the United States was countered by another system of racial segregation during the early 1900s in the United States, when the Irish and the Germans continued to be segregated and racialized as ethnic "others."[2] The other side of his English family, however, comes from old money made from the 1890s to the 1940s through the H. B. Glover Co. overall factory. Almost as large as the World Trade Center, this massive factory outfitted almost every farmer in the Midwest and then switched to making uniforms for the U.S. army during World War II. The factory was controversial because of the famous Unionized Women Strike in the late 1890s, during which his great-great-grandfather (ab)used his political clout to fight off powerful labor unions. Even though my father and his family still reap the benefits from this factory, he always stubbornly wanted to prove that he could make it on his own (his strong work ethic is a refusal to use these privileges yet also embodies the "American" frontier ideology that anyone can pick oneself up by the bootstraps, a phenomenon that disavows racial and class privileges).

While my father remembers listening to his father's stories of racism against them as a German family, he identifies with his mother's side, the English family who shares a history with Colonel Glover, George Washington's right-hand man. His strong family connection to the building of the United States—first outfitting farmers and then both armies during the Civil War—is part of the deracialization of his German and English roots and serves to naturalize the sense of ownership and historical claim he feels as a white male and citizen. While Mexicans continue to build the nation as workers in the fields, nannies, domestics, governors, professors, scientists, and poets, they continue to be racialized as bodies of excess, bodies that drain the system rather than being visible as the backbone of the communities they work in and the very fabric of the nation.

While Mexicans and indigenous peoples were native to the Southwest, a territory of Mexico before the 1846–48 war, they are othered as immigrants and outsiders, while others take on the label of "pioneers," those who bring vision, progress, and modernity to people who continue to occupy that which is imagined as undeveloped, naturally wild, and backwards. As I peel back my family layers, I find no pure place to go back to; all of my relations embody legacies of conquest and resistance.

My parents' divergent immigrant histories paint their genealogy, the sense of who they are today. My father repeatedly tells my brother and me the story of his mother's family history to incorporate into us the idea that, like him, we are meant for big and great things. My mother, conversely, held onto the hope that if she assimilated (however unevenly and sometimes not at all) into the white world, her children might have it much better than she did. For this reason, my brother and I did not learn how to speak Spanish (although we understood it fluently) until college. She tried her best to protect us from the harsh days in Texas during the late 1950s when the Catholic nuns would swat the Mexican kids caught speaking Spanish in the hallways or classrooms. She always protected us from being Mexican, hoping that our middle-class neighborhood would surround us with the safety and privilege of whiteness. Yet this entrance into a privileged world came at a price. She married into this world and was continually reminded that she belonged only marginally, through marriage, not blood. Thus, my father excluded her from this genealogical past.

I promised myself that I would never do what my mother did, to think of myself as the woman who must sacrifice herself for her husband and family. I wanted to be like my auntie Alicia, the one who lived by the beach, bleached her hair blonde, had her own career, and never married. That is what feminism was when I was young—refusing to be dependent on a man, following your dreams, leaving the "Virgen complex" and most of my Mexican culture behind, and definitely never marrying.

This changed when I learned to understand my mother's world through the stories written by women of color about the generational conflicts that arose between mothers and daughters, from the old and new worlds. In *Loving in the War Years*, Cherríe Moraga tells the story of her painful relationship with her mother in a culture that privileges men and sons over daughters. Chicanas are taught to think of themselves as *Malinchistas*, sellouts, if they do not put men first. It took me a long time to understand how the world my mother came from left her few alternatives for a life outside the dusty circle of racism and oppression in which she grew up. She was immersed in a culture that told her she must keep up the pretense of feminine docility, of subservience to the husband, the father, and the holy spirit. I finally understood that her frustration with my casual fashion and demeanor reflected the disparaging geographic and cultural zones between California and Texas that separated us. My calm and highly motivated demeanor reminded her of my father, and while she could not reach him, she laid her unfulfilled dreams onto me, her imperfect daughter, who grew up in Southern California and refused to wear curls, thick makeup, dresses, and loud colors reminiscent of an idealized femininity for Mexican women in San Antonio. Even after my father left, she maintained this fixation on the ideal even as her reality resembled the matriarchal figure of my grandmother, whose husband died when my mother was young, leaving my *abuela* and her daughters in charge of the finances, cooking, and raising a very large family.

While the women in my family are strong, patriarchal codes of womanhood hold a tight grip on women's roles. Once I understood the history of my mother's actions and ideals, I was angry and hurt that my father did not treat her better, that she did not expect more for herself, and that our relationship was marred by this long history of patriarchy. This connection between my mother and me was important because she kept me grounded in a world that split open, and she was all I had when my father and brother moved away my first year of high school. I learned to be a woman, a feminist, and Mexican through and against her, a woman I fiercely loved and from whom I also felt estranged.

My parents' antagonistic relationship left me unaware of where to stand, without feeling as though I was taking sides, marking my line in the sand and crossing over, as if I could never return. Yet I did not belong completely to either side. I knew that my success in life mirrored societal benefits as well as my father's limited affection. Love was not conditional for my mother, yet she always tried to push me over to the other side, the white side where I could escape the hardships and pain she encountered in her life. I was never good enough for my mother because she was never good enough for my father, who thought I was good enough as long as I was not like my mother. As long as I measured myself against white standards, as long as I kept the brown girl inside of me silent, I was accepted. My body felt torn apart like the conquest of Mexico, conflicted between the white world of privilege and the brown world in which I identified and learned to question privileges, policies, histories, and perspectives that excluded and subordinated others. I had to survive in this contentious environment and thought the way to do this was by choosing to be either Mexican or white. But I was both, and I could never pass as just one or the other. I identified more with my father's more liberal and outspoken ways than with my mother's conservatism born out of years of training as a Catholic in Texas. My father was not indoctrinated in traditional gender roles; instead, he pushed me to succeed in school and supported my decision to go to graduate school. He always believed in me, and he even lent me money when I was twenty to start a funky little shoe store. Yet to adopt a white identity meant "forgetting" the pain deep down that I too was a second-class citizen as a Mexican and as a woman. I was caught in the body of a brown woman who could not look up to my mother's role nor our place as Mexicans in the larger white middle-class community I grew up in. While my decision to go to college appeared to validate my father's middle-class value system, I saw it as a space to dream outside the constrictions of domesticity and traditional gender roles. It was ironic, then, that when I decided to go to college, it was my mother who forced me to apply to colleges outside of Los Angeles. On one level I was entering her American dream, while she also worried that I would become "like them," too white and too unfeminine.

My departure to San Diego State University in 1989 initiated my growth as a woman of color. It was not until I cracked open Gloria Anzaldúa's books *Borderlands/La Frontera* and *Haciendo Caras/Making Face, Making Soul* in 1993 that I started to feel more awake, empowered to name what I had sensed for many years.[3] Finally, women of color were exposing the white world and the status quo of the university with their defiant tongues. Anzaldúa's courageous voice gave me, a mixed-race woman caught in multiple border zones, the historical and political context to understand why I felt severed from myself, from my family, and from the academy, as if I could not claim any place to stand. I learned to turn the world upside down and to find strength and power in standing between conflicting histories and cultures. What she called "la facultad," the ability to see more clearly from below, from multiple perspectives, was my strength, my world since I could remember.

I knew how to see the world through the lens of both the colonized and the conqueror and knew that power relations between the oppressor and the oppressed were much more complicated than the universal male versus female paradigm implicit in the term *woman* that feminism pursued. It was my experiences with my family, as a woman of color in a world that pushed me to be white, that drew me to this kind of feminism that insisted that race, gender, class, and one's national affiliation are central to how we see the world. My opposing family worldviews set the stage for me to identify with other women of color who saw themselves as outside mainstream culture and feminism in myriad ways. Thus, my personal life *became* political after I connected my ostracism with a larger historical, cultural, economic, and social framework. Once I realized the violent process of erasure that I had experienced in a school system that elided any diverse interpretations of history and cultural worldviews, I felt an urgency and political commitment to learn and teach to others what had been stolen from me.

As an undergraduate, I was part of an English department in the early 1990s that was split between the "old school" proponents of dead white male writers and the "new school," who brought me into contact with women of color writers and my own buried identities. I could not see myself as a meaningful part of the academy because I had no connections to the physical place, nor to the mythical legacies written about in the "classics" and taught in courses on "American" literature. Like many others, we learned to adventure, love, and travel with Anglo male characters from cultures and times much different from our own. Chicana feminist texts spoke out against the "aura of innocence" in the academic literary canon as well as Chicanas' exclusion from white women's feminist movements of the 1960s and 1970s. While it has been popularly understood that second wave feminism was a white women's movement, revisionist scholarship, such as that by Becky Thompson, argues that women of color were actively working toward political projects during the late 1960s and 1970s and beyond.[4] Thompson argues that during this time women of color worked in three areas: mixed racial movements, autonomous feminist organizations, and white-dominated feminist groups. In an attempt to reverse the idea that women of color's feminism came from white women, Thompson argues that much of the antiracist white women's collaborations came from working with women of color feminists. Others such as Angela Davis trace a feminist legacy back to the nineteenth century, when slave women intimately knew the connections between race and gender.[5]

I entered feminism at a time when multiracial coalitions defined the present and future of feminism(s) as coming out of women's personal exclusions and multifaceted activism. I took for granted that a feminist perspective envisioned the world through an interdisciplinary axis in which race, class, and gender were central to women's struggles. Through these women writers, I forged an identity as a woman of color, not only though my mixed racial background but through a political consciousness that awakened me to a life aimed toward social change. The reaction against identity politics came at a time when people of color were entering the academy in greater numbers. Rather than to espouse essential identities, identity politics is a way to strategically mobilize alliances with other women of color activists who fought for a more open understanding of feminism as it intersects with race, class, culture, age, religion, sexuality, nation, and gender.

During this time, in the early 1990s, the cultural wars spread across campuses, forcing divisions among faculty in our English department at San Diego State University. The literary "canon" was under attack as questions of alternative histories, race, gender, and multiculturalism were just beginning to be theorized as a necessary part of education. And it did not help that I was at a university in one of the most conservative Californian political climates, where Governor Pete Wilson led an anti-immigration campaign that came to fruition in 1994 when California passed proposition 187. This proposition delineated the racial, class, and gender boundaries of citizenship in an attempt to deter Mexican immigrants from crossing into California (and San Diego specifically) by taking away medical and public services and education for "illegal" workers and their children. It was amid this climate that my professor Ian Barnard, who was a temporary hire at the time, brought the voices of women of color into the classroom. Teaching his first class, he did not realize that the majority of students would resist Anzaldúa's texts, *Borderlands/La Frontera* and *Making Face, Making Soul/Haciendo Caras*, with such strong opposition. In a classroom that was conservative, middle-class, and mostly white, I was one of the few students who saw these texts as positive and life-changing. Even two Mexican-national female students rejected Anzaldúa as definitely *not* Mexican, as low class, nonacademic, offensive, and crude. They challenged the professor in class as to why he had them read such tasteless books that misrepresented "true" Mexicans and Mexico more generally. A white male student dropped the course and sent the professor hate letters threatening to beat him up for trying to sneak his "queer" politics into class through Chicana lesbians.

Chicana feminist writers spoke to me in a way that I thought my mother would identify with, but was surprised to learn she vehemently rejected. That is "low-life" stuff, she would say, mimicking her mother's insistence on steering her children away from those who were dark-skinned and low class, including Chicanas who wore lots of black makeup and sprayed their hair into big webs that defied even the strongest wind. During my mother's generation in Texas, Chicanas/os were marginalized and framed as the abject by aspiring middle-class Mexican Americans who hoped for acceptance by mainstream Euro-American culture. In California during the 1980s and 1990s, however, the term *Chicana* became popularized as a working-class aesthetic and self-proclaimed affiliation for *mujeres* who fought alongside working-class women. It was also a designation for those who wanted to claim a politicized identity and history as *transfrontera mestizas,* or those of mixed racial heritage labeled from across both sides of the border.

When I look back now, I wonder why these texts spoke to me differently than they did to the rest of the class. Unlike the Mexican students who saw themselves as part of the dominant class in Mexico as well as in the United States, I was uncomfortable trying to "pass" with the white middle class. I always felt "out-of-place" and thus identified with the other kids of color who were meant to feel like they did not belong. These women wrote about their marginal place across different spaces such as through the church, in their families, in the academy, in the feminist movement, and in the United States. I felt something powerful move inside me, as the stories I read turned what was private and solitary into a public and widely shared sentiment that was larger than life. It was through women writers and their feminism that I developed the skills to speak up, to refuse to let others make me feel like I was only partially good enough, that my skin was either too light or too brown. Academia was an imperfect "home" for the homeless, those of us who work toward making visible the multiple exclusions, erasures, and injustices in our lives and those around us. This was feminism, a political consciousness that was personal and public, particular and universal, a way of life that shifted sometimes with great force and other times slowly and as quiet as the wind.

Coming from such disparate family histories helped to broaden and balance my perspective on race and privilege. I intimately knew what it was to be poor, to be from a lineage of wealth and prestige, to be comfortable in my grandmother's home where too many people were squeezed into too small a space, as well as to exist in the quiet and tidy home of my father's family. Feminism could never be as simple as following a checklist of qualities, such as protesting or having a career outside of the home. I learned how to see things in their complexity, to connect where we came from with where we move toward and sometimes arrive, and to move comfortably and often uncomfortably between worlds. I could not understand how my mother saw herself as a woman without understanding how this was tied to her experiences as a Mexican in the very racist state of Texas in the 1950s and 1960s. These intersections were the center that made sense to me as a mixed racial woman who never felt completely at home in a white identity, nor in a Chicana one, nor in the academy. I felt the most alive with others who were seen and saw themselves as "misfits," "queers," "*foresteros*/outsiders," demanding that we be given space to vocalize our experiences.

The antagonistic attacks against the professor and the texts by women of color sharpened the lines for those of us on the margins of the academy. I developed a critical relation with the English department and with the university system, the place where I had become transformed and politicized in the first place. Choosing to align myself with women of color writers was both liberating and frustrating, because as a light-skinned *mujer* who did not speak Spanish at the time, I always felt I had to pass some "authenticity" test to be considered a "true" Latina. Yet it was liberating to find an outlet for the injustices I felt and saw and lacked the language to describe. It was confusing, too, to feel like I had to position myself against a homogeneous white culture that I knew was more complex. I went to a couple of MEChA meetings on campus—a student run organization for Chicanos in higher education—but could not identify with the patriarchal and nationalistic construction of a Chicano identity that defined itself as against the dominant white culture, while perpetrating women's subordinate roles as part of the movement.[6]

In the early 1990s, my racially feminist perspective paralleled a larger explosion of hip-hop culture. I found a more dynamic home through the multiracial hip-hop music and fashion scene I was actively engaged with in downtown San Diego. As the co-owner of a shoe store in the offbeat area of San Diego—where deejays spun music, artists sprayed graffiti on the walls, and music artists frequented—I also came into being as a feminist woman of color in a multiracial community in which I thought the sky was the limit. Unfortunately, however, I found the ideal of multiculturalism in the late 1980s and early 1990s worked against me as a female woman of color. As I was coming into myself as a mixed-race Latina, white boys saw me as exotic, and my political views of what this racial and ethnic claim meant dissipated under sexual desire. And after five years of participating in an underground movement where young people were talking about race, racism, politics, and revolution through music, fashion, and dance, I found myself confronting the limits of my role selling platform shoes, shell-toed Adidas, and vintage clothes. The initial thrill at the possibilities for change was dampened by the need to sell to survive and the fact that capitalism needed difference to survive and then deflated it as something that was equally accessible to all who could afford to buy it. It was time to move on.

In 1994, I went to a small San Diego café to see Ana Castillo talk about her new book, *Massacre of the Dreamers*.[7] Like other Native, African and Asian American feminists at the time, Castillo resisted a Western-centric notion of history and progress by drawing on her own brand of feminist indigenous belief systems. She uncovered pre-Aztec deities such as Coatlicue and Tonantzin, deities that were appropriated by an overly masculine Aztec warrior society and then by patriarchal Catholic Spanish conquistadors. Part of the process of eradicating legacies of racial and sexual conquest was accomplished through a process of uncovering histories in which women and their sexuality were valued in indigenous cosmology and everyday lives. I wanted to learn more about my history, wanted to have the tools to further my goals of radicalizing people's minds in a similar way as I had become radicalized in the university. My inner transformation had begun in my family, but it was at the university that these latent feelings became conscious to me as a political project toward change. I decided to get a master's in Latin American studies to learn more about women and feminism across the first world/third world divide.

While I thought that the Latin American studies program at the University of Arizona in 1996–98 would be a lively place to exchange perspectives with a diverse student body, when I entered the program, I was the only student of color. It was here, however, in courses that spanned the Americas, that I was forced to face my own U.S.-centric bias that led me to believe feminism was a radical movement brought about by U.S. women of color during the 1960s and 1970s. I found an interesting hierarchy among those who studied and taught courses on Latin America (mostly Euro-American scholars) and the assumption that only those who were Chicana/o or Mexican American studied the "local," or grounded, experiences of the U.S.-Mexico borderlands. At the time, few faculty or students from Latin America made up a critical part of the conversation or theoretical framework. In a similar vein, transnational and global projects are "globally circulated" from the United States outward, although this perspective is in a state of flux as the occupants of the United States continue to change. But this dominant position within the United States is enabled by privileges of citizenship within the wealthiest nation, which give us access to particular perspectives, a wealth of resources, and a historical legacy that mark some of us as local and others as cosmopolitan.

Almost all of my classes were cross-listed in women's studies, so I developed my program with a minor in women's studies. Gender and women were always central to my interests, yet women's studies departments were dubious "homes" for me; not only were there few programs that offered graduate degrees, but I had learned to be skeptical of mainstream women's studies politics through my entrance as a woman of color feminist. Furthermore, most of the more radical faculty of color were straddled between departments and marginally affiliated with the department. While I was only marginally aware of the schism between "official" middle-class feminism and a more diffuse idea of how women enacted their own version of feminist activism and survival tactics, I delved into the lives of early feminists in Mexico: La Malinche, Sor Juana Inés de la Cruz, las madres de la Plaza del Mayo, and indigenous Zapatista women. Feminism could be using your power as a mother to demand justice for the disappeared, it could be entering the nunnery to escape marriage (and/or sex with men), it could be starting a soup kitchen for people in the community, or it could be selling your body to feed your kids. One of the earliest feminist conferences, bringing hundreds of mostly middle-class women together, was in Yucatán, Mexico, in 1916. An array of radical and conservative Mexican women came together to debate better working conditions for domestic workers, better education and health for women, as well as women's right to vote and participate in the political process. While I had considered women of color feminism as a challenge to "Western" feminism, I realized that feminism was much different on the other side of the border.

I became interested in cross-border conversations and activism, and interactions between Chicanas and Mexicanas. In one of my early graduate courses at the University of Arizona, Adriana Estil introduced me to the way Chicanas attempted to think about making cross alliances through the feminist theoretical paradigm of Chela Sandoval.[8] Rather than replace the margins for the center as the privileged space from which to gaze, scholars such as Sandoval theorized instead for making strategic alliances across differences depending on the needs of the community. To avoid replacing the center with yet another form of domination, she labeled these constantly shifting movements as "guerilla tactics." Even though differences between women can be great, we must politically unite through a feminist political commitment to speaking from diverse marginal places. The idea of "guerilla tactics" was a way of life for me. I realized that as my identity changed in different places and in relation to different people, I would have to creatively navigate each situation with different tools, defenses, and tactics, a strategy that, women of color feminists reminded me, did not mean I was less of a feminist. I thought back to my mother and understood that she had a different set of tools than I did, and grew up in a different generation with different codes of what it meant to be a Mexican woman. Guerilla tactics were also important later in my academic career in learning to understand feminism across national borders, class backgrounds, and racial milieus.

Women in Mexico are influenced by feminism in the United States, and Chicanas by women in Mexico, but very unequally. The uneven circulation of knowledge across borders makes it more challenging for us in the United States to even access books from Mexico. Rosaura Sánchez and Beatrice Pita identify the role the United States and Europe play in the production of knowledge through the NAFTA trade agreement. As NAFTA opens Mexico's borders to foreign investment, publishing houses are bought out by foreign investors, increasing the circuit of foreign texts and decreasing the market for local production.[9] The politics of how information travels accentuates the uneven dispersal of knowledge. Yet feminism continues to thrive across the Americas with or without knowledge of feminists in the United States. I learned to interpret feminist struggles not through static definitions of Western empowerment, but through the spectrum of ways that women came into contact with larger structures of power in their everyday lives and experiences. To complicate the hegemonic production of knowledge and power emanating from the United States, we need to build more alliances with academics, activists, and institutions outside the United States. Rather than merely looking at knowledge from new places, we need to share and collaborate in the production of knowledge , so that transnational projects do not reproduce violent erasures of "others" while we profit and develop our professionalization on the backs of other people's lives.

Tools of the Mestiza Trade

As a mestiza feminist, I learned a new world of women's theorizing, resistance, and politics from across the border and through new medi-
ums. Only certain women had access to written books; thus, I turned to
popular culture, from art, to documentaries, to magazines, to soap op-
eras, and to film, to examine women's expressions and representations.
I wanted to find connections between Latinas on both sides of the U.S.-
Mexico border. I realized that border conflicts in the United States were
de-politicized through a romantic union between an Anglo man and a
Latina. Differences were minimized through middle-class romance narratives in which love (and assimilation) conquered all. In Mexico, class
differences came to light between lower-class women who were told to
be creative survivors, even if this meant becoming a prostitute, and mid-
dle- to upper-class women who were expected to seek out romance with
men who promised upward mobility.[10] Thus, feminism was not only lived
differently by women but institutionalized unevenly through popular
culture and social expectations.

Despite my enthusiasm for the project, some in the Latin American
studies department were skeptical at the time as to whether a project
that crossed the U.S.-Mexico border could be considered Latin American studies. Because of the need to demarcate boundaries between disciplines, borderlands were a threat, a liminal zone that put in question
the distinctiveness of this area studies. There was little discussion of how
contemporary U.S. imperialism resembled colonial processes in Latin
America or of how Mexicanas and Latinas from the United States shared
a feminist consciousness or experiences. I decided to find an academic
home in American studies and feminist studies for their support of interdisciplinary methods and transnational research projects.

I applied to PhD programs in ethnic studies, Chicano studies, and
American studies. I chose to pursue a PhD in American studies at the
University of Minnesota in 1998 because American studies was an interdisciplinary field informed by ethnic studies and feminist debates and
was critical of the United States' imperial role at home and abroad. I resisted the boundaries of area studies because in Latin American studies
at the time there was little discussion about how intertwined the United
States and Latin America were economically and culturally and about
how each place was crisscrossed by migration, policies, and globalization. While the United States is also an "area" of study, I was much more

interested in how dominant national narratives intersected with racial, gender, and class politics in the United States as well as across national contexts. I learned how central race, sexuality, and gender were to de-marcating the boundaries of the nation, or what Benedict Anderson has now popularly labeled "the imagined community."[11]

While my feminism began with women of color, I was later taught a linear history of feminism through texts and discussions about feminism in both American studies and women's studies at the University of Min-nesota. The first wave of feminism was popularly conceived as beginning in the United States by white women during the suffrage movement of the 1920s, and then by both white women and women of color in the 1960s and 1970s. Since then, exciting scholarship has reevaluated the assumption that feminism began in the United States and that race was not a significant part of the equation for feminists fighting for equal-ity. Louise Michele Newman makes important connections between the way suffrage feminists leveraged power through racial divisions between themselves and the "racial degenerates" in other countries that needed to be "civilized" and "saved." Thus, Newman hones in on white women's feminism in their efforts to civilize immigrants at home, concurrent with the United States' need to assert itself as an imperial power abroad.[12] Newman brings back the centrality of race to early feminist organizing.

Again, I turned to the feminist studies department for classes and a second home. Yet, the department was troubled by academic approaches to the theoretical legacies of feminism. Is it to be taught through a linear trajectory, assuming a seamless cause and effect from the second wave to the third wave? Who would be included and who excluded? Who originated certain theories? There was a division between those who did "high" feminist theory (usually embedded in masculine ideas about knowledge production) and those who produced *rigorous* theory from their personal lives. For example, even though Donna Haraway coined the catchy phrase "situated knowledges," this same idea had been dis-cussed by Moraga, Anzaldúa, and others earlier who talked about doing "theory in the flesh" (1981). We graduate students entered this debate in the core feminist theory class. Our professor decided to approach this debate by allowing our interests to steer the course, thus opting for the "hands-off" approach. While this ideal approach looked appetizing in "theory," we were left with a "melting pot" understanding of feminism disconnected from larger discussions of historical social movements, power, hegemony, and the deleterious effects in the academic tradition of the race for theory.[13] While feminists theorized about situated knowledge, we were left with an eclectic array of women's theoretical contributions without any grounding in where these debates came from. In a department that must continually justify its existence in an academic milieu dominated by masculine ideas of producing universal rather than personal theory, feminists were challenged by how they would define their theoretical contributions to the larger academic community.

The struggle with how to define and teach women's studies courses continues to challenge departments across the United States. In many classes, women of color become the "final frontier" to end with in the class rather than the beginning. And the assumption that women of color feminism was based on a critique of their exclusion from white women's movements leaves us recentering the history of feminism as a white women's movement. To escape putting women of color in the position of resistance based on identity politics, rather than as the site of radical critique, would require centering the course on current debates and scholarship that have pushed women's studies to question new theoretical paradigms and exclusions, and how activism is imagined and carried out. Women of color do not simply mark another addition to the legacy of feminism in the United States, but as Lee argues, "Women Studies became a 'field' when it realized its racial exclusions." She also argues that women of color can shed this reactionary stance (of finding a pure site to gaze from without being seen) by acknowledging their own blind spots. Three examples she raises are (1) being U.S.-centered, (2) relying on civil rights as the place for change (thus excluding Native Americans), and (3) emphasizing "unity" and thus obscuring other legitimate modes of conceptualizing change.[14]

The idea that disciplinary boundaries come into sharp relief when exclusions are made visible resonates with the new direction of American studies, moving from a discipline that reinforced the United States as an exceptional nation to one that recognizes the United States as embedded in racism and imperialism. American studies developed out of a cold war era that hoped to solidify national boundaries; Inderpal Grewal and Caren Kaplan understand feminist studies' national preoccupation as having a similar historical trajectory.[15] Freedom and democracy for *all* were ideologies steeped in the formation of "whiteness," ideas and practices that were built on the backs of people of color (such as the violent disavowal of Native and Mexican land, slave and women's labor). Even the desire for suffrage and women's rights were masked as the rights for middle-class Euro-American women. Feminist work needs to break this U.S.-centered paradigm by looking at the common and uneven links among patriarchies, colonialisms, racisms, and feminisms across national contexts.[16] A transnational framework emphasizes linkages rather than comparisons, what Ella Shohat calls the "relational approach" that "operates at once within, between and beyond the nation-state framework."[17] Much earlier, Chandra Mohanty similarly defined third world feminism of the 1990s as

a world which is definable only in *relational* terms, a world traversed with intersecting lines of power and resistance, a world which can be understood only in terms of its destructive divisions of gender, color, class, sexuality, and nation, a world which must be transformed through a necessary process of pivoting the center . . . for the assumed center (Europe and the United States) will no longer hold.[18]

Mohanty is also concerned with how we theorize feminism in relation to women with different histories and relations to colonial and state structures. Mohanty poses the question of whether third world women share a particular history (she expands the "third world" to include poor women of color in the United States). She says, "What seems to constitute 'women of color' or 'third world women' as a viable oppositional alliance is a *common* context of struggle rather than color or racial identifications."[19]

I have found even "women of color" feminism and borderlands theory from the 1980s to be similarly limiting in their U.S.-centric vision. Yet, it was borderlands theory, the idea that people live between borders, nations, cultures, languages, genders, and racial constructions, that initiated my interest in the ways Chicanas and Latinas across the United States and Mexico share political visions, experiences, and patriarchal systems while also coming from different state regimes and nations. Perhaps it was fate that I stumbled on those Web sites advertising hot, sexy (yet marriageable) Latinas to predominantly white men from the United States, which set in motion my dissertation project. In this project, I examine the cyber-bride industry as a contemporary contact zone between the United States and Mexico where new kinds of migration patterns, constructions of selfhood, and transnational constructions of race, gender, family, nationhood, and sexuality are forged. The simultaneous desire and repugnance surrounding the U.S.-Mexico border have always intrigued me. It is not a coincidence that backlashes against Mexican laborers coincide with the "Latino craze" or that multi-culturalism was heralded during a time of intense anti-immigrant senti-ment. While men from the United States seek in Mexican women what they feel they lack in themselves and the culture around them, they are also reminded of their superiority in the presence of the "other." I took to heart this simultaneous production of self and other that Anzaldúa, Morrison, Hegel, hooks, Said, and others speak about. Mexican women also seek what they lack in themselves and their culture in men from the United States but are faced with a sense of emptiness once they move to the United States that accompanies such extravagant lifestyles. Further-more, they see how men who once basked in their differences turn it on them by trying to get women to leave their worlds behind and become "Americanized." I have felt this deep down from both my mother and father. This contradiction goes deep into the conquest and continues through imperial and global processes that bring these two nations, cul-tures, and people into uneven contact with each other.

Feminism on the Run

I have spent the past ten years or so traveling across the United States to attend graduate schools, I have traveled back and forth to Mexico for research, and I have now returned to California as a dissertation fellow at the Chicana/Latina Research Center at the University of California, Davis. During a time when theorizing prioritizes the mobile, this kind of roving lifestyle and career call for creative strategies for learning how to live our feminist visions for change, as well as the desire for families and communities (in whatever form we create them). In these times of flux, I am continually questioning what feminism is and how I live feminism through my academic, personal, imaginative, and activist life.

My participation in Capoeira—an Afro-Brazilian martial arts/dance group—equips me with a vision of transnational feminist praxis for fu-ture generations who sometimes have to be mobile and want to connect with the local communities in which they live. Capoeira is a hybrid mar-tial arts/dance some say originated with the African slaves of Brazil, who practiced defense movements while the slave owners were out of sight. Upon their return, the slaves would feign dancing to hide their resist-ance for the day they would set themselves free. The songs we sing, the instruments we play, and the kicks and rhythms we practice are a form of remembering, through the body, mind, and spirit, this history of colonialism and resistance now taken up by communities in the United States, Mexico, Japan, and around the world. Whatever city I move to, my partner and I take part in an active and multiracial community committed to social change. We use music, dance, and our voices to speak out against injustices, such as most recently protesting against the war in the Middle East. Capoeira changes form as it travels from Brazil to the United States and back again, incorporating local politics while also conserving the spirit of resistance and history of oppression from which it gathers energy. Its origins remain contested and continue to be rewritten by those who participate.

Women's participation in Capoeira grows stronger and poses a critical challenge to those *mestres*/professors who insist on preserving the patriarchal roots of Capoeira and marginalize women's participation. Yearly women's workshops in Oakland and global chat discussions continue to raise consciousness and push for the importance of women's contributions in democratizing this art form that combines martial arts, gymnastics, yoga, and postmodern dance forms in a way that blurs gender, national, and geographic boundaries and origins. Even as a site of struggle, Capoeira nonetheless serves as an alternative model for putting transnational feminism into practice by fusing local and transnational activism. Together, we remember that globalization is not new but part of a longer history of colonization in which we defend multiple struggles for self-determination.

Thus, for me, feminism has been a road of flux, of *mestizaje*, of being in-between, and of crossing borders, and a process of returning to how my own family history connects to present-day global circuits of desire, marriage, and migration. As long as knowledge continues to be envisioned as a commodity that helps us climb the corporate academic ladder—rather than a process of liberation, change and self-definition—the radical qualities of the university will be wiped out.[20] My own transformation as a feminist within the university commits me to fighting to keep this institution as an important place for social change and liberation.

I no longer see feminism as having to make a choice between my family and the academy, between activism in the classroom and in the streets, and as having to exclude men. In some ways, my life has come full circle. My parents now live together after fifteen years of separation, and I have recently married a wonderful man who has similarly learned to understand the complexities of feminism as a struggle that he must also engage. I will not be confined by someone else's version of feminism and will continue to critically question what it means in different places, times, and situations. I refuse to give up my family and community for the academy or the academy for my family/community. Both exist within me and continue to bring me balance and wholeness.

Notes

1. Ana Castillo used an *X* instead of a *Ch* to emphasize the linguistic, cultural, historical, racial, and spiritual connections between Chicanas in the United States and indigenous female legacies across the Americas. The Spanish language to this day utilizes many Nahuatl words such as *chocolate,* which were written with an *X* rather than a *Ch.* See Ana Castillo, *Massacre of the Dreamers: Essays on Xicanisma* (Albuquerque: University of New Mexico Press, 1994).

2. For more on this topic, see Matthew Frye Jacobson, *Whiteness of a Different Color: European Immigrants and the Alchemy of Race* (Cambridge, Mass.: Harvard University Press, 1998).

3. See Gloria Anzaldúa, *Borderlands/La Frontera* (San Francisco: Spinsters/ Aunt Lute, 1987); and Gloria Anzaldúa, ed., *Making Face, Making Soul/Haciendo Caras* (San Francisco: Aunt Lute Foundation Books, 1990).

4. Becky Thompson, *A Promise and a Way of Life: White Antiracist Activism* (Minneapolis: University of Minnesota Press, 2001).

5. Angela Davis, *Women, Race, and Class* (New York: Vintage Books, 1981).

6. MEChA stands for *Movimiento Estudiantil Chicano de Aztlán*/Chicano Student Movement of Aztlán. MEChA is a national organization that came out of the social movements of 1968, when Chicano students were fighting not only for equality for all Chicanos but for the creation of Chicano studies departments across the United States. Chicano students held a conference at the University of California, Santa Barbara, to develop a master plan for the creation of a curriculum and the related auxiliary services and structures essential to facilitate Chicanas and Chicanos in institutions of higher education.

7. See Castillo, *Massacre of the Dreamers.*

8. Chela Sandoval, "U.S. Third World Feminism: The Theory and Method of Oppositional Consciousness in the Postmodern World," *Genders* 10 (Spring 1991): 1–24.

9. Sánchez and Pita use a study by Nestor Garcia Canclini on the effects of NAFTA on Mexican cultural productions. See Rosaura Sánchez and Beatrice Pita, "Mapping Cultural/Political Debates in Latin American Studies," *Cultural Studies* 13, 2 (April 1999): 295.

10. See Jean Franco, "The Incorporation of Women: A Comparison of North American and Mexican Popular Narrative," in *Studies in Entertainment: Critical Approaches to Mass Culture,* ed. Tania Modleski (Bloomington: Indiana University Press, 1986).

11. There are many feminist critiques of Anderson's "imagined community" that specifically question who has the power to "imagine" the nation and how

gender, race, and class influence the kind of nation that is disseminated. See Partha Chatterjee, *The Nation and Its Fragments: Colonial and Postcolonial Histories* (Princeton, N.J.: Princeton University Press, 1993); and Caren Kaplan, Norma Alarcón, and Minoo Moallem, eds., *Between Woman and Nation: Nationalisms, Transnational Feminisms, and the State* (Durham, N.C.: Duke University Press, 1999).

12. Louise Michelle Newman, *White Women's Rights: The Racial Origins of Feminism in the United States* (New York: Oxford University Press, 1999), 21.

13. See Barbara Christian's early critique of how theory has become a central commodity of production in the academy and is central to processes of inclusion and exclusion, such as whose voice carries legitimacy, who gets heard, and how knowledge is constructed. Barbara Christian, "The Race for Theory," *Cultural Critique* 6 (Spring 1987): 51–63.

14. Rachel Lee, "Notes from the (Non) Field: Teaching and Theorizing Women of Color," in *Women's Studies on Its Own: A Next Wave Reader in Institutional Change*, ed. Robyn Wiegman (Durham, N.C.: Duke University Press, 2002), 96.

15. Inderpal Grewal and Caren Kaplan, "Transnational Practices and Interdisciplinary Feminist Scholarship: Refiguring Women's and Gender Studies" in *Women Studies on Its Own*, ed. Wiegman, 69–70.

16. Ibid., 70.

17. Quoted in ibid., 76.

18. Chandra Mohanty, Ann Russo, Lourdes Torres, eds., *Third World Women and the Politics of Feminism* (Bloomington: Indiana University Press, 1991), 2, emphasis in the original.

19. Ibid., 2.

20. Chandra Mohanty, *Feminism without Borders: Decolonizing Theory, Practicing Solidarity* (Durham, N.C.: Duke University Press, 2003).

10. Between Wind and Water

Thinking about the Third Wave as Metaphor
and Materiality

Hokulani K. Aikau

I encountered the turbulent waters of feminism relatively
early in my academic career. As an undergraduate in women's studies
in the early 1990s, I learned that the "safety" of a feminist space could
be as destructive and dangerous as a harbor where a small boat anchors
to escape a storm only to be thrashed about and nearly toppled. It was
a Sunday evening and a special session of the women's studies executive committee convened to discuss allegations of students (myself included) interfering with a professor's academic freedom. At the time,
I did not really understand the meaning of academic freedom or how
course evaluations could interfere with it. During the first half of the
meeting I was so upset by the discussion and implicit threat that I might
be expelled from college that I dissolved into tears. Shortly thereafter
we took a break. In the dim light of the hallway, a second generation
feminist sociologist, Dair Gillespie, was the first to comfort me. She put
her arm around my shoulders and with a strong, reassuring squeeze, she
looked into my tear-filled eyes and said, "Honey, to be a feminist in the
academy you'll need to grow tits of steel." That was over ten years ago
now, and I have realized that tits of steel are essential armor for being a
feminist in the academy, but, as we also know, with prolonged exposure
to salt water steel begins to rust.

By the time I arrived at the University of Minnesota in 1997, I had put
my armor away. The volatility of the feminist academy seemed behind
me. Trained as an undergraduate in women's studies at the University
of Utah and as a master's student at the Center for Research on Women
(CROW) at The University of Memphis, I came to Minnesota taking
feminism for granted.[1] Further, I entered a graduate program in American studies and a university where feminism seemed to be in the water
like fluoride. Minnesota housed not only the nationally recognized Department of Women's Studies but also an influential research center,
the Center for Advanced Feminist Studies. And most of the graduate

courses I took as well as the professors who taught them were influenced by feminism. So, after depositing my armor on the shelf, my thinking about metaphors for feminism began to shift.

This shift was prompted, in part, by my participation as an invited panelist for an "Author Meets Critic" session of the American Sociological Association in August 2000. The panel featured the three founding members of CROW—Elizabeth Higginbotham, Bonnie Thornton Dill, and Lynn Weber—and I was invited to speak as a representative from the "next generation." At that time I was unfamiliar with the literature on third wave feminism, and after reading more about this new, emerging cohort of which I was supposed to be a part, I was left feeling more confused than when I began. Why was it called "third" wave? And how was the third wave supposed to be distinct from the second? I did not let this confusion sway my enthusiasm at being able to share the stage with my mentor from The University of Memphis, Elizabeth Higginbotham. I went to the conference, did my presentation, but left with a nagging suspicion that something was missing in the literature on third wave feminism.

After the conference, I left for a research trip to Hawai'i. Sitting on the beach I began to wonder more about the metaphor of waves and how they were being used to describe consecutive generations of academic feminists. Where do waves come from? How do they operate? As I sat and watched wave after wave roll onto shore, I wondered how we could tell when one wave begins and another ends. According to surfers, waves come in sets of three or more with the third wave being an ideal one to catch and ride to shore. The first few waves allow the surfer to read the size and speed of the waves that will follow. The surfer does not worry if she does not catch the third wave or if the set fades out before reaching shore because she knows that more will be coming on the horizon. In the surfer's understanding of the materiality of waves, she looks to the horizon in eager expectation of not one but rather sets of *many* waves.

Within the historiography of twentieth-century feminism in the United States, waves often serve as a metaphor for the large-scale and highly visible involvement of women in social movements that brought about dramatic transformations in women's access to social, political, educational, and economic opportunities. Historian Sara Evans, for instance, describes how women's collective activism has dramatically changed American society in the past forty years as a "tidal wave."[2] In her usage, the tidal wave stands in for forty years of social, political, and economic change. The current literature by and about third wave feminists also uses the term *wave* to distinguish their vision of feminism from that of the second. In their writings, the third wave refers at once to forms of political activism, theoretical work, scholarship, and a particular birth cohort—feminists who were born between 1964 and 1975.[3] In their understanding, the third wave represents changes in politics, scholarship, and generational cohorts.

In this essay, I argue that thinking about waves as both materiality and metaphor is productive for looking broadly at structural forces that shape academic feminism and for describing fully the variety of experiences, politics, and forms of feminism that exist within a single feminist generation. In making this argument, I suggest that generations and waves should not be used interchangeably but, in fact, offer two distinct vantage points from which to view feminist legacies and trajectories. In my reconceptualization, generations represent a particular cohort of people, while waves work as a metaphor for the movement and relocation of theories, politics, methods, and ways of knowing across time and place. While generation relies on time as a distinguishing characteristic, taken alone it cannot fully describe the complex interplay of forces that affect when an individual encounters feminism, how one receives feminist ideas and politics, and the style and form of feminist politics one subsequently advances. The materiality of waves, however, requires us to pay attention to historical time *and* place. It shows us how energy is carried forward from previous forces and how it changes as it encounters obstacles, shores, and currents. Rather than think about the "second" and "third" waves as separate physical entities that we can count from the shore, as third wave writers often do, I suggest that feminists look to the horizon for the variety of waves that comprise a wave train in order to understand the multiplicity central to feminist legacies and trajectories.

This vision of waves allows us to see how one generation of feminists can be produced from a multiplicity of waves created out of larger generating forces. As I argue, reading waves as materiality offers a more complex view of the variations that exist within a single generation of feminists and begins to offer a way to trace the legacies of feminism through time and across space. In what follows, I begin with a brief examination of the scientific basis of waves. Next, I offer a reading informed by this thinking about how different waves of feminist thought swelled and ebbed upon two different academic shores during the late 1970s and early 1980s. Finally, I highlight two ways the materiality of waves can be used to trace feminism's legacy by drawing from my own personal encounters with feminism as a third "wave" feminist.

Understanding Waves, Understanding Feminisms

Waves can be found on any body of water. Waves can be as small as the ripples that form on the surface of the milk as my cat laps up her treat. They can be as big as a tsunami, a seismic sea wave that is formed from earthquakes below the sea's surface. The energy produced by seismic sea waves has the power to destroy buildings, docks, trees, and people. As I have suggested, when feminists use the term *wave* to describe successive generations of feminists and feminisms, they are describing waves as if they exist in isolation from one another. Here, I briefly examine the scientific basis of waves in order to illuminate how the materiality of waves serves as a more effective way of describing the force of feminisms on feminist generations. As I suggest, the language of waves enables us to better understand the fluid waterscape of feminisms. What are the origins and behaviors of waves? What are their structures and characteristics? How do they change as they encounter the ocean floor or a coast or an island? I begin with a brief discussion of waves, how they begin, their basic anatomy, and their varying types. Then, I go on to suggest how the wave metaphor can be useful for understanding how the varieties of feminisms made their way to two institutions: the University of Utah and The University of Memphis in the late 1970s and 1980s.

How does a wave begin? Although the specific origins of waves vary, waves begin when a disturbing force or generating force is introduced to a body of water. Wind, landslides, sea bottom faulting or slipping, moving ships, and even thrown objects can be generating forces. Let me begin with a simple example. When a stone is thrown into a perfectly smooth lake, waves form at the point of disturbance and flow away from the center. As the rock falls toward the bottom of the lake, water is displaced, but almost immediately water rushes back to fill in the space of the displacement. The motion of waves is caused by the oscillation of water particles that propels waves across the surface of water. The greater the disturbance, the larger the wave height, the greater the diameter of the orbit of the water particles, and the further the wave will travel. One important note is needed: "the water that composes a wave does not advance with it across the sea; each water particle . . . returns *very nearly* to its original position."[4] In this way, waves are external forces that act on the water particle; an equal and opposite restoring force acts on the water in order to restore it to equilibrium or the level of the undisturbed surface. For small waves, surface tension is enough to bring the water back to equilibrium. For larger waves created by storm centers or seismic activity, gravity is the restoring force.[5]

Taking a closer look at the institutionalization of feminism at the University of Utah (U of U) and The University of Memphis (U of M) in the late 1970s illustrates how different feminist trajectories can be understood by applying a wave metaphor. As feminists left the "streets" and got jobs at various universities across the country, these waves broke onto academic shores.[6] In some cases, the waves were strong enough and consistent enough for their energy to be harnessed to create an institutional feminist impact. At the University of Utah, a feminist wave touched down in the 1970s, and by 1977 enough energy was harnessed to create a program in women's studies. When it began, the program brought a Marxist and socialist feminist agenda to the curriculum. At the U of U, they have been able to continue to harness the energy from feminist waves to continue its forward progression. In 1991 when I took my first core course, the winds of change had begun to blow the curriculum in new directions. The curriculum had already adapted to the influence of third world feminist critiques as well as postmodern literary criticism. The winds of change were able to maintain a constant level of energy even as new waves broke onto shore.

Also in the late 1970s, the waves of feminism were crashing onto the shores of The University of Memphis. The founders of the Center for Research on Women (CROW) were greatly influenced by the social justice movements of the 1960s. Having encountered race relations theory and feminist theory as graduate students or as activists, they brought with them to the university a critique of race that focused on men and a critique of feminism that focused on white women. When Bonnie Thornton Dill began working at Memphis State University in 1978, there was no women's studies program. Soon after her arrival, various women faculty were able to lobby the administration for money to pay for a part-time coordinator who would coordinate cross-listed courses under the title women's studies.[7] When CROW was established in 1982, it became the central feminist presence on campus. With its dual focus as a research center and its attention to the intersections of race, class, and gender, it had a very distinctive look. Unlike the feminism that had white middle-class women as its object, CROW supported research that recognized race, class, and gender as interlocking systems of power and privilege. As a research center, CROW assisted faculty at the university in developing feminist research projects, spearheaded community-based research projects, and became a clearinghouse for research on women of color and southern women. In addition, the center trained graduate students, like myself, in feminist research methods where our point of departure was intersectionality.

In these examples, the waves that crashed onto these two universities' shores did not lose energy. Rather, other winds came up, bringing new energy to the waves. These examples also illustrate how different generating forces produced and propelled different waves of feminism onto each institution. At each university, there were also times when the wave entered shallow water, forcing it to change its shape. At CROW, they began to "feel" bottom with the appointment of a new dean in the late 1990s. Elizabeth Higginbotham, the interim chair of CROW while I was at Memphis (1994–96), left the university to take a job in sociology at the University of Delaware in 1997. When I asked why she left, she told me that although it was a difficult decision, she felt that under the new dean, she would not be able to continue to do the kind of work that she valued.[8] As waves begin to feel the sea floor, the orbit of the water particle begins to flatten out, creating an elliptical shape. The energy of the wave gets compressed, and the height increases as the wavelength shortens to accommodate pressure from below. If the height of the wave increases beyond the maximum allowable for the shorter wavelength, the wave will break. I think Elizabeth had to leave CROW before the break. CROW continues to exist, however, performing different institutional roles. Elizabeth has been able to transfer the energy she put into CROW into other endeavors at the University of Delaware.

First Encounters with Feminism

I often feel as though I happened upon this academic path accidentally. When I look back to how I found my way to college and women's studies, I imagine that I am a water particle being carried along by the energy of feminism. As Rachel Carson notes, the distance a water particle travels is not far, for the wave returns it very nearly to its original position. The story of my first encounter with feminism is a parallel travel narrative. I graduated from high school in 1988 and left home to become a nanny in

St. Louis, Missouri. This year-long experience along the banks of the Mississippi River broadened my horizons and opened my eyes to the many possibilities available to me. It was while working as a nanny that I first realized that a college education was attainable. My plan was to apply for admission to the University of Utah, where I could be close to home but far enough away to still feel as though I was on my own. As plans go, mine was a simple one with modest expectations. I was admitted to the university, where I declared an art major and began school in fall 1989. My first encounter with feminism was when I took my first women's studies course in 1990, an elective called "Sex Roles and Social Change." For the first time in my short college career the texts that I read and the discussions we had in class had relevance to my personal experience even when my experiences did not quite fit. With gender at the center of the analysis, my experiences as a young woman raised within the Mormon Church resonated with the battles waged by second wave feminists, but my Hawaiian family life was still much different from other families'. The following year, I enrolled in the course "Martin Luther King and the Civil Rights Movement." It was there that I learned the language of racial oppression and was able to make the historical connection between the racial identity movements of the 1960s and the women's movement. In this course, I adopted the language of African American oppression and resistance to begin to understand my experiences as a biracial Hawaiian woman where skin color combined with colonization to produce the oppressive atmosphere within which I was raised.

It was in the shadow of the Church of Jesus Christ of Latter-day Saints (also know as the Mormon Church or LDS Church) that I came out as a feminist. One of my apartments in college was located equal distance between two conservative institutions—the state capitol building up the hill and the LDS temple down the hill. Nestled between these two bastions of conservatism one autumn night in 1991, I called my parents to give them the news. I talked first to my dad and then was handed off to my mom so she could deal with me. I enthusiastically told them my good news; I had declared women's studies as my major. In the two years that I had been at the University of Utah I had been an art major, a math major, and a secondary education major. I was excited to have finally found an intellectual home. They did not share my enthusiasm. As my spirits began to fade, I looked out onto the magical scene of downtown Salt Lake City. The light from the street lamps and buildings filtered through the moisture in the air to soften the hard edges of the LDS church office building that soared in the foreground and smoothed out the sharp points of the temple's spires in the background. But there was nothing to smooth over the hard edges of my father's words. In his view, my decision had put my membership in the church and my eternal salvation in jeopardy and placed into question the possibility that I would spend eternity with my family in heaven. In his estimation, if I was a feminist, I could not be a faithful Mormon. I learned several years later that my parents' response had more to do with their automatic association of feminism with lesbianism. When I came out to them as a lesbian in 1995, they were not surprised because in their minds when I told them I was a feminist, I was also telling them that I was a lesbian. Whereas, for my parents, the backlash against feminism in the 1980s had effectively linked feminism to lesbianism, for me, feminism was not "dangerous" but transformative, both personally and intellectually.[9]

From 1991 to 1994, I was introduced to what would become the canon of academic feminism. We read Simone de Beauvoir and Luce Irigaray, Cherríe Moraga and Gloria Anzaldúa, Patricia Hill Collins and Toni Morrison, and countless others including influential male theorists such as Freud, Lacan, Foucault, and Marx. My transcript from the U of U reads like a critique of disciplinarity: we challenged the transparency of history in "Women in History since 1870," we critiqued discursive boundaries of both feminist theory and literary criticism in "Feminism with and against Critical Theory," and in "Advanced Feminist Research Methods" we challenged the objectivity of social science research.

The women's studies program inspired me to become politically active on campus while it inspired many of my peers to become politically active in the feminist community off campus. I became involved in and cochair of an undergraduate student committee to adopt a diversity component to the liberal arts education requirements. The initiative passed the faculty senate during my last semester at the U of U in 1994. As a passionate student, I was encouraged by faculty to become actively involved in the governance of women's studies by becoming a member of the Student Advisory Committee (SAC). As my introductory story illustrates, there I learned some hard lessons about the limits of academic collegiality. Unlike other departments and programs on campus, women's studies included student participation in the governance of the program and in their written constitution. By the time I became active in SAC, the committee had practically become defunct with lack of participation. Along with a couple of other enthusiastic majors, we decided to revitalize SAC and increase student participation in the program. One aspect of SAC responsibilities included overseeing course evaluations. One member of SAC decided to look over past evaluations and found that one professor in particular had consistently received weak teaching evaluations for the courses she taught in women's studies. The SAC member brought it to the attention of the student committee, and we decided to bring it to the Women's Studies Executive Committee as a student concern.

At the time, I had no way of knowing that we were walking into a storm. As one of two student representatives on the Women's Studies Executive Committee, I would be bringing the issue to the faculty along with the student who initially identified the problem. What came of this inquiry is a long and painful story that spans several months. At the initial committee meeting, most of the faculty members were supportive of students' concerns about the problem of allowing instructors to continue teaching for the program when their evaluations indicated that they were poor or ineffectual teachers. There were, however, a few faculty members who were not. One relatively new member of the faculty was stunned to learn that students had access to such information. She argued that access to evaluations should be restricted, especially from students who could use them as weapons against vulnerable (junior) faculty. The program chair was equally upset by our query. She concurred with this professor, claiming that in the wrong hands (namely, ours) evaluations could destroy a professor's career (they could be next). In their estimation, students wielded a considerable amount of power, and if not held in check, faculty careers could be destroyed. Although their opinions were in the minority of the group, the chair had the power to control the direction we all took next. She decided to pursue her own investigation—an investigation of the students who brought the allegations forward—my friend and myself. A short time after this initial meeting a second meeting was called to discuss the matter further.

My introductory story tells how the second meeting went. On that night, I felt tossed in wildly erratic and dangerous directions by forces outside of my control. I imagine that this is what happens to water particles in a storm; unrestrained energy tosses them around as the storm wreaks havoc around them. After that experience, I no longer saw women's studies as the calm in the storm, a safe harbor. I learned the hard way that even in the safety of a feminist space—which women's studies had been for me—undergraduate students are vulnerable to the whims of petty administrators and faculty. Although this near expulsion from college was a painful experience, I learned a valuable lesson in how to pick my battles and how to be strategic when fighting them. One lasting drawback of these experiences is that I have also become cautious and a little skeptical when entering "feminist" spaces. As a third generation feminist, I have the luxury of continuing to do feminist research and teaching outside of women's studies. In all, my experiences at the U of U were formative. My classes and the mentoring I received provided a lasting foundation for future experiences in the academy.

When the opportunity to go to graduate school at The University of Memphis came up, I still was not confident in my skills; I was not the captain of my craft, and my story reflects that uncertainty. Once again, when I look back on this time in my career, I describe the events that led to my move to Memphis to begin a master's program in sociology as an accident. Despite my successes, I still did not believe that I was the kind of person who went to graduate school.

From Water Particle to Rider of Waves

In summer 1994, I left home again and traveled to Memphis, back to the Mississippi River valley. Eager to see what the mighty Mississippi had for me on this voyage, I went to the Center for Research on Women (CROW) in the Department of Sociology at The University of Memphis without really knowing the full weight of its significance. The initial funding for CROW came from a grant from the Ford Foundation, which in the early 1980s was providing seed money to start centers for research on gender and race across the country. Lynn Weber, Elizabeth Higginbotham, and Bonnie Thornton Dill note that unlike the research centers established around the same time at Duke University, the University of North Carolina, Chapel Hill, and University of Washington, CROW took as its point of departure that "race, class and gender are *power relations* of dominance and subordination that are socially constructed and historically specific and that are *primary* forms of social organization."[10] Its mission was to "validate and promote the views of women of color, working-class women, and other groups that experienced oppression along multiple dimensions."[11] Unlike at the U of U, where the intersectionality of race, class, and gender was taught as one of many frameworks, at CROW the faculty and my fellow graduate students provided this as the model for incorporating intersectionality into research. And finally, their pedagogy reflected their personal and political commitment to collaboration.

In addition to the training I received in putting intersectionality into practice through pedagogy and research, I also inherited the precious gift of collaboration. Collaboration is not solely linked to joint authorship as much as it is connected to the idea that intellectual work is not a solitary process. At CROW the graduate students proofread each other's papers, bounced ideas off one another, boosted one another's confidence when it started to wane, and let loose and played together when the work was done. We provided a support network for each other that went beyond the halls and walls of CROW, stretching into our personal lives as well. Together, we fell in love, got divorced, started new relationships, built lifelong friendships, and made Memphis our home. It was a place that bridged what can often be a painful divide between the personal and the academic.

I came into my own as an academic feminist while at CROW. It was there that I was able to merge the feminist foundation I had from Utah with a commitment to intersectional research and teaching. It was at Memphis in the mid-1990s that I became a third wave feminist. While at the University of Utah and throughout my time at The University of Memphis, I was carried along by two wave trains, or groupings of waves. Attention to the divergent histories of feminism on these two college campuses emphasizes the different impact feminist waves can have. At the University of Utah, feminist waves were harnessed in 1977 to produce a women's studies program that introduced students to the feminist canon. At The University of Memphis, feminism took the form of a research center that provided support to feminist faculty and trained graduate students. Although the generating forces for each tradition may have been different, at both Utah and Memphis the wave trains have been sustained by prevailing winds. I was trained to read and navigate these waves, and they have combined, through wave interaction, to produce the kind of feminist I am today. When I arrived on the shores of The University of Memphis, I felt myself to be a water particle controlled by the energy of waves. I left Memphis ready to ride feminism's waves. I was prepared to chart my own journey and had developed the skills to handle whatever the academic sea would throw at me. I built my vessel from the intellectual tradition of intersectionality taught at CROW and filled it with the nourishment that comes from collaborative research.

With a chart plotted, my vessel built, and provisions loaded, I left Memphis and traveled upstream, against the current of the Mississippi River to Minneapolis.

Winds, Currents, and Third Waves: Interdisciplinarity in American Studies

Winds, currents, and waves have an interdependent relationship in the earth's oceans. Currents are pushed by the wind and affect the surface flow of water. Currents transport water along semipredictable paths across the ocean, following the hemispheric wind patterns that guide them. In the academy, we talk about intellectual currents as a metaphor for new theories or the institutionalization of well-worn ways of knowing. Adding currents to our metaphorical understanding of how energy and water move helps us to think about the many forces that shape knowledge production at a particular institution. My life history prior to graduate school shaped what I hoped to find at the University of Minnesota, my approach to research, and the alliances I sought out. Not only was I in motion, but the university itself, far from a homogeneous entity, was crisscrossed with differences according to discipline, and even within disciplines. Below I describe how I interacted with some of the currents I discovered at the university.

I have to backtrack some to describe how I came to be traveling up the Mississippi River to Minneapolis. I began the arduous task of applying to PhD programs in fall 1996. After earning a master's degree, I stayed in Memphis an additional year, teaching in the Department of Sociology. In my search for programs, I found out what a privileged and sheltered education I had received thus far. After leaving Utah and Memphis I was warped. My understanding of the field of sociology looked far more diverse and critical than it really was. I began my search by looking for sociology programs that focused on qualitative research methods, specifically those that had faculty who did ethnography, as well as programs that were feminist friendly and whose courses and faculty reflected a commitment to the intersectionality of race, class, and gender.

The enormity of the task became quite small rather quickly. I realized almost immediately that if I stayed in sociology, I would not easily be able to replicate my experience at CROW. But I held strong to my commitment to find a PhD program that would support the kind of research I wanted to do. In the end, I applied to only five programs, four sociology

PhD programs and one American studies program. I surprised myself by applying to the University of Minnesota's American Studies program. I had not heard about the program—not surprising since American studies was originally founded by and continues to be dominated by historians and literary scholars—but was interested in the kinds of work the graduate students were doing and the support they gave each other. I was also intrigued to learn that the American studies students at the University of Minnesota had established an organization, Más(s) Color (an acronym for Minnesota American Studies Students of Color), that acted as a watchdog and support group for graduate students of color. I realized that American studies at Minnesota was the kind of place I would be able to do Native Hawaiian cultural studies and that applying to this program would also mean entering a landscape that had become a battlefield over the politics of race. I was not deterred by students' stories of the political battles that had been waged. In fact, I had come to expect them. I was energized by the fact that graduate students of color organized themselves and demanded changes in the program. Having encountered and weathered many storms myself while an undergraduate, I was sympathetic to their struggle and knew that I could contribute to and further their cause. I also knew what it was like to be in a supportive environment; I knew the benefits of graduate student collaboration and faculty mentors.

I began the PhD program in American studies fall semester 1997. I entered the program during a time of transition, when the winds of change were beginning to blow. Whereas my cohort of eight had two students of color, more recent cohorts have seen an increase of students of color, reaching nearly 50 percent. The department's commitment to diversity goes beyond student representation in admission and is reflected in the developing field of postnationalist American studies that dominates the research of both graduate students and faculty. The focus on a postnationalist American studies builds on theoretical currents in the field that call for a critique of the history and legacy of United States imperialism. In addition, postnationalist theory calls into question the boundaries of the nation/state and calls for attention to both the local and global. My research on the construction of a uniquely Mormon Polynesian identity through migration and tourism is part of the intellectual current that brought the feminist wave I rode onto the shores of American studies at the University of Minnesota.

The trend in American studies at Minnesota toward a postnationalist framework is similar to a current bringing a new intellectual tradition to the program. Like the flow of water, ideas pass in and out of institutions and academic departments depending on the winds and currents. In my own research I have moved from the land-based metaphors developed by Chicana feminists, such as Gloria Anzaldúa, toward water metaphors, such as waves and currents.[12] My examination of the imperial relationship between the United States and Hawai'i through the lens of tourism and cultural preservation efforts by the Mormon Church recognizes that processes of racialization cannot be limited to nation/state boundaries. To study the relationship between travel and tourism between the United States and Hawai'i, a new model for boundaries and borders is needed. As exciting and transformative as the work in Chicana/o studies is, one limitation of borderlands discourse is that it is a land-based metaphor. The notion of borderlands does not travel as well beyond the continental boundaries of the Americas.

Despite the feminist-friendly and ethnic studies–centered focus of American studies at Minnesota, I was reminded that we must always be on the lookout for gatekeepers. I was surprised to find my work blocked at the borders of the American Studies Association. I had come to believe that the national association was a place where feminists and ethnic studies scholars had found an intellectual and institutional home.[13] I was excited by the conference theme and by the diversity of panels and presentations. I did not expect to have my access blocked by a border patrol. Although I had been nurtured in supportive departments, as an interdisciplinary feminist and antiracist scholar I had been warned that I could expect to encounter the coast guard patrolling the academic sea. What I was surprised by was that the border patrol in American studies at the national level did not object to my feminist critique or my focus on Hawaiian cultural preservation at a tourist site. Their objection was focused on the fact that I study the intersectionality of gender, Hawaiian culture, and the LDS Church.

My dissertation, "Polynesian Pioneers: Twentieth-Century Religious Racial Formations and Migration in Hawai'i," traces how conversion to the Church of Jesus Christ of Latter-day Saints is simultaneously a racial formation. I had planned to use the oral histories I had collected earlier that year to look at the intersection of work, religion, and race through the stories told by former Polynesian workers at a tourist attraction. A salient feature of the ethnic identities that these workers have of themselves is their membership in the LDS church. So for me to talk about the racial formations that happen at this tourist site, I also have to contend with how religion informs this process. Imagine my surprise to be informed by a member of the program committee that my paper was not accepted in part because other members of the committee were suspicious that I would turn my presentation into an opportunity to proselytize for the church. There were also other, more pragmatic reasons why the paper was not accepted that had to do with fit. My paper crossed the boundaries of so many fields—Native Pacific cultural studies, religious studies, leisure and tourism, and work—that they were hard pressed to find a place for it.

I tell this story to illustrate how I had been lulled into a false sense of security. The programs where I had received my training had been supportive of me. I harbored the belief that there was a sociology program out there that wanted someone like me: a scholar of color who did intersectionality as well as interdisciplinary research, and who had a commitment to feminist and antiracist pedagogy. The training I received at Utah, Memphis, and Minnesota had prepared me well to navigate the sometimes turbulent waters of academia. This story also illustrates how third generation feminists, like myself, set sail from these early ports of call but set off in new directions. My attention to the intersections of race, gender, religion, and nation on the currents of postnationalist American studies carried me into a treacherous harbor of the national association. My research topic also brings me full circle. As mentioned at the beginning of this essay, when I came out as a feminist, I was carried away by third wave theories and methods, taking me farther from my family of origin. In wave theory, water particles oscillate as the energy that waves generate carry them along but ultimately return them very nearly to their original position. Currents, on the other hand, direct the flows and movement of water itself. One of the greatest advantages I have experienced as a third wave feminist has come from the feminist waves and intellectual currents that inform my dissertation topic and that simultaneously return me "very nearly" to my "original position"—I came home.

"Each water particle . . . returns very nearly to its original position"

I began this essay with a story of how I came to have tits of steel and how, after I arrived at Minnesota, I decided that I could deposit them on a shelf. When I started reading and researching feminist waves, I realized that putting them away was foolish. I have since learned that tits of steel are necessary not solely to be a feminist in the academy but also to protect me as I fight other battles. When I was given my tits of steel, I was told that to be a feminist in the academy would require a lot of hard work. I came to Minnesota and found that feminists who came before me weathered the fiercest storms and that the calm seas that I encountered were a product of their labor.

I also began this narrative reflecting on how water particles are carried along by the energy of waves. When I first began college, I saw myself as a water particle carried along by the energies of feminist waves. These waves took me away from home, literally and figuratively, as I "came out" as a feminist under the shadow of Mormonism. My story has come full circle. Just as water particles rise, move forward, fall, and rise again, I have returned very nearly to my original position. It is now 2005, and I write this conclusion from my desk in the women's studies program at the University of Hawai'i at Mānoa, where I am an instructor. But I come to this point changed. I no longer see myself as a water particle but as a navigator of academic seas. I left the University of Minnesota unsure upon which academic shore I would disembark. I have ridden the waves of academic feminism and interdisciplinary research to this point, and I feel ready to put my craft in dry dock as I get settled. When I began this journey, I was saddened to be taken so far away from home. But now, I know that the path I took was circular; through research, I found my way home.

In previous trips to Lā'ie, before I began traveling to Hawai'i to do research for my dissertation, this place of my birth felt foreign. I knew I was not supposed to feel this way. When I was twenty-four years old, I went with my family to Hawai'i. It was the first time I had been "home"—I was raised to call Hawai'i "home" even though it did not feel like it—since our small family had moved to Utah in 1973, when I was three years old. By 1994 the family was no longer small. Keawe, Māpuana, Maui, and Kemalia were born on the mainland and joined the three of us, Keala-Jean, myself, and Kenikenihia, who were born in Hawai'i. Keala-Jean's husband and two children were also on this momentous family vacation. Despite being with my entire family in the town where I was born, I felt like a stranger in this place. As we toured around the town, Mom and Dad showed us the home where our grandparents lived, the park where one of the houses we had lived in once stood, and the beach that Mom used to take Keala-Jean and me to when we were babies. Despite this nostalgic tour, there was nothing familiar about this; it did not feel much like home.

During winter 2002, I spent seven weeks, Monday through Friday, reading the oral histories of Lā'ie community members and former Polynesian Cultural Center workers archived at special collections at Brigham Young University, Hawai'i. On days when I left the library early, I could hear the canoe pageant underway at the adjacent Polynesian Cultural Center. During this visit I stayed with an aunt, who lived just off campus in faculty housing. Some days when I finished with my research, I felt restless and had to walk. I toured around town, following an imagined map taken from the stories I read about in the archives. This was a different kind of nostalgic tour. The road, Naniloa Loop, that I took to get from auntie's house to Hukilau beach, where I went to read, used to be the railroad line that took men and women to work in Kahuku on the sugar plantation, and children to the movies on Friday nights. The shortcut that I took to get to the grocery store, Puuahi Street, was once the only road into the village. They planted trees at the end of the road; now it is a dead end; the main entrance to Lā'ie was moved to Hale Laa Boulevard, which is the road that leads to the LDS Temple. All of the house lots along Iosepa Street were allotted to those families who in 1917 returned to Lā'ie from living in Iosepa, Utah. The paved-over roads that I walked down were no longer nameless. The familiarity I now feel comes from these stories of a time long past but still living in the words stored in the archives. Before there was the college, there were watermelon patches. Before there was the Polynesian Cultural Center, there were taro patches. Before there was a park that housed a double-hull canoe, there was a house, my house. Lā'ie is now home. I feel the spirit of my ancestors when I walk those streets. Their stories of the train, of visions above watermelon patches, of harvesting taro, of fishing in the sea, of dances at the cultural hall, of the souvenir stands along the road, of building the temple, the college, and the center are carried on the wind. I hear their voices whispering to me, reminding me to listen. If I listen, I will learn. So I listen. I listen for their voices to call me home again.

Notes

1. I would like to thank Lauren Rauscher, Melissa Fry, Elizabeth Higginbotham, Bonnie Thornton Dill, and Lynn Weber for sharing their reflections on the Center for Research on Women at The University of Memphis with me. I

dedicate this piece to Lauren Rauscher, Andreana Clay, and Alex Washington, who were central to my transformation as a person and a scholar.

2. Sara Evans, *Tidal Wave: How Women Changed America at Century's End* (New York: Free Press, 2003).

3. Jennifer Baumgardner and Amy Richards, *Manifesta: Young Women, Feminism, and the Future* (New York: Farrar, Strauss, and Giroux, 2000); Silvia Evangelisti et. al., "Generations: Women's Tradition and the Handing Down of History," *Symposium* 49 (Summer 1995): 130–35; Susan Fraiman, "Feminism Today: Mothers, Daughters, Emerging Sisters," *American Literary History* 11, 3 (Fall 1999): 525–44; Susan Gubar, "What Ails Feminist Criticism?" *Critical Inquiry* 24 (Summer 1998): 878–902; Susan Gubar, "Notations *in Medias Res*," *Critical Inquiry* 25 (Winter 1999): 380–96; Leslie Heywood and Jennifer Drake, eds., *Third Wave Agenda: Being Feminist, Doing Feminism* (Minneapolis: University of Minnesota Press, 1997); Lisa Maria Holeland, "Against Generational Thinking: or, Some Things That 'Third Wave' Feminism Isn't," *Women's Studies in Communication* 24, 1 (Spring 2001):107–21; Devoney Looser and Ann Kaplan, eds., *Generations: Academic Feminists in Dialogue* (Minneapolis: University of Minnesota Press, 1997); Rebecca Walker, ed., *To Be Real* (New York: Anchor Press, 1997); Robyn Wiegman, "What Ails Feminist Criticism? A Second Opinion" in *Critical Inquiry* 25, 2 (Winter 1999): 362–79; Jacqueline Zita, introduction to Special Issue on Third Wave Feminism, *Hypatia* 12 (Summer 1997): 1–6.

4. Rachel L. Carson, *The Sea around Us* (New York: Oxford University Press, 1989), 114; emphasis added.

5. Alyn C. Duxbury and Alison Duxbury, *An Introduction to the World's Oceans* (Reading, Mass.: Addison-Wesley Publishing Company, 1994); Heather Hathaway, *Caribbean Waves: Relocating Claude McKay and Paule Marshall* (Bloomington: Indiana University Press, 1999).

6. Barbara Laslett and Barrie Thorne, eds., "Life Histories of a Movement: An Introduction" in *Feminist Sociology: Life Histories of a Movement* (New Brunswick, N.J.: Rutgers University Press, 1997).

7. Bonnie Thornton Dill, personal communication, April 19, 2002.

8. Elizabeth Higginbotham, personal communication, November 2001.

9. On this backlash, see Susan Faludi, *Backlash: The Undeclared War against American Women* (New York: Anchor Books, 1991).

10. Lynn Weber, Elizabeth Higginbotham, and Bonnie Thornton Dill, "Sisterhood as Collaboration: Building the Center for Research on Women at the University of Memphis" in *Feminist Sociology: Life Histories of a Movement*, ed. Barbara Laslett and Barrie Thorne (New Brunswick, N.J.: Rutgers University Press, 1997), 230; emphasis in original.

11. Ibid.

12. Gloria Anzaldúa, *Borderlands/La Frontera* (San Francisco: Spinsters/Aunt Lute, 1987).

13. Mary Helen Washington, "'Disturbing the Peace': What Happens to American Studies If You Put African American Studies at the Center?" Presidential Address to the American Studies Association, October 29, 1997, *American Quarterly* 50, 1 (March 1998): 1–23.

11. "I Thought She Was One of Us!"

A Narrative Examination of Power and Exclusion
in the Academy

Wendy Leo Moore

WHEN my husband and I became serious, he called his parents to tell them that he was planning to marry a white woman (I am white, my husband is African American). I had already "met" his parents over the phone on several occasions, but we were concerned about what they might think when they found out I was white. His mother and father were both very supportive and loving in their response, but I remember his father's response particularly clearly. When my husband told him I was white, he expressed surprise and said, "I thought she was one of us!"

My experience as a third generation feminist can be analyzed through the feminist lens of intersectionality. As bell hooks notes, "[n]owadays it has become commonplace for individuals doing feminist work to evoke gender, race, and class, it is often forgotten that initially most feminist thinkers, many of whom were white and from privileged backgrounds, were hostile to adopting this perspective."[1] For me, finding my way to feminism necessitated looking through the lens of race. Because of my life experience, growing up white in an African American community, I saw race first. White middle-class feminism did not make sense to me.[2] But through the works of scholars like bell hooks, as well as Patricia Hill Collins, Gloria Anzaldúa, Bonnie Thornton Dill, and Evelyn Nakano Glenn, I came to view sexist oppressions as deeply connected to systems of racist oppression. Making that connection and becoming aware of the multiple structures of power and oppression in society have been crucial to my development as an academic. But the path I took, which began from a critical race perspective, was/is confusing to many people. Typically white women do not see race first.[3] So the aptly chosen words of my father-in-law, "I thought she was one of us," are a sentiment that I have encountered from many people in my life, and from many people in academia. But the words of my father-in-law were meant to be inclusionary and supportive, suggesting that we were alike in sharing many perspectives. By contrast, in academia, not being "one of us" meant that I was an outsider. The power structures I bumped into in my experiences in graduate school in sociology and in law school taught me that not being "one of us" has painful consequences.

This essay is a personal narrative that examines the situational consequences of not being "one of us" in the academy. It explores my own "coming of age" as a feminist while dealing with the pain and anger that goes along with working, and learning, in a hostile academic setting. Richard Delgado says that "stories or narratives told by the ingroup remind it of its identity in relation to outgroups, and provide it with a form of shared reality in which its own superior position is seen as natural. The stories of outgroups aim to subvert that reality."[4] Beginning with the development of my standpoint as a white woman growing up in a working-class and poor African American neighborhood, and examining my experiences in academia from that standpoint, my narrative attempts to subvert many natural assumptions perpetuated by a white male–dominated academia. In doing so, this work critically examines systems of power and exclusion in the academy, a project that I believe all feminist and antiracist scholars must continually undertake.

Standpoint: On Becoming Not "One of Us"

Essential to my own understanding of my academic experience is a recognition of my particular standpoint when I entered academia.[5] In the 1970s and 1980s, I grew up the only child of a single mother, and one of the few white people in a neighborhood that was predominantly African American and working- and lower-class.[6] My mother, who was strongly influenced by feminism as well as the civil rights movement, moved us into this neighborhood because she wanted me to live in a community that was not all white and because she was able to find affordable housing there. My mother was the only biological kin that I interacted with daily. My father and my mother's extended family all lived outside of the state (or outside of the country in the case of my father's family). Because my mother struggled to support the two of us completely on her own, I became involved in adoptive kin relationships with many people in the community, who took me into their families and their lives. Most of these people were African American.

When I was a child in grade school, two people had a deep impact on my life and my perception of myself as a young student. One was a counselor at my grade school, and the other was the principal of the school. Both of these African American women mentored me and worked to encourage me to become critically engaged in my education. My counselor, Marci Wade, would pull me out of classes twice a week and bring me into her office to talk and write poetry. She told my mother that sometimes, if she was having a particularly hard day, she would pull me from class just so we could talk, because I always brightened her day. I spent time with Marci every week throughout grade school, and she brightened many of my days, becoming one of the most important people in my life as a young child. My principal, Shirley Keiser, also spent a great deal of time with me when I was in grade school. She would keep me after school with her to help her with chores around the school so that I would not go home to an empty house (because my mother was working).[7] Even after I graduated to a new school, I would take the bus to her school and stay with her until her workday ended.[8] To this day I see Mrs. Keiser from time to time, and she keeps up with my whereabouts through my mother.

These two African American women stood in sharp contrast to the white teachers in my schools. For those white teachers (both men and women), I was too loud, I was not properly dressed and preened, and I questioned their authority too much. I did not represent what a little white girl was supposed to represent (in fact, I was not even very little—I was six feet tall by the time I was in the eighth grade). These teachers criticized me, and they frequently berated my mother for not giving me proper training. But the support that they failed to give me I got from Marci Wade and Shirley Keiser. They gave me confidence, they advocated for me, and they helped my mother negotiate the criticisms from teachers. Marci Wade and Shirley Keiser have remained important to me throughout my life.

Another person who influenced my life, perhaps even more than Marci Wade and Shirley Keiser, was my mother's mentor in college. Dr. Robert B. Bailey III was a professor of sociology at the University of Wisconsin-River Falls. As the first African American man to receive a Fulbright Scholarship, in 1952, he received his master's degree from Birmingham University in England and went on to get his PhD in 1958 at the University of Utrecht in the Netherlands. His dissertation, *Sociology Faces Pessimism,* was published by a German press, and he spoke four languages fluently (and was proficient in several others). When he returned to the United States to find an academic job in the late 1950s, he encountered a great deal of racism in the academy, despite his impecca-ble credentials. As a result, he took a teaching position at this small state school in Wisconsin. One of the starkest contradictions of my life is the fact that my godfather, who was always a loving and ardent supporter, found his way into my life as a result of white racism. He was the most brilliant and thoughtful man I have ever met, and in a world without rac-ism he would most likely have received a position at an elite university. But because he was teaching at an almost exclusively white university in a small Wisconsin town, he met my mother and became her friend and mentor, and eventually became my godfather.

Doc, as we called him, was a guiding force in my life. While I knew him all my life, he became a mentor to me when I was in high school. Able to be loving even when he gave criticism, he taught me to think crit-ically about my environment and question normative assumptions. His ability to push me, yet at the same time remain totally supportive, was a unique quality. Given his own life experience and his ability to mentor, I doubt he would ever have pushed me to conform to normative ideals of white womanhood. In fact, he adored my challenges to whiteness, and I think he knew, though we never discussed it, that challenging racist norms required me to also challenge gender norms. Doc was the most influential person in my decision to become a sociologist. He died on the day that my daughter was born, June 4, 1993, and his mother (Great-Gran Bailey—who turned 106 years old in May 2006) said that he had lived just long enough to see my daughter into the world.

These extended kin were extremely important to my life, my con-struction of self, and my understanding of the world in which I live. These people took me into their lives and gave me the love and acceptance that every child needs. But it was not long before I learned that while this black community was one that I recognized as my own, I was not "one of us." In *Black Feminist Thought*, Patricia Hill Collins discusses the role of black women working as servants in the homes of white people. She de-scribes their experiences as that of the "outsider-within," suggesting that they were racial outsiders, but they were located within family structures in white people's homes, which often gave them an insight into white-ness and demystified white power.[9] In many ways my experience was that of the outsider-within. Unlike the black women that Collins described, who were in exploited positions as outsiders, the power relationship in my experience was reversed. Rather than being in an exploited posi-tion, I was (and still am) the beneficiary of unearned privilege from what

Feagin calls the "racist relations" of the United States, which are structured upon white supremacy.[10] Yet, because of my status as an outsider-within in the black community, I developed a nuanced understanding of white supremacy and the contradictions of racial oppression, just as the women Collins described had.

As a child, race became the most salient axis of my identity, and I became very critical of whiteness. The contradiction, of course, was that this process occurred at the same time that I benefited from my whiteness. I learned about white privilege as a recipient. Area police saw me as someone they wanted to protect, not harass. Store clerks saw me as a potential sale, not a potential thief. School administrators saw my bad behavior as a momentary lapse of judgment, not as indicative of my essence. I saw white privilege everywhere—because I benefited from it, and many of the people I loved did not. I did not appreciate this unearned privilege; instead, I saw it as something that marked me as different from those I cared most about.

Still, I shared that socially constructed but biologically conceived designation of white. The possibility remained that within a white community I could become "one of us." Unfortunately, what I found in my interactions with most white people was that the words of David Roediger are indeed true:

It is not merely that whiteness is oppressive and false; it is that whiteness is nothing but oppressive and false. . . . Whiteness describes, from Little Big Horn to Simi Valley, not a culture but precisely the absence of culture. It is the empty and therefore terrifying attempt to build an identity based on what one isn't and on whom one can hold back.[11]

To be a white "one of us," I had to ignore white privilege and white supremacy and be complacent about both structural inequality and expressions of prejudice and stereotyping. I had to accept the benefits of race privilege without ever naming them. When I failed to ignore or to be complacent about racism in interactions with other white people, I met with disapproving comments or gazes and sometimes exclusion.

My outsider status was situational. In the community in which I grew up I was racially different, but I shared many similar experiences. When my father-in-law said, "I thought she was one of us," he implied that he recognized a similar perspective and shared set of values. His words were inclusive. When I encountered comments from white people who said the same, the process was reversed. They thought I was "one of us" because I looked biologically white, and that meant that I was supposed to behave in particular ways. But when I did not share their values, perspectives, and experiences, especially on issues of racial inequality, they looked on me with a sense of betrayal. Their perspectives were exclusionary.

When I entered graduate school at the University of Minnesota, I learned that not being "one of us" often meant exclusion. My godfather had given me the tools of critical analysis that made me a good sociologist. But what he did not prepare me for was the power of the normative white perspectives I would encounter once I got into academia.

The Sociology of "Us"

As a new graduate student in the sociology department at the University of Minnesota in 1995, I was continually made uncomfortable (even confused) by assertions that I must be neutral and objective in my sociological work and in academic discussions. I was *not* neutral about issues of social exploitation. I believed that my standpoint offered unique insights into domination and social stratification and ought to be valued as a component of knowledge claims. Further, I was convinced that what was being sold as "objectivity" actually meant support for a system of knowledge production that was deeply entrenched in power hierarchies that did not confront important issues of race, class, or gender oppression. But I was unable to articulate these contradictions in a way that was acceptable enough to be "heard" by the majority of the faculty, all of whom were white, and most of whom were male.[12] This caused a constant tension in my graduate education, because I needed the acceptance of these people in order to get through my graduate program. What I experienced on entering the department was an odd mix of praise and sanction. Looking back now, I see this combination as a form of discipline, in Foucault's sense of the word, designed to reconstruct me—to shape me into the image of a white woman who could be "one of us" in the "discipline" of sociology.[13]

In one of my first required classes in the graduate program, I wrote a proposal outlining the research I planned to conduct for my master's thesis. The project was an examination of the ways students of color and white students interact with one another and negotiate disagreements about race in courses on race relations. An upper-level graduate student (who was a white man) was the teaching assistant for the course; he read and critiqued my proposal. At the end of a page full of praise for my solid writing and organizational skills, he said, "Is this really about race, or do you just want it to be?" I was so shocked by the comment that I was unable to respond. He did not provide a critique of my work but instead challenged my ability to define whether race played any role in the dynamics of these courses. His critique suggested that I had the capacity to do sociology, but that my biases about race made me see a race problem where one did not exist. His comments implied that I could be a good sociologist, but only if I abandoned my impartial focus on race.

During this same semester, I was taking another class with a senior professor, who sanctioned me in a much stronger and paternalistic manner. This professor would have public conversations with other faculty (two of the people on my committee and one fellow graduate student told me they had heard him making comments) concerning how smart he thought I was and how much I contributed to his class. Yet when I turned in a paper to him that examined Michael Omi and Howard Winant's racial formation theory, he informed me that this was not "really theory," and he suggested that I examine the works of George Simmel and Hubert Blalock instead.[14] Once again the message was that I had the potential to be "one of us," but I had to relearn how to think about race and become less critical—more neutral—concerning racist exploitation in my theoretical framework.

I viewed these incidents (as well as others more subtle and too numerous to mention) as acts of social control designed to encourage me to conform to acceptable racial norms in the discipline of sociology. According to those with the power to judge my credentials, either I was too sensitive about race, and so I saw it as relevant in places where it was not, or I was not "sociological enough" in my approach to race-related questions. As a result of these kinds of discipline, I began to view the world of graduate education in sociology as racialized. Ruth Frankenberg notes,

Whiteness . . . has a set of linked dimensions. First, whiteness is a location of structural advantage, of race privilege. Second, it is a "standpoint," a place from which white people look at ourselves and others, and at society. Third, "whiteness" refers to a set of cultural practices that are usually unmarked and unnamed.[15]

Whiteness defined the space of this sociology department in which I was a graduate student. With an almost completely white faculty and graduate student population, the department was physically a very white space in comparison to my life.

In addition, the way that race was theorized and discussed was entirely different from what I had experienced. Yet most of the people in the department were unwilling to examine (or mark) the influence of whiteness in this process. And not only were people in the department unwilling to critically examine whiteness and race, but it was made clear to me that it was not legitimate for me to be critical of race and white privilege in the discipline of sociology. When I attempted to do this, those who had given me praise, with sanctions, pulled away—and again I received the exclusionary gaze that said, "I thought she was one of us."

During this period I also read the works of feminists of color, but gender oppression still did not seem very salient to me. Over time, in my reading, I began to see sexist oppression as connected to racist oppression. However, I saw some white women in the sociology department who appeared to be identified by white men as "one of us" in the discipline of sociology. Their position served to solidify my sense that racist oppression was a more powerful form of social stratification than gender oppression. But in my second year I received an everyday education about the intersections of race and gender that made me understand that I had been wrong about the dynamics of gender oppression; my standpoint had caused me to miss the structural consequences of gender oppression.

Power, Exclusion, and the Consequences of Not Being "One of Us"

In contrast to my interactions with the majority of the faculty in the sociology department, my advisor, Jennifer Pierce, supported me academically and encouraged me to bring my standpoint to my work in sociology. She gave me the resources to both find my academic voice on issues of race and discuss it in a way that bridged the worlds of academia and my real life. In my second year of graduate school she went up for tenure and promotion. At the time I had no doubt that she would get tenure. I realize now that I was naive about the racialized and gendered power structure that was solidified in the department.

In the first semester of my second year, a fellow graduate student (and a friend) found me in the computer lab and told me that the faculty had voted, twelve to seven, to deny Jennifer tenure. What followed this decision in the department was a painful explosion of emotions among faculty and graduate students. Many graduate students were outraged by the decision, but others, working with faculty members who had voted against Jennifer, set about to justify the case against her. There was an immediate split in the department between those who supported Jennifer and those who did not. Discussions with faculty soon revealed who had been in her favor and who had not. And several professors who had voted against Jennifer discussed the decision publicly in their classes with graduate students. The problem as they viewed it was that Jennifer's work was considered feminist and that feminist scholarship was not sociology.[16]

From observing her experience I began to realize that while there was space within the discipline of sociology for white women, in this department that space was limited to white women who would "buy into" the system as it existed.[17] I realized that movements toward gender equality in the academy (and elsewhere) were being constructed and delineated by white men. It was not a gender equality defined by women on their terms or one that seriously challenged normative views about gender. Instead, what was being sold as gender equality was the right for women to participate in patriarchal structures. This form of "gender equality" had male-defined boundaries, and if one did not stay within those boundaries, there were negative consequences. Jennifer had challenged the normative structures of the department, and the consequence for her was that those in power denied her tenure and threatened to seriously harm her standing as an academic. Reflecting on her experience, I began to suspect that one of the reasons I had received the level of praise that I had in the department was that I had not openly stated a commitment to feminism. As a white person my commitment to antiracist work had not been taken seriously. The continued sanctions on my perspectives on race suggested to me that many people in the department regarded my commitment to antiracist work as a passing phase that would disappear with the proper discipline. But as a white *woman*, had I openly embraced feminism at this point, I am not sure that these same people would have believed I could be dissuaded. As a result, my self-identification as a feminist became necessary at this point in my life. I realized that gender oppression could not be separated from racial oppression. Both were systems of power and domination that were mutually justifying, and often distinctions between gender oppression and racial oppression were difficult to make.

My experience with the faculty during this time made me feel powerless in the department. I became disgusted with the coercive attempts at social control and the racialized and gendered use of power to exclude people and perspectives. I realized that there were real and painful consequences to being not "one of us" in sociology. Consequently, I decided to leave sociology and go to law school. But before I left, the dean overturned the faculty decision in Jennifer's tenure case, and she was granted tenure in the sociology department. The summer before I started law school, Jennifer encouraged me to come back; I was close to getting my PhD, and she suggested that I get a law degree and then come back to finish in sociology. She convinced me that I could find a space in sociology and do the kind of teaching and research that I wanted, and that she would help me to do this. I decided that I would go back, and when I got to law school, I was glad that I had made this decision. Sexism and racism were even more prevalent and less questioned in the law school than in sociology.

Race, Gender and the Boundaries of "Us" in Law School

Lani Guinier, Michelle Fine, and Jane Balin concluded on the basis of their research at the University of Pennsylvania Law School that "[t]here is something about the law school *environment* that has a negative academic impact on female law students.[18] They go on to say, "learning to think like a lawyer means learning to think and act like a man."[19] While Guinier, Fine, and Balin do not examine race, there are suggestions in their work that indicate that learning to think like a lawyer—to be "one of us" in law school—really means learning to think and act like a *white* man. This was my experience in law school; law school, like graduate school, was a sexist and racist space.

Everything about law school indicated that to be "one of us" was to be a conservative elite white man. Five-foot-tall portraits of old white men in the large law school classrooms seemed to be looking down at you each time you entered a room. Plaques outside every room indicated the law firm or corporation that had donated money to build it. There was a "Northwest Airlines Staff Lounge" and a "Toyota Courtyard." There was an unspoken assumption that work at a corporate law firm was more valuable than public interest work. And there were the many racialized and gendered interactions between professors and students.

In my final year of law school, tired and emotionally bruised by the entire experience, I took a course that examined issues of criminal sentencing facilitated by a professor at the law school. The class was two semesters, and in the first semester it was a regular seminar in which we read sentencing theory and met to discuss. In the third week of class the professor called me to his office. He told me that he was impressed with my comments and that he wanted to help my career. Specifically he told me that I should consider a clerkship after law school and that he could help me get one: I knew that this was a good recommendation because he worked closely with many judges and his wife was a judge. During that semester my grandmother became ill, and it became clear that she was going to die. For her to die at home, members of my family would have to care for her during her last days. I spent two weeks helping my grandmother so that she could die in her own home, and when I went back to school, I went to this professor to explain why I had been gone and to ask for an extension on the paper I was to write for the class. He granted me the extension, but he was not happy about it, and he told me that in life we have to create priorities for ourselves—and it was unfortunate that I would now be behind. He made it clear that a decision to care for my grandmother in her dying days did not fit with his notion of priorities. Just as I had been in graduate school, I was being disciplined, receiving praise with sanctions, this time pushing me to conform to a patriarchal work ethic.

The second semester of the class was set up such that we met for three weekend-long conference sessions, during which students (myself included), judges, attorneys, and some community corrections administrators discussed real cases and the appropriate sentences for offenders.[20] At the first session I discovered that all of the judges, attorneys, and community corrections administrators invited to participate were white (there were three students of color in the class). As we discussed the cases before us, each person was invited to comment on the case and discuss how they would sentence the offender. During that three-day session I was shocked and saddened by a general level of apathy on the part of the judges concerning the severe racial disparities in the criminal justice system. At one point a white male student brought up the issue of racial disparities in sentencing, and a white woman judge said, "What should I do? Every time a black defendant is before me should I let him go?" Discussion throughout served to completely dehumanize people who violated criminal laws, and failed to acknowledge any connection between action and social structure.

Although I felt alienated by the discussion and thought it represented only a white elite perspective on the criminal law and criminal justice, I continued to raise issues of race, class, and gender inequality as we discussed the cases. At the conclusion of the first three-day session we had a dinner—a social event to end the academic discussions. At that dinner I was relatively cheerful. While few people had agreed with me, I felt as though the majority had been respectful. During the dinner, one of the judges, a white man, introduced me to his wife by saying, "This is the Commie Pinko I told you about." I laughed, ignoring the offensive comment, and shook her hand. He then apologized for calling me a "Commie Pinko" and told me that I reminded him of his daughter, who was off in Africa working for the Peace Corps. He went on to say that both myself and his daughter were young idealists, but we would be exposed to real life soon enough. At the time I thought he was paternalistic and condescending, suggesting that I was merely going through a "liberal phase" and that I would at some point change my perspective and accept social inequalities without question. I merely smiled and walked away.

In the second session of the course I became more uncomfortable as one student, a white woman, went on and on about the fact that "criminals have caused harm" and they must be "punished" for that harm. I suggested that we consider the social context of the crime and the person who violated the law. She responded saying that she felt that "all that context is merely mitigating factors, and that it is not really relevant at sentencing, because when it comes down to it, they violated the law, and they have to be punished." Her comment upset me, but I did not respond right away. As the session progressed, however, I continued to be disturbed by her comment, the perspective it represented, and by the general failure in the discussion to draw any connection between the decisions people were making about sentencing and the racial disparities in the criminal justice system.

Later in the session, as my frustration escalated, I could not resist commenting, so I said that I wanted to respond to the comment she had made. I said that while it is true that people who commit crimes do cause harm, other types of behaviors that are not sanctioned by criminal law cause harm. And I told everyone that my husband and my daughter are African American and that periodically individuals do and say things that are racialized or racist—and that this causes harm to my family. But more often than not when I talk explicitly about the harm that racism causes, people respond by saying that we have to consider social context and the social factors that lead people to do and say racist things—a sentiment that had been expressed during the seminar. Yet in the case of an action that is criminally sanctioned, we felt comfortable dismissing any conversation about social structure.

The white woman student, whose comment I was referring to, began to cry and said that she was not a racist. I was shocked by her response, and I said to her, "I think you have misunderstood me, I was not talking about anything you said about race, the race example was merely an analogy. . . . But I was talking about how we respond to criminal defendants and whether we consider the structural issues that lead to criminal behavior, I was not . . ." I was unable to finish my sentence because I was interrupted by the judge who had called me a "Commie Pinko." He said loudly and angrily, "Are we finished here?" I stopped, in shock, and looked at him. He said, referring to me, "Now I understand what her problem is, she has a huge chip on her shoulder, and she is very rude, and if we are finished, I would like to go home." The professor said, "I don't want you to go home, I want you to stay, and I want to discuss the [next] case." The judge yelled, "Then tell her to shut up and let's get on with it." The professor looked around the room and said, "Are we ready to discuss the [next] case?" After a long pause another student said, "Maybe we should take a break." Without any other comment the professor said, "five-minute break."

I felt tears welling up, so I dashed into the bathroom so no one would see me cry. A few minutes later, another student in the class, an African American woman who was a close friend, came to the door to ask me what had happened. She had been in the bathroom when the discussion took place and was shocked to hear what the judge had said. She told me that I should leave and not stay for the rest of the session, and she went back to the classroom and gathered my things for me. As I was leaving, I walked past the professor and told him I was leaving; he said that he did not want me to leave. When I told him I was leaving whether he wanted me to or not, he said that the judge who had interrupted me had apologized to him and that he was planning on apologizing to me. I said that it did not matter. As I was walking out, the judge was walking back in, and he attempted to apologize. I said, "It doesn't matter," and he said, "Yes, it does." As I walked out, I thought to myself how ignorant he was. He thought I was saying that what he *did* did not matter to me, but I was saying that his *apology* did not matter to me.

Before that judge learned that my husband was African American, he saw me as a white woman who was perhaps misguided by liberalism at the moment but was very much like his own daughter and was thus "one of us." I had been critical of racism and the criminal justice system throughout all of the sessions, I had spoken many times, and I had passionately disagreed with others in the room. While the judge was not in agreement with my criticisms of structural inequalities, he assumed a commonality between us, which caused him to believe that with the proper discipline I could fit in. But when I revealed that my husband and daughter were African American, and at the time I was noticeably pregnant, I believe I challenged his conception of the community of "us." Ruth Frankenberg says, "[I]nterracial relationships symbolically challenge the boundaries of communities structured by race and culture. . . ."[21] She further notes that interracial relationships between white women and men of color challenge white patriarchy in that white men lose control over white women's bodies, an important component of the power dynamics of sexist oppression. When I spoke about my African American husband and daughter and my family's experiences with racism, his reaction was so severe and emotional that he publicly shouted that I had "a chip on [my] shoulder" and should be told to "shut up." I cannot be certain what made his reaction so powerful, but I suggest it was related to what Frankenberg asserts: a loss of control over his perception of community boundaries and over my body, the body of a white woman who reminded him of his daughter. This judge had been disciplining me, praising me while at the same time sanctioning my repeated challenges to inequality in the criminal justice system. When I revealed that I was involved in an interracial relationship, the judge gave up on this strategy of praise combined with sanctions and instead forcefully sanctioned me by attempting to remove my status as an insider in the law school seminar.

The next week, I went to see the professor of the seminar to discuss what had happened and to inform him that I had decided that I would not return for the last session. The professor's first response was that while the judge may have acted inappropriately, I should not let that affect my experience in the class. I told the professor that his response was a perfect example of the kind of analogy I had been making in the class when I had been rudely silenced. I said, "If [the judge] had pushed me and broken my wrist, in violation of the law, you would not ask me to come back to that class. But since it was merely an act of racism, I should ignore it and ignore the emotional pain it caused me." The professor responded by saying that he did not think that what the judge had said had anything to do with race or racism. I asked, "How do you explain his saying that 'now he understands what my problem is' and I have a 'chip on my shoulder' if he was not reacting to my stating that my husband and daughter are black?" To this he answered that I had been "emotional" in my comments and that people did not respond well to shows of emotion. Then he said that maybe my level of emotion was due to my "condition" (referring to my pregnancy). And finally he said that I was "fairly inartic- ulate" in my comments, something that he said was "unusual" for me.

The professor seemed to be suggesting that the comment of the judge was not about racism but that it was about sexism, and that this form of sexism was justifiable in the context of a law school seminar. I was sanctioned by the judge because I was emotional and inarticulate— a common charge against women. And according to the professor, I was probably "emotional" because of my "condition": an emotional, inarticulate, pregnant woman. Given my rejection of the proper gen- dered boundaries of law school discussions, it was justifiable to sanction me, although the judge might have been a bit severe. I had challenged white patriarchal authority in that room, and now the professor insisted that I understand and consent to the abuse that this transgression had caused. I told the professor that it was true that I had been emotional, and I thought that it was a shame that more people were not emotional about issues of racism. And I told him that as a student in the process of learning, I reserved the right to be inarticulate in classroom discus- sions without being abused. He acknowledged my comments but told me that he must insist that I come to the last session of the seminar, a clear indication that he did not understand my perspective. On a final condescending and paternalistic note, he told me that he would be very disappointed in me if I allowed this interaction with the judge to prevent me from attending the last session.

I left his office, and after consulting with counsel at the university's Equal Employment Opportunities Office, I wrote a letter to this profes- sor, informing him that I would not come to the final session of the semi- nar and that under the circumstances my decision should not affect my grade. In it I said:

I am writing you this memorandum to inform you that I will not be attending the final sentencing seminar session. Given the personal attack on me and my viewpoint . . . I do not feel that the seminar is a learning environment where I can freely express my opinions and concerns about the criminal justice system and sentencing. Further, I believe that the reaction to [the judge's] comments was not commensurate to the extreme offensiveness of his comments. . . .

The professor never responded to this letter. I received the equivalent of an A in the class, the grade that all students received (we were graded as a group), but no one ever contacted me about the event again. No one who was in that session ever made an attempt to publicly rectify what had happened. Looking back, I realize that I violated three norms in that classroom—the first was that, as a white woman, I told a white man, who had likened me to his daughter, that I was married to an African American man—defying racialized gender norms. Second, I had been a loud and assertive woman, who refused to defer my point of view. And third, I had refused to consent to the law school norm of neutral rationality. I refused to be silenced in that classroom—but I paid a price, including losing valuable contacts for a judicial clerkship and being ostracized from a group of law students whom I had to see every day in my final semester of law school.

The year after I graduated from law school, this professor retired. His secretary sent out a blanket mailing to all students who had been in his sentencing seminar to invite them to come to his retirement party; I did not receive an invitation. Several students from the class, with whom I still had contact, commented that he must have specifically asked his secretary to remove my name and not invite me, as everyone else had gotten invitations. This was my final reminder from law school that I did not belong.

Returning to Sociology: Using Anger; Finding Voice

Returning to the PhD program in sociology, I have found that in many ways I am still an outsider. I was gone for three years, and the composition of the faculty has changed. Many of the professors who were there in my early years of graduate school, and with whom I had battled, have retired or left. I do not know many of the newly hired junior faculty or the new graduate students. My advisor, Jennifer Pierce, moved her tenure line to American Studies after her tenure battle. My dissertation chair, Rose Brewer, who fought a tenure battle of her own in sociology years before, had moved her tenure line to the African American and African Studies Department even before I entered the sociology department. My experience working with faculty members who seem often to find themselves thought of as not "one of us" in their disciplines has taught me something very valuable about academia. There are safe spaces in academia for conservative perspectives, and there are safe spaces for liberal perspectives. But critical perspectives, perspectives that seek to mark whiteness, to challenge male norms, to name power and rage against inequality, frequently do not find safe spaces in the academy. There are negative consequences, potentially career-threatening consequences, for asserting critical race/gender/class/sexuality perspectives in academia. Those consequences range from being the subject of a gaze that says, "I thought you were one of us," to being denied tenure. I believe that this skews the academic discourse on issues of race, class, gender, and sexuality. The spectrum of ideas and knowledge in the academy is unbalanced both because power structures drive out individuals with critical perspectives and because other individuals avoid raising critical perspectives for fear of reprisal.

Despite the risks involved in engaging a critical perspective and confronting authority, I have not given up my battle to become a critical scholar. Critical race theorist Derrick Bell says that if we live our lives allowing small indignities to pass without challenge, we may fail to step up when serious human rights are at stake.[22] The experiences I have had in academia may or may not be perceived as small indignities, but I have been unwilling to remain silent about the pain they have caused me and the way in which being an outsider has been a constant struggle. Through my experience in academia, I have found and developed my own voice, a voice to challenge the normative "realities" of the academy. As a white woman, a critical race theorist, and a feminist, I have experienced exclusion in the academy. But I have also benefited from race privilege. Faculty in both sociology and law school, who began by seeing me as an insider and said that I was gifted and talented, changed their perspectives about me when they learned that I would be openly critical of racist and sexist structures. In doing so they revealed their bias. My talent, in their eyes, was contingent on my buying into their construction of society, sociology, and law.

I began this narrative with the words of bell hooks, reminding us that feminists today frequently evoke the intersections of race, class, gender, and sexuality, but that we must remember that this was not always the case. An important critique of second wave feminism came from women of color and poor white women who noted that the movement was dominated by white middle-class women. Race and class privilege

allowed middle-class white women to define feminism and gender oppression while their own whiteness and class locations went unmarked
in their work. Women of color and poor white women were made to feel
as though they did not belong in the feminist movement and could not
be "one of us" unless they bought into feminism as defined by women
in a social location very different from their own. My narrative offers an
example of the ways in which systems of power in the academy continue
to operate to exclude race and gender critical perspectives. As a self-defined feminist, one who came to feminism as a result of seeing the intersections of racist and sexist oppressions, I believe that it is an essential
task for me, and for all feminists, to be constantly reflective concerning
issues of power and exclusion—in all forms. My hope is that the third
wave of feminism will pave the way for an academic space where those
who have experienced exclusion can find a place where they can truly
be "one of us."

Notes

1. bell hooks, *Feminist Theory: From Margin to Center,* 2nd ed. (Cambridge,
Mass.: South End Press, 2000), xii.

2. For example, in her *The Feminine Mystique,* Betty Friedan asserts that the
major problem facing women is that they had been taught to think of themselves
in terms of their roles as wife, mother, and homemaker, and that despite being
surrounded by new luxuries in appliances and electronics, they still felt alone and
misunderstood because this image did not acknowledge their humanity outside
of their sexual relation to man. This image did not capture the life experiences
of any of the women I knew, many of whom were divorced, all of whom were
in the workforce, and very few of whom were surrounded by elaborate home-
making electronics and appliances. As a result of the implied white middle-class
woman in her assessment of the problems of women, Friedan's construction of
feminism did not seem to deal with the issues I found relevant. See Betty Friedan,
The Feminine Mystique, 20th anniversary ed. (New York: Norton, 1983).

3. See, for example, Ruth Frankenberg, *White Women, Race Matters: The
Social Construction of Whiteness* (Minneapolis: University of Minnesota Press,
1993).

4. Richard Delgado, "Legal Storytelling: Storytelling for Oppositionists and
Others: A Plea for Narrative," in *Critical Race Theory: The Cutting Edge* (Philadelphia: Temple University Press, 1995), 64.

5. Here I employ Patricia Hill Collins's concept of standpoint as meaning
an interpretation of my experiences and ideas based on the locations of my lived
experience within a racialized social structure. Patricia Hill Collins, *Black Feminist Thought: Knowledge, Consciousness, and the Politics of Empowerment* (New York:
Routledge, 2000).

6. During the 1970s and 1980s the phenomenon of an increasingly isolated poor black inner-city community, which sociologists Douglas Massey and Nancy Denton describe in *American Apartheid,* was in progress. However, in my youth, in the inner-city St. Paul Summit-University community there was still a sizable working/middle-class black community that lived side by side with the poor unemployed and underemployed community. Since that time, that neighborhood has experienced gentrification. White people have moved into the central city, artificially driving up property values, causing rents and property taxes to skyrocket. The result has been that a neighborhood that had a long history as a black neighborhood is becoming increasingly white, and the black community living there (especially the poor) has largely been driven out. Douglas Massey and Nancy Denton, *American Apartheid: Segregation and the Making of the Underclass* (Cambridge, Mass.: Harvard University Press, 1998).

7. Looking back, I cannot be sure why Mrs. Keiser took me under her wing in this way. She did tell my mother that it was because she thought I was an interesting child and she enjoyed having me around. I suspect it was also because she felt that I was in need of someone to support me, and she decided that she would be that someone.

8. In the mid-1970s the schools were set up so that J. J. Hill, the school where Mrs. Keiser was principal, housed grades K–3; then students moved on to Longfellow for grades 4–6, and then on to junior high. I continued to go to Mrs. Keiser's school on a regular basis into my junior high years. See Massey and Denton, *American Apartheid.*

9. Collins, *Black Feminist Thought.*

10. Joe Feagin, *Racist America: Roots, Current Realities, and Future Reparations* (New York: Routledge, 2000).

11. David R. Roediger, *Toward the Abolition of Whiteness* (New York: Verso, 1994).

12. Professor Rose Brewer, an African American woman, was in the sociology department, but after a nasty tenure battle she had her tenure line moved to the African American and African Studies Department. She remains an adjunct faculty member in the sociology department.

13. Michel Foucault, *Discipline and Punish,* trans. Alan Sheridan (New York: Vintage Books, 1995).

14. Michael Omi and Howard Winant, *Racial Formation in the United States: From the 1960s to the 1990s* (New York: Routledge, 1994); Hubert M. Blalock, *Toward a Theory of Minority-Group Relations* (New York: John Wiley and Sons, 1967); Georg Simmel, *Conflict* (Glencoe, Ill.: Free Press, 1955).

15. Frankenberg, *White Women, Race Matters,* 1.

16. See Jennifer Pierce, "Traveling from Feminism to Mainstream Sociology and Back," this volume.

17. See Maxine Baca Zinn, Lynn Weber Cannon, Elizabeth Higginbotham, and Bonnie Thornton Dill, "The Costs of Exclusionary Practices in Women's Studies," *Signs* 11, 2 (Winter 1986), for a discussion of a similar form of inclusion and exclusion in women's studies.

18. Lani Guinier, Michelle Fine, and Jane Balin, *Becoming Gentlemen* (Boston: Beacon Press, 1997), 9; emphasis in original.

19. Ibid., 29.

20. This section of the narrative, concerning my experience in the second semester of this seminar, is largely drawn from records of the event that I created at that time in the expectation that they might be needed for legal action against the law school and the professor of the class.

21. Frankenberg, *White Women, Race Matters,* 100.

22. Derrick Bell, *Confronting Authority: Reflections of an Ardent Protestor* (Boston: Beacon Press, 1994).

12. A New Wave, Shifting Ground

Women's Studies PhDs and the Feminist Academy,
from the Perspective of 1998

Dawn Rae Davis

UNTIL the late 1990s, the existence of women's studies exclusively depended on the multiple disciplinary constituency of its faculty—scholars who earned doctorates in traditional disciplines and longer-standing departments.[1] However, contours of disciplinary location and identity are in transition with the advent of women's studies doctorates, who represent a new wave of development within the feminist academy broadly and its topographies of knowledge.[2] For the first time in the three decades of feminisms' academic history, women's studies has become a primary institutional location for the doctoral training of feminist scholars. It now produces knowledges and expertise reflective of disciplinary standards, methods, and specializations (required by training at the level of doctorate education) specific to the field. Both interdisciplinarity and a concentrated, exclusively feminist focus of study are central to defining women's studies as a site of advanced degree training distinct from the training feminist scholars obtain in other disciplinary locations (although often supplemented by minor degree training in women's studies). Consequently, a primary impact of the development of PhDs in women's studies is on the cross- and multidisciplinary dynamics that have characterized both faculty affiliations with women's studies and graduate training in women's studies programs. Correspondingly, these impacts bear on feminist histories of migration between women's studies and other disciplines where scholars' professional identities and research are also (and, in many cases, primarily) located.

Feminist communities are as yet in the early stages of recognizing and engaging with the impacts of these emerging disciplinary contours and how they will affect the traditional cross-disciplinary movements of feminist scholars in and out of women's studies. To an extent, changes becoming evident in hiring preferences have begun to highlight some of these impacts in terms of disciplinary affiliations that we can anticipate will increasingly characterize future women's studies faculty.[3] Those of us who are currently in women's studies PhD programs and who have recently obtained women's studies doctorates are positioned experientially at the crest of this new wave of disciplinary transition in ways that uniquely impact and inform our perspectives. As a result, we are acutely aware of a generational shift taking place across epistemological, identity, and cultural topographies pertaining to ways that the feminist academy has traditionally positioned women's studies and perceived it to function. This generational shift cannot be fully comprehended by examining women's studies alone or by focusing primarily on distinctions between second and third waves in the feminist academy generally. Instead, it must be understood in the context of the unique historical relationship that women's studies has shared with the broader feminist academy, and, in particular, how that relationship had been conditioned by disciplinary affiliations and identities.

Focusing on the feminist studies PhD program in women's studies at the University of Minnesota and the experiences of my cohort during the program's inaugural year of 1998, I will share some of my perceptions regarding practices and topographies historically associated with the field and currently in transition. As more doctoral programs are instituted, other locations are likely to confront issues and produce insights particular to them. So although transitions initiated in 1998 at the University of Minnesota are not necessarily identical to other institutions or uniformly relevant, the story of my cohort's and my experiences that first year reflects a number of generational factors embedded in the multidisciplinary history of the field. Sharing aspects of our local story, I will profile shifting contours of identity governing disciplinary relationships between women's studies and the feminist academy to argue that the emergent disciplinary identity represented by the PhD in women's studies challenges perceptions widely held by earlier waves of the feminist academy. As I have already suggested, the generational story that these perceptions tell is largely a result of cross- and multidisciplinary dynamics, and it reveals issues of space and place that are epistemologically, culturally, and institutionally material.

Attempting to understand how these issues defined several transitional factors encountered by our program's first-year cohort in 1998, my colleagues and I began to see that they were specifically related to contrasts between the locations of our academic training and those of earlier feminist generations within the institution. Past generations of feminist scholars received doctoral training in programs other than women's studies and migrated between women's studies and other disciplinary locations over the course of their careers and professional identities. In contrast, many women's studies PhDs will have been primarily or solely in the field all along and immersed in its particular scholarship throughout their academic careers. Of the first-year cohort of the University of Minnesota's feminist studies PhD program, for example, all five students majored in women's studies as undergraduates, and two of these entered the program with master's degrees in women's studies also.[4] This is a distinct contrast to the academic training of our department's current core faculty members and most of its affiliated faculty. Differences between faculty and students in terms of the locations where they obtained their academic training produce significantly different experiences and perceptions regarding the disciplinary identity of women's studies. These locational distinctions warrant analysis in the context of generational shifts created by the new wave of feminist scholars that women's studies doctorates represent.

Contentions of 1998: The National Scene within Local Transitions

While the feminist academy has witnessed new waves specific to women's studies programs and departments before, between 1997 and 1998 the number of women's studies PhD programs increased by 50 percent (half a decade after the first PhD programs began at Clark and Emory universities in 1992 and York University in 1991).[5] The program at the University of Minnesota was one of two begun in 1998. The other was at the University of Iowa. The University of Washington initiated their program in 1997. These years also coincided with the completion of doctorates by the first students in the older programs and their entry into the job market. This combination—the sudden proliferation of new PhD programs and the advent of feminist scholars holding never-before-available PhDs in women's studies—garnered wide attention within the feminist academy and the National Women's Studies Association (NWSA) on disciplinary issues pertaining to the field and its graduate training. Feminist scholars raised new concerns regarding the distinctiveness of women's studies scholarship, methodologies, and epistemologies.

It was quite frightening to enter a brand-new program in the midst of this scrutiny reflected by contentious national debates that questioned the intellectual merit of the very degrees we were undertaking. In asking whether or not women's studies PhD programs should exist, a central issue addressed by the 1998–99 debates was the disciplinary capacity of women's studies to produce knowledges demonstrative of the expertise and specialization required at the level of doctoral training.[6] Questions expressed considerable concern regarding the depth, legitimacy, and adequacy of knowledges produced by the field. It was particularly unsettling for my colleagues and me (who had considered the professional risks of this new, "unproven" women's studies degree but had nonetheless optimistically decided to pursue it) that these concerns issued from feminist scholars who were themselves affiliated with women's studies education. With only one exception, scholars on both sides of the argument (in the published debate) had obtained their doctoral training in long-standing or traditional disciplines[7]—a fact duly noted by my colleagues and myself. We were genuinely concerned by the disciplinary perspectives some of the interlocutors revealed in terms of feminist ownership and identity regarding the institutional location of women's studies and its knowledges.

Closer to home, amid sizable transitions initiated in our local context, we found ourselves concretely situated by changing cultural, disciplinary, and epistemological topographies. Because 1998 marked such a noteworthy national development in the field as well as wide discussion of its implications at the same time our local context saw the introduction of a new PhD program, my cohort was uniquely positioned by both national and local contexts in an important transitional moment. Several of the transitions we experienced locally reflected issues of ownership and identity similar to those we perceived the national debates to highlight. We began to understand them specifically with regard to the multidisciplinary constituency of both our department and the Center for Advanced Feminist Studies (CAFS) and the historical relationship between them. The University of Minnesota is home to a vital feminist community of scholars and a thirty-year-old women's studies program, facilitated by the presence of CAFS, which has served for twenty years as an umbrella entity bringing together feminist faculty and graduate students from diverse disciplinary locations. CAFS also administered a long-standing graduate minor degree program in women's studies, certifying graduate scholars from disciplinary locations as diverse as those of CAFS-affiliated faculty. Structurally, CAFS represents a cross- and multidisciplinary space for feminist scholars, knowledges, and research interests, serving in many ways as a second domain for feminists in the academy in addition to their primary disciplines. Similarly, the CAFS's graduate minor program was also a second institutional home for developing feminist scholars primarily located in traditional disciplines.

Most CAFS-affiliated scholars embody a relationship within dual domains of emphasis: one strongly informed by a primary discipline, and the other within the feminist focus of their work. As I mentioned earlier, this dual emphasis contrasts with the exclusively feminist focus of study and interdisciplinarity that are primary constitutive elements of women's studies scholarship and training. This contrast represents one of the most important factors marking scholars primarily located in women's studies as different from their feminist colleagues across the academy. It is important, however, to point out the compatibility of the academic space provided by CAFS with the multidisciplinary identities of its faculty and students obtaining minor degrees. In the absence of a women's studies master's or doctoral program, the CAFS minor degree program was entirely compatible with producing feminist scholars whose research was defined by primary disciplinary identities outside women's studies but whose work also included important feminist components, methodologies, and/or an explicit focus on gender. The CAFS graduate program prepared future feminist faculty at the same time that students' primary disciplines regulated and administered their doctoral programs, research, and dissertations. In other words, the site of feminist knowledge and supplemental training provided by the CAFS minor program was additional to the disciplinary training scholars obtained in their home departments.

The diverse disciplinary context of CAFS in terms of preparing future feminist faculty for women's studies positions prior to 1998 can be witnessed across a spectrum of institutions. In the absence of women's studies doctorates, women's studies has often looked to scholars with supplemental feminist training and minor degrees (or to those with a consistent feminist emphasis in their work) as the strongest candidates to fill its faculty positions. Although most graduates of women's studies minor programs (nationally) acquire appointments in their primary disciplines, some acquire joint appointments in those disciplines and in women's studies. Due to the limited size of most women's studies programs and departments and the fewer lines of hire generally available to them, significantly fewer acquire appointments solely in women's studies. However, the concrete aspect of hiring trends points out how women's studies doctorates and PhD programs may contribute to shifting lines of distribution pertaining to disciplinary emphases and institutional resources. Certainly at the University of Minnesota, where the doctoral program had emerged from the long-standing minor degree program, we were feeling a number of material transitions in 1998. As CAFS transferred its resources for graduate student training over to the women's studies department, its administrative budget and staffing were altered, and its overall mission was somewhat adjusted. The first months at Minnesota brought surprising experiences that mirrored concrete and cultural transitions in ways that highlighted generational factors and specifically made issues of disciplinarity visible to my cohort and me.

Space, Place, Home, and Disciplinarity: What We Ran Into

Our earliest awareness of transitions related to space, place, home, and disciplinarity came directly through our participation in the women's studies graduate student advocacy group, which before 1998 was made up of CAFS minors—many of whom had been affiliated with CAFS a number of years. Significantly, these students had benefited from being the sole graduate students associated with women's studies in terms of funding opportunities available through teaching and research assistantships. Joining the student advocacy group both as newcomers to the department and as a new generation of women's studies (and feminist) scholars, we were in the minority in terms of numbers; however, the different relationship to the institutional site of women's studies that we embodied immediately surfaced in our discussions. Our presence directly affected the security of the relationship older CAFS minors had had with departmental resources before 1998,[8] and students expressed varying degrees of acceptance of the changes. As my colleagues and I asserted the distinctiveness of our relationship (as the program's majors) with the department and its resources in the course of articulating our agendas, some minors expressed a sense of being displaced from what had become an important second home for them in the academy. They were concerned about the financial impact and also that they would not obtain valuable teaching experience in women's studies that made them stronger candidates for women's studies faculty positions upon completion of their programs of study.

All of us were somewhat surprised, I think, by the broader implications of our discussions around resource issues. For example, when my colleagues and I encountered the sense of entitlement regarding resources that some older minors expressed, we considered for the first time how the history of women's studies is such that it has been largely constituted by affiliates who in traditional disciplines would be considered "outsiders" or peripherally associated with a department under which they pursued a minor program of study. We began to realize that claiming women's studies as our primary institutional "home"—asserting our specific relationship to the department's resources and teaching opportunities and articulating distinctions between our training needs and those of minors in the program—reflected subtle reorientations regarding place, entitlement, and ownership. Within a few months, the new majors withdrew from the group in order to define and articulate our own advocacy needs, because it was clear that our relationship with the department engendered a different agenda than that of students minoring in the program and was not productively addressed collectively.

Later that year, a concrete space issue developed that also became a compelling example of both cultural and material adjustments underway. Although it arose with regard to everyday practices, it suggested a more extensive metaphor reflecting both identity and epistemological issues related to space, place, and "home" in the context of the feminist academy's association with women's studies. Our department and CAFS were located on the same floor of the building that housed them and shared some staff and office space. In that joint context, women's studies had always provided office space to student instructors and teaching assistants (who before 1998 had been solely CAFS minors). However, with seven new PhD students (including four of us teaching for the department that first year) requiring office space—along with the guarantee of office space made by the department's initial offer letters to its new majors—the distribution of space among both majors and minors became a point of contention.[9] While some majors and minors agreed that the unique history of women's studies' dependence on scholars from other programs—in terms of filling its teaching positions—made a compelling case for sharing office space, some majors strongly asserted that minors should utilize office space within their own major degree programs/departments and that women's studies majors were entitled to (own) their own space in their home department.

The deliberation regarding graduate student office space was not without some tension. Some faculty agreed that PhD students were entitled to their "own" space, and some cited the history of the department's relationship to its minors and were unwilling to support the needs articulated by its majors. This particular space issue represented more than important material shifts at the level of lived experience. Cultural, disciplinary, and epistemological topographies pertaining to ownership, academic identity, and place were also shifting. These transitions highlighted more starkly (than what had been considered before 1998 in the Minnesota context) how women's studies and its scholars are distinctly located in ways that differ from our colleagues variously located elsewhere in the feminist spaces of the academy. Importantly, this issue of location signaled a distinctly generational shift regarding perceptions of disciplinary space and place in connection with identity. For many of the PhD students, women's studies had always been their primary institutional place and source of disciplinary and scholarly identity, and from the perspective of their experiences, it was definitively not a site in and out of which they traveled cross-disciplinarily. Consequently, they perceived the space of women's studies as markedly distinct from other feminist spaces in the academy.

The office space issue, along with this broader implication (equally reflected by our experience with the joint minor-major student advocacy group around funding resources), presented a new hierarchical development for women's studies and the feminist academy. PhD students perceived and asserted an unprecedented privileged entitlement and access to women's studies, its space, knowledges, and resources that established a hierarchical relation between majors and minors. On the part of feminists who have generally opposed such hierarchies, the appearance of these differences in the very maw of the institutional space conceived as the academic arm of feminist activism and celebrated for its radical alternatives was jarring, to say the least, and predictably challenging for some to accept. To reckon with hierarchies of place, identity, and ownership specifically within the domain of women's studies truly brought an impact created by women's studies PhDs straight plunked down in the middle of the home place of academic feminism in our local context.

"Home" and Other Evidence of Generational Disciplinary Histories

As my colleagues and I negotiated the effect of these jarring occurrences on our own experiences, as the very bodies and subjects whose presence had been responsible for bringing them to bear at "home" in our local space, we had numerous conversations. These were heated, passionate exchanges.[10] Many of them took place in the very office now defined by official departmental protocol as our "own"—not an irrelevant factor. I suspect that the analyses that emerged from our conversations were enabled not only by the collective effort to establish our own work space and by identity issues of which we became aware in the process, but by the privacy and distinct sense of home we enjoyed in a space specifically designated for our work as developing women's studies scholars. Out of a particular focus on "home," we began to discuss how a generational dynamic was evident in an association between "home" and women's studies in the cultural imaginary of the feminist academy.

We began to see how the dual domains characteristic of women's studies faculty engendered a home metaphor detrimental to understandings of the distinctiveness of women's studies scholarship. Many older generations of feminists in the academy often regarded women's studies as a second "home" and a nonprimary site of scholarship and academic identity. Distinctions between women's studies and the other disciplinary domains of feminist scholars are related to professional responsibilities but also to professional rewards available within primary disciplines, their professional organizations, and professional journals identified with established disciplines. For many feminist faculty, women's studies has continued to be a secondary, nonprimary domain for their scholarship and professional identities and rewards.[11]

The perception of women's studies as a secondary "home" to feminists in the academy reflects two important historical factors: the relationship between the field and the diverse disciplinary identities of older academic waves, and the marginalized status both of the field and of feminist scholarship generally. However, the prevalence of this perception within feminist quarters negatively contributes to a further marginalization of women's studies scholarship within the broader disciplinary contexts of academic feminism and reveals hierarchical rankings that are not often recognized and rarely remarked upon. Even though affiliation with women's studies and publishing in feminist journals demand significant commitments of time additional to what scholars give to their home departments and disciplines (thereby increasing their workloads), perpetuating the notion of women's studies as a secondary home to feminists in the academy also plays into feminizing tropes of home as hearth and refuge. Such metaphors suggest a space of haven removed from the corruption of (academic) commerce and the hierar-

chies of patriarchal disciplinarity and its canonical laws. Within this metaphorical field, women's studies becomes a feminized space of safety for
(the comparatively private and cloistered) exchanges of feminisms and
somewhat a step removed from the more public domains of scholars'
primary professional identities. The hearth-refuge connotations, in contradicting the additional concrete burden of labor entailed by participating in women's studies (as well as in one's primary discipline), duplicate
the "double-shift" discourse related to the feminization of housework.[12]
In ways I find very significant, this takes the feminization of the space of
feminist and gender studies in an unfortunate direction and reinscribes
gendered hierarchies of work and work space within a private/public
distinction. Moreover, feminizing the space of women's studies within
feminisms' own discourses of disciplinarity inscribes the primary, traditional disciplinary domains of feminist scholars within spaces marked
by masculinity, privileging both the traditional disciplinary and public
power of masculine space, knowledge, and professionalism.

Two colleagues (Jodi Horne and Sara Hottinger) from my first year
cohort and I wrote papers that first year for an NWSA conference panel.
In them, we emphasized the dangers of "home" when conceived as a notion of refuge in the context of what women's studies—as a unique site
of knowledge and scholarship—offers to the feminist academy more
broadly. We argued that for current PhD students in the field, "home" is
not necessarily a safe place to be with regard to professional rewards and
status within an institutional structure that continues to regard women's
studies as a "marginal" space capable of producing only idiosyncratic
knowledges.[13] In light of the professional risks students entering wom-
en's studies PhD programs were taking, we wished to caution against this
notion of refuge and safety. We sought to displace the "home" metaphor
within the feminist imaginary by drawing attention to changes in its top-
ographical meanings related to professionalization brought about by
doctoral training in women's studies. We also wanted to raise awareness
regarding disadvantages that result when one's primary institutional
"home" bears the markings of marginality celebrated from within the
feminist academy's own ranks. Such celebration further devalues the
PhDs that are produced by the field and that we ourselves are very invested in valuing.

When we presented our panel ("Home Has Never Been So Dangerous: The PhD in Women's Studies") at a CAFS colloquium the following year and collectively emphasized issues of professionalization with

regard to legitimizing the disciplinary location of women's studies in
the context of its doctoral training, we anticipated many of the objec-
tions that were raised in the discussion period following. Indeed, our
papers were conceived precisely with the goal of confronting them.[14]
However, we found ourselves confronting one concern, raised by a core
faculty member from our own department, that summarized a generational bias so boldly that I think it caught all three of us off guard. She
commented that our emphasis on professionalization was startling and
concerning because of the conservatism she perceived it to express. We
readily acknowledged that this concern reflected a historically celebratory attitude toward women's studies as a radical place of marginality
within the institution, but, more reluctantly, we found it reflective of
a bias that demonstrated a certain contradiction. Namely, this faculty
member, like all her current colleagues in the feminist academy at Minnesota, had already achieved and benefited from the privileges of a professional identity via the credibility of her own doctorate degree conferred by an established, traditional, or long-standing discipline. Like
that of her contemporaries, the professional accreditation by which this
faculty member had obtained her position and entitlements represented
indisputably ratified value legitimized within the perceptual field of the
institution. Was she suggesting that her own professionalization within
her particular doctoral degree program and the benefits and privileges
it conferred demonstrated less conservatism than the professionalism
to be acquired within the doctoral degree programs of women's studies? My colleagues and I were not asking for a more conservative professionalism than what current faculty had already achieved in terms of the
credibility and legitimacy associated with disciplinary identity conferred
by a doctorate.

Introducing a new professional identity produced exclusively from
within the domain of women's studies is necessarily subjecting the home
metaphor to renovations. The point is not to detract from the commitment many feminist scholars have had to women's studies programs and
the extensive labor many feminists have devoted to developing and sustaining them over the course of the past three decades. Neither is it to
minimize the role of minor graduate degree and certification programs
with respect to developments in the field. There would be no PhD programs in women's studies in the current institution without the ground-
breaking, challenging, and dedicated work of older generations of feminists in the academy. Rather, the emphasis here is to direct attention

to how PhDs in the field are dynamically challenging ways that older generations have positioned and perceived women's studies. It is also to highlight a visible collusion between the function of disciplinary identities and perceptions that actively marginalize women's studies, obscure its distinctiveness, and are implicated in current practices with negative impact for doctoral programs and the future of the field.

Critiquing the "home" metaphor at the same time that we were reclaiming it under a new generational definition helped us see how women's studies has historically functioned as a cross-disciplinary site of feminist engagement in ways that obscure the particularity of women's studies knowledges and interdisciplinarity. The multidisciplinary histories of women's studies faculty contribute to perceptions of women's studies as a cross-flow "interdisciplinary" space, open to all feminists from different academic disciplines similarly. In addition, interdisciplinarity has often been articulated as an "anti-disciplinary" position, a notion compatible with conceptions of feminist scholarship as "against" the disciplines and women's studies as a particularly celebrated place of anti-discipline.[15] Due to the nexus of cross- and multidisciplinary histories, women's studies has not been widely perceived to function within its own disciplinary rules and emphases. Those of us trained throughout our careers primarily and exclusively within the field regard this perception as inaccurate.

However, challenges inherent to initiating a brand-new PhD program (and articulating disciplinary issues entailed by program development) demonstrated that generational perceptions of the distinct disciplinary emphases of women's studies differed among our core faculty.[16] Again, the transition from training minors to training doctoral students played a key role. Although our junior faculty members did not receive their graduate training in women's studies, they were of a feminist generation closer to the age of graduate students strictly in terms of the number of years they had participated in the academy (this generational reference is unrelated to chronological age). They appeared readily flexible in the transition from training minors to also training majors and to the specificity of the new disciplinary identity represented by PhD students. Senior faculty from earlier academic generations, in contrast, had experienced the disadvantages of doing feminist scholarship in the years when the environment was much more hostile to work on gender. Their experiences were also conditioned many more years by the particular disciplines in which they were trained and in which their scholarship was (and in many cases continued to be) located. Lastly, senior faculty had embodied the "academic arm" of feminisms in the early years of women's studies programs and conveyed a sense of ownership over women's studies to which, indeed, they were entitled in ways their junior colleagues were not.

However, both our junior and senior faculty represented an important contrast to the PhD students precisely in our generational location within the field itself pertaining to the focus of our undergraduate and graduate training and scholarship. That is, we younger scholars (who came directly out of women's studies undergraduate and master's programs) identified exclusively with women's studies as our primary disciplinary domain. Neither our junior or senior faculty had similarly been located by women's studies training or been the recipients of a women's studies education to the same extent. We were indeed, indirectly, the generational offspring of our senior faculty, inheriting their legacy and labor directly via our women's studies educations, but our experiential relationship to the field and its knowledges was entirely different. This difference was very apparent as we attempted to share our perceptions with senior faculty who, to a significant extent, regarded us as "identityless" with regard to disciplinarity.[17] It was often challenging to communicate how our uniquely different set of experiences in women's studies engendered in us a very firm disciplinary identity specific to the field and its interdisciplinarity distinct from the cross- and multidisciplinary dynamics historically characteristic of previous generations.

With substantial efforts on the parts of both students and faculty in the early years of the program on development issues, the department's history of training graduate minors presented perhaps the most challenging and concrete sites of generational negotiation pertaining to disciplinary issues. As the department transferred the basic curricular structure of the CAFS training program for minors over to the PhD program, the fundamental multidisciplinary history of women's studies and its minor and certificate degree programs presented a stark contrast with the training needs of doctoral students. Training students with the purpose of supplementing their primary disciplinary training with feminist discourses and emphases as well as with feminist methodologies that transformatively build on the research methods of traditional disciplines (feminist methods in the social sciences, feminist literary studies, feminist ethnography, feminist history, etc.) entails markedly different curricular needs than training students primarily within the focus of women's studies. While the interdisciplinarity of women's studies scholarship benefits from cross-disciplinary feminist methods and training, the radical reorganizations of knowledge and objects of study that characterize the field, its interdisciplinary focus and practice, and the related emphasis on synthesis entail distinct methodologies that cannot be captured solely by feminist alterations to traditional disciplinary methods (or, as some have coined it, the "add and stir" approach).[18]

Similarly, an additive approach to women's studies curriculum (women in literature, women in history, women in the arts, women and the law, the sociology/psychology of women, etc.) optimizes the multidisciplinary constituency of women's studies faculty and serves the educational needs of graduate students by providing a feminist focus of study corresponding to a number of disciplinary fields in which graduate non-majors are located. However, the multidisciplinary structure of an additive approach is limited in terms of supplying a curricular structure conducive to interdisciplinarily focused specializations of feminist study, the needs of which are better met by courses that integrate across disciplinary fields to stage topics focused by particular discourses. Women's studies PhDs also have significantly more curricular needs in the context of feminist theory than do minors supplementing their disciplinary training. However, the program had transferred the basic feminist theory core course (previously required by the minor degree) to the PhD program without developing additional courses solely focused on theoretical training.

A major focus of development since the inception of the program in 1998 has been adjusting a curriculum that served the minor program (very well) to better serve the specific training needs of the interdisciplinary doctoral program. A number of significant changes have been effected, and students (especially those entering the program in recent years) are benefiting from them. Considering the young age of our program, the department has responded very quickly to the curricular needs of its majors, hammering out rather extensive changes through its committees for approval. I dwell on these factors not to detract from the considerable strength of the women's studies PhD program at Minnesota, which is very much due to the strength of its faculty and its willingness to address development issues, but rather to delineate important ways in which the multidisciplinary histories of the feminist academy—intersecting at the site of women's studies—have had an impact on the contour of women's studies education in a generational context and galvanized critical attention within the new program at Minnesota. The process of transitioning out of multidisciplinary models and curricular structures is integral to remapping generational topographies of knowledge between women's studies and the feminist academy. Developing better feminist understandings of differences between the cross- and multidisciplinary past of the field and the particular disciplinary identity being defined by its PhD training—as well as better recognizing how migrations into women's studies entail crossing into a distinctive disciplinary space (representing specific standards, methods, and objects of study)—is critical to the future of women's studies and its PhD students and programs.

By Way of Concluding: The New Wave and Solid Ground, Three Years Later

In 2001 I participated in a working conference attended by North American Women's Studies scholars at Emory University to focus specifically on articulations and visions of the PhD in women's studies.[19] The interrogations of 1998–99 questioning the merit of women's studies PhDs had moved to a more productive level. The conference focused on grappling with articulations of the knowledge field, research standards and methods, the training needs of students, the career opportunities for which they were being prepared, and administrative challenges facing PhD programs. Moving onto this new terrain of discussion was exciting for PhD students at the conference. However, the extent to which the multidisciplinary history of the feminist academy's association with women's studies informed discussions about research methods and the epistemological topographies of the field revealed inadequately narrow understandings of the distinct disciplinary contours and interdisciplinary practices with which my colleagues and I in doctoral programs identify.

Several plenary panelists demonstrated a disturbing tendency to veer off the specific focus of the conference on PhD programs and instead to discuss general women's studies curricular issues and concerns regarding the role of feminist activism to women's studies broadly. The frequency with which feminist activism was made a point of discussion reflected the strength of women's studies' history as an academic site of activism. In the context of the conference, however, it also expressed resistance to the expanding degree of professionalization and intellectual development within the field. Suggesting that the intellectualist context in which some women's studies doctoral students locate their research will inevitably result in a reduced activist focus within the field overall seemed an overdetermining assessment. When expressed by feminists, holding both doctorates and academic positions themselves, the concern seems extremely misplaced. I was reminded of the faculty response to my colleagues' panel at the CAFS colloquium in Minnesota regarding conservatism, and I heard the same contradictory logic expressed in this concern about activism. If acquiring a doctorate has not restricted these scholars' own interests in feminist activism, it seemed extremely unlikely that acquiring a women's studies doctorate would in any way inherently restrict feminist activism.[20] Again, scholars (holding doctorates themselves) who may, to varying degrees, professionally benefit from migrating between women's studies and traditional disciplines conceive women's studies to be a home place of radical refuge—raising issues of place, space, and identity and demonstrating an active marginalization of the field approved by the feminist academy's own members.

In the final plenary session, I was relieved when one of the conference organizers called attention to aspects of the conference proceedings that, for me, were representative of marginalizing effects. Summarizing the scope of focus covered by the previous two days of discussions, she pointed out the tendency to veer off the topic of issues specific to PhD programs and asked participants to think about what might have been motivating an apparent resistance to maintaining this focus. PhD students at the conference had discussed this resistance in a student-only conversation the previous night, sharing experiences from our local contexts regarding the shifting generational ground of disciplinary histories (reminding me very much of the conversations of my cohort three years earlier at Minnesota). Clearly, generational contours were affecting disciplinary issues related to PhD programs across a range of local contexts. In the last moments of the final plenary, one PhD student at Emory eloquently captured the spirit of the historical moment and generational relationships in which many of us attending the conference understood ourselves to be participating. She articulated the responsibility of PhD programs and students to carry on and give witness to the traditions and work of earlier feminist waves in the academy. And she described the exciting opportunity for older waves of feminist scholars to see PhD students in women's studies as the inheritors of their achievements who would innovate new terrains of feminist scholarship.[21] I felt my own short history within the newest wave of women's studies scholarship and the challenges of transitions since 1998 surge with the possibilities of shifting ground and the sagacious strength of generational legacies. We are here, the speaker seemed to say, in the very compelling present of the feminist academy, not to plant our feet but to keep moving, looking both forward and behind to see that generational convergences are themselves a sustaining source of visionary movement and feminist possibility.

Notes

I would like to thank Hokulani Aikau and coeditors Jennifer Pierce and Karla Erickson for comments on drafts of this essay, and Lisa Disch, Amy Kaminsky, and Eden Torres for comments on an earlier version. I would also like to thank Lisa Disch and the Center for Advanced Feminist Studies for the opportunity to present a version of this essay at the CAFS colloquium series. My appreciation goes to Helen Longino and Jacquelyn Zita for conversations in 1998 that helped me understand generational dynamics and to my colleagues in the first-year cohort, with special thanks to Sara Hottinger and Norma Juarbe-Francescini and most especially to Jodi Horne for the education and insights they helped me acquire. A note of thanks to Frances Wood also for permission to refer to her extemporaneous eloquence.

1. In 1998, this history was reflected by nearly all women's studies faculty in North America, including those at the University of Minnesota, none of whom received their doctoral training in women's studies. It is important to note that a multidisciplinary constituency is not uncommon to other interdisciplinary programs, such as Chicano studies, African American studies, and American studies. The critical difference with regard to women's studies is its marking by the particular signifier that operates to unify that multiplicity, namely, "feminism." The unifying force of that signifier contributes to ways in which the distinctiveness of women's studies (as an institutional site) and its scholarship is often obscured.

2. I use the term *feminist academy* to identify the impact of feminist thought, methods, and practice on the U.S. and North American academy subsequent to the women's movement of the late 1960s and the 1970s and to refer to a constituency of faculty and graduate students, located at multiple sites across the disciplinary terrains of the academic institution, for whom feminist practices and perspectives are identifying aspects of scholarship and personal and professional positionalities.

3. My personal attention to job announcements reveals that increasingly since women's studies PhDs entered the academy's hiring market, many announcements by women's studies departments distinctly specify a PhD in women's studies (and a particular topical focus as well that is sometimes stated by reference to a traditional disciplinary domain) or a scholar with comparable

feminist training and gender-focused scholarship (also sometimes stated by reference to a topical area or traditional disciplinary domain). This distinct specification regarding women's studies PhDs is also increasingly appearing in job announcements for non–women's studies departments that are particularly seeking a feminist scholar to teach topics of gender.

4. Two additional students joined the program in its second semester, transferring from other University of Minnesota PhD programs. Both of these students held master's degrees from a gender studies program.

5. The University of California, Santa Barbara, initiated a doctoral emphasis accredited through its women's studies department in 1991.

6. *Feminist Studies* 24, 2 (Summer 1998). These debates were also the focus of one of the plenary panels the following summer at the NWSA conference in 1999, and it was one of the most strongly attended plenaries of the conference (although I am not citing statistical evidence but only sharing my own personal appraisal).

7. Angela Bowen, who acquired her doctorate in women's studies at Clark University, was this exception; Angela Bowen, "Testifying: My Experience in Women's Studies Doctoral Training at Clark University," *Feminist Studies* 24, 2 (Summer 1998). Bowen was also the only scholar who received doctoral training in women's studies who spoke on the plenary panel that focused on these debates at NWSA's annual conference in 1999; Angela Bowen, "An Interdisciplinary PhD in Women's Studies: What's Not to Like?" paper presented at National Women's Studies Association Annual Conference, Albuquerque, New Mexico, 19 June 1999.

8. It is important to note that we did not encounter similar resistance to our presence by those students in their first year of study in the women's studies minor program; I think part of what enabled us to begin to formulate understandings of our experiences in the student advocacy group was the differences in dynamics we registered between new minors in the program and those who had been CAFS minors in years before the PhD program. It is important to say also that much of what we encountered can be attributed to "growing pains" with regard to adjustments in terms of impacts on CAFS minors, and nothing related to the individual personalities of these students was reflected by the dynamics we encountered.

9. With the admittance of two additional students to the program in the second semester, our cohort grew from five to seven.

10. Jodi Horne, Sara Hottinger, and I were the primary participants in these conversations, but also Norma Juarbe-Francescini. Importantly, we were all in the introductory-level core courses required by our program, whereas our other three colleagues had transferred to the program at more advanced stages of graduate work, having already completed the core courses as CAFS minors or having had the core course requirement waived.

11. Many are affiliated women's studies faculty, teaching a course in women's studies annually or on a less regular basis, and serving on the committees of women's studies programs and departments at the same time that their appoint-

ments and the bulk of teaching and administrative responsibilities are within their home departments, and very often they are members of the professional organizations of their primary disciplines (rather than of NWSA, for example).

12. See Arlie R. Hochschild, *The Second Shift* (New York: Avon Books, 1990).

13. Jodi Horne, "Women's Studies, Disciplinarity, and Interdisciplinarity as Method and Positionality," and Dawn Rae Davis, "Between What It Is Correct to Say and What Is Actually Said: Women's Studies as Interdisciplinary Marketplace," unpublished papers, presented at the Center for Advanced Feminist Studies Colloquium, University of Minnesota, 1999; NWSA annual conference, 1999; and National Teleconference on the Education of Women Conference, 2000.

14. In brief, the papers addressed (1) issues related to the depth of knowledge available within the field, (2) the legitimacy of specialized knowledges to be acquired through a women's studies PhD program, (3) misidentifying the distinction between the interdisciplinary practices of women's studies scholarship and multi- or cross-disciplinarity within feminist practices broadly, and (4) uncritical perceptions that take for granted the accessibility of women's studies (and its knowledges) with regard to feminists scholars primarily located by other disciplines.

15. My colleague Jodi Horne has argued that interdisciplinarity, as a politicized concept in the context of academic feminism, provides a positionality of radical otherness within a celebrated marginal space with respect to the academy; Horne, "Women's Studies, Disciplinarity, and Interdisciplinarity as Method and Positionality."

16. Of course, these are not precisely uniform across all the department's core and affiliated faculty, and there are a number of exceptions. But to the extent that some consistent patterns are visible, the generational factors I am describing are generally applicable.

17. The PhD program had in fact been designed to address this perception by requiring a secondary supporting program. Optimally that program would mark a student's training with a traditional disciplinary affiliation.

18. I thank Hokulani Aikau's editorial comments on this essay for bringing Gloria Bowles's apt coinage to my attention. See Gloria Bowles and Renate Duelli Klein, eds., *Theories of Women's Studies* (New York: Routledge and Kegan Paul, 1983).

19. The title of the conference was "The PhD in Women's Studies: Visions and Articulations" (October 2001).

20. The continuing contentions (extremely visible in NWSA) regarding activism, which significantly devalue feminist intellectualism, do not meet with enormous empathy or support among many PhD students. Many of us would like to work in the highest intellectualism available to us because that is where our research interests lie. Equally, many locate their research interests elsewhere. Most PhD students in women's studies with whom I have talked are pursuing academic careers; however, there is nothing specific to the PhD in women's studies

that prevents feminist activism to any degree greater than other doctoral programs in which feminists across the academy have earned their PhDs. Similarly, there is nothing specific to the PhD in women's studies that privileges intellectualism to a degree greater than other doctoral programs. Nor is there anything specific to the women's studies PhD that prevents doctoral students from pursuing careers in sectors other than academia.

21. The student was Frances Wood, from Emory University's women's studies PhD program.

13. Negotiating Feminist Futures

Transgender Challenges and Contradictions of a PhD in Feminist Studies

Sam Bullington and Amanda Lock Swarr

*Women's studies are still growing, offering to more and more
women a new intellectual grasp on their lives, new understanding
of our history, a fresh vision of the human experience, and also
a critical basis for evaluating what they hear and read in other
courses, and in the society at large.*

Adrienne Rich, "Claiming an Education"

As Adrienne Rich pointed out so eloquently, at its inception
women's studies elicited promise and optimism. Now, more than twenty-
five years later, the future of the discipline is in question, as the categories and premises on which it rests are being challenged and revisited.
Two of the most pressing concerns for contemporary feminists are the
"professionalization" of the field and the contestations posed by transgender studies. These seemingly separate areas of concern have rarely
been seen in the same light; however, both have been similarly viewed
as challenging the basis of feminist politics as well as crucial to the continued growth and development of the field. Currently, the institution
of PhD programs in women's studies is conceptualized alternately as a
necessary development or an unwelcome institutionalization of feminist ideologies, while the newly emerging transgender studies is often
seen as a threat to the idea of "woman" on which women's studies rests
or, alternately, as a key to the future of feminist theorizing and thinking
about gender. In this essay we address the similarities in the politics of
these interventions. Following Rich's edict, we assert that women's studies still offers students and faculty the radical potential to explain their
experiences and critically reevaluate their perspectives on the world. In
our view, feminist histories, activism, and theorizations of social justice
are critical to negotiating feminist futures.

Tensions over the terrains of feminism and directions for the discipline of women's studies are not new. Neither are generational debates

and conflicts in which fields such as ours are redefined. We both find ourselves caught in the middle of these two generational debates within feminism whereby people make assumptions about our allegiances based on our calendar and academic "ages," the nature of our research, and physical appearance that does not necessarily match our commitments. This paper demonstrates the oft-noted ways that identifications are contextual, creative, relational, and ever-changing but also the ways in which early loyalties and understandings can remain threaded through shifting circumstances, creating inconsistencies and tensions that demand new strategies to integrate.

The two of us came to similar ideas about feminism and similar political commitments during different decades and through very different means. While graduate students at the University of Minnesota, we were both members of the committee that formed the feminist studies PhD program, and both eventually transferred to this program from anthropology, although five years apart. Neither of us neatly belongs to our feminist generation—the third wave—for similar and different reasons, but at least in part due to our relationships to transgender concerns and our hopes for the future of women's studies.

Sam identifies as a transgendered lesbian feminist, an identification that makes total sense to hir, but one that has become increasingly unintelligible to others as trans and feminist communities have become more polarized, leaving hir feeling between worlds.[1] This feeling finds expression in several areas of hir personal and intellectual life, as ze finds hirself not only between genders but also between feminist generations and between academic disciplines. Just as many second wave feminists identified politically as lesbians, regardless of the nature of their sexual feelings, Sam often politically identifies as a woman despite hir relationship to hir own gender and body. Amanda has been solidly situated in the field of women's studies since her college days in the early 1990s and identifies as a feminist lesbian. She was the first women's studies major at Bucknell University and the first feminist studies PhD candidate at the University of Minnesota. Although Sam shares Amanda's love of and commitment to women's studies, ze has remained on the fringes of academic feminism since hir early college days, having an ambivalent relationship to women's studies as an academic field, in part due to hir ambivalent relationship to the category of "woman." Whereas Sam identifies as transgendered in hir personal life, Amanda's dissertation project took up transgender queries intellectually. Her research, at times, works to undermine the categories underlying women's studies; therefore, Amanda has concerns that in the view of some second wave feminists her political commitments might be overshadowed by the subject matter of her research. Sam has more worries about how to personally position hirself on the job market, including what ze would wear to a job interview as a transgendered person applying for a women's studies position.

As the two of us learned in working to create the University of Minnesota's feminist studies PhD program, we can create feminist spaces and institutions, but we cannot control what others decide to do with what we have helped to shape. Our vantage points were as a PhD major (Amanda) and a PhD minor (Sam) during this transition. While our goal has been to make traditional disciplines be more like women's studies, rather than the opposite, such objectives at times have put us in tentative relationships with those who are interested in "professionalizing" the field. Our hopes for the future of women's studies are strongly rooted in activism and indebted to the activist movements from which it emerged.

Amanda's Feminist Politicization

I can trace the origins of my commitment to feminism to my mom's *Ms.* magazines and her "ERA YES!" button and, as a teenager, my own involvement in pro-choice politics. But my identification as a feminist activist and academic began in earnest in my first women's studies classes as an undergraduate. During my first semester at Bucknell University, I remember being asked to define feminism as a class assignment, an exercise that brought me to the realization that, indeed, I was a feminist myself.

To me, activism was an integral part of feminism; I took the edict "the personal is political" very seriously and applied this idea to my life and choices. Perhaps in part because of the conservatism of Bucknell's political culture and student body, I became involved in campus activism working to change the injustices I was learning about. Within my first few years at Bucknell, I had organized a bus trip to Washington, DC, to a national pro-choice rally, planned numerous campuswide demonstrations against homophobia and sexual violence, become vegan, and been arrested protesting a hazardous waste incinerator.

While initially interested in liberal feminist politics, I soon became disillusioned with the possibilities for social change that could take place within such a framework. I was most influenced by radical thinkers like Audre Lorde and Adrienne Rich,[2] and I would spend weekends at the library reading black feminist theory[3] and personal manifestos of radical feminists and lesbian separatists.[4] These works and my activist experiences solidified my sense of connection between my daily life and my political convictions.

Unfortunately, this was the early 1990s, and my largely conservative peers, though occasionally involved in activist events I helped to plan, were not making the personal identification with feminism that I was. In fact, many of the students at Bucknell were openly hostile, such as one who carved a swastika on the door of the Lesbian, Gay, Bisexual Programs office where I worked, which increased my sense of alienation and purpose as a social justice activist. Consequently, my primary influences and collaborators were not my peers but the books I read, most of which constituted "second wave" feminism, the few other radical activists on campus, and the faculty members who mentored me, many of whom were second wave feminists themselves.

I read about the third wave of feminism as well, of course, and was able to meet feminist icons such as Rebecca Walker and Naomi Wolf when they spoke on my campus. But I felt disappointed by their liberal politics and what I perceived as lack of commitment to the radical activism I was finding so empowering. Thus, I created my own path as inspired by and deeply connected to second wave feminism but generationally located in, while disconnected from, the third wave. Thanks to the work of my feminist foremothers in the academy, I was the beneficiary of extensive institutional support for my radical intellectual work while at Bucknell, but these resources were not concurrent with a sense of feminist community. Without a department or even a program to guide me, but following the advice of my feminist mentors, like Marilyn Mumford and Glynis Carr, in 1995 I became the first student to graduate from Bucknell with a major solely in women's studies.

In fall 1995, I enrolled in the anthropology PhD program at the University of Minnesota, drawn to Minneapolis by the established feminist communities of the Center for Advanced Feminist Studies (CAFS) and Department of Women's Studies. Through CAFS I was able to pursue a minor in feminist studies, while the MacArthur Program funded much of my graduate studies and allowed me to simultaneously become part of an international community dedicated to social and environmental justice.[5] Although based in the Department of Anthropology and thus still not located among feminist peers, I found a community of MacArthur graduate students dedicated to social justice as well as feminist mentors among the University of Minnesota's faculty. I began speaking to the faculty about the possibility of initiating a PhD program in women's studies at the University of Minnesota. When I started my graduate studies, there were only three PhD programs of this sort in the United States, and my hope was that if such a program could be developed at the University of Minnesota, I could be part of its first cohort.

Sam's Feminist Politicization

In 1985, I came to feminism, as many did, in an Introduction to Women's Studies class. Many students are drawn to women's studies courses as spaces to learn more about themselves; however, I did not readily identify with the subject of women's studies. Although my motivation to take the course came from my excitement and trepidation at having recently become involved in my first sexual relationship with a woman, unfortunately my initial response to registering for a whole class about women was boredom. I felt I had nothing in common with women, and I could not relate to them at all. In fact, I was quite resentful that I had to be a woman at all. I had grown up feeling that I was a boy, with plans of being a baseball player, until the onset of puberty brought those dreams crashing down. Growing into a woman's body meant learning how to make do with what I had, beginning a silent lifelong struggle of negotiation, compromise, and accommodation.

Feminism helped me learn how to do more than make do. Mid-1980s feminism at the University of California at Santa Cruz taught me to value women, women's experiences, and women's bodies. Although in high school I did not believe that women were oppressed and used to have heated arguments with my best friend over her support for the ERA, in college I proudly identified as feminist and even tentatively began politically identifying, at times, as a woman. I learned that my relationship to my own body was not merely individual but political as well, and learning to accept my body as it was, without bowing to social or internal pressures to change it, was a radical political act. This early training continues to influence my choices around how to express my transgendered identity.

We form our understandings of ourselves through the language and categories that are available in that space and time. Although clearly sex reassignment surgeries existed in 1985, I had no knowledge of them, much less of any options beyond the gender binary. What I did find in college were theories of homosexuality as a "third gender," so I tentatively began to call myself "gay" (I thought lesbian was too gendered) and became increasingly involved in gay activism. Had I grown up in a different time or had access to different information—for instance, if I were currently coming out "queer"—my attention might likely have been otherwise directed, prompting perhaps radically different choices about my body, my politics, and my life path.

Perhaps because of my contentious relationship to gender, for me feminism was never entirely, nor even primarily, about gender. Instead, after reading authors like Audre Lorde, Alice Walker, and Adrienne Rich, I thought feminism was about radical social change, about power and oppression, and about justice.[6] It was about listening to and learning from those who had different experiences than mine and finding a place for my own feelings of difference. Finding feminism was part of my overall politicization, and this feminism was fundamentally activist oriented. Being a feminist for me was strongly associated with lesbianism, due to my own personal trajectory, but also with my being a vegetarian, antiracist, antiwar, and antidieting. Feminism linked me to other struggles for social justice. As an environmental studies major, I campaigned door to door for clean water with CalPIRG; when a friend developed environmental illness, I educated other students about disability rights. And living in Santa Cruz, known for its large homeless population, I worked closely with a soup kitchen.

Although Amanda drew her energy from books, I found my inspiration in what was happening around me and the political culture of my particular location. Thus, my understandings of feminism were not only specific to my generation, sexual orientation, class and educational background, race and nationality but were also regionally and institutionally specific. In the mid-1980s, students at UC Santa Cruz were dancing to "Free Nelson Mandela" and sleeping out at the library to pressure the UC regents to divest from apartheid South Africa. In the nearby San Francisco Bay Area, AIDS was wiping out an entire generation of gay men. I worked with ACT UP, interned at the Santa Cruz AIDS Project, and organized a visit by the Names Project AIDS Quilt to Santa Cruz. I understood, and continue to view, all of these issues as feminist political issues.

When I decided to pursue a graduate degree in the mid-1990s, inspired by reading Susan Faludi's *Backlash,* I only considered schools with strong women's studies programs.[7] Although I had wanted to obtain a women's studies PhD, there were not many options at that time, and ultimately I was accepted instead at the University of Minnesota in anthropology, an institutional affiliation I chose because of the presence of the Center for Advanced Feminist Studies.

However, within just a few years, women's studies faculty began to talk about the possibility of creating a PhD major at the University of Minnesota. Amanda and I, having been active in CAFS, volunteered to serve on the committee responsible for drafting the PhD. CAFS had provided a wonderful sense of community for us and support for our work; I imagined a new doctoral program would facilitate more of the same and even better. In addition, we hoped that we might be able to transfer into this new program ourselves.

Conundrums of a Feminist Studies Doctoral Program

Although we began from drastically different places, with Amanda's appreciation of her mom's pro-ERA button and Sam arguing against the ERA in high school, we ended up in similar locations. We both cultivated a commitment to a feminism strongly rooted in similar kinds of activism, in part through reading the same feminist intellectuals, such as Audre Lorde and Adrienne Rich. We both were deeply connected to second wave feminist politics and felt indebted to feminist scholars and activists who had created the spaces and opportunities we were now able to utilize. We regarded these feminist foremothers as role models to emulate and respect, not as "dinosaurs" to rebel against. While Amanda came to her position through books and individual feminist mentorship within the conservatism of Bucknell University, Sam was galvanized by hir environment and the radical politics ze was surrounded by at UC Santa Cruz.

As a result, Amanda came to the University of Minnesota optimistic and hungry for feminist community, possessing the tools to create it if need be, as she had had to do at Bucknell. Sam arrived at the University of Minnesota ready to be more engaged with feminism intellectually. Ze expected to find feminist community, engaged political activism, radical pedagogy, and like-minded people because ze had never experienced anything different. Sam had never needed to position hirself as a feminist because ze had been surrounded by those who understood feminism in similar ways. While in the early 1990s, Amanda was publicly challenging prominent third wave feminists on campus, Sam was between college and graduate school, working as a freelance writer for feminist and gay and lesbian publications in Santa Cruz. Ze was discovering womyn's music festivals and the separatist politics of radical feminist writers like Sonia Johnson, largely unaware of the challenges that third wave feminists were posing.[8]

Despite our different journeys, in 1997 we found ourselves in the same location, both pursuing doctorates in the Department of Anthropology at the University of Minnesota, both pursuing feminist studies minors through CAFS, both receiving much of our academic and personal support through the MacArthur Program, and both part of a small committee working to institute a PhD program in feminist studies at our university. The hard work of this committee was done by faculty members Helen Longino, Jennifer Pierce, and Edward Schiapa. Over the course of one year, the committee surveyed existing doctoral programs, planned the curriculum, wrote numerous proposals, and garnered faculty and institutional support.

One of our roles as the graduate students on the committee was to ascertain student interest in the proposed doctoral program and to inform students about the work of the committee. We held meetings for those who wanted to learn more about potentially enrolling in a PhD program in women's studies, and we surveyed the CAFS minors and women's studies undergraduates to learn their perspectives. Overall, we received positive responses, and almost all students supported the creation of such a program.

Soon afterward, the faculty successfully presented the committee's case to the administration. The dedication of the faculty made a lot of hard work happen quickly, and by fall 1998 a new PhD program in feminist studies was part of the curriculum at the University of Minnesota. The committee made a conscious decision to name the degree "feminist studies" to reflect a political commitment to feminist politics and to represent the diversity of scholarship within the discipline of women's studies. We cannot speak for the committee, but the two of us thought that naming the PhD program "women's studies" might not centralize scholarship outside of traditional studies of "women." On the other hand, "gender studies" seemed too generic and apolitical, and we feared it would facilitate the misinterpretation that the field of women's studies was too focused on women and needed to more fully include men, which was not our view.[9] In our opinion, "feminist studies" offered an alternative to these choices. It allowed for studies of women and of social justice beyond "women" and "men," and it reflected our commitment to feminist politics that placed social justice and activism at its core.

The Transition: Amanda's Experience as a Major

For me, the institution of this new program meant completing a master's degree in anthropology and applying to be part of the first cohort of feminist studies doctoral students. I was thrilled to be returning to women's studies as a major, and I hoped that the new doctoral program would finally allow me to have feminist peers with convictions about academic and activist feminisms and their transformative possibilities that were similar to my own.

However, the advent of the doctoral program brought with it tensions that I did not anticipate. As other PhD programs in women's and gender studies were beginning to emerge on campuses around the country at this time, our new program was seen as representative of new directions in women's studies and academia more broadly.[10] This placed us at the center of debates about the future of the field itself, furthering tensions between women's studies' activist origins and its institutionalization as well as raising concerns about the disciplinary training of those shaping women's studies' professional future. Far from being the panacea I imagined, the new PhD program raised issues of resource access and foregrounded concerns about exclusion and inclusion (in the department and in women's studies as a field), which Sam discusses below. Beginning in 1998, the program both displaced CAFS minors and challenged students and faculty to articulate new directions for feminist studies.

I consequently found myself in the midst of difficult debates about the needs and perspectives of feminist studies majors and minors to which there were often no easy solutions. Some PhD students perceived this conflict as one of limited financial resources and saw majors in direct competition for these resources with CAFS minors. But prior to the introduction of the doctoral program, CAFS graduate students had not only benefited from but had also shaped women's studies at the University of Minnesota, where their labor was necessary and valued, as Sam details below. For many of the students and faculty members, a disagreement over office space, from which minors were eventually barred, had troubling undertones. The committee, especially Sam and I, had envisioned the new feminist studies program as a place for collaboration; barring minors from the office space seemed to delineate new boundaries around feminism rather than establishing feminist communities. I did not expect that the initiation of the feminist studies PhD program would virtually eliminate the multidisciplinary feminist community we cherished in CAFS and leave many feeling alienated and despairing about the future of women's studies. However, I was simultaneously conscious of the need for feminist studies doctoral students, including myself, to have the training and support necessary for the completion of graduate degrees in this new field. Students based in the Department of Women's Studies needed to be able to count on the department for financial support, and such a shift necessitated adjustments to hiring policies and job availability.

Before 1998, I envisioned the PhD program as an arena through which students would experience feminist studies at its most transformative. To me, this new program was an opportunity to disrupt the hierarchies and expectations of academia and, instead of mirroring the difficulties many students find in traditional departments, to envision feminist pedagogies, theories, and actions, and to put them into practice. After the inception of the degree, many conversations within the department centered on "professionalization" and how to best prepare graduate students receiving doctorates in feminist studies to enter the job market. Feminist studies programs have a responsibility for this eventuality, but I believe that they have a concurrent responsibility to feminist principles of social and economic justice. For me, discussions about professionalization need to be couched in terms of class politics and communal responsibilities. Elucidating the implications of professionalization and writing about recent developments in ethnic, black, and women's studies programs, Chandra Talpade Mohanty points out: "[The] individualization of power hierarchies and structures of discrimination suggests the convergence of liberal and neoconservative ideas about gender and race in the academy. Individualization, in this context, is accomplished through the fundamentally class-based process of professionalization."[11]

Attention to class and community has been critical to the development of the field and needs to be at the forefront of considerations of how it should continue to develop. Pursuing a different but similar tack, Jean Robinson claims that the professionalization of women's studies has contributed to the erosion of the "themes of participation and community that were the foundations of early Women's Studies."[12] The institutionalization of graduate feminist studies need not reduce the strength of feminist activism and commitments, but it does require careful attention to social justice–based ideals within feminist communities and a vision not only of how feminists fit into the academy but how we can continue to transform it.

Thus, for me, placing myself in these debates included consideration of the histories of women's studies as a multi- and interdisciplinary field that challenges academic assumptions and boundaries. I recognize that those faculty who first imagined women's studies over thirty years ago, while receiving their doctorates in traditional disciplines, have shaped the field and will continue to do so, as will feminist scholars all over the academy. I also celebrate, and indeed have benefited from, the opportunity to obtain my doctorate in feminist studies. I feel well-trained and prepared to teach and conduct research that is interdisciplinary and takes women's studies seriously as a discipline, not as an addendum to scholarship done in a traditional department. I hope that the advent of increased numbers of doctoral programs in feminist studies will open up conversations about new possibilities for global social change and intersectional analyses within and outside of the field.

The Transition: Sam's Experience as a Minor

Although I had thrived in my anthropology major at UC Santa Cruz, the anthropology department at the University of Minnesota was not a nurturing environment for me. While the department was not explicitly antifeminist, during my second year, the one professor who taught feminist anthropology was denied tenure, making her at least the second feminist scholar in less than five years to be fired from the department. Her departure left only a handful of faculty who broadly dealt with gender in their work, and none who worked from an explicitly feminist political perspective.[13] As an Africanist, my choices were similarly bleak. There was only one professor, on the verge of retirement, who had studied in Africa, but his last trip to the continent had taken place in the 1960s. Thank goodness for Amanda!

Amanda arrived in the department during my second year. We were drawn together by our common interests as lesbians, feminists, Africanists, and activists. It was wonderful to again have a peer, and we unofficially advised one another, did directed readings together on LGBT anthropology, and honed our collaboration skills. As we both became increasingly involved with CAFS and MacArthur, we became less and less engaged with our home department. As we each had been trained in interdisciplinary programs as undergraduates, we conceived of ourselves as feminist ethnographers more than anthropologists, and we found, through MacArthur and CAFS, the mentorship, funding opportunities, and vibrant intellectual and political community to compensate for the lack of support we felt in anthropology.

Because I regarded CAFS and MacArthur as my intellectual training grounds, when faced with the decision about whether to transfer from anthropology to the feminist studies PhD program, I minimized the relevance of my home department. I assumed that I would be doing the same work, with the same people, and with the same kind of support regardless of where I was located institutionally. Thus, I was willing to remain in anthropology, while Amanda transferred to the new PhD program, in part due to considerations about the job market. I never imagined that the disciplinary border crossing that I had been doing would become problematic, because feminists straddle disciplinary boundaries all of the time. I never viewed feminist studies as a bounded discipline itself, nor could I have at that time imagined that there would be feminists demanding such boundaries.

In retrospect, I should have realized that boundaries were what we were creating. That was ultimately what all those proposals to the administration were about—not my naive vision of expanding the feminist base and possibilities at the University of Minnesota but instead about asking for official permission to regulate the training and creation of something called a feminist doctoral scholar, with university rules about what that means that were not even within the control of the women's studies department. However, I could never have anticipated that the push for such regulation would come from the first cohort of feminist studies PhD students themselves.

The introduction of the feminist studies PhD had dramatic effects not only on my personal and academic life, but on feminist institutions and communities at the University of Minnesota. With the institutionalization of the new major, CAFS turned over control of the minor program to the women's studies department. The university administration took this as an opportunity to question the continued necessity of CAFS and began to gradually withdraw its funding. Currently, after its more than twenty years as a vibrant feminist community, CAFS's future is uncertain, and it has narrowly escaped closing on several occasions. At any rate, the kind of feminist community I had experienced pre-1998 disappeared with the arrival of the graduate major.

This, in and of itself, would have been devastating for me, even if the feminist studies PhD had brought a nurturing intellectual and political community to replace CAFS. However, it became immediately clear that the incoming cohort of doctoral scholars had very different notions of feminism than I did. First of all, although Amanda and I shared a definition of feminism as fundamentally rooted in activism, within the community of new students we were definitely in the minority. I first encountered this in a required feminist history class. I was surprised to find that although I was excited about the course and felt lucky to have curriculum in which I was so personally interested, after suffering through anthropology core theory courses, other students regarded the class not as a gift but as a burden. I watched with irony as the third wave queer undergraduates dismissed second wave feminism, seemingly oblivious to the fact that such a history is what enables their own queer choices. But it was more difficult to witness the outrage of several of the new feminist studies PhD students who demanded to know why they were required to take a course on the history of an activist movement that had nothing to do, in their minds, with their intellectual agendas at the university.

Instead, it became increasingly clear to me that the main agenda of most of the new cohort was what they called the professionalization of women's studies. Establishing such legitimacy involved, among other things, making the field more responsive to continental theory and more detached from its activist political history. In other words, women's studies could become more respectable if it became more like other disciplines. My naive hope was that the creation of the feminist studies PhD would work toward fundamentally altering the way knowledge is produced and disseminated in the university system. I wanted other disciplines to become more like women's studies, an agenda that seemed at odds with the desires of this cohort of new students.

Part of the professionalization of women's studies was also carving out a unique territory for feminist studies PhD students to claim. Again, my vision that the new PhD program would expand the terrain of feminist studies at the University of Minnesota was fundamentally in opposition to the expressed needs of the new feminist doctoral students. What resulted were disturbing "turf wars" that played out between CAFS minors and the PhD majors around specific resources. The first battle, of course, was over jobs; prior to the establishment of the PhD program, the relationship of the women's studies department to the CAFS minors was symbiotic. Graduate students received assistantships to supplement those they could obtain elsewhere as well as valuable teaching experience. The department had a steady pool of labor to support their curriculum and drew on graduate student expertise, often at the last minute, to offer a rich variety of courses, supplement the interests of departmental faculty, fill in for those who were on sabbatical or otherwise unavailable, and assist faculty with overenrolled courses as teaching assistants.

Speaking personally, I rarely taught in the women's studies department simply because I needed a job. Once I moved away from anthropology, I had steady employment teaching composition and often took on women's studies courses in addition because the department needed help and because I enjoyed them. I taught in women's studies because I was committed to the department, because I felt a sense of loyalty and a desire to build such a feminist institution. It was what prompted me to volunteer for the PhD committee in the first place.

However, with the arrival of the new PhD students, departmental resources and opportunities went to them, abruptly severing the symbiotic relationship between the department and the CAFS minors. This move seemed entirely understandable, given the constraints of how departmental resources are allocated university-wide. However, given the dramatic change in policy, it might have been handled delicately. This, of course, was not the case, and the new majors, rather than forging alliances with those who had been displaced by their arrival, chose to make further territorial and hierarchical claims, insisting, for instance, that they have their own office space rather than one shared by other feminist graduate student instructors. From the vantage point of a minor, such as myself, this move felt a bit presumptuous, not only disregarding the particular feminist history of the University of Minnesota but similar histories within women's studies departments generally.

The new cohort's prioritizing of their own personal and professional advancement left me feeling rather alienated, as it was entirely at odds with my larger ambitions for academic feminism. Just as I did not teach in women's studies as a graduate student just for a job, my career objectives are not merely about academic self-promotion. Rather, my role models are my mentors, Carolyn Martin Shaw at UC Santa Cruz and the late Susan Geiger from the University of Minnesota, feminist scholars who published their first books late in their careers due to their commitments to feminist institution building, student mentoring, and political activism. Scholars such as Carolyn and Susan, as well as Charlie Sugnet, also at the University of Minnesota, often sacrificed their own professional success to create social change and to mentor the next generation, and these priorities seemed to differ markedly from the focused ambitions of the current generation of feminist graduate students as well as of many younger faculty.

Thus, my experience of the transition to the feminist studies PhD program was primarily negative. Working on the PhD committee, I had felt a sense of hope and excitement, a sense of belonging, even feeling almost central in the department in some ways as part of its history making. My commitment to women's studies seemed clear and my contributions valued. However, with the advent of the PhD program, I became relegated to "just a minor," back on the fringes, my contributions and commitment to the department dismissed and forgotten. While academic feminism at the university had previously facilitated my intellectually blurring of boundaries in ways similar to how I feel personally with regard to gender, my experience of the new PhD program was that the gates dropped, the security systems were initiated, intruders were turned away, and the kind of fluidity I was seeking became increasingly impossible.

One of the arguments the feminist studies doctoral cohort made to lay claim to a special relationship to feminism was that they were the only ones solely located there. As those who were really serious about women's studies, who were willing to risk their careers, they should be the ones to set the agenda for the future of the field. And so they, in my view, turned their energies inward, became exclusive, created boundaries around who are "real" feminists, and patrolled that territory, marking insiders and outsiders, defining themselves against those they opposed, and thus replicated the very dynamics that they were quick to criticize as second wave.

And their arguments felt so familiar. Many second wave lesbians have been criticized for their intolerance of bisexual women, in particular what they regarded as bisexual "fence-sitting." I, too, had doubted the seriousness of bisexual women, interpreting their fluidity as lack of commitment or indecision. How could I truly trust them, I thought, if they could merely float in and out of queer spaces and seemingly easily return to spaces of privilege when threatened? I did not understand bisexuals to be undertaking the same kind of risk that I thought that I was as a lesbian. However, what I have come to understand is that those of us who truly straddle social categories and political locations (like bisexuals, transgendered people, and feminist scholars located in traditional disciplines), who do not fit neatly into any of the choices that are presented, experience not a lack of risk but instead multiple risks to accompany our multiple positions. And such multiple positions do not represent a lack of commitment but instead lack of exclusive commitment, which is something altogether different.

Although I may experience moments of male privilege when I am assumed to be a man in my daily life, it is always undermined by the risk of being "found out" and the potential hostility, even violence, that could ensue. Although I may have been located for the majority of my academic career thus far in a traditional discipline, seemingly able to move in and out of feminist spaces at my discretion, the very fact that I was multiply located disqualified me from many of the privileges or protections a traditional discipline might have been able to offer. For instance, although I was never overtly accused of being "disloyal" to anthropology, I was explicitly told by the Director of Graduate Studies of the anthropology department that I should not expect any funding from anthropology because he believed that MacArthur students were "overfunded." Further, once the feminist studies doctoral program was initiated and created a hierarchy disadvantaging those who were not majors, my location became less one of feeling multiply situated—or in both—and more the experience of being without a location—or in neither. As Naomi Scheman writes about being normatively gendered, there is security, and thus a different kind of privilege, in being singly situated, even if it is a position that is marginalized, such as being in feminist studies, being a woman, or being a lesbian.[14]

I had taken for granted that doing feminist work, I would not feel constrained by disciplinary boundaries. But I learned firsthand what is at stake in debates over understandings of feminism. In a very different context, Madhu Kishwar analyzes how women organizing in India must position themselves as feminists by Northern definitions in order to have access to NGO resources, even holding to agendas that are not their own.[15] Clearly, access to resources was a flashpoint issue between the new feminist studies majors and CAFS minors, like myself, but so was agenda setting, professional survival, and, for me, personal survival as well. Being on the margins of feminist studies, I felt adrift and "homeless" for several years. However, in recent months, I have claimed my space within academic feminism, finally transferring officially into the feminist studies PhD program to finish out my graduate career. In five years, I have surely been sobered as well as humbled, and I am ready to learn from my experience. The challenge remains, however, of how to forge alliances with those whose feminist agendas are very different from my own, first rooting out any remnants of elitism in my own thinking and behavior.

Transgendered Conundrums

The problem of transsexualism would best be served by morally mandating it out of existence.[16]

We crossed a red clay county road separating our tents from the wood posts, wire fences, and candy-colored tents of the Michigan Womyn's Music Festival. There are six of us, gender outlaws all, queued up like so many tenpins before the smiling woman in the ticket booth. The Michigan Womyn's Music Festival is about to meet the Transexual Menace.[17]

Academic feminism has a long and rather unfortunate history of mishandling transgendered issues. In 1979, radical feminist scholar Janice Raymond wrote a scathing attack on transsexuals, whom she claimed were wolves in sheep's clothing (male-to-female) or antifeminist defectors (female-to-male).[18] Although scholars like Suzanne Kessler, Wendy McKenna, and Anne Fausto-Sterling pioneered sensitive studies of trans issues, Raymond became the archetype of feminist hostility to transsexuals, and other prominent feminists, such as Mary Daly, Sheila Jeffreys, and Claudia Card, have been sympathetic to her views.[19] These scholars have propagated hurtful and dismissive assumptions about transsexuals, failing to acknowledge trans agency and the complexity and multiplicities of trans experience and neglecting to similarly interrogate their own identities. Such feminists and others influenced by their ideas have portrayed transgendered individuals as irrelevant or even antithetical to feminist politics and as entirely different creatures, ignoring other ways feminists may refashion our bodies (through cosmetic surgery, dieting, piercing, tattoos, etc.) and missing the continuum and parallels between transgenderism and 1970s feminist androgyny. Such feminists have accused transsexuals of uncritically adopting conservative medical paradigms of gender and have focused on transgenderism as gender play instead of a substantive and carefully chosen life path. Although, as feminist scholar Cressida Heyes writes, "many transgendered people are daily the victims of the most intense and public attempts to discipline gender in ways feminists have long criticized," trans people have been seen by many as threatening to feminism.[20]

Similarly, and no doubt largely in response, many transgendered activists have viewed feminism as threatening to trans people and have targeted feminists as arch enemies. In the past decade, some of the most heated feminist "border wars" have taken place at the Michigan Womyn's Music Festival, where transgendered activists have repeatedly held protests over the festival's "womyn-born-womyn only" policy, even physically storming onto the land to disrupt the womyn-only space. After decades of having to be authenticated by the medical establishment, transgendered folks are understandably tired of being told by others whether we are appropriate, woman enough, man enough, acceptable. However, the combative style in which trans activists have taken on lesbian feminists, such as in the quotation above in which Transexual Menace activists approached the Michigan Womyn's Music Festival like they were going to war, undermines the potential for solidarity. These tactics have shown some activists to be indifferent to the personal and political importance of women-only space, as well as demonstrating ignorance of the range of gender diversity that has long existed in such spaces. Many of those who attend the festival annually have been gender outlaws for decades.

It disheartens us that feminist communities that have been so formative and important to our own survival have been so dispassionate and shortsighted when it comes to transgender issues. And it disheartens us that trans communities that we belong to or are allied with have been so disrespectful and shortsighted in labeling feminism and feminist spaces as special enemies of trans people. Trying to position ourselves over the past decade as transgendered/trans-allied lesbian feminists, straddling communities that are intensely threatened by one another, has been fraught with difficulty.

Sam's Engagements with Transgenderisms

In February 1995, during my first year of graduate school, I went to the most life-changing lecture I have ever attended. Transgendered social justice activist Leslie Feinberg was visiting the Twin Cities in the first of many subsequent appearances. During a talk that was later memorialized in a photo in Leslie's book *Transgender Warriors*, Leslie laid out a global history of transgendered people and shared hir own transgendered life experiences.[21] I wrote the following in my journal after hir visit:

Listening to the talk, I kept getting chills as I remembered experiences I hadn't thought about in a long time, feelings I'd long since filed away as unresolve-able. The heat of self consciousness was rising in my face, as I felt like I was in a spotlight, convinced that everyone in the audience could see that Leslie was speaking directly to me. I'm still wrestling with exactly where I place myself on this continuum between man and woman, what kind of identity feels important to me. I don't know that I understand enough about transgendered experi-ence to label myself as such, but I definitely identify with being "differently gendered." I want to make peace with this female body that I live in, but I am glad to be an "other" and don't see a need to obscure that. I don't think I neces-sarily want to be a "man," but I don't think I'll ever really identify as a "woman" either. (spring 1995)

It was so empowering to finally have language to characterize my experi-ence, and to learn of others similarly situated. It was as revolutionary to me as when I first became a feminist and discovered that so many of the struggles I faced and thought were personal idiosyncrasies were actually societal gender oppression.

For the third time, I felt like I had found a home. Coming out as a lesbian feminist in college gave me not only a way to understand the world and to place myself in it but also a community, a culture, and a politics. Making a place for myself in academic feminism as a graduate student expanded and refined my politics and understandings of the world, a space that felt like home until the creation of the PhD major changed the terrain. Discovering the language of transgenderism felt like another home, one that expressed so many of the ambiguities I had felt throughout my history as a feminist. However, again, it has proven to be not such an ideal fit.

Transgendered communities have increasingly been replicating within our own spheres the very same dynamics that are protested every year at the Michigan festival. When Feinberg spoke at the University of Minnesota in 1995, transgenderism was understood to be an umbrella category representing the experiences of a wide range of people who fell out of traditional gender expectations for very different reasons, includ-ing transsexuals, butch lesbians, effeminate gay men, drag kings and queens, transvestites and cross-dressers, as well as those for whom there was not a ready category of identification.[22] Transgenderism in 1995 en-compassed individuals who were interested in moving from one side of the gender binary to the other, calling the naturalness of that binary into question, as well as those, like myself, who felt more or less stable in their understandings of themselves as between, both and/or neither.

In the decade that has intervened, transgenderism has come to be more narrowly associated with transsexuals. Specifically, hierarchies have arisen within transgendered communities, privileging those who have altered their bodies through surgery and/or hormones and carving separatist-type spaces for various transgendered identifications. For instance, national transgender conferences generally prioritize issues surrounding physical transitions and provide spaces limited to certain people. According to the Web site of the FTM 2004 Gender Odyssey conference, "only folks who find themselves personally aligned with the identity, issue, or circumstance listed . . . [should] access this space."[23] Even in 1994, trans author-activist Kate Bornstein described an "unspoken hierarchy" of gender outlaws, expressing sadness about the paucity of groups that "encompass the full rainbow that is gender outlawism."[24] And these divisions are represented in the infrastructure of many transgendered communities, such as those in the Twin Cities—one of the largest and most protected clusters of transgendered folks in the country.

For instance, there is a group that I belong to for trans men, those born female who are or are interested in living as men.[25] Those in the group generally take on male names and pronouns, are interested in "passing," often adopt conventional ideas about masculinity, and have completed, are in the process of, or, usually at the very least, are planning to undergo hormonal treatment and/or surgery. It is entirely understandable that those who have transitioned or are preparing to transition would want a separate space to talk about issues relevant to that experience and to gain support and information. However, those who are not interested in wholeheartedly embracing maleness are relegated to the group called "All Genders," which includes most anyone touched by transgenderism, including the partners of transgendered folks, and it is clear in hearing people talk about the groups that the trans men are considered the "real" transgendered people. At trans community events, such as a local monthly cabaret, the trans men can frequently be found outside in the parking lot, building the sets, while their generally traditionally feminine girlfriends can be found in the kitchen, organizing the food. I wholeheartedly support every person's right to choose their own gender and sexual expressions and have no judgment about those who make different choices than mine.[26] However, until we live in a world where "man" and "woman" are equal choices (and there are other viable options), such decisions, in my mind, are not just matters of individual self-expression but have implications that demand, for me, that they be weighed carefully and seriously. Sadly, I have not found much of a "third" space within a community whose very premise is as a "third" option.[27]

Ironically, such dynamics are remarkably similar to the ones I experienced in the context of the creation of the feminist studies PhD. There I found a parallel elimination of a "third," more fluid space and, in its place, similar types of hierarchies and spoken and unspoken boundary delineation. And just as I was rendered inferior in my relation to feminist studies as "just a minor," I also feel inferior as a transgendered person for my decision to forgo, at this juncture, altering my body (ironically due in large part to the great influence my feminist training had on me). Whereas I knew early on that I was not a "real" woman, I find myself now wondering whether I am a "real" transgendered person. Unless I decide to change my body, it is likely that I will not be perceived by some as authentically transgendered.

Straddling these identifications has become more stressful and disheartening as lesbian feminists and transgendered communities have become increasingly combative, making my position in both strained and at times unrecognizable or seemingly untrustworthy. For example, I drive past Camp Trans every year as I go to the Michigan Womyn's Music Festival, where Transexual Menace activists, after crashing the gates, come up to me to teach me about what transgenderism is and to tell me that there are no trans people welcome on the land. Just as I seem to be invisible to other trans activists at times, I also fear, as I prepare to go on the job market, that, in a masculine suit with a masculine name, I will be misunderstood by other feminists, my potential employers.

Although challenging, my strategy in occupying this complex subjectivity has been to honor all parts of myself as well as the formative influences that have led me to claim various identities. I strive to make peace with the disharmony within me at the same time I strive to make peace with the disharmony that surrounds me, abstaining, to the best of my ability, from amplifying the negativity—no matter how juicy and compelling—and resisting the pressure to definitively choose a camp—a gender, a discipline, a generation. Although this sounds familiarly like a third wave refusal to embrace labels and categories, that is not the spirit in which I undertake such a choice. I have politically identified as a "woman." I have claimed lesbian and feminist and transgender identities. But I see no need to, and must constantly resist the urge to, reconcile these divergent subject positions, to make coherent their ambiguities and inconsistencies. Instead, I choose to embrace the ambiguities, to see strength in my ability to blur boundaries and straddle categories. This is not a place of lack of commitment or clarity or passion but represents my commitment to a larger vision for which I do not even have language—yet.

Amanda's Engagements with Transgenderisms

Like Sam, I came to understand the category of "transgender" through personal reflections on my own gender identifications and intellectual work on gender, sex, and sexuality. Through my academic scholarship, especially my dissertation project, and my activist involvement I entered numerous conversations and debates, collaborations and struggles. Initially, I found this engagement exciting and inspiring, but over time I became wary of tensions between feminists and trans people, often positioned oppositionally.

My first experiences with issues self-defined as "transgendered" came through activism. In the mid-1990s there was a vibrant trans community in Minneapolis in the process of defining itself, and, initially, I saw myself as part of this community. I was excited about the possibilities for envisioning gender outside of the traditional boundaries of "men" and "women," which, as a lesbian, did not fit me at all. However, I was also discouraged by the hierarchies I felt were developing in trans communities. Like Sam, in my experience those who passed most effectively and surgically or hormonally modified their bodies were seen as most "authentically" transgendered, and those defining themselves between gendered/sexed categories were often dismissed in ways I found alienating. But I was still optimistic about the empowering and revolutionary potential of trans identifications for me personally and for the way I understood the world.

I worked through my concerns and questions about transgendered issues in much the same way I came to feminism and lesbianism—through books. I read as much as I could: trans autobiographies, activist writings, and theory. I also thought about how a newly emerging "transgender studies" intersected with feminism. The sex/gender categories on which feminism and women's studies rested were being undermined in some ways, but transgender studies also offered new ways of thinking about feminisms beyond "women's oppression." They pointed to different ways of understanding gendered/sexed categories and to the importance of intersectional analyses of gender, sex, and sexuality. But, at the same time, trans people's lives and experiences were also being used as fodder for advancing feminist theory. An academic focus on the theoretical implications of "transgenderism" was generally accompanied by inattention to the daily struggles and agency of trans people.

Self-identified feminist and transgender activist-scholars have rarely engaged in constructive collaborations. Since the 1970s, many second wave feminists have felt upset by trans issues, and their defensiveness in protecting gendered categories was often vehement. Feminist initiatives have largely advanced redefinitions and revaluations of existing gender/sex categories. On the other hand, many trans communities seemed to operate without attention to structural inequities outside of gender/sex on which intersectional feminist analyses were built. While trans scholarship and activism have often looked to eliminate sex/gender categories altogether, "gender play" often accompanies disregard for lived experiences of sexism, racism, and classism. Inattention to feminist histories that resulted in social change around gender/sex also worked against the collaboration of feminist and transgender studies.

In the midst of these conflicts, I was beginning a dissertation project that fell in the middle of these fields and communities. Based on my preliminary research into a rich history of South African communities of gender variance and the promises of the transition from apartheid to democracy, I decided to talk to South Africans about their lives at the borders of gender/sex in this context. Thus, my dissertation addressed communities of people in South Africa who did not easily fit categories of "man" or "woman." Though not self-identified as "transgendered," as the word has little significance in South Africa, these communities included marginalized people from all races and classes who faced difficulties including medical experimentation, forced surgeries, legalized discrimination, underemployment, family rejection, and high levels of violence. However, my research sought to highlight South Africans' articulate understandings of their experiences and genders and their strength in creating the lives they envisioned for themselves, rather than positioning them as "victims" of their circumstances. Working with these liminal communities allowed me to merge my activist and academic commitments, as well as to envision new bridges between feminist social justice and trans politics based on analyses of intersecting identifications.

Living in South Africa for one and one-half years with friends at the edges of sex and gender systems and making frequent return trips there did not facilitate my relationships with trans communities in the United States. In the late 1990s I was disheartened by the politics of trans communities; the vocal proponents of these communities, despite their radical views on gender/sex, seemed to me to be largely white and middle-class, focusing on U.S.-based issues that felt worlds away from the concerns of my South African friends. Further, I felt nervous about entering into conversations within trans academic and activist communities; too often, there seemed to be "right" answers that were difficult to discern, and little room for constructive conversations without attacks. In the midst of conversations about the problems of identity politics, in many contexts postoperative transsexuals' identifications positioned them as most representative of trans movements.

I felt ambivalent about these conversations and foci. Simultaneously, my work with transsexual, intersexed, gay, and lesbian South African communities also put me at the fringes of women's studies and feminist communities. Despite changes over the past twenty years, feminists still place analyses of women's lives, writings, and theories at the center of the movement and field. In spaces ranging from conferences to the job market, my work with trans and gender nonconforming people meant that I was sometimes met with suspicion and skepticism by some second wave feminists. I felt that my loyalty to feminist politics and to women's issues as the center of the field was also questioned and problematized. It seemed as if I did not fit easily anywhere.

However, it was my passion for my work and my relationships with trans and feminist friends that kept me engaging with these two conflicting camps. Like Sam, I came to terms with locating myself where these disparate communities and positions overlapped. I continue to reconcile feminist politics and transgender concerns in my own way, despite others' views. And in the past ten years feminist and transgender studies have changed a lot, too. Much of feminist theory now rests on considering the borders of sex, gender, and sexuality, especially in conversation with other social categories. There are a number of feminist academics who trans activist-scholars consistently cite and whose work they embrace. Trans communities in the United States have changed significantly, too, with race and class slowly coming to the forefront of

314 Sam Bullington and Amanda Lock Swarr

the issues recognized as most pressing. Trans activists and scholars are centralizing the issues, ranging from health care to legal discrimination, that affect trans people of color and poor people most acutely.[28] And of course there are many ways trans and feminist concerns overlap, especially in transgendered feminists/feminist trans people's lives and perspectives. So perhaps the possibilities for collaboration and reconciliation that highlight social justice, trans oppression and resistance, and fresh ways of understanding intersectionalities seem brighter now, too.

Toward Feminist Futures

Second wave feminists recognized the importance of creating safe spaces to foster new kinds of identities, to heal from histories of oppression, and to speak to specific kinds of experiences. They were, and still are, vigorously criticized for this practice—for being exclusionary, for patrolling the borders of categories of identification and thus discouraging individuality, and for supposedly disempowering themselves and others by focusing too much on their oppression. Two of the main groups who have been most vocal in their criticism of such second wave politics and practices have been third wave feminists and transgendered communities. However, through this examination of our own experiences at the University of Minnesota and in feminist and transgender communities generally, we argue here that these two groups are currently engaging in some of the very same politics and practices as those they criticize. This, of course, is perfectly understandable and acceptable. Throughout the history of social organizing, groups who have felt excluded in one context have readily gone off and formed their own spaces and movements. However, we argue that third wave feminist doctoral scholars at the University of Minnesota and some transgendered communities do so without self-reflection on the ironies of their position. As feminists who both participate in and feel excluded by such politics, we have offered lessons from our own experiences in straddling categories, debates, and generations.

Notes

1. Sam chooses to label hirself as neither woman nor man in this chapter by using terms such as "ze" instead of she or he, and "hir" instead of his or her.
2. Audre Lorde, *Sister/Outsider* (Freedom, Calif.: Crossing Press, 1984); Audre Lorde, *Zami: A New Spelling of My Name* (Freedom, Calif.: Crossing Press,

1982); Adrienne Rich, *Blood, Bread, and Poetry: Selected Prose, 1979–1985* (New York: Norton, 1986); and Adrienne Rich, "Claiming an Education" in *On Lies, Secrets, and Silence: Selected Prose, 1966–1978* (New York: Norton, 1979), 233.

3. bell hooks, *Ain't I a Woman: Black Women and Feminism* (Boston: South End Press, 1981); Gloria T. Hull, Patricia Bell Scott, and Barbara Smith, *All the Women Are White, All the Blacks Are Men, But Some of Us Are Brave: Black Women's Studies* (Old Westbury, N.Y.: Feminist Press, 1982); Barbara Smith, *Home Girls: A Black Feminist Anthology* (New York: Kitchen Table Women of Color Press, 1983).

4. Valerie Solanas, *S.C.U.M, Society for Cutting Up Men, Manifesto* (New York: Olympia Press, 1968); Leeds Revolutionary Feminists, *Love Your Enemy? The Debate between Heterosexual Feminism and Political Lesbianism* (London: Onlywomen Press, 1981); Sarah Lucia-Hoagland and Julia Penelope, eds. *For Lesbians Only: A Separatist Anthology* (London: Onlywomen Press, 1988).

5. At the University of Minnesota, I was a MacArthur Scholar with the Interdisciplinary Center for the Study of Global Change from 1995–2003, a program dedicated to the themes of justice that underlie my academic work. The MacArthur Program provides graduate students with scholarships and facilitates discussions and seminars among a select group of graduate students and faculty committed to political equity in the global south and in marginalized communities in North America and Europe.

6. See Lorde, *Sister/Outsider*; Alice Walker, *You Can't Keep a Good Woman Down: Stories* (New York: Harcourt Brace Jovanovich, 1981); and Rich, *On Lies, Secrets, and Silence*.

7. Susan Faludi, *Backlash: The Undeclared War against American Women* (New York: Crown, 1991).

8. Sonia Johnson, *Going Out of Our Minds: The Metaphysics of Liberation* (Freedom, Calif.: Crossing Press, 1987).

9. For a discussion of more recent considerations in naming such departments, programs, and degrees, see Robyn Wiegman, "The Progress of Gender: Wither 'Women'?" in *Women's Studies on Its Own* (Durham, N.C.: Duke University Press, 2002), 106–40.

10. Robin Wilson, "PhD Programs in Women's Studies Proliferate on the Campuses: But Some Scholars Worry That Choosing a 'Non-traditional' Field Will Limit Students' Prospects," *Chronicle of Higher Education*, November 27, 1998.

11. Chandra Talpade Mohanty, *Feminism without Borders: Decolonizing Theory, Practicing Solidarity* (Durham, N.C.: Duke University Press, 2003), 199.

12. Jean C. Robinson, "From Politics to Professionalism: Cultural Change in Women's Studies" in *Women's Studies on Its Own*, ed. Wiegman, 208.

13. In fact, one, my former advisor, was also denied tenure last year.

14. Naomi Scheman, "Queering the Center by Centering the Queer: Reflections on Transsexuals and Secular Jews," in *Feminists Rethink the Self*, ed. Diana Tietjens Meyers (New York: Westview Press, 1997).

15. Madhu Kishwar, "Why I Don't Call Myself a Feminist," *Manushi*, December 1990.

16. Janice G. Raymond, *The Transsexual Empire: The Making of the She-Male* (Boston: Beacon Press, 1979), 178.

17. Riki Anne Wilchins, *Read My Lips: Sexual Subversion and the End of Gender* (Ithaca, N.Y.: Firebrand Books, 1997), 109.

18. Raymond, *The Transsexual Empire*.

19. Suzanne Kessler and Wendy McKenna, *Gender: An Ethnomethodological Approach* (New York: Wiley, 1978); Anne Fausto-Sterling, *Myths of Gender: Biological Theories about Women and Men* (New York: Basic Books, 1985); Mary Daly, *Gyn/Ecology* (Boston: Beacon, 1990 [1978]); Sheila Jeffreys, *The Lesbian Heresy: A Feminist Perspective on the Lesbian Sexual Revolution* (Melbourne: Spinifex, 1993); Claudia Card, *Adventures in Lesbian Philosophy* (Bloomington: Indiana University Press, 1994).

20. Cressida J. Heyes, "Feminist Solidarity after Queer Theory: The Case of Transgender," *Signs* 28, 4 (2003): 1094.

21. Leslie Feinberg, *Transgender Warriors: From Joan of Arc to RuPaul* (Boston: Beacon Press, 1996).

22. Leslie Feinberg, public presentation, University of Minnesota, Minneapolis, February 1995.

23. See "FTM 2004: A Gender Odyssey," conference in Seattle, www.transconference.org; also "Southern Comfort," conference in Atlanta, www.sccatl.org. There are very good reasons for such exclusive spaces, given the personal nature of the issues under discussion, as well as the titillation, curiosity, objectification, and exploitation surrounding transsexual and transgendered people in popular media and culture. However, there also might be very good similar reasons for female-born women's spaces (like the Michigan Womyn's Music Festival).

24. In Bornstein's view, the parameters of the hierarchy include the following: "Postoperative transsexuals (those transsexuals who've had genital surgery and live fully in the role of another gender) look down on: Pre-operative transsexuals (those who are living full or part time in another gender, but who've not yet had their genital surgery) who in turn look down on: Transgenders (people living in another gender identity, but who have little or no intention of having genital surgery) who can't abide: She-Males (a she-male friend of mine described herself as 'big tits, lots of make-up, and a dick.') who snub the: Drag Queens (gay men who on occasion dress in varying parodies of women) who laugh about the: Out Transvestites (usually heterosexual men who dress as they think women dress, and who are out in the open about doing that) who pity the: Closet Cases (transvestites who hide their cross-dressing) who mock the post-op transsexuals." Kate Bornstein, *Gender Outlaw: On Men, Women and the Rest of Us* (New York: Routledge, 1994), 67–68.

25. This group also welcomes FTMs who have not transitioned or are not planning to, but discussions are usually reserved for issues related to living fully as men.

26. I understand myself to be simultaneously and serially both man and woman, as well as neither. Although physically I embrace my masculinity, I am not particularly interested in behavioral cues of masculinity and find myself, as

a feminist, concerned about the sexism and misogyny of many FTM transsexuals, as well as many butch lesbians. Although I embody masculinity, I critique the uncritical deployment of it.

27. I find recent changes in the group and the Twin Cities FTM community more broadly to be encouraging. The designator "gender queer" has emerged as a new umbrella term for wide-ranging expressions of gender (although the hierarchy of "just gender queer" versus "really transgendered" remains), trans/trans romantic relationships have become more visible, and transmen are identifying as feminists in the present (instead of just joking about their former lives as feminists/lesbians).

28. Viviane K. Namaste, *Invisible Lives: The Erasure of Transsexual and Transgendered People* (Chicago: University of Chicago Press, 2000), 27; Dean Spade, "Resisting Medicine, Re/modeling Gender," *Berkeley Women's Law Journal* 18 (2003): 15–37.

14. On Taking Feminism for Granted

Reflections of a Third Generation Feminist

Karla A. Erickson

IN preparation for this volume, I researched the institutionalization of women's studies at the University of Minnesota because I wanted to "hear" what the discourse "sounded" like during the 1970s. What I found was a historical document proposing to create a department of women's studies back in 1972. They wrote:

> The systematic oppression of women in society at large is present in all its details at the University. It is manifested in these facts: we are cut off from our roots, female culture, our history and contributions both individual and collective, have been systematically excluded from study just as Black, Chicano, and Indian cultures have; we have been brainwashed by the male biases and sexism which dominate every sphere of academic life; we lack access to the centers of power and thus have no control over our own destinies; we continually have been denied the necessary knowledge for the development of the skills needed to change our situation.[1]

I say "back" in 1972 because the year this group of feminist professors started their push to institutionalize feminism as an academic department, I had not yet been born. Thirty years later, I have been privileged to study within an institution profoundly influenced by the work they did to create and maintain feminist spaces. I pursue my own research questions against the backdrop of an institution that houses not only feminist studies but also African American studies, American Indian studies, and Chicano studies. And in the same tradition of building institutional space for intellectual pursuits, in 2002 the University of Minnesota introduced a minor in Asian American studies. I describe the presence of these departments as a backdrop to my larger story because institutions are sometimes said to "house" ideas, but the official structure of academe is only one aspect of what shapes us as scholars and teachers. As they argued in 1972, the connections and collectivities between individuals and around a sense of shared ideas and history provide an important touchstone for us as feminists, as professionals, and as people. The choices we make regarding who we align with, which questions we choose to ask, and what we choose to give back once our training is complete are shaped by an intersection of the "necessary knowledge" that they alluded to in 1972 and the private journeys—intellectual, emotional, and physical—on the road to our own place within the academy.

The story I have to tell comes full circle from the feminist founders making their argument the year before I was born, to three decades later, when I sit housed in the relative security their efforts produced. Unlike them, I get to speak of feminist networks and roots in terms of presence, not absence. As a third wave feminist, I have legacies to refer back to that have occasionally allowed me to take feminism for granted. My story is also tinged with the challenge of trying to be "feminist" at a time when feminism is declared dead,[2] under attack, and out of date, when the struggles that remain look small and tedious compared to the golden era of the second wave; today the branches of the feminist tree are spread wide enough that sometimes we ache for a centralized effort, for a war cry, for a shared concern around which to rally. My generation is one of feminism(s) that attempt to honor lived experience in all its multiplicity, contradiction, and intersection. As such, I cannot hold myself up as representative of anyone but myself and my own story, which begins and ends here at the University of Minnesota, where I have made my intellectual home. I use "home" in keeping with bell hooks's notion that "Home is that place which enables and promotes varied and ever changing perspectives, a place where one discovers new ways of seeing reality, frontiers of difference."[3] In this way, "home" does not speak to an idealized, sanitized, safe haven from the outside world but rather a space from which one can better perceive where one is in relation to others, to imagine a future and to percolate change. Unlike other feminist travel tales, mine involves little geographical movement. Instead, against the backdrop of Minnesota green and glimmering lakes, I have mainly traveled in my thinking. Mine is a story of passing through seasons of intellectual growth from beneath the trees lining the Mississippi River to the prairies of Illinois, from the lazy green of suburbs to the city—leaving home only to return again, changed.

Homecoming

In fall 2001, I drove from my home in Minneapolis to join my old group of girlfriends for homecoming festivities at my alma mater, Illinois Wesleyan University in central Illinois. One of the great joys of that weekend was seeing my closest friends from my undergraduate years walk across campus one more time as grown women. But the most rewarding moments of that weekend that was filled with traces and echoes of my most private past were spent in faculty offices, where I returned to visit the three women who had trained me. A decade had passed since I began my undergraduate education in 1991, and it had been six years since the May day in 1995 when I donned green robes to receive my bachelor of arts in English and women's studies.

In 1991, I was able to pursue a major in women's studies only through a design-your-own-major loophole. Since then, these three women along with other feminist scholars on campus have institutionalized women's studies so that students who enter Illinois Wesleyan today can pursue a bona fide major or minor in women's studies, and all students have access to a much broader spectrum of courses under the umbrella of women's studies.

That is not how things worked in the four years I spent at this rather conservative, quiet little campus in central Illinois, which continues to open its doors to a student body that consists of primarily white upper-middle-class, academically gifted students from Chicago. Back then, women's studies was offered as a minor that could be assembled from the limited course offerings available each semester. Most of the relevant courses were taught by the three women I worked with during my tenure there, and outside of that small umbrella of course offerings, instructors seemed content to teach a less nuanced story of the past and present; feminist issues received little play and, when taught, were often relegated to a token week out of the semester. The ensuing decade had wrought many changes, some quiet, some loud.

One thing that was not different was the line of students waiting outside Georganne Rundblad's door in the sociology department. Hers was always one of the most welcoming spaces on campus: a water pitcher on the table, menus from a new ethnic restaurant (a luxury in the culturally homogeneous town of Bloomington-Normal), and pictures of her life and work made her office a place where both the academic and the personal were acceptable topics of conversation. Georganne (nicknamed "George") really knows her students, and I was astounded at how well she remembered me, the courses I had taken with her, my friends at the time, and how she had chosen me to lead her class when she was away due to cancer. She had prepared for my visit with questions about my work, a request to talk with one of her current students about the state of American studies, a copy of a multicultural anthology she edited, and videotapes by her students from her social welfare documentary course. I was returning as the prodigal daughter (especially to her) because my path had come full circle to closely resemble her research interests. Privately, I had also modeled my own teaching style and persona in the classroom on her example. George was known for being approachable while also possessing a formidable intellect; she was always "up" on everything, and as I scanned her bookshelves, I saw that although she was already tenured, she had continued to read absolutely all the newest scholarship in her field. She was interested in my dissertation project, which stands at the crossroads of gender and labor, as do her own research interests. Without prodding, she introduced me to the chair of her department as a possible candidate for a job that was opening up in two years. As always, George's enthusiasm for the questions I was pursuing was remarkable. This time I was returning just one step away from being a colleague rather than her student, but her treatment of me and her other students had never suggested anything less than equal status. Her active support was to be expected. It was representative of who she was as a teacher and was in keeping with her goal of remaking the academy, both by planting seeds of feminist concerns in all her students and by aggressively pursuing the hiring and advancement of feminists within her institution.

Alison Sainsbury's brand of feminism was quite different from George's, although they were then and remain friends and allies. She had been housed in the English department when I attended Wesleyan, where she most notably taught Third World Women Writers in a way that transported a white-faced classroom of privileged American undergraduates into the complicated experiences conveyed by writers like Bessie Head, Nawal el Sadaawi, Alifa Rifaat, and Salwa Bakr.[4] Alison's approach to my visit was to update me on "the good fight." She had moved in the intervening years and was the director of women's studies, for which she received one course release, leaving her with seven courses to teach a year. She was still hot on the trail of the administration, who had recently fallen out of her favor (again) for positively alluding to an article that had cited Wesleyan as one of the best schools for males to attend. Schools were measured on a male-friendly scale according to the ratio of men to women (better odds if there was a sixty female/forty male split, like there had been for thirty years at Wesleyan); the article also surveyed student groups and course offerings to determine the degree of feminist activism on campus, the presence of which was portrayed as threatening to men choosing between possible schools. Wesleyan had tried to use the article as another feather in its cap for the purposes of recruitment, and Alison had called a press conference to let people know what they were up to this time. In the 2001–02 academic year, she was also teaching a course that included books with titles like *Breasts: The Women's Perspective on an American Obsession, The Clitoral Truth,* and *Woman: An Intimate Geography* and that, among other things, required students to develop an intricate understanding of female genitalia, how women's bodies are put together, and an overview of the long history of how medicine has treated female anatomy.[5] She was frustrated by the level of apathy she discovered in incoming students, and while she still fought to instill feminist outrage and inspire action in her students, she was growing weary and made mention of better days when at least one student in each course "got it."

In 1991, that student had been me. I remember being a little intimidated by what I would now label her second wave approach to feminism; she was a rabble-rouser, a troublemaker, the first to grab the microphone and make some noise when she noticed injustice, and there was plenty of it going on at Wesleyan in terms of race, gender, and class, all of which interested Alison. I remember feeling riled up personally by Alison's teaching and yet still a little afraid when it came time to transfer ideological convictions into action, as in, you mean I have to do something about this too? But I also vividly remember the day that Alison cried when she explained to us that Bessie Head, an African writer, died of an infection due to lousy health conditions in her hometown. She cried because an illness with a simple cure in our nation had wiped out an incredibly important voice from Africa. Bessie Head was one of the women Alison introduced us to for whom her voice was her truest possession, and now she had been silenced by a highly curable illness. I realized that for Alison, teaching was not an exercise that prepared us for a job, and literature was not just words on a page; for Alison, sharing stories was a form of activism. Her passion was infectious. Alison encouraged my faith in the importance of telling one's own story, which feminists have long identified as the key to empowerment, and which happens even here, when we use personal narratives to frame our life histories and entry into feminism.

And finally, I met with April Schultz in the history department, who had become my intellectual model and guide because she had been trained in the graduate program I eventually came to call home, the Department of American Studies at the University of Minnesota. Her dissertation advisor, David Noble, was not only my intellectual grandfather, but over a decade after she began her graduate training, he became one of my committee members as well. The bond that April and I had shared as student and teacher during my time at Wesleyan had been deepened by a sense of a shared intellectual kinship; we had been indoctrinated into a particular understanding of American studies. We had been trained interdisciplinarily, which had shaped our research projects, but had also, for both of us, blended seamlessly with the discipline-crossing nature of women's studies.

April was one of the leaders and also part of the inspiration for the recent development of an American studies program at Wesleyan, an unusual development for such a small institution. I celebrated this as an advance because I knew that an American studies program led by April would house courses that taught alternative and multicultural histories that would address postnational and global concerns and that would foster understandings of how American racism, sexism, homophobia, and classism have developed over time and continue to work through channels of power in our nation. Having just visited my other two mentors, I was struck by April's use of institutionalization as her primary vehicle for promoting a feminist politics. April fostered a feminist vision and politics first and foremost through the texts she asked students to read and in the stories she presented *as* American history. For example, she taught a course titled "Women, Work, and Leisure," which traced women's "official" participation in the marketplace and unofficial leisure activities through the past two centuries to help students understand how changing opportunities shaped the lives of women over time. The texts she used always assumed a recognition of women as historical actors and wove in historical narratives from multiple sources like journals, letters, and official records. In addition to the scholarship she exposed students to, she also quietly sought out, as she had done with me, students to pursue undergraduate work in women's studies and tapped budding scholars for graduate school. Her guidance played a profound role in my choice to become a professor, and, thankfully, because my department has been very supportive of my work, helped lead me to American studies at the University of Minnesota as my academic home.

Mentors, Modeling, and Feminist Spaces

Who are we to the people we teach? The vignettes I recount about the women who taught me tell one sliver of the work they have done over the past twenty-five years, first as students and now as professors and activists. I realized as I sat across from them discussing my "progress" in my own graduate work that as an undergraduate I had no idea what institutions they had attended, I understood very little about the ideological divides and political leanings of different disciplines and departments although I recognized the divisions, and for the most part, I took what I needed from each of these three women, drawing from them examples and ideas and passion alternately to form my own path and my own feminist politics. But I certainly did not *know* the women who trained me as I know the other women in my life. The power differential at the undergraduate level prevented me from ever even turning my gaze toward them as women, despite the work all three did to involve themselves in the community of students and to break down institutional hierarchies. Had I known then what I know now, I would have considered how their position as 2.5 generation feminists had shaped their training and continued to shape the work they did in their scholarship, their classrooms, and their office hours. While I borrowed different skills, notions, and questions from each, it also never occurred to me that they differed significantly in the way they expressed their feminist convictions and the avenues through which they practiced a feminist politics.

During my stay at Wesleyan, Georganne, Alison, and April were three of the five professors I would have labeled "feminist," but I only talked of them as feminists in protected circles where I knew it was safe. Against the backdrop of the Reagan-Bush era, Illinois Wesleyan remained safely wrapped in a conservative politics that required only occasional nods to political correctness. In Minnesota, the dramatic move to the political right that had taken root nationally was often mourned and to some degree resisted by local politics. By contrast, amid the uninterrupted flatness of fields and roads that make up central Illinois, feminism was still a bad word. To be a feminist at that college in central Illinois in 1991 was to be a femi-nazi, dangerous, and, most important to me at the time, anti-male and therefore not fit to date. It is interesting that when word got out that we might be up to something deemed feminist that we were *not* punished by being labeled dykes or lesbians because the "threat" of a visible homosexual presence on campus was at that time still unspeakable. Gays and lesbians were invisible, just like the people of color on campus. Being a feminist was punished by being perceived as "trouble" in a situation where heterosexuality was not only assumed but the only recognized sexual orientation.

The secure dominance of white heterosexuality was reinforced socially by the students but also maintained through recruiting patterns that were very evident when I worked for the admissions office,[6] and reinforced by conservative student groups on campus and the reigning power of the Greek system. More than fifty percent of all students at Wesleyan were part of either a sorority or a fraternity, which meant that the school year was punctuated by the calendar of the Greeks, that social life was monopolized and defined by the Greek houses, and that heterosexuality was not just the norm but was the context within which all social life on campus played out. So being a feminist, and subsequently dangerous to date, was a high price to pay. It meant that we had fallen out of the social net; we were freaks just like the other unmentionables: the unassimilated people of color and even to a large extent the few working-class folks (scholarship kids) whose job involved more than attending class and partying. It was within this context too that these three women did the important work of inspiring, identifying, and cultivating a new generation of feminist scholars under less-than-friendly circumstances. When I think back to how I developed a budding feminist politics, I remember many compromises, a close circle of friends with whom I committed to staying independent (not joining a sorority), and the strong support of these three women.

At Wesleyan I simultaneously grew into a self-proclaimed feminist while for the first time in my life being met with daily, if not hourly, reminders that women were indeed not equal and quite unimportant. I encountered this attitude in the unevenness of Greek culture—women moved to houses to be trained to be ladylike, follow rules, and rein themselves in, while men moved to houses to enjoy the freedom of brotherhood unencumbered by a parent's or girlfriend's eye. I encountered a deep silence regarding all minority groups in many of my mainstream (read nonfeminist) courses that became increasingly difficult to bear as my feminist convictions gained strength. As a matter of fact, one of the courses, Human Sexuality, which counted toward my major in women's studies, not only failed to address homosexuality, but I was also told that my paper on date rape and the consequences that violence toward women has on their sexual development was not an acceptable topic for a course on human sexuality. The possibilities for research were reined in by subtle means; in this class, my vantage point on the prevalence of rape was considered a cultural analysis that did not fit within the biological/physical lens within which human sexuality was presumably focused.

At the same time that I was seeking courses that allowed me to pursue my feminist-informed interests, I was struggling not to give up my work as an advocate for victims of domestic violence at the local courthouse. Despite training regarding the cycle of domestic violence and the existence of one of the only safe houses in the surrounding towns, officers continued to ignore or debate women's stories of abuse on 911 calls, and many of the judges I stood before with my clients refused to grant orders of protection on even the second or third documented incident of abuse. More than just frustrated by the inertia I witnessed, at age twenty I felt intimidated and miserable regarding the constant joking by attorneys and police about the women who were abused, the attempts they made to separate me from them as a "different sort" of woman, and the degree to which many of the women still working in the system to protect these women had come to believe that they had to make incredible sacrifices and in many ways play along with stereotypes of women's complicity in violence—of them "deserving it"—in order to simply save these women from being beaten to death.

These stories formed the counterbalance to what happened in safe spaces like George's, Alison's, and April's classrooms, to the discussions that took place in dorm rooms, and to the progress we did make in protecting women, in conducting marches, and in influencing laws and policies at the city and campus level. My story, taking place in the years it does and in the cities and institutions it does, is uneven. I felt safer and more confident that women could do anything when I was young, wrapped in the benign privileges of middle-class liberalism in Minnesota. When I arrived at college, I was exposed to an articulated feminist vision at precisely the time I most needed those tools to make sense of the contradiction between my awareness of my own and other women's capacities with the way women in general and myself specifically were being treated during the early 1990s in central Illinois.

Mediated Politics

My undergraduate years prepared me for what came next; however, my story of taking feminism for granted begins much earlier than that. Two sources provided foundations for my feminist convictions; the first was a supportive, unencumbered childhood in the quiet green of the suburbs of Minneapolis, and the second was the media images and words with which I fed my growing girl mind. As a third wave feminist, I got in touch with the vitality of Friedan, Gilman, Rich, hooks, and Steinem through the music of the Indigo Girls, Ani DiFranco, and Sarah McLachlan. I first imagined gender equality with the help of *Free to Be You and Me* and *Sesame Street*. Passing through a history-poor educational system, my interests and attitudes were shaped by Spike Lee's and Oliver Stone's on-screen visions, and more recently by films like *Boys Don't Cry* and *American History X* as visual negotiations with our nation, then and now. And I don't think I am alone: for many of us raised in the 1970s and 1980s and trained in the 1990s, popular culture was the first bridge we crossed toward a politicized understanding of our gender. "Billy Has a Doll" from *Free to Be* and "I Am Woman" by Helen Reddy played in my home while I was deciding whether to join Girl Scouts or T-ball. Though I did not know until college why feminists were too often denigrated as "bra burners," I had already internalized the idea that beauty pageants and Barbie were bad for my health.

While I have sought out interdisciplinary programs to pursue my interests because it is the way I know the world, I also feel particularly at home in a department like American studies that takes seriously the role of popular culture in shaping individual and group identities. I believe that departments and disciplines that fail to consider the role of the media in knowledge production and reception for incoming students stubbornly make their approach to the world seem antiquated. For example, I learned about the Holocaust first through *The Diary of Anne Frank*, second through the fiction of Primo Levi and Elie Wiesel, and third through Steven Spielberg's *Schindler's List*. While I have read hundreds of pages of history on the Holocaust since that time, it is these meditations on the meanings of the Holocaust and visual representations that stick with me. These images and the Indigo Girls' song "Jacob's Ladder" about the victims of the Holocaust prepared me to connect with—rather than divorce myself from—the pile of shoes in the Holocaust Museum in Washington, DC, which I visited in fall 2001.

Our media culture is often blamed for overwhelming us with digestible visuals and narratives to the point of numbness. While this can be true, the profound impact of images and interactive media must be intermixed with, not placed in competition with, the "flatter" history in ink. For feminists my age, as for all of us labeled "Generation X," part of our shared history, part of the way we nod to each other across difference or recognize a joint past is through popular culture and the meanings we found and carried with us from television, music, and movies. I understood Gerda Lerner's *Creation of Patriarchy* when April taught history with it because I had already read the *Mists of Avalon,* a novel about the King Arthur legend told from the point of view of the women. In Alison's course, I researched female genital mutilation in Africa as compared to domestic violence in the United States after reading the short stories of Bessie Head and Salwa Bakr in combination with *The War against Women* and *Sexual Politics.* I worked as a legal advocate for victims of domestic violence after I read "Rape Poem" by Marge Piercy because it was one way I felt I could make the world safer for other women and therefore safer for me. Peggy McIntosh's notion of the "backpack of privilege" was made tangible to me in Judy Grahn's masterpiece, the poem "A Woman Is Talking to Death." Toni Morrison's novels, more than any theory I have read, brought race home to me, making racism as built on slavery real to me. Her *Beloved* in combination with *Crossing the River* by Carl Phillips provided me with a linguistic, narrative representation of interlocking hierarchies. I came to see the impetus for the Holocaust, slavery, and the treatment of AIDS carriers as intimately connected through the desire to exclude and to construct identity through the repression, expulsion, and even extermination of the not-me. I studied history as a result of novels like these, using my coursework to wrap facts around the essence of historical memory I discovered in these texts. Popular culture, as such, is part of what laid the groundwork for my early excursions into feminist inquiries.

The Culture of Home

As academic feminists, we are sometimes encouraged to think of our histories as primarily movements through texts, schools of thought, and the tutelage of particular instructors or scholars. One of the significant differences between myself and the feminists labeled second wave is the stage of life during which I was first exposed to a feminist belief system. For me, the media was an early vehicle for thinking about women as powerful and unstoppable, and for imagining a more equal world. The work of first and second wave feminists is what made it possible for young girls and women to be exposed to the narratives and visions that accompanied me through my youth. That wave has continued; today my undergraduate students have multiple feminist visions to choose among, and the existence of pro-feminist media is even more taken for granted by them than it was by me. My movements, from home, down a couple states, across the pond to England, and back home again were less dramatic physically than intellectually. The short journey to Illinois made me aware of the local conditions that had shaped my childhood, while a semester in England helped me identify the privileges and assumptions that accompanied my American citizenship.[7] While I did not travel far, the experience of arriving home again—changed—brought many of the forces that had shaped me to light.

Though I would not have called myself a feminist until I met Alison, April, and George, looking back, I was certainly a feminist-in-training. Beginning in elementary and through high school, if I was given an option, I always selected paper topics that addressed women's experience, from abortion rights to date rape, from the beauty industry to reproductive technology. Again, the space and the people who inhabited it as instructors mattered to my first forays into feminism. Trained in the liberal Minneapolis public school system where teachers, although still paid poorly, were highly valued and supported, I was met with a lot of support for my early research interests. And while no feminist I know can tell a perfect story of familial reception of a feminist politics, clearly both my parents thought of women as important, relatively equal people in our culture and also gave my burgeoning interest in women's rights and questions of gender justice fair play.

Raised in a household where education was not simply valued but held up as the ultimate tool for self-empowerment, and surrounded by examples in my family and school of strong women, at an early age I did believe that girls could do anything because there was little evidence to suggest otherwise. Minnesota is known for the strength of its public school system, and especially in the suburbs of Minneapolis where I grew up, the schools catered to the young and promising. It was wonderful to be labeled "gifted" during the 1980s in Minnesota: interdisciplinary, hands-on courses were designed specifically for us to ensure that we were never bored or hungry for new knowledge once we had been fast-tracked through the general requirements. When I arrived at Wesleyan, it was clear that my public education had paralleled and in some ways surpassed the private, college prep high schools that many of my classmates had attended in Chicago.

However, the special status of the "gifted" in the Minneapolis school system at that time is one example of the narrowness of the home culture that was so conducive to my upbringing. The opportunities I took for granted as a child were part of a larger system of white middle-class liberalism that pervades Minneapolis and that is incredibly beneficial to a certain group of people, of which I was luckily a member. In many ways, Minneapolis is a politically progressive area; the emphasis on public services, from free and perfectly maintained parks, to clean and safe downtown streets, to an innovative public school system, makes for a comfortable, affordable life supported by the shared, if somewhat weak, liberal leaning that has been the hallmark of the state for the past fifty years, from Hubert Humphrey through Walter Mondale and continuing today in the wake of the untimely death of Senator Paul Wellstone. In Minnesota, the Democratic party is still called the DFL—for Democratic-Farmer-Labor Party. Many Minnesotans take pride in maintaining a liberal politics that falls left of the Democratic platform, and in claiming a long history of voting for liberal candidates, in contrast to voting patterns in other states. The world I moved through looked like an equal playing field, where anyone could get a leg up, but this illusion was in part maintained by the relative homogeneity of Minnesota in comparison to other urban centers. While the Minneapolis metro area has grown increasingly diverse during the three decades I have lived here, many of the spaces I moved through were white middle-class spaces, and so the promise of equality was in many ways an untested one.

My movement from home, to college, and back again complicated my vision of for whom the "supportive" environment in Minneapolis was set up, and who fell through the nets that had always caught me. For example, I became aware of the degree to which I had been raised in a queer-friendly culture when my friends from Chicago were astounded by the prevalence and overtness of gay and lesbian shops, clubs, and hangouts when they came to visit. While my four years in central Illinois helped me to appreciate the rather unusual culture of gender equity that pervaded in the public schools that trained me, I became increasingly aware of what had been left out of my experience and my vision of a more equal world. For example, I was appalled to hear from a college friend that she had been warned not to move to Minnesota because she was African American and the general sentiment among friends and family was that Minnesota was a very unfriendly and potentially dangerous place to be black. I did not want to see my home as a place where it was relatively safe to be gay but somewhat dangerous to be black. The warnings she received about how isolating Minnesota culture could be for African Americans provided me with a new awareness of just how white most of the spaces I moved through had been. My introduction to feminism was in many ways easy; the path was smooth for me. During my early education I was comfortable feeling what bell hooks calls the "good feminist vibes" of a complicit white feminism.[8] My journey through feminism has been marked by removing layers of blindness and guilt to make space for a feminist vision that extends beyond the limited realm of young, intelligent white middle-class women for whom Minneapolis, during my growing-up years, had been a playground.

When I say that I have too often taken feminism for granted, it is a brand of feminism that might be called white middle-class liberal feminism, or perhaps better labeled "complacent feminism." Part of my ability to take feminism for granted has included my ability to "pass," to mask and unmask myself as a feminist. More importantly, both in my early education and at Illinois Wesleyan University, our ability to stake feminist claims and make progress on gender equity issues and the spaces in which I felt safe to perform a strong femininity and be taken seriously were predicated on a willingness to stop at questions of justice along lines of gender. What has been harder, and far less taken for granted for me, is developing an intersectional feminism that pays simultaneous attention to how power is wielded through gender, race, class, and sexuality.

My youth and training set me up to expect that I would be taken seriously and that my complaints regarding inequities according to gender would be heard, while at the same time, my social position and the culture of my home set me up to be blinded to the freedoms I experienced as an educated white middle-class American feminist. Revealing these gaps and oversights and the blindness that accompanies privilege has at times made me feel stupid and complicit. Many times I felt that I had been lied to or misled when the limits of my training were revealed, when I came face to face with the questions I had not been encouraged to ask. In response, I developed a syllabus for a course I call Working Through Whiteness. The course description begins:

The goal of "Working Through Whiteness" is to take on the labor of interrogating and attacking racism by making whiteness visible. Racism is still one of the foremost social problems plaguing our nation. Racism is perpetuated by a system that prevents white people from honestly engaging with what it means to

be white in a racist nation. This course is committed to not only looking—peer-
ing, if you will—at whiteness, but breaking down the historical advantages of
whiteness and the present-day costs of the "possessive investment in whiteness."
We will work together to break through the silence, fear, and anxiety surrounding discussions of racism, and particularly of what it means to be white. The
course will culminate in presentations which hone our ability to see whiteness
as it is expressed in popular culture, and to begin to define what it would mean
to develop an antiracist identity: to simultaneously be white and work against
racism. This is important work: challenging—at times intimidating—but re-
freshingly real. I invite you to accompany me on this journey through the white
wall, and I look forward to learning from and working with you.

My syllabus is designed with the culture of my home in mind; this course
is still necessary for much of the student body at the University of Minnesota in a way that it might not be elsewhere.[9] I feel that it is my particular
responsibility—considering my own legacy of blindness and privilege—
to help usher students through the process of passing through their own
privilege, to help them avoid being paralyzed by guilt when they encounter the silences and limitations that accompany their own position.

   This work of moving through whiteness, because it has been my own
struggle, galvanizes me as a teacher.[10] Part of my "good fight" is to take
the complacent feminism that empowered me and to complicate it early
on, to teach the contradictions of culture, to reveal the intricacies of experience as crosscut by privilege and oppression along more than simply gender lines. At times I am apologetic that it has taken me so long
to begin to "get it," but part of what I teach in my courses is inspired by
one of my mentors, David Noble. At the age of seventy-six, David reminds his students that he must combat his internalized racist and sexist
tendencies every day. Often his students will ask a question about what
helped him overcome his racism, and he replies that he never did, that
the work of being white and antiracist is a daily practice that is never
finished. In 1998, I had the honor of teaching with David. For the final
essay assignment, he proposed that we ask students to link one of the
fictional characters to historic events and listed three of the main male
characters as options. When I suggested that he give students an option
to write on *either* a lead male character or female character for their final
paper, David was quick to change the assignment, and then, laughing at
himself, he reminded me, "As I've said before, sexism has been the last
to go." David is a model of continuing to peel away the layers of what we
cannot yet see. He has remained on the cutting edge of new thought and
scholarship throughout the five decades of his career.

My finding an intellectual home here began with my contact with David, who exemplified change over inertia. In comparison, one of my favorite male professors at Wesleyan in a moment of professional terror grabbed my hand and said, "Karla, Camille Paglia is writing me out of a job." This was 1994, and Paglia's *Sexual Personae* was all the buzz in central Illinois.[11] Rather than celebrating the potential of her work, he felt that her interdisciplinary use of literature and the way her work absorbed what was once literary criticism into a larger cultural studies analysis were endangering his decades of responding directly and solely to texts. As English departments had been elsewhere for many years, Wesleyan's department had come under attack for its "relevance." His response was to feel fear and to stay with that fear, to continue to do what he felt he knew rather than claim the opportunity and even—I would argue—the responsibility of expanding himself, of transforming with the times. I respect both this man and David, but I felt more at home in a department where David was the flag bearer of our disciplinary development. He often referred to himself as the Ghost of American Studies Past, but he was very, very present. More than that, he had grown, grown into a feminist, in fact. His most recent book, *Death of a Nation*, provides one of the most cutting-edge analyses of the United States under postnational conditions available today.[12] He takes his students' ideas, learning, and development seriously, but he also gives back when it is his time, through his example and through his scholarship.

I rely on David for inspiration, particularly at moments when I feel frustrated by a renewed awareness of how much I, and we as a nation, have left to do to even approach equality. At times I feel frustrated, as do many of my students, that we have not come further, that our legacy as Gen X and beyond is to continue to work on the promises and dreams of the 1960s that have not been realized. We have not cashed the check of equality that Martin Luther King Jr. talked about: women cannot count on feeling safe on the street or receiving equal pay for equal work, and despite the rhetoric of a classless society, one of the greatest changes in my lifetime has been the increasing divide between the rich and the poor. This is exhausting work precisely because change is so slow to achieve, and precisely because it involves progressively dismantling and replacing the silences and possessive investments that accompany our own privilege.

I offer my Working Through Whiteness course in the hope that making the work of dismantling racism overt will help students earlier in their journeys, that like feminism, change will be facilitated by a group of students who encounter models of moving through whiteness earlier than I did. I offer it too, in the tradition of David Noble, of embracing change over inertia. Perhaps this is how "waves" are constructed. I never liked "waves" to describe feminism because it sounded like something that just happened naturally, like an inevitable force. There is nothing inevitable about the progress that has been made possible by the "waves" of feminists who have proceeded me; in fact, the advantages and possibilities that lay before me were achieved through intense struggle, high personal cost, and a constant cycle of advance and backlash. Just as I have benefited from the official and unofficial mentoring of second wave feminists, I hope my students can pick up where my early work leaves off: at the challenge of making feminism attentive to injustice along all lines of privilege, not simply gender. The work we do today toward a more nuanced, informed, intersectional, transnational feminism is demanding, exhausting, and exhilarating, both in our private struggles to engage what we are positioned to see and know and in the teaching we do in our classrooms to assist our students in similar intellectual journeys.[13]

Returning Home

I came "home" in 1995 after graduation from college. My hometown felt different to me, having traveled both physically and intellectually in the intervening four years. I had completed the first step of my training toward my career goal and had during my senior year experienced my first serious setback toward my ultimate goal of becoming a professor. My intellectual development had taken place within an aura of white liberal complacency more broadly, but personally, I had also been coddled and celebrated so frequently that I was not properly prepared for rejection. In 1994, I prepared to apply to graduate school and arrogantly assumed that I would be welcomed into my program of choice. So when the American studies program at the University of Minnesota denied me entrance for the 1995 academic year, I was left without a backup plan as to how to proceed. Whereas my scholarship had been lauded as exemplary at Illinois Wesleyan University, I was surprised to discover that my training was insufficient to move me onto the next level of training.

While my sense of entitlement regarding my desirability as a PhD candidate and the subsequent range of emotions I experienced in the next year, when I was unwillingly out of academe, are particular to my story, the way my private aspirations intersected with the flow of minds and bodies through academe is significant to the story of feminist generations. In looking back, I see clearly that the choices I made earlier in my life affected my entry to graduate-level work in ways I did not expect back then. As a valedictorian and a National Merit Scholar in 1991, I had my pick of any undergraduate institution, and I knew it. I was opposed to what I saw as the elitism of the Ivy League and did not apply. Northwestern in Chicago and Pomona in California were the most elite institutions I applied to because my search was guided by a sense of needing to find an intellectual home and a place that felt like the right fit for what I considered the college journey. As a result, I did not "trade in" my spotless academic credentials for entry into a prestigious program. Instead, I followed both my intuition and funding. Illinois Wesleyan University had one of the best scholarship programs for National Merit Scholars in the country. As the daughter of teachers, I had my family's support, but we fell into the middle territory between not qualifying for financial aid and not being able to afford the exorbitant cost of a college education out of pocket, so money was a concern.

I believe I received a fairly good education at Illinois Wesleyan, although it was not as rigorous as at times I wished it was. What it did provide, as promised, was a community, and a place where I did a lot of stretching and maturing as an individual. While I was satisfied with what my four years had produced, my application hurt for the lack of prestige attached to my alma mater. In short, I believed that my individual merit would carry me through to my goal, but I had not taken into consideration how much institutional affiliations shape opportunities in academe. My experiences point to an internal divide in the academy—between elite and nonelite institutions—that create tracks from which it is difficult to diverge.

I learned more about the politics of "the big time," as one of my professors called it, and much more about being a scholar during my master's work at Hamline University. Much like Wesleyan, Hamline is a small liberal arts university located in St. Paul, Minnesota. There I pursued interdisciplinary coursework under the rubric of "liberal studies." I became interested in labor, deepened my understanding of class, and benefited greatly from the opportunity to put interdisciplinary learning into practice. When I applied to the University of Minnesota again for the 1998–99 academic year, I was undoubtedly better prepared to not only survive but flourish in a PhD program.

While I am grateful for the path my education took because what first appeared as a detour ended up being an important stepping stone in my development, it also reminds me of some of the problems associated with who has access to higher education and through which channels. While it is certainly not true that only candidates from elite institutions are accepted at the University of Minnesota or anywhere else, having attended a well-known, reputable undergraduate institution is a conventional criterion for admittance. At eighteen, I did not understand that by following my gut, I was unwittingly giving up professional currency, and I was weakening my ability to move from one strong institution to another. So even though I was satisfied with my education, it did not show well on paper. While this is one minor example, my experience fits into a larger range of choices that young scholars might make, in part as a reflection of feminist convictions. For example, someone might choose to work with a particular scholar at a less elite institution, money constraints might make it impossible for someone to attend a particular institution, or someone might choose an institution based on a feminist-friendly curriculum or campus. Any of these choices could affect subsequent training in terms of how institutions flow into one another and how "quality" is recognized in the academy.

Many third wave feminists have not yet tried their wares out on the job market, but from the past we know that women in general and particularly scholars with a reputation that includes a feminist politics hit some land mines on the way to being hired and getting tenure. What I am suggesting is that the sacrifices reported by feminist professors regarding how thin they must spread themselves, the risks they must take to teach what they want to teach, and, as Jennifer Pierce explains in her essay, the intense backlash they can experience are part of a larger process of being disciplined by the academic process by which certain career trajectories are made easier by the recognizability of an institution, of "big names," and of the sorts of questions one asks. In 1998, when I was first placed on the wait list and eventually admitted, I felt like I had slipped into the "big time" through the backdoor, overcoming "weak" institutional affiliations with further evidence of my commitment to the profession and my ability to produce quality scholarship. Even having arrived where I wanted to be for the next step toward my career goal, my entry into graduate school was shaped by a feeling of having sneaked in under the radar. I am certain that it is not an uncommon feeling, but it set me up to go after my PhD with intensity, because I felt I had to prove that I deserved what felt like institutional upward mobility.

Imagining a Feminist Academy

In her 1991 dissertation on the socialization of women's studies scholars in the 1980s, Sharon Nero argues that involvement in the women's movement provided "the formal knowledge and skills, and the informal and 'professional' socialization for these [second generation] scholars."[14] While my upbringing prepared me to be receptive to a feminist line of thought, and my undergraduate training sparked my interest and introduced me to key questions within feminism, only as a graduate student have I moved fully into my own as a feminist scholar. This final step in my socialization has provided me with my chosen arena in which to "give back" rather than simply receive feminist ideas and support. Located in a liberal American studies department, my interests have been encouraged since the day I arrived at the University of Minnesota, but for me, academic work is only ignited through a simultaneous engagement with people, and most often, with other women.

Having first encountered academic feminism at Wesleyan, one of the most startling discoveries on my return home was how central feminist considerations were to the training at both Hamline and the University of Minnesota. Here, feminism was not a dirty word. There was nothing hush-hush about feminism, and only the most outdated, "old-school" professor taught in a format or with texts that ignored a multicultural nation or the conditions of oppression and domination. Here the texts that April, Alison, and George used in their courses were assumed to be significant contributions to any canon, not radical interventions in the curriculum. Having become a student at institutions with very different clientele and leadership, I was suddenly in the middle of the political spectrum rather than unspeakably on the left, as I had been at Wesleyan. These conditions allowed me to pursue my questions and scholarly concerns with more ease and allowed me to push the limits of my inquiries.

In spite of the many benefits of a feminist-friendly learning environment, I at times felt less inspired—conducting feminist research without a fight did not have quite the same thrill as it had had in a more toxic setting. Over time I have come to think that feminists in my age group—third wave or third generation—at some point in their training and eventual move into positions of leadership commonly find themselves in the privileged position of taking feminism for granted. For us, unlike for the generations of feminists who have come before us, not everything requires a good fight: there are spaces in which it is safe for us to speak our minds and institutions where the issues addressed under the rubric of women's studies are not foreign or marginalized but included across the curriculum; there are, indeed, places where the "old school," which I characterize as parlaying a dominant male WASP version of the past and present, really seems to be antiquated, on its way out, and losing power. We encounter these feminist-friendly places along the way, which is not to say that we do not have to fight for our convictions, for the right to define ourselves in opposition to cultural stereotypes and gender trappings, or that we are able to pursue our careers and interests uncontested. But not every step of our experience as feminist scholars is fraught with challenge, as might be said of the generation of women who trained us, and certainly of first wave feminists in the academy.

One of the key differences at the University of Minnesota was that there was a strong enough feminist cohort among the faculty that I could choose among feminist scholars who could support my work. Unlike at Wesleyan, where Georganne, Alison, and April were the only feminist scholars on campus, at Minnesota, the feminist presence crisscrossed the academy. The University of Minnesota houses the Center for Advanced Feminist Studies, one of the oldest feminist centers in the country, which supports a press that publishes progressive scholarship and for a while was the home of *Signs: Journal of Women in Culture and Society* (1990–95). These are institutional traces of a history of feminist work that had paid off by the time I arrived in 1998 not only in the explicitly feminist departments but also across the disciplines.

Since I arrived at the University of Minnesota, a PhD in feminist studies has also been implemented, further solidifying the place of feminism within the university. But for third generation interdisciplinary scholars like myself, the spectrum of feminist professors at the university has provided another significant advantage in that we do not necessarily have to take courses under the rubric of women's studies in order to pursue our research interests. The legacy of struggle to create room for feminist concerns as reflected in the excerpt from 1972 that opens this essay was the outcome of a small contingent of strong, determined feminist faculty three decades ago. In the intervening years, feminist academics have been hired in almost all the major departments, and in "younger" and interdisciplinary programs like American studies, it is not unusual to have more than just a token feminist scholar.

The strong historical presence of feminist concerns, faculty, and institutions at the University of Minnesota invariably affects the admission of a new wave of feminist scholars looking for a supportive environment in which to pursue their training and research interests. But these newly arrived feminist scholars do not always make their homes within the women's studies department. While I did pursue a minor in feminist studies, I experienced the relative privilege of a wide range of courses that addressed feminist concerns or applied a feminist-informed analysis to their object of study. In part as a result of my having these options, I have established contacts, touchstones, and mentors in places other than feminist studies. I believe that those who declare academic feminism dead have themselves taken for granted that feminist work must call itself first and foremost feminist and must be explicit about an originating feminist impulse. This tension around what "counts" as feminism was an ongoing sore spot in the two-semester course Feminist Theories and Methods, which I took during fall 2001. This course sequence was designed to be the first step toward a feminist major or minor, but due to my course choices, it was the last course I took before moving into my dissertation work. As such, I was familiar with many of the central questions driving the course, questions that have plagued feminism from the beginning: What is feminism? What is feminist scholarship? What is feminist pedagogy? What is feminist methodology? Answers to these questions are invariably tied up with how we choose to do our work, and how we identify ourselves professionally and personally. Thus, the stakes are high. For me, the course was a reminder of why I think feminism is most effective when it is diffused across the disciplines and legitimized in multiple sites. When feminism, which began as a cross-disciplinary critique of the academy, tries to form itself into a traditional discipline, to name its methods and theories, and to establish criteria of what "counts" as feminism, it loses its critical edge and becomes entangled in navel gazing, losing the impetus for change. However, even for many feminists in my generation, women's studies remains the only safe space to pursue their interests and to openly profess a feminist politics. The options available to me in terms of courses, faculty, and funding allowed me to work within a feminist framework, keeping gender at the center of my scholarship while moving across disciplines.

I think we third wave feminists are blessed with an opportunity to be feminist and to pursue feminist research without having to be "housed" in women's studies. I was lucky enough to have one of the top programs in American studies located in my hometown, so my choice of program was influenced primarily by the way that my search for an intellectual home combined with a desire to return to my circle of friends and family. As a native of Minneapolis, I did not necessarily need the immediate support of my cohort and colleagues in the same way graduate students who had just moved to Minnesota did. I was not lonely, and due to the politics and intensity of my many lifelong relationships, the friendships and partnerships developed through my graduate work contributed to but did not supplant my private reserve of support and intellectual camaraderie.

Up until now I have not spoken of cohorts and the private array of friendly faces and great thinkers we gather around us to feed our minds and spirits. While the people we choose as mentors and guides are incredibly influential to the work we do and how we perform it in the academy, our cohort, the people we enter and move through graduate training with, have a profound influence on how we understand our place in our discipline, in recent intellectual debates, and in the academy as a whole. I have had the luxury of being part of an intense and collaborative group of eight individuals who began with me in 1998. We have supported each other intently but easily, pushing each other without a tendency to compete mercilessly. When I think about the tides and currents of thought in the academy, I recognize the connections between our seemingly disparate research interests. We have made it through the rigors of graduate training together by honoring a need for fun and by treating each other as friends and equals, not as competitors, and our individual visions have been expanded by that camaraderie. When I think of the eight of us as one slice of a larger contingent of scholars trained in the early and mid-1990s, I feel invigorated by the potential we have to change not only our fields but the academy itself, the way that knowledge is conferred, the nature of collaboration, and the balance between teaching, learning and scholarship. As we each conclude our training at the university, our time of thinking together in the same space comes to an end, and yet the traces of the questions we have been exposed to or formed together travel with us in our imaginations. As such, my cohort is engrained in me and my approach to the work of being a professor.

When I say that I enjoyed the opportunity provided by feminists crisscrossing campus, I mean both in terms of representation in various disciplines and in terms of multiple generations. Unlike Wesleyan, where change was slow in part due to a conservative agenda and in part due to the slow pace of new hires, as a public university, the University of Minnesota was arguably decades ahead of other schools. My training has been enriched by exposure to multiple generations of feminist scholars in various disciplines and subsequently by my familiarity with how feminisms play out in practice. An ongoing push to make this institution feminist friendly has also resulted in the placement of multiple generations of feminists. Because feminism had only recently "arrived" at Wesleyan, the three feminists who trained me there were all in their thirties and represented a particular generation of the feminist movement in terms of the time during which they were trained. By contrast, at Minnesota, feminists from each subsequent wave teach and conduct their research, making for a more nuanced representation of the larger history of feminism as embodied in our feminist faculty. The range of options available to me at this level is one of the advantages of being a third generation feminist. There are moments at the university when the informal networks of feminist scholars across generations combine with official, institutionalized feminist debates, publications, talks, and courses to offer a vision of what it could feel like to work in an academy where feminism was appropriately taken for granted.

During my PhD training, I was privileged to feel supported and surrounded enough to toy with the vision of a feminist academy, but that optimistic outlook should not mask the ongoing challenges present at the University of Minnesota or camouflage the potential missteps I feel I took along the way. At this moment in feminism, when central concerns and approaches are not necessarily shared (if they ever were), the ability to choose between feminists with whom to work is especially important. Having benefited from such powerful mentoring at the undergraduate level, I arrived at the university with my eyes peeled for a feminist scholar to be my mentor. I described my search for a leader as a process of carefully combing the ranks for someone who modeled feminist scholarship and a commitment to teaching and with whom I felt comfortable. My first year I came up empty. My second year, I encountered a prominent scholar who calls herself feminist and who expressed an interest in my work and in acting as a guide for my training. Having no official leader, I found it difficult to trust my instinct not to respond favorably to her professional advances. My hesitancy was based on her personal politics, which to me seemed to contradict her professed feminist politics: she treated graduate students as her personal assistants, she used her classroom as a place to show how important she was rather than to facilitate her students' development, and she played favorites, reaching out to some "lucky" students like myself and ignoring or even chastising the students she felt were not significant enough to warrant her attention. Although she professed to be a feminist, I felt that specific behaviors went against my own expectations regarding collaboration and support between all feminists, regardless of our "standing" in the system. For example, when I did go to her office to chat, as she often invited me to do, before beginning, she would hand me money and ask me to walk down the hall and get her a Diet Coke. I referred to the reading list for her course as "Professor and Friends" since she taught her own and her friends' scholarship often to the exclusion of other feminist texts that addressed the same issues. Like most young graduate students, I was trying to make my way through the landscape of graduate school, trying to make sense of competing stories about what counted in a mentor in terms of prominence in the field, personal relationship, shared research interests, and disciplinary affiliation. In other words, I was torn between my intuition and instinct and the need to market myself for a future job. This professor had picked me out of the flock, so to speak, and so it was difficult to choose to walk away from her extended invitation at a time when I did not know what lay ahead for me, but I am glad I did.

In my third year Jennifer Pierce, who had recently transferred her tenure line from sociology to American studies, returned from sabbatical. I took two courses with her in fall 2000: her practicum on interdisciplinary teaching and the first of a two-semester course on gender and labor. I immediately appreciated her approach to the classroom as a space where students' voices and the trying out of ideas were welcome, and I quickly came to recognize how the questions she was asking regarding gender and labor provided a vehicle for me to bring together my interest in gender roles with changing norms of identity formation under postmodern conditions. More than anything, I felt that Jennifer and I saw eye to eye on what we were all doing sitting in this classroom, working in academe, and choosing college teaching as our careers. I experienced, as I had with George, Alison, and April, an "aha" moment in each of her classes, where the texts she selected felt purposely picked to advance my inquiries, and where I felt challenged to advance my thinking in a supportive environment.

Once I asked Jennifer to be my advisor, the rest of my training fell into place. I already knew two of the key members of my committee, so all I had been lacking was a leader with whom I had a good working relationship but who also shared my intellectual interests. But Jennifer provided more than that. One of the huge perks of being her advisee is becoming part of the web of feminists not only across campus but across the nation with whom she has both professional and personal ties. My involvement in Jennifer's dissertation group, the speakers who visited, the scholars she introduced me to at conferences, and the combined reading list accumulated from all these people made me feel for the first time like I was truly part of a feminist academy.

Teaching Barefoot and Giving Back

I feel at home now in an academy within an academy, carefully constructed but nonetheless present and available to me. For the first time I am involved in a community of feminists (and, specifically, of female feminist scholars) that had until now either been imagined or pieced together, and that involvement has advanced my confidence, my agenda, and my activism in my classroom, which for me is the site of my own giving back. When other undergraduates were making choices between professions (because that is primarily what Wesleyan trained for, the only recognized life trajectory) like law and economics, when career counselors asked me what I wanted, I said I envisioned a classroom where I could teach barefoot. This dream was influenced by Alison, who in a moment of passion, would occasionally—unconsciously, I think—fling one of her shoes under her desk, and rather than "righting" herself, she would kick the other shoe off, so she would be lecturing and circling barefoot in her classroom. As a student, I hungered for those moments of intellectual stimulation, and I hoped that someday I could be that kind of teacher. Changing sides, moving from the role of student to instructor has secured me in the knowledge that I am just as passionate about being the "teacher" as being the "learner," as much as those roles can never be static. I have found my professional home in the classroom, and the joy and energy that I receive from my calling are a rare luxury in a time when few people get the privilege of doing work that they are called to do. So, teaching barefoot functions as my image of engaged and engaging teaching.

The image of teaching barefoot serves as my symbol for who I hope to be in the classroom, while the words "giving back" remind me of my other mission—dare I say, responsibility—as I move into the ranks of the professoriate. Giving back is my reminder of the debts I owe to the people who helped me get here, to the brink of having the privilege of standing in front of a classroom, of belonging to a faculty. An institutional history of the University of Minnesota will reveal documents, departments, arguments, and employment patterns that confirm a feminist presence that has grown, transformed, and spread and is not going away. The formal and informal networks that the women writing in 1972 were arguing for are to a large extent in place today. The presence of these feminist legacies began with feminist pioneers in the academy like the women who wrote that document, but early accomplishments have been expanded and maintained through subsequent generations, waves, and cohorts of feminist scholars who have committed themselves to helping each other as part of a feminist politics. This energy, carried forward, is what produces a broad-reaching, diversely expressed feminist presence across the University of Minnesota and prevents us from getting stuck in complacency. While many scholars who point to feminism as a stalled revolution would say that the consciousness-raising groups that fueled many of the social changes of the 1970s are over, I would argue that the energy associated with these groups is still generated in the informal networks that feminists establish and expand in order to work around and through official channels.

Carrying this energy forward is one of my prime motivations for remaining in academe. I want to repay the feminists who have come before me by offering the same access to resources, emotional and intellectual support, and shared vision to my students and the scholars who will follow me. This expectation is made explicit by both my advisor Jennifer Pierce and Jeani O'Brien, the former chair of American studies. Anytime I stumble through small speeches of gratitude for her guidance, Jennifer reminds me that my thanks to her should take the form of giving back. When I passed my preliminary exams, Jennifer was there, as always, to celebrate with me, my friends, and my cohort as we gathered in spring 2001 beneath the budding trees, drinking beer and listening to the crack of ice breaking up in the Mississippi River. Jeani came too and paid for my small celebration. Her presence and sponsorship of my celebration are just one example of the many ways that feminists in the academy offer mentorship with no official payback or connection. When she paid for my party, in conventional Scandinavian outrage at acts of generosity, I argued, "You don't have to do this!" and Jeani just shrugged her shoulders and reminded me to give it back. I take the charge seriously. More than that, I feel grateful for my membership in the academy at large and particularly in this feminist academy, both real and imagined, where I feel at home. I think we all experience gratitude for our work, which is both grueling and unending, but which for us is incredibly meaningful, often rewarding, and at times an amazing way to make a living.

It is a driving philosophy among the five people who form my committee that we pass down to our own students the respect, delight, and intensity we see modeled in our own mentors, and this approach creates a tangible history of intellectual legacy, as we and our ideas build on each other. The purpose of this volume of essays is to understand the uneven transmittal and transformation of feminism across generations, and while I am sure not many third wave scholars can tell as rosy a story as mine, we can each work to improve the institutions and world we pass on to the students who enter our classrooms.

I know from graduates of other programs that my experience is not the norm, and the cumulative effect of feeling at home in my discipline, my institution, my department, my chosen committee, and my cohort has provided and will continue to provide me with confidence and the desire and impetus to give back, to work to create similar conditions for my own students. This experience is part of the many contributions that Jennifer Pierce makes to this institution. She works to make sure that her experience is only a cautionary tale and that we arrive in our profession armed with the tools necessary for success and a careful combination of confidence and healthy skepticism regarding the potential perils of academe. As I begin my career at Grinnell College, I am buoyed by the hope that my entry into the academy will feel unencumbered, that I will, once again, feel like women, and specifically feminists, are recognized and will perhaps—someday—be welcomed into the academy.

While my hope for the future is to be part of a push by third generation feminists to build a feminist academy, my plan in the meantime is to perpetuate these pockets of hope, promise, and security for my students in my classroom, in my office hours, and within the sphere of my influence. I do this work based on a conviction that as feminisms transform and evolve, these pockets of giving back and working forward will join up once again to form a feminism that is connected but not united, committed to pursuing feminist concerns while leaving space for the multiplicities, contradictions, and fluidity of culture and experience. My conviction is not ahistorical, because my arrival here, at this desk, writing this essay, experiencing the power to tell my story with no holds barred is built on the back of three generations of feminists who have believed that the work they did made a difference, and it has for me and my own generation of feminist scholars.

Notes

To the strong women who, whether they identified as feminists or not, personified strength, I dedicate this work. To my grandmother Phyllis, who taught me to be unapologetically strong; to my mom, Cathie, who raised me to believe there were no limits; to my sister, KT, who is my touchstone; to my best friend, Danielle, without whom I would not have made it to this point; to Lu, who made feminism and everything else fun; to Colleen, who proves you do not need the theory to live the reality; and to Hoku, Jennifer, and Janet, who remain for me models of the strength and insight that three generations of feminists in the academy have made possible. Thank you.

1. "A Proposal for a Women's Studies Department," University of Minnesota, Minneapolis, 1972.

2. The 1990s were marked by many declarations that feminism was dead. While many of these deliberations took place in academic texts, in June 1998, *Time* magazine emblazoned its cover with the question, "Is Feminism Dead?" thereby exposing a wider readership to a sense that feminism was in danger or fading. See Ginia Bellafonte, "Feminism: It's All about Me!" *Time,* June 29, 1998, 54.

3. Michelle Fine, *Disruptive Voices: The Possibilities of Feminist Research* (Ann Arbor: University of Michigan Press, 1992), 99.

4. Alifa Rifaat, *Distant View of a Minaret* (Portsmouth, N.H.: Heinemann Educational Books, 1983); Nawal El Sadaawi, *Woman at Point Zero* (London: Zed Books, 1983); Salwa Bakr, *The Wiles of Men and Other Stories,* trans. Denys Johnson-Davies (Austin: University of Texas Press, 1992).

5. Carolyn Latteier, *Breasts: The Women's Perspective on an American Obsession* (Binghamton, N.Y.: Haworth Press, 1998); Rebecca Chalker, *The Clitoral Truth: The Secret World at Your Fingertips* (New York: Seven Stories Press, 2002); and Natalie Angier, *Woman: An Intimate Geography* (New York: Anchor Books, 2000).

6. The institutionalized sexism and racism that I observed at the admissions office could be the subject of an essay in itself. Examples include discussing students' appearance more than their grades when trying to "construct" an incoming class, and wining and dining athletes of color because we needed to "improve those numbers." It is no surprise that because students of color were viewed as numbers, not people, Illinois Wesleyan University's ability to retain them after the initial honeymoon stage of recruitment was weak: many students of color left after their first or second year.

7. I studied for a semester at the University of Sheffield. My understanding of feminism, education, and nationalism was affected by my time there; however, for the purpose of this essay, my time in England is mainly significant as a point of comparison that eventually became integrated into how I understood my intellectual and physical home.

8. bell hooks, *Teaching to Transgress: Education as the Practice of Freedom* (New York: Routledge, 1994), 184.

9. Although the course was designed for the University of Minnesota, I had the opportunity to teach it, instead, at St. Olaf College in January 2004. I believe that the opportunity to examine how race privilege reproduces itself was also very important for the student body of St. Olaf. The course was well received by students.

10. While intersectionality requires us to look simultaneously at interlocking systems of privilege, for me, whiteness is the primary marker of other privileges; it links with class, education, and ease of occupational and social mobility and therefore provides an excellent jumping off point from which to address various forms of difference. I focus on whiteness as a category needing interrogation because it has been my greatest challenge to disrupt my own possessive investment in racial privilege. Many of my students have also grown up in white spaces, and so it becomes one of the primary hurdles to their own intellectual development and ability to understand and negotiate difference.

11. Camille Paglia, *Sexual Personae: Art and Decadence from Nefertiti to Emily Dickinson* (New Haven, Conn.: Yale University Press, 1990).

12. David Noble, *The Death of a Nation* (Minneapolis: University of Minnesota Press, 2002).

13. Some of these exemplary works include Anne McClintock, *Imperial Leather: Race, Gender and Sexuality in the Colonial Conquest* (New York: Routledge, 1995); Chandra Talpade Mohanty, *Feminism without Borders: Decolonizing Theory, Practicing Solidarity* (Durham, N.C.: Duke University Press, 2003); Patricia Hill Collins, *Black Feminist Thought: Knowledge, Consciousness, and the Politics of Empowerment* (New York: Routledge, 2000); Gloria Anzaldúa, ed., *Making Face, Making Soul/Haciendo Caras: Creative and Critical Perspectives by Feminists of Color* (San Francisco: Aunt Lute Books, 1990); bell hooks, *Feminist Theory: From Margin to Center*, 2nd ed. (Cambridge, Mass.: South End Press, 2000); and Toni Morrison, *Playing in the Dark: Whiteness and the Literary Imagination* (New York: Vintage Books, 1993).

14. Sharon Ann Nero, "The Professional Socialization of Women's Studies Scholars: A Case Study of the University of Wisconsin System" (PhD diss., University of Minnesota, 1991), 11.

Contributors

Hokulani K. Aikau is assistant professor of political science at the University of Hawai'i at Mānoa. She received her BS in women's studies and sociology from the University of Utah in 1994, her MA in sociology from the Center for Research on Women at The University of Memphis in 1996, and her PhD in American studies from the University of Minnesota in 2005. Her dissertation research was supported by a Ford Foundation Fellowship as well as a MacArthur Scholar Fellowship. She is now revising her dissertation into a book, tentatively titled *Negotiations of Faith: Mormonism, Native Hawaiian Identity, and Struggles for Self-Determination.*

Sam Bullington is assistant professor of women's studies and geography at the University of Missouri. He completed his PhD in feminist studies at the University of Minnesota; his dissertation is titled "From the 'Rainbow Nation' to the 'New Apartheid': Sexual Orientation and HIV/AIDS in Contemporary South African Nation-Building." He is cochair of TransVoices, one of the only transgender choruses in the country, and participates in HIV/AIDS, feminist, and trans activism.

Susan Cahn is associate professor of history at the State University of New York, Buffalo, where she teaches U.S. women's history and the history of sexuality. She is the author of *Coming On Strong: Gender and Sexuality in U.S. Women's Sport,* as well as articles on lesbianism, women's sports, adolescence, and chronic illness. She is finishing a manuscript on adolescent girls' sexuality and its social and political implications for southern history.

Dawn Rae Davis obtained her PhD in feminist studies from the University of Minnesota. Her dissertation, "Decolonizing Love: Feminist Subjects and the Ability of Not Knowing," is a philosophical examination of relationships between knowledge, love, and public spheres of social transformation from a postcolonial perspective. She was awarded the University of Minnesota's Stout-Wallace fellowship and an American Association of University Women Dissertation Fellowship. She received her BA in women's studies and American studies at the University of California, Santa Cruz. Her work on love has been published in Hypatia.

LISA J. DISCH is professor of political science, former director of the Center for Advanced Feminist Studies, and former *Signs* editorial board member at the University of Minnesota. She has published *Hannah Arendt and the Limits of Philosophy* and *The Tyranny of the Two-Party System*. She received her PhD in political science from Rutgers University in 1988.

KARLA A. ERICKSON is assistant professor in sociology at Grinnell College. She received her PhD in American studies, with a minor in feminist studies, at the University of Minnesota in 2004; her MA in liberal studies from Hamline University in 1998; and her BA in English and women's studies at Illinois Wesleyan in 1995. She is working on a book that examines the role of gendered labor in the service sector. Her work has been published in *Symbolic Interaction, Space and Culture,* and *Qualitative Sociology.*

SARA EVANS is Regents Professor of history and one of the founding members of the Center for Advanced Feminist Studies at the University of Minnesota. She is a pioneer in the area of women's history and was the first scholar hired in women's history at Minnesota. She is the author of *Personal Politics: The Roots of Women's Liberation in the Civil Rights Movement and the New Left, Born for Liberty: A History of Women in America,* and *Tidal Wave: How Women Changed America at Century's End.*

ELIZABETH FAUE is professor of history at Wayne State University. She is the author of *Community of Suffering and Struggle: Women, Men, and the Labor Movement in Minneapolis, 1915–1945; Writing the Wrongs: Eva Valesh and the Rise of Labor Journalism*; and several essays on gender, labor, and history. She is working on a book, *Solidarity and Allegiance: Political Conflicts about Nation, Class, and Gender.*

RODERICK A. FERGUSON is associate professor of race and critical theory in the Department of American Studies at the University of Minnesota. He is the author of *Aberrations in Black: Toward a Queer of Color Critique* (Minnesota, 2004).

PETER HENNEN is assistant professor of sociology at The Ohio State University at Newark. His research interests include masculinities, embodiment, and gendered sexuality; he is working on a book on gender and sexuality in three gay men's subcultures. His work has been published in *Gender and Society* and the *Journal of Contemporary Ethnography*. He received his PhD in sociology from the University of Minnesota in 2002.

TONI MCNARON is professor emerita of English at the University of Minnesota. She is the former director of the Schochet Center for GLBT Studies, former chair of the Department of Women's Studies, former director of the Bush Program for Excellence and Diversity in Teaching at the University of Minnesota, and one of the founders of the Center for Advanced Feminist Studies. She is author of *Poisoned Ivy: Lesbian and Gay Academics Confronting Homophobia, I Dwell in Possibility: A Memoir,* and numerous other books and articles.

WENDY LEO MOORE is assistant professor of sociology at Texas A&M University. Her research examines the gendered and racialized dimensions of professional socialization in elite American law schools. She is also an attorney. She received her JD from the University of Minnesota Law School in 2000 and her PhD in sociology in 2005.

JEAN M. O'BRIEN is associate professor of history and the former chair of American Studies at the University of Minnesota. Her work is in the areas of American Indian studies and colonial American history. She is the author of *Dispossession by Degrees: American Indians in Colonial New England.* She is an enrolled member of the Minnesota Chippewa Tribe (White Earth Reservation, Mississippi Band) and received her PhD in history from the University of Chicago in 1990.

JENNIFER L. PIERCE is associate professor of sociology and American studies, a former director of the Center for Advanced Feminist Studies, and a former editorial board member of *Signs: Journal of Women in Culture and Society* at the University of Minnesota. Her publications include *Gender Trials: Emotional Lives in Contemporary Law Firms* and a coedited anthology, *Is Academic Feminism Dead? Theory in Practice*. She is working on a book tentatively titled *Racing for Innocence: Whiteness, Corporate Culture, and the Backlash against Affirmative Action* and on a collaborative project with M. J. Maynes on the uses of personal narratives in the social sciences. She received her PhD in sociology from the University of California at Berkeley in 1991.

FELICITY SCHAEFFER-GRABIEL is assistant professor of feminist studies at the University of California, Santa Cruz. She received the University of California President's Postdoctoral Fellow in the Latin American and Latino Studies Department at the University of California, Santa Cruz, and is revising her dissertation on the Internet marriage industry between Mexico, Colombia, and the United States. She received her PhD in American studies at the University of Minnesota in 2003.

ANNE FIROR SCOTT is W. K. Boyd professor emerita of history at Duke University. She was an early contributor to the history of American women, beginning with an article published in *South Atlantic Quarterly* in 1962 and a book, *The Southern Lady*, published in 1970. The latter, still in print, came out in a twenty-fifth anniversary edition in 1995. She has published several other books and numerous articles, and is writing a book about the nearly forty-year correspondence between Pauli Murray and Caroline Ware.

JANET D. SPECTOR is professor emerita of anthropology at the University of Minnesota. During her twenty-five-year career at Minnesota, she taught anthropology and women's studies, which she chaired from 1981 to 1984. She was one of the founders of the Center for Advanced Feminist Studies at the University of Minnesota. She also served as assistant provost of academic affairs, a position created to provide leadership to the university in its effort to improve the campus climate for women. She pioneered the development of feminist archaeology in the late 1970s and early 1980s, and her articles on feminist archaeology have been reprinted in numerous anthologies published in the United States and abroad. She is the author of *What This Awl Means: Feminist Archaeology at a Wahpeton Dakota Village*.

AMANDA LOCK SWARR is assistant professor of women's studies at the University of Washington, Seattle. In 2003 she received her PhD in feminist studies from the University of Minnesota. She was a Mellon Post-doctoral Fellow at Barnard College of Columbia University from 2003 to 2005, where she taught in women's studies. She has recently published articles in *Signs: Journal of Women in Society and Culture* (with Richa Nagar) and *The Journal of Homosexuality*, and her current research addresses sexuality, sexual violence, and HIV/AIDS in South Africa.

MIGLENA TODOROVA received her PhD in American studies, MA in political science, and BA in American studies from the University of Minnesota. She grew up in Sofia, Bulgaria, and came to the United States as a college student in 1993. She is currently working on a book titled *Becoming White in the Balkans and What That Says about Race in the United States*.

Index